FEAR
ON TRIAL

John Henry Faulk

S I M O N   A N D   S C H U S T E R

New York, 1964

Third Printing

Library of Congress Catalog Card Number: 64–22407
Designed by Betty Crumley
Manufactured in the United States of America
by The Book Press, Brattleboro, Vermont

To the three persons, Texans all,
who influenced me the most in respecting the liberated mind
and the joys and responsibilities of citizenship:
my mother and father and J. Frank Dobie.

FEAR
ON TRIAL

1

This is a story of violence. Not violence involving physical brutality, lust, or bloodshed, but a more subtle kind of violence—the violence of vigilantism. In a society that has achieved rule by law, rule by vigilantism is a violence not only against those immediately affected but against society itself. Like all stories of violence, this one took place against a background of intrigue and fear. The story began, for me at least, with a telephone call.

Sunday, February 12, 1956, was a gray, cold day in New York. Just after lunch my wife, Lynne, and I decided we would brave the wintry weather and take our children to Central Park, a block away. Though there were only three, and small ones at that—Johanna was seven, Evelyn six, and Frank Dobie four and a half—if they didn't get out for an airing at least once a day, they seemed more like three hundred very large ones. Then, after we got the last snow suit zipped up and were ready to go, I changed my mind and decided I had better stay home and work.

I had a radio show on WCBS, the flagship station of the Columbia Broadcasting System, in New York City. It was a one-hour show each afternoon, five days a week, and it was pretty much a talk program. I spun a few yarns, reminisced about my childhood in Texas and commented on the news of the day and the foibles of the world. I wrote most of the material for it myself, and Sundays were reserved for getting together the stuff for the following week. On this particular Sunday, I also wanted to work up some ideas for a television show that my business manager, Gerald Dickler, thought we had a very good chance of selling. I had been putting it off for several weeks, and I was determined to get it done that day.

Lynne herded the children out, and I sat down at my desk to write. The phone rang. It was Val Adams, a radio and television columnist for *The New York Times*. He apologized for bothering me at home on Sunday and then asked if I had seen the bulletin that AWARE, Inc., had just issued, attacking me for pro-Communist activities.

"This is the first I've heard of it, Val. When did you get it?" I asked with a tightening sensation in my stomach.

"I got it in yesterday's mail. They just put it out," Val replied. "Thought maybe you might want to comment on it."

"What do they say?"

"Oh, it attacks your Middle-of-the-Road slate in the union. Singles you out in particular—you and Collingwood and Bean."

"Could you read it to me, Val?"

"Well—" he hesitated—"it's pretty long, four or five pages. It's their usual drivel. Lots of rhetorical questions about your patriotism. That sort of thing. They list some alleged pro-Communist affiliations you're supposed to have had."

"I'd like to see it, Val, if I may. I don't want to comment on it until I've read it. How about my coming by and reading it to-morrow?" I guess my voice betrayed the anxiety I felt, in spite of my efforts to conceal it.

"Sure, Johnny. I'll leave it at the reception desk. I hope I didn't upset you."

"Oh, it doesn't upset me," I said. "I don't know what it's all about yet. I'll talk to you after I've read it." And I thanked him and hung up.

I hadn't been honest with Val. It did upset me. It also made me mad. I knew good and well what it was all about, too.

All performers in radio and television—actors, singers, dancers, announcers, and the like—are required to belong to the American Federation of Television and Radio Artists, known familiarly as AFTRA. I had belonged since 1946, when I first came to New York from Texas to become a radio performer. I had paid my dues regularly, but I had never been very active in the affairs of the union until 1955. I became active at that time only because of AWARE, Inc.

AWARE had been organized back in 1953. It called itself "an

organization to combat the Communist conspiracy in entertainment-communications," and it operated as a vigilante committee, putting out bulletins from time to time, accusing performers in radio and television of Communist or pro-Communist activities. It had played havoc with the careers of dozens of performers; any performer it attacked was blacklisted throughout the industry. AWARE also was a powerful influence in the affairs of AFTRA—in fact, they almost completely dominated AFTRA in New York.

AFTRA had been founded in New York in 1938, and although it became a national union with strong locals in Chicago and Hollywood, the New York local was the largest and strongest in the union. The governing body of the New York local was a thirty-five man board of directors, whose members were elected from the membership every December, to serve throughout the following year. From the early 1950s, this board of directors had been controlled entirely by one faction of the union. The same group was elected year after year, and they made anti-Communism a big issue. A number of them, including Vinton Hayworth, the president of the New York local in 1955, were officers of AWARE, Inc.

In the AFTRA election of 1954, a slate of candidates ran against the entrenched board of directors. The insurgents were soundly trounced, and shortly after the election AWARE put out a bulletin attacking their patriotism. This bulletin was dutifully circulated to all the employers in radio and television, and it laid the groundwork for the blacklisting of those AFTRA members whom it attacked. It also served as a stern warning to other members of the union; anyone who wanted to run in opposition to the AWARE-supported slate of officers had better think twice.

The AWARE-supported faction, however, did not have control over the feelings of the membership of the union. In March of 1955, at a membership meeting of the New York local, a resolution was offered to condemn AWARE for its unwarranted interference in AFTRA affairs. It was a stormy meeting. One union member after another got up and blasted away at AWARE and its destructive practices. Not one member of the board of directors spoke against AWARE; on the contrary, most of them defended it.

The membership voted overwhelmingly to condemn AWARE, but the AFTRA board of directors remained in office.

Instead of heeding the obvious desire of the membership to curb AWARE's influence and oppose the blacklisting of union members, the board of directors started mumbling that the vote to condemn AWARE was part and parcel of a Communist plot. They even suggested that the House Un-American Activities Committee come to New York and hold hearings. Sure enough, the HUAC announced it was coming to New York in August. It subpoenaed some fifteen members, most of whom had signed the petition to condemn AWARE. It was about this time that I began to take an active interest in AFTRA's affairs.

That summer, 1955, I was living on Fire Island with my family. Fire Island, with its wide sandy beaches and casual, informal way of life, is a favorite summer place for people connected in one way or another with show business. Practically every group I ran into, whether on the beach or at one of the cocktail parties that are a hallmark of Fire Island summer life, was talking about the goings-on in AFTRA and the vote to condemn AWARE. Orson Bean, who was just beginning to win fame as a talented actor and comedian, lived near me on Fire Island. We had long talks about AFTRA affairs and agreed that we ought to do something about the board of directors and AWARE. Then and there we decided that we would run for office against the incumbents the following December. We knew that even if we were elected to the board, we wouldn't have much chance of changing things, since there would be thirty-three other members of the board to oppose us. But at least we could make our voices heard; we could dissent.

Charles Collingwood, a news commentator at CBS, had his summer home nearby. He was a friend of mine, and I talked to him about the matter. Charles had never been very active in union affairs either, but he felt pretty much the way we did. He agreed to run with us, and his wife, actress Louise Allbritton, said she would join us too. The more we talked about it the more enthusiastic we became over our chances of stopping AWARE's blacklisting. Charles said if we were going to run we might as well get a whole slate of officers to join us.

Toward the end of the summer Bean had to go off to Philadelphia to open in *Will Success Spoil Rock Hunter?* While he was gone

Charles and I rounded up Garry Moore, Faye Emerson, Janice Rule, and a number of other well-known performers who belonged to AFTRA, and got them to run on our slate. It wasn't easy to find people who would join us, since there was a great deal of fear of reprisals from AWARE.

We managed, however, to get thirty-three people in all. We called ourselves the Middle-of-the-Road slate and put out a statement setting forth what we hoped to do for the union. We called it "A Declaration of Independents." Among other things, we declared that while we were opposed to Communism we were also opposed to the blacklisting and intended to do something to put a stop to it. The announcement that there was a Middle-of-the-Road slate in the election running against the AWARE-supported slate created quite a stir among the AFTRA membership in New York.

At election time, in December of 1955, we swept into office with a flourish. The Middle-of-the-Road slate won twenty-seven of the thirty-five seats on the board. This meant that we were firmly in control of the New York local as far as numbers were concerned. The constitution of the union provided that the president, five vice-presidents, a secretary and a treasurer were to be elected from the board of directors by the membership. A couple of weeks later Collingwood was elected president, Bean first vice-president, and I was elected second vice-president of the local. We took office in January of 1956.

We had rough sledding from the start. Most of us were inexperienced in the administration of union affairs and had a great deal to learn. But the biggest problem we had was the strong and continuous opposition we met. We had soundly defeated the AWARE-supported faction of the union, but we hadn't silenced them. In fact we had only stirred them up. Several of their strongest and most effective members were among the eight who had been re-elected to the board. There was Clayton (Bud) Collyer, who for years had been a big wheel in AFTRA and a leading spirit in the old administration. There were Alan Bunce, Rex Marshall, and Conrad Nagel. They had all been officeholders in the union for years and had the advantage of experience. They offered unyielding opposition to everything the Middle-of-the-Road slate undertook to do, both at board meetings and outside. There was also Henry Jaffe, who for years had been the legal counsel for AFTRA, both local and national; he made no secret of his dislike for the Middle-of-the-Road slate. Although he was only an employee of the union, not a member, and consequently was not entitled to vote, he attended every board meeting and never hesitated to speak—usually in opposition to us. To add to our problems, a couple of weeks after we had taken office, the House Un-American Activities Committee, in its annual report, let go with a blast aimed at the Middle-of-the-Road administration. It declared among other things that the issue of blacklisting was being used by the Communist forces to reinfiltrate the union. This report was released to all the papers and was widely publicized.

Now, to top it all off, hardly a month after we had taken office, AWARE, Inc., had come out with the bulletin (the one Val had just called me about) attacking the Middle-of-the-Road slate.

As I sat down at my desk again after Val's call, I was filled with anger—anger that AWARE would pull such an underhanded trick. I thought of where the bulletin would go and who would see it. God-amighty, this could get *me* blacklisted! I went to the phone and called Gerald Dickler, my business manager, at his home and told him about Val's call.

"You expected AWARE to do something like this, didn't you, Johnny?" he asked.

"I don't know, Gerry, I guess I did. Of course, I haven't read the thing yet. Val said I could pick it up at the *Times* office in the morning."

"Well, we can't do anything until we have seen it," Gerry said, "but you'd better bring it over to me just as soon as you get it in the morning." I didn't like the worried note in his voice.

When I started working again on the notes for my show, my mind kept wandering back to the matter of being blacklisted. I tried to concentrate on my program, but before long I would be thinking of the bulletin again. I grew irritated with myself; I didn't want to admit it, but I was feeling a little scared. After all, I reasoned, if AWARE has branded me subversive, I ought to be indignant, *mad*. I was damned if I was going to be scared! I resolutely sat down in my chair and began writing again. I started a short piece, for use on my program the next day, about Boots Cooper, an old boy down home whom I had known years ago.

Boots was a big old overgrown smart aleck who claimed he wasn't afraid of the devil himself. One afternoon while Boots was fishing by himself up on Barton Creek, Buster Rollins rigged himself up in a wagon sheet and came tearing down through the pecan trees behind Boots, screaming like a Comanche Indian. Boots dropped his fishing pole and made a new path through the bushes heading for home. The next day, in front of all of us, Buster was teasing Boots about being scared of a man under a wagon sheet. Boots smirked, "Hell, I knowed it was you. I warn't skairt. I was just mad. I was good and damned mad 'cause you come there scarin' the fish away." Buster wagged his head, "Guess that's right, Old Boots was really mad. So mad he ran five miles all the way home, 'fore he could get control of his temper." *I* felt better when I finished writing that piece.

2

Val Adams had left the AWARE bulletin with the receptionist at the *Times* office. As I picked it up the next morning I got the same angry-scared feeling that had followed Val's call the day before. I hailed a cab, gave the driver Dickler's office address and sat back. My hands trembled a bit as I tore open the sealed envelope and unfolded the bulletin. I noticed that it was even longer than I had anticipated—some five and a half pages, single-spaced on legal size paper. It was headed "AWARE, INC. An Organization to Combat the Communist Conspiracy in Entertainment-Communications." It was dated February 10, 1956, and was presented as a "News Supplement to Membership Bulletin, AWARE Publication 16."

It started off by saying that in a recent AFTRA election, "a caucus styling itself 'middle of the road'" had won twenty-seven out of thirty-five seats, "choosing its candidates by two standards: their opposition to AWARE, Inc. and also their opposition to 'blacklisting and Communism.'" Then it advised that "the term 'blacklisting' is losing its plain meaning and becoming a Communist jargon-term for hard opposition to the exposure of Communism."

There followed a paragraph stating: "The 'middlers' attack on AWARE and relative silence on Communism require some comment." Then it called attention to the fact that the "unqualifiedly anti-Communist slate was defeated for the first time in eight years," and that Charles Collingwood was elected president, Orson Bean first vice-president, and I second vice-president. It suggested that there was an apparent ambiguity in the Middle-of-the-Road's position relative to the Communist issue and asked rhetorically:

16

Will the "middlers" enforce AFTRA's constitution which bars from union membership those who maintain membership or knowingly aid the Communist party or other officially designated subversive organizations?

Will they enforce AFTRA's National Rule, which provides disciplinary measures against union members who refuse to answer when asked by a Congressional committee if they are or have been Communist Party (CP) members?

After listing the names of fifteen members of the New York local who had refused to cooperate with the House Committee on Un-American Activities in August and October of 1955, it demanded:

What will the "middlers" do about enforcing AFTRA's Constitution and National Rule against these 15?

The bulletin went on to say that we had been critical of AWARE but had said nothing about the "many CP fronts that have operated in the entertainment field," and it added: "Silence is sometimes more eloquent than words." It related how AWARE had been condemned by AFTRA membership the year before, hinting that the condemnation was a dark Communist plot, but it magnanimously declared that "AWARE did not then, and does not now, suggest that to be opposed to AWARE is necessarily to be pro-Communist. It is a tragic fact that most Communist successes have come about with the help of non-Communists won over by slogans."

After these preliminary remarks it got down to the business of working me over, saying that after I had begun to organize the Middle-of-the-Road slate, the Communists had abandoned their plans to run a slate and had left the field open for us to oppose the "unqualifiedly anti-Communist ticket." Then came the paragraph that really hooked into me.

John Henry Faulk was further quoted as saying that "all (middlers) were chosen for their opposition to Communism as well as their opposition to AWARE." In most cases, this may well be true. But how about Faulk himself? What is his public record?

There followed seven allegations:

[1] According to the Daily Worker of April 22, 1946, "Jack Faulk" was to appear at Club 65, 13 Astor Place, N.Y.C.—a favorite site of pro-Communist affairs.
[2] According to the Daily Worker of April 17, 1947, "Johnny Faulk" was to appear as an entertainer at the opening of "Headline Cabaret," sponsored by Stage for Action (officially designated a Communist front). The late Philip Loeb was billed as emcee.
[3] According to the Daily Worker of April 5, 1948, "John Faulk" contributed cabaret material to "Show-Time for Wallace," revues staged by the Progressive Citizens of America (officially designated a Communist front) in support of Henry A. Wallace's candidacy for the presidency of the U.S. Although Wallace was the officially endorsed candidate of the CP, by no means all his supporters were Communists or pro-Communists. What is in question here is support of any candidate given through a Communist-front setup.
[4] A program dated April 25, 1946, named "John Faulk" as a scheduled entertainer (with identified Communist Earl Robinson and two non-Communists) under the auspices of the Independent Citizens Committee of the Arts, Sciences and Professions (officially designated a Communist front, and predecessor of the Progressive Citizens of America).
[5] Vol. 3, Nos. 1 & 2, of the Bulletin of People's Songs (officially designated a Communist front) named Faulk as one who had sent greetings to People's Songs on its second anniversary.
[6] "Johnny Faulk" was listed in a circular as an entertainer or speaker (with Paul Robeson and two others) to appear at "Spotlight on Wallace" to be held in Room 200 of the Jefferson School of Social Science on February 16, 1948. The Jefferson School has been found by the Federal Government to be what it is, the official training school of the Communist conspiracy in New York.
[7] "John H. Faulk" was a U.S. Sponsor of the American Continental Congress for Peace, staged in Mexico City, September 5–10, 1949, as shown by the official "call." The Congress was later described by the HUAC as "another phase in the Communist world 'peace' campaign, aimed at consolidating anti-American forces throughout the Western Hemisphere."

Having dispensed with me, the bulletin turned to Bean and Collingwood. It pointed out that Orson Bean had done a satire on the House Un-American Activities Committee as recently as August 1955 and reported on a letter by Charles Collingwood in January in answer to the HUAC's attack on the Middle-of-the-Road administration. The bulletin also summarized the HUAC counsel's public reply to Collingwood.

> Tavenner further stated that there is not only no blacklist at all, but some of the named individuals have been finding it easy to secure employment. He added: "It is significant to note that the election of the so-called anti-blacklist candidates in the recent AFTRA election [the 'middlers'—A.] has been greeted enthusiastically by the Communist press."

The bulletin ended by expressing great dismay that President Collingwood would dare take issue with the HUAC.

This, then, was the AWARE Bulletin. It was a cleverly constructed piece of work. The way it had positioned my name in sentences with "Communist Party" and "Communist front," its use of phrases like "officially designated a Communist front," and its skillful mixing of half-truth and falsehood suggested the work of a hand skilled at innuendo.

I sat pondering the matter as the cab moved slowly through the mid-morning Manhattan traffic. I had a vague, uncomfortable feeling of guilt. But I had done nothing wrong. Why should I feel guilty? What was I going to do? Run up and down Madison Avenue, buttonholing people and declaring that whatever they might believe, the AWARE bulletin was false? Of course, this would be ridiculous. I realized at that moment that I was going through the frustrations and anxieties that had been experienced by countless other performers when they had found their names linked with subversion by AWARE.

Up in Gerry's office, I handed him the bulletin. He took it without a word and began to read. I occupied myself by gazing at the framed photographs of other clients of Gerry's: Lowell Thomas, in Tibet; H. V. Kaltenborn, at his desk; Pauline Frederick, at a microphone.

Gerald Dickler was not only my business manager, he was my friend and professional adviser. He had a definitive knowledge of affairs in the radio and television industry, gained through years of intimate association with those media. I relied heavily upon him and his guidance, and I had profited greatly by his direction. He was also intimately acquainted with the affairs of AFTRA, and had been for many years. He knew all of the personalities and the conflicts in the union. He had cautioned me against getting into the AFTRA squabble. "You've got a career to look after, Johnny. Besides, you're up against a tough, experienced crowd. They're professionals. You're not." When we had won the election he had told me, "It's a fluke, Johnny. Your Middle-of-the-Road slate is a sandlot team. You have accidently beaten the New York Yankees for one game. Watch out for 'em. The men who have controlled this union for many years have a vested interest in keeping that control. They're not about to let you and your Middle-of-the-Road slate take that control away from them."

As Gerry finished reading the bulletin he removed his horn-rimmed glasses and looked at me with a troubled frown.

"This is bad, Johnny. It could mean real trouble."

"Yes, I know. What do you reckon my first move should be?"

"I think you should take this to Sam Slate at WCBS at once. Get it to him before the AWARE crowd does. Sam's on your side. Ask him what you should do at CBS about it."

"I'll take it to him as soon as I leave here. Do you think CBS will stand by me, Gerry?"

He nodded. "Yes, I think they'll stand by you—that is, for a while. They don't want to lose you. They don't like AWARE any better than you do. They won't do anything unless they begin to get some real pressure from the agencies or sponsors. Then it will probably be a different story."

"How long do you think that will be?"

"It's hard to tell," Gerry said thoughtfully, "hard to tell. They really can't risk firing you outright. Can't afford it. It would leave them open to too much public criticism for letting AWARE pressure them. And, if they did that you would have a legal action against them. The blacklisting business doesn't work that way."

"And besides, Gerry," I said hopefully, "I'm pretty well liked there at CBS. I happen to know that most of the executives there don't like AWARE any better than I do. Maybe they'll line up with me in this fight."

Gerry shook his head. "There's not an executive at CBS that is your enemy, Johnny. There's probably not a one there that likes

AWARE. But on the other hand, there is not a single one of them that wouldn't fire you if a decision is made to do so. Don't forget that."

"I thought you just said they wouldn't fire me—that is, outright. What other way is there to fire a man?"

"The way this thing works, Johnny, is subtle and strictly behind the scenes. The networks and the agencies want to avoid making an issue of it. So they ease along until a legitimate reason comes. A reason that sounds perfectly logical on the surface. Then they let a man go. However, you take this on up to Sam Slate. See what he has to say."

"Well, if I get fired from CBS, or even if I don't get any more work, I could certainly prove it was because of this damn bulletin."

"That's where you're wrong, Johnny. There's not an executive in radio or television in New York today who would come in and say he had fired you or refused to hire you because of this. They simply wouldn't do it."

"Who do you suppose went to all the trouble to write this damn bulletin, Gerry? To get up all this nonsense? It must have been a lot of work."

"Vincent Hartnett, in all likelihood. He's the mainspring of AWARE. He and Laurence Johnson of Syracuse helped start AWARE, you know. Hartnett makes his living out of this sort of thing. He's a pro."

Indeed I did know. I had never set eyes on Vincent Hartnett. But his name was legend on Madison Avenue in those years. He was not only one of the founders and moving spirits of AWARE, but he had published a book back in 1950 called *Red Channels.* In this book Mr. Hartnett purported to reveal the extent to which the international Communist conspiracy had penetrated the communications industry. Although the book's authors were careful to point out that the persons who were listed inside its pages were not necessarily Communists, or Communist sympathizers, or even subversive, the book had a devastating effect on the careers of dozens of performers whose names were listed in it. *Red Channels* became something of a semi-official guide for employers in the radio and television industry—a guide in the sense that it was widely used in deciding whom not to hire. It made money for Mr. Hartnett.

Mr. Hartnett's friend Laurence Johnson owned a number of supermarkets. He and Mr. Hartnett shared the political philosophy of Senator McCarthy. But Mr. Johnson was not merely a philosopher; he was also a man of action. Sponsors who advertised in radio and television had to sell their products through Mr. Johnson's supermarkets. When Mr. Hartnett protested the appearance of an actor or an actress on a program which was sponsored by a company whose product was sold in Mr. Johnson's store, Mr. Johnson obligingly went to the sponsor himself and demanded the artist's dismissal.

I pounded my fist into my palm and declared, "Well, one thing's sure! I'm not going to sit and do nothing! I figure maybe we can get the union lined up behind this thing. After all, it is their fight as much as it is mine. It's their fight more than it is mine, really."

Gerry pursed his lips and gazed at me speculatively. "That's right. It's very important that AFTRA support you. But to be perfectly candid with you, Johnny, I don't believe that you can get AFTRA to act in this matter."

"Why? After all, we swept into office on an antiblacklist ticket. The membership censured AWARE only last year. Our Middle-of-the-Road slate has been attacked by this bulletin. We're in the majority on the local board. We're in control, at least here in New York."

"That's the hell of it, son"—Gerry shook his head—"you're not in control of AFTRA. Not even in the New York local. Henry Jaffe, Bud Collyer, and the men who have run AFTRA for years are in control. They don't like you one damn bit. You'll certainly get no help from them. On the contrary, they will take advantage of this AWARE bulletin to completely undo the Middle-of-the-Road slate. This bulletin is calculated to panic your entire slate. That's one of its purposes. It will probably succeed there."

His observation irritated me.

"Now wait a minute, Gerry. Remember last fall when we started our Middle-of-the-Road slate? Practically everyone, you included, said that we could never defeat Bud Collyer and his crowd. But the membership supported us. If the Middle-of-the-Road slate stood together then, if we stood firm then, why not now?"

"You might as well face it, Johnny. You Middle-of-the-Road boys have been under attack since you were first elected. This is simply the crowning blow. Every member of the Middle-of-the-Road slate knows as well as you do that this bulletin goes to executives in agencies and networks. That fact alone would be enough to scare most of them to death, start them thinking of ways to become disassociated from you and the Middle-of-the-Road slate. Not only that, but remember, your slate has already had its defectors. Take Luis Van Rooten and Cliff Norton, two of the most vocal members of the slate when it was running for election. They've both been voting with Collyer and his clique since you have been in office. They have not supported a single one of your Middle-of-the-Road resolutions at board meetings. You had better stop right now and reflect on the fact that you haven't been able to get one clear piece of action on a single one of the promises that you made to the membership when you asked for election."

I knew that Gerry was right. He went on to predict that in a fight against AWARE's bulletin, there would be many members of the Middle-of-the-Road slate who would publicly denounce the slate and me. They would do it in a frenzy of fear of being tarred with the same brush that had tarred me. Then he took a slightly more optimistic tone.

"I'll tell you what we should do right now, Johnny. Let's go over the list of names of the Middle-of-the-Road slate who you know will stand with you in this fight. Don't waste your time on the Van Rootens and the Nortons. Get hold of Collingwood and Bean, Garry Moore, Faye Emerson, Del Horstmann, Ronny Graham, and the others. Tell them how important it is that you all stand together in this and not let the opposition pick you off one at a time. But you're going to have to move fast."

"I'll do that at once, Gerry," I said. Then a thought occurred to me. "You know, come to think about it, since I'm the main target of this AWARE bulletin, it's kind of embarrassing for me to go around to my slate members and ask them to get into the fight. I sure wish that some of them would volunteer to pick up the cudgels themselves. It puts me in the position of asking them to help pull my chestnuts out of the fire. I don't like that. What if they won't do it?"

"You have no choice, Johnny," Gerry said. "Somebody has to take the initiative in this thing and do it fast. It's no time to stand on formalities. Of course if they won't stand with you, you'll be in the soup. So will they, for that matter."

"If they won't support me, what then, Gerry?"

"Then, I'd say, you'd better forget the union and start looking out for number one. If you can't rally enough members of the Middle-of-the-Road slate, or other union members, behind this fight, you'd be a damn fool to keep going. In fact you wouldn't have any choice but to start to figure out a way to save John Henry Faulk's hide, and forget AFTRA. You'd have but one way out there. You'd have to make peace with AWARE. Kiss and make up."

"The hell you say!"

"I know how you feel. I guess it's pointless for me to tell you this, because I know you won't do it. But I'm telling you right now that if you don't do it, you can start looking for some other kind of work."

I started to argue the point with him, but thought better of it and changed the subject. Shortly after, I took the bulletin and left his office.

Sam Slate was program director of WCBS and my direct superior. He was the one who had hired me, back in 1951. We had remained close personal friends since that time. I frequently visited in his home and he visited in mine. He had been born and reared in Columbus, Georgia. After he was graduated from the University of Georgia, he became a newspaper reporter. Later, he became interested in radio, and, among other things, worked for BBC, before becoming program director with WCBS. He was a crackerjack radio executive and a literate one, besides. He had earned the respect not only of the BBC but of his CBS colleagues as well. He had an enlightened, civilized attitude on social and political affairs. We had discussed them many times. I knew that he resented the inroads that McCarthyism had made in the radio and television industry and had little use for the ridiculous anxieties of some of his colleagues about controversial matters. I respected him and I trusted him.

I had discussed my intention of running for office in the union with him, before we ever launched the Middle-of-the-Road slate. I had felt that, as my employer, he had a right to know what I was planning to do. Especially since it could possibly affect my professional standing. He had agreed that AFTRA should be cleaned up for the benefit of the whole industry and was quite pleased when our slate won.

I went in and handed him the bulletin. He puffed his cigar as he read it. Then he put it down on his desk, frowning.

"That's a hell of a note isn't it, Johnny? This bunch is sore at you because you licked them in that union election." I nodded. He smiled.

"Most of those things they claimed you did were nearly ten years ago. Couldn't they find any current subversion to charge you with?"

"I guess not." I relaxed. "But I wanted you to see it, Sam. If there's anything there you want me to explain, I'll be glad to do it. After all, I think you've got a right to know what's true and what's false about it."

"I don't think it's worth paying any attention to, Johnny. It's all hogwash. Hell, you've been here five years. You're no more red than I am. I personally don't think anybody pays the slightest bit of attention to these fools."

He pushed the AWARE bulletin toward me, then said, thoughtfully, "But you know, you'd better take that in to Carl Ward. Let him see it too. Just so he'll know what it's all about in case he gets a call on it or hears about it from somebody else. If he wants to talk to me about it, tell him I'll discuss it with him."

Sam was so unperturbed and so understanding about it that I began to feel that Gerry and I had overdramatized the whole thing. I thanked him and took the bulletin over to Carl Ward's office. Carl was general manager of WCBS. I knew that he was a cautious man where company policy was concerned, but I knew that he liked me. He had been brought to New York from Minneapolis by CBS and had done well as general manager of the station. Our social contacts had been confined to company or sponsors' cocktail parties. He had always treated me with good will and respect. I had no idea what his political opinions were or whether he even had any. I had a strong feeling that he did not have the least interest in the union's affairs, nor the rights or wrongs of blacklisting—except where such matters affected the interest of WCBS.

As I handed him the bulletin, I explained that I wanted him to be acquainted with its contents before he heard of them from some other source. He thanked me and started reading it. He was obviously not interested in the labored matter with which it dealt, for he had only scanned it. As he folded it and handed it back to me he was smiling.

"I notice they said that Collingwood is a CBS news commentator, Johnny, but they don't even mention you in connection with WCBS. You ought to speak to them about that. Thanks for bringing it in to me."

I was feeling pretty good as I went into my office and sat down at my desk. The reaction of Sam Slate was reassuring. And Carl Ward's reaction was certainly nothing to be alarmed about. As far as I was concerned, I had come through the first step and it had not been unpleasant at all. Neither Slate nor Ward asked me if the charges were true or false. I appreciated that.

I called Gerald Dickler. "Mission accomplished, Gerry," I said. He asked how it had gone. "Well, I showed it to Sam Slate and Carl Ward. Sam was almost jovial about it. Put his finger right on the trouble spot—our beating the AWARE crowd in the union. He said not to pay it any mind." Gerry grunted approvingly.

"Okay, Johnny. You've at least got that matter attended to. You've done everything you can there. Now I think you ought to get in touch with Collingwood and Bean and a couple of others on your slate. Get on it right away."

After I finished doing my program that afternoon, I started calling up the members of the Middle-of-the-Road slate. I caught myself joking about the bulletin. Each member, in turn, expressed himself strongly on the matter. Each one wanted to do something at once. Perhaps, had I not been so confident and self-assured, I would have detected a note of anxiety in the voices of several of those whom I called and would have been forewarned of some of the things that were to come. However I did not. I felt too good.

I finished my telephone calls and prepared to leave the office. Just as I was closing the door behind me, the telephone rang. It was Nelson Case, a prominent and successful announcer. He had worked hard for the Middle-of-the-Road slate and had been effusive in his praise when the slate won. His voice sounded strained as he asked me if I would write him a letter stating that he was not a member of the Middle-of-the-Road group and that he had never been one. It was such a strange request that I thought for a moment he was joking. But his voice had a note of impatience and anger. I explained that I didn't consider it my role to write him such a letter. If our side had a leader at all, it was Charles Collingwood. I told him I would ask Charles to write him a letter. He asked me if I would have Charles do it at once. I told him, of course—if Collingwood wanted to do it. I couldn't force him to do so. He said that he thought he had better call Collingwood himself, and I agreed with him. After he hung up, I stood for a moment, baffled. Suddenly, I understood it. He had probably seen the AWARE bulletin.

3

Ten Middle-of-the-Road members of the local board of directors had agreed to meet at my apartment on the night following my talk with Sam Slate and Carl Ward. As the time for the meeting approached, I became jittery about what their reaction might be. In fact, I was more concerned with their reaction than I had been the day before about Slate and Ward. And I had reason to be uneasy. I had worked long and hard with the Middle-of-the-Road slate and I had been proud of the victory we had won. I hated to see all our efforts go down the drain. I knew that the coming meeting was most crucial. I understood full well that a strong aggressive position in the face of AWARE's attack was our only way out, that a defensive attitude would be fatal to any effectiveness we might have in union affairs. AWARE, like McCarthy, could only operate on the offensive. That's why they followed one policy alone—*attack*. They trafficked in fear. I knew that if the Middle-of-the-Road slate allowed fear to influence its actions, we were done for. But I was not at all convinced that I woud be able to communicate this to my fellow board members. I was not a good politician and I knew it.

While we were running for office, the program of the Middle-of-the-Road slate had been clear and positive. We had been united in purpose, and we had given little thought to what our opponents were saying. With the issues clearly presented, the membership emphatically endorsed our program by giving us an overwhelming majority in the election. But despite the unmistakable mandate we had received, we thereafter undertook, in a fatuous gesture of magnanimity, to rationalize and modify our position. We appointed members of the opposition to key positions, and we sought their views on measures for the fulfillment of our promises to the membership. The opposition, of course, took full advantage of our ingenuousness, and we paid dearly for it in the days ahead.

And now it was clear that the showdown had come. AWARE had openly attacked the top three officers of the local and had cast a cloud of doubt over the entire Middle-of-the-Road slate. It offered a perfect chance for the Middle-of-the-Road slate to stir the union into an all-out attack on blacklisting. I knew that our failure to go on the offensive now would mean the rapid dissolution of our slate.

As the members arrived, each one read the bulletin. Del Horstmann, a board member who had worked long and hard with the Middle-of-the-Road slate, declared at once, "Hell, this is nothing more than a stupid attempt to intimidate and scare us into silence. We ought to take it and shove it down their damn throats." Orson Bean suggested that we should call up Godfrey Schmidt, the president of AWARE, before the local board and question him about this antiunion action. Schmidt, a lawyer, was a provisional member of AFTRA. We decided against this, agreeing there was nothing that Schmidt would like so much as to get up before our board and denounce us. Horstmann then suggested that a strong resolution be passed immediately by the local board, warning employers that AFTRA would investigate any refusal to employ a performer who had been attacked by AWARE. It was agreed that a committee should draw up such a resolution at once.

Someone suggested that a special board meeting be called for the purpose of considering the resolution. This brought on the first signs of division. Several members said that a special board meeting might antagonize the opposition, who would charge that we were using the local board for factional fights.

I had remained silent up until that moment, but now I felt constrained to say, "The matter of blacklisting is not a factional matter. If Collyer and his friends want to sit and do nothing about blacklisting they're entitled to do so. But the Middle-of-the-Road slate pledged the membership that it would take action against blacklisting and we'd better get at it."

We debated the matter back and forth. There were enough of us to demand such a meeting, but several members were strongly opposed to the idea. One said, "If you make a sharp issue of this by calling a special meeting, Collyer or one of his bunch is sure to demand that you and Collingwood and Bean answer the AWARE charges before the local board is asked to pass such a resolution. What would you say to that?"

"Well, I want to make this matter very clear. I will be happy to discuss any of the allegations with members of my slate. I feel I owe that to you. However, I have resolved that I will not, under any circumstances, affirm or deny any of these allegations in a hostile atmosphere. It is my position that AWARE has no right whatever to publish such allegations against any citizen, including me. I do not believe that AWARE's purpose is to expose Communist infiltration. They are simply trying to destroy our effectiveness in the union. That's their purpose pure and simple. The only circumstances under which I would answer these allegations publicly would be in a court of law where AWARE would be held responsible for having made them." It was finally decided that the antiblacklist resolution should wait for a regular meeting of the local board.

The gathering adjourned on a less than positive note but, all in all, I was not disappointed with it. Later that evening Dennis Patrick, one of the members who had been present, called me to ask me confidentially if I was or had ever been a member of the Communist Party. I assured him that I was not now and never had been. Furthermore, AWARE didn't think I had either.

A couple of days later Orson Bean called to say that he had just been told by his agent that the AWARE bulletin had gotten him into trouble with Ed Sullivan. Bean had made many appearances on the Sullivan show and had other appearances scheduled, but Sullivan had told Bean's agent that he could not use Bean again till he, Bean, had done something about the AWARE allegations. This caused alarm and distress in the Middle-of-the-Road slate. Some thought that Bean should have it out with Sullivan and the advertising agency, and take the matter to court if they did not give him satisfaction. It seemed to be a clear case of an artist being blacklisted and being told why. However, Bean's agent did not think that a lawsuit was a wise course. Sometime later, Orson Bean withdrew from the Middle-of-the-Road slate. Being a man of integrity he gave his candid reason for doing so. His professional advisers had made it clear that remaining on the slate would seriously harm his career.

We had placed a lot of store in our antiblacklisting resolution. It was duly introduced at a regular board meeting. The opposition, together with the Middle-of-the-Road members who had gone over to their side, reacted as though we were inviting Khrushchev to join AFTRA. An opponent pointed out that he had served on the board many years and that it had carefully avoided taking a position on blacklisting that could in any way be construed as pro-Communist. Now here we were trying to pass a resolution which would put AFTRA in an uncompromising position on the matter of blacklisting. What if AWARE attacked somebody who was really a Communist or pro-Communist and that person became blacklisted? Would we then go to his support? Just the thought of such a thing was too much for him. He sat down and closed his eyes and shook.

We pointed out that each case would be investigated individually and judged on its merits. We also pointed out that the AFTRA constitution had safeguards against Communists belonging to the union. Furthermore, it was our obligation as officers charged with the responsibility of protecting the membership to presume that all members in good standing were entitled to our protection until such time as authorized and legal agencies of our government had proved they were not.

Our arguments fell on deaf ears. It was like yelling "Whoa" to a runaway mule. We stood by our guns, however, and the resolution was finally passed.

During the next few weeks I did not hear a murmur of disapproval from my employers at CBS. On the contrary, everything seemed to be going along fine there. I became so involved with trying to get action started in the union that I almost forgot that my personal affairs had been jeopardized.

One of the reasons that I continued to work so hard in the union was that I knew if we lost, it would be due in part to my own inadequacy. I understood very well that there were many mitigating factors over which I had no control, but I felt frustrated at my inability to rally support. I was loath to face the unhappy fact that many of the Middle-of-the-Road members had lost their appetite for the fight against AWARE.

This fact became very apparent to me after Henry Jaffe and I had an encounter at a general membership meeting some weeks later.

Jaffe suggested that I could best parry AWARE's attack on me by immediately bringing charges against members in the union who were suspected of having Communist ties. He pointed out that, since I was the principal target of AWARE's attack, I should take this action personally.

I suspected that Jaffe's motive was to get the Middle-of-the-Road slate involved in a hopeless morass of legal entanglements that would take up so much of our time we would have little chance to do anything really constructive in the union. I pointed out to him that a member who was brought up on charges for violations of the union's rules had a right to hire counsel and demand a full hearing. This would take on the aspects of a full-fledged trial. It would even be necessary for us to subpoena witnesses to testify against the performer.

As Jaffe continued to talk, I realized that he was quite sincere and really believed that he was suggesting a way that I might escape AWARE's attack. He suggested that I call Congressman Francis Walter, chairman of the House Un-American Activities Committee and tell him that I wanted to press charges against some AFTRA member of the union who had been identified before the HUAC as a Communist. He then said that he, Jaffe, could help locate several members of the New York local of AFTRA who had given evidence on their fellow members before the Committee. We could get these informer members to come and testify against the member on trial. I thanked Jaffe for his suggestion, without mentioning the revulsion that I felt at such an idea.

Immediately after the meeting I called several members of the Middle-of-the-Road slate together to tell them about Jaffe's suggestion. To my amazement and disappointment, several of them felt that it was a wise solution to our problem. When I argued that I could never be a party to buying my personal security at the expense of another performer's reputation and career, one of the members said:

"Hell, Jaffe's just saying that if you are really anti-Communist you can show it by taking some action."

We discussed the matter for an hour or so without coming to any conclusion. It was clear that the opinion of the Middle-of-the-Road slate was too sharply divided for comfort. I went home depressed and frustrated.

There was a great deal of sentiment in the Middle-of-the-Road slate for taking action under our National Rule. This rule provided that members of the union who had defied the House Un-American Activities Committee could be subjected to discipline at the discretion of the board of directors of the local to which they belonged. Charles Collingwood consulted some of the best legal minds in the country concerning the constitutionality of such a rule. He was advised that there was a serious question as to whether a member of the union could be disciplined for exercising his constitutional rights and that the matter should be examined at great length. Charles was cautioned that if the union did take the action against a member and the action was unconstitutional, the member would have a real action against the union for damages. Collingwood then appointed a committee, with me as chairman, to study the matter and report back to the board on what action, if any, should be taken.

We had been timid in the matter of a legal counsel for the New York local. Mr. Henry Jaffe had been counsel for AFTRA for many years and had the enthusiastic support of the faction which opposed us; in fact, he was so closely identified with the opposition that many members of our slate felt that he should be replaced by an attorney more congenial to our point of view. The anti-Jaffe forces represented a considerable majority on the board of directors and they now demanded that Jaffe be fired at once. Both Collingwood and I argued against this, saying that in all justice, and for the sake of Jaffe's professional reputation, he should be allowed to resign. Collingwood and I prevailed. Collingwood had a meeting with Jaffe on the subject and Jaffe agreed to resign as counsel of the New York local and agreed to give as his reasons that he desired to devote his time to his private law practice and to production in television.

The announcement of Jaffe's resignation set off a first-class earthquake. The Bud Collyer faction reacted as though we had announced we were dissolving the entire union, rather than merely allowing its counsel to resign. Jackson Beck, an announcer who had supported the Middle-of-the-Road slate in its early days, came charging into my office at CBS and demanded to know what we meant by firing Jaffe and replacing him with Harry Sacher, a lawyer who had been disbarred for defending eleven Communists on trial. He refused to tell me who had told him this piece of idiocy. I began to receive phone calls, both at home and at my office, from unnamed persons who announced that they knew for a fact that Jaffe had been dismissed on the instructions of the Communist Party. Ed Sullivan joined the chorus through his column in the New York *Daily News*. He announced that sinister forces in the union were seeking to take over, and urged the membership of AFTRA to attend a coming membership meeting, alerting them that there were real dangers in store that they must be prepared to counteract. Garry Moore called me to say that Bud Collyer and Henry Jaffe had come to visit him and asked him to present a resolution calling for a unanimous vote of confidence for Jaffe. Garry said that he did not know Jaffe and knew little of his reputation, but that Collyer and Jaffe had seemed so agitated he had agreed to do so.

The membership meeting was held on the afternoon of April 11, at the New York City Center. When I arrived I realized that it was a near record turnout, with a heavy sprinkling of AWARE members and their supporters. As customary, the board of directors sat on the stage, facing the membership. Collingwood first recognized Garry Moore, who introduced his resolution asking for a vote of approval for Jaffe. This was followed by one Jaffe partisan after another coming to the microphone with a ringing tribute to Jaffe and his great services to the union. Most of the speeches contained thinly veiled attacks on the Middle-of-the-Road slate. Those of us who had been responsible for Jaffe's resignation could do little but sit and smart. I rationalized that at least we had gotten rid of him. That was the important thing.

As the pro-Jaffe sentiment reached a fevered pitch the resolution was passed. Charles Collingwood seemed relieved when the vote was finally taken. He came to the rostrum to continue the business for which the meeting had originally been called. I glanced around at the faces of my fellow board members. They seemed to be as relieved as Collingwood that this part of the meeting was completed. I felt fatuous and ineffectual indeed to think that we who were ostensibly in control of the local board had had to sit by stupidly while our opponents turned the meeting into an all-out rally for Jaffe. I didn't realize that the Jaffe part had just been a curtain raiser.

I saw Dick Stark, an announcer and one of the original Middle-of-the-Road board members, go forward and ask Collingwood for the floor. He desired to make a very important statement. Collingwood told him that this was out of order, but he allowed him to speak. Mr. Stark then delivered himself of a ringing denunciation of the Middle-of-the-Road slate, charging that a faction on the local board had been holding secret caucuses, and were trying to pass resolutions which were contrary to the best interests of the union. He carefully avoided specifying what the resolutions were. He confessed that he had once been deluded into running with the Middle-of-the-Road slate but that he was now disillusioned and sought the counsel of the union members as to what he should do. I seethed with indignant fury. Stark knew as well as I did that he had not attended more than two board meetings since we had taken office and he had never expressed the slightest disagreement with our actions or policies. This was obviously a put-up job. His speech set off a mighty rumble among the members. I leaped to my feet to answer him. Garry Moore restrained me, saying that Bud Collyer actually had planned much worse for us and that Stark was being mild. I told Garry that I didn't care what Bud Collyer did—I *expected* him to oppose us. But I wasn't going to sit by and listen to a man who had voluntarily joined us publicly misrepresent the facts.

Collingwood recognized me and I went to the microphone. I was too furious to make a coherent speech. Even if I had, it would have done no good. The sentiment of the meeting was running strongly against us. As I gazed out over the faces I saw only cold disdain. Ed Sullivan and a hard core of our opposition were sitting in the front rows, staring up at me with unfeigned contempt. A terrible feeling of impotent rage overcame me as I sat down.

Cliff Norton, another member of the Middle-of-the-Road slate, went to the microphone and, like Stark, denounced the slate and disassociated himself from it. Those Middle-of-the-Road members who remained firm were so bewildered and confused by the proceedings that they said nothing. Collingwood, always strictly neutral when he was presiding over a membership meeting, could only comment that it seemed highly inappropriate that such matters should be discussed at a membership meeting.

I departed, alone and depressed. I sensed that this was the end of any fight against AWARE in the union. It was probably the end of the Middle-of-the-Road slate. We had tangled with the wrong boys. They had shown us what *real* fighters could do.

When I got back to my office at WCBS I received a phone call from Art Woodstone, a reporter for *Variety*. He told me that he knew what had happened at the meeting and asked me if I had any comment on it. I asked him how he had found out so quickly. He informed me that he had been told about it the day before. I didn't bother to ask him who had told him. I knew.

The following morning Ed Sullivan's column in the *Daily News* was to carry a fulsome report of the heroic onetime fighting marine, Dick Stark, and the heart-warming exhibition of his courage.

As I sat there at my desk reflecting on the chaos that had overtaken our Middle-of-the-Road slate in the union, Sam Slate sent word to me that I should meet him at once in Carl Ward's office. I discovered that the union was not the only place where I was losing.

4

When I got into Carl Ward's office, I found him sitting behind the desk, looking as if he had just lost a good friend. Sam Slate was standing near the window, fingering his cigar and frowning. It turned out that we had lost something just about as close to Carl as a friend: an account. Carl told me he had just learned that Laurence Johnson was in New York, going up and down Madison Avenue, seeing my sponsors and demanding that they withdraw from my show. I was still so punch-drunk from the drubbing I had received at the union meeting that afternoon that I could only mumble: "Well, I'll be doggone."

"This is serious, Johnny," Carl said, "Very serious. Libby's Frozen Foods account just canceled today. It looks like you'll lose Libby's Canned Vegetables account this week, too. If Johnson forces all these people off your show, you'll lose your commercial value to the station." Carl was courteous and concerned. He was also correct in his manner. He wasn't mad at me. And he wasn't indignant at Laurence Johnson. He was upset at losing an account.

"How'd you find out about it, Carl?" I asked.

He shook his head quickly. "I'm afraid I can't tell you. I'm sorry. I hope you won't press me on that."

"Carl," I said, "you've seen that damn bulletin. You know it's a bunch of trash. It's a shame to let a man go around with that thing and destroy my livelihood without getting back at him somehow or other."

"Perhaps," he said, "you could take this bulletin and answer each one of the allegations. Put it in the form of an affidavit. We could give it to our salesmen to give to any sponsor who raises a question about you. If there are things in there that you didn't do or are just plain lies, say so. If there are things that you did because you were a chump or a dupe, say so. Shoot straight. An affidavit might help."

We talked for a few more minutes about the affidavit and I went back to my office. I pulled the AWARE bulletin out of my desk and looked at it. I was sore at Ward and Slate for taking what I thought was a pretty indifferent attitude toward my interest in the matter. But when I got to thinking about it, I realized that they were really trying to help me. I had a lot of good sponsors, which meant a lot of money for the station. If for no other reasons than those of good business, Ward and Slate would try to hold on.

I tried to size up my situation. I thought of the union, and the shambles that had been made of my efforts there. And now it looked like I was getting kicked out of a job too. I might as well admit that I wasn't any great shakes at the business of fighting for causes. I couldn't handle the union. I couldn't even handle the matter of holding on to my own job.

To hell with it, I thought. If the world won't be saved, dammit I'm not going to break my back trying to save it. I'm going to look after my own interests. I'll answer this doggone bulletin. I'll give them what they want. Make them feel good. Maybe get Dickler to call up AWARE. He could tell them that I'd made a mistake, and wanted to call the whole thing off. At the moment I felt utter defeat.

I took up the AWARE bulletin and started reading it again. Carl Ward had said to answer its allegations candidly. Very well, I would do just that. As I read and reflected, a tiny thread of light began to trace through my consciousness. There was nothing to answer. There were no real allegations. It didn't say that on a certain day and in a certain place, John Henry Faulk had engaged in a Communist conspiracy or made a speech that was Communist propaganda. AWARE claimed that its purpose was to "combat the Communist conspiracy" in radio and television, but in this bulletin, AWARE didn't show one instance in which I had uttered a single word or thought, on radio or television, that could be pointed to as being Communist propaganda. I was being asked to say "I didn't," without knowing what it was that I supposedly had done. Someone had merely written, "You did." Was this their method? If so, they were as dangerous as conspirators against liberty, freedom and democracy in America.

I stared at the AWARE bulletin. I felt a slight nausea that I had even for a moment considered giving it respectful thought. Ward and Slate wanted to help me. They wanted an affidavit. I would give them one. And it would be candid.

My spirits soared. I went dashing home and sat down at my desk to start work on the affidavit. I worked almost all night, and this is what I wrote:

This affidavit is being made at the suggestion of Mr. Carl Ward of WCBS.

I have been employed by station WCBS for the past five years and by CBS Network for one year in 1946–1947. In the intervening four years, I was employed by WOV and WPAT, and under the auspices of Columbia Lecture Bureau, lectured nationally before various women's and patriotic and civic organizations. Prior to my coming to New York City in 1946, and after my graduation from college, I taught at the University of Texas, spent a year overseas with the American Red Cross with American forces, and two years in the United States Army as an enlisted man.

During all of this time, I was continuously before the public eye. In addition to the many thousands of broadcasts on radio and television, local and national, I appeared at several thousand dinners, conventions and functions as an entertainer and M.C., many of them at the request of CBS and WCBS. Most of them were in furtherance of my professional career and my employers' public relations.

There has been no criticism (aside from criticism of my shortcomings as a performer), from any source whatever, about anything that I have ever said or done at any of these functions, on the air, or anything I said or did elsewhere. On the contrary, as WCBS knows, both they and I have received many letters of commendation for such public services, and citations from such groups as the Daughters of the American Revolution, the National Press Club of Washington, D.C., and Jewish, Catholic and Protestant organizations, as well as many civic and educational institutions. Although I am primarily a humorist, the usual subject of my lectures has been Our American Heritage, in which I stress the enormous advantages an American citizen has over people of other countries.

For the past ten years, I have been a member of AFRA, which, since 1952, has been known as AFTRA. Last December, I was elected a member of the Board of Directors of the New York Local of AFTRA and then elected second Vice President of the Local. That board, at a meeting on March 22, 1956, adopted a resolution as follows:

"Whereas, the membership of the New York Local of AFTRA endorsed the proposition 'that its local officers should oppose denial of employment by discriminatory and intimidating practices, especially by outside organizations,' in the recent local elections; and

"Whereas, Aware, Inc., has, in spite of a vote of censure by the local membership, continued to circulate allegations of a derogatory nature about members of the union;

"Be it resolved that the employers of AFTRA members be forthwith advised in writing by the Executive Secretary that any discrimination by any such employer against any member of AFTRA on the basis of charges made by Aware, Inc. or any person or group exercising similar functions, will be promptly investigated and made subject of appropriate action by the Local Board."

This resolution was in accordance with the platform on which I and twenty-six other members of the Board ran. We took office under a mandate from the membership to effectuate Plank #5 of what was denominated a "Declaration of Independents," in which we said: "We solemnly pledge . . . to oppose denial of employment by discriminatory and intimidating practices, especially by outside organizations."

Prior to that campaign and my election to the Board, and the Board's beginning to effectuate its opposition to discriminatory employment practices, there had not been one single charge, insinuation or complaint concerning my Americanism and complete loyalty to my government. However, there are those who have decided to make AFTRA their victim and seemingly I have been chosen as one of the first three of the new Board members of AFTRA to be attacked as part of this plan to control our union.

There has been on file for the past five years in the offices of CBS my signed statement, along with those of all other CBS employees, that I was not then, nor at any time a member of the Communist Party, nor of any Communist Front, nor of any of the long list of organizations whose names were imprinted on that CBS form. I repeat now, and under oath, that I am not now nor have I ever been a member of the Communist Party.

Shortly after the new Board took office and began to put into effect the platform on which it ran, a business corporation, Aware, Inc., which in the past has tried to institute a blacklist of performers and has so been condemned by the membership of our union by a vote of nearly two to one, began to circulate scurrilous rumors concerning the newly elected Board. In Aware Bulletin #16 of February 1956, a series of innuendoes and falsifications were made concerning the three top officers of the Board, Charles Collingwood, Orson Bean and myself. Apparently the hodgepodge of allegations made in this bulletin is the reason for your inquiry. I do not believe for one minute that CBS has any intention of becoming a party to the effort of Aware to institute or continue a blacklist in this industry.

Frankly, I do not consider the allegations made by Aware of any relevance or importance. I have worked at CBS for a number of years, and there are many executives, commentators, performers in this organization, well-known civic and religious leaders in New York and elsewhere, as well as members of the New York Local Board of AFTRA, who are perfectly willing and competent to advise CBS and anyone else whom it might concern, on my personal integrity and my attitudes. I have always believed in the American system of government, in due process and in Constitutional liberties, and I will be the last man to betray those principles upon which our government was founded. I was raised a member of the Methodist church, and still am. I grew up as a practicing democrat and I expect to continue that way.

As a member of the New York Local Board of AFTRA, I am pledged to combat discriminatory practices in the industry and I will continue to fulfill that pledge whatever the consequences to me personally may be. Our union is approaching negotiations in a friendly but firm manner. I am confident that the efforts of Aware to destroy the effectiveness of the newly elected Local Board, through personal attacks on its officers or by singling out particular members of the Local Board will arouse nothing but direct resentment and will serve to alert the membership to what is in reality an effort to control our union.

[signed] JOHN HENRY FAULK

The next day, April 13, 1956, I had the affidavit notarized and took it in to Carl Ward. Then I sat down to chat with him about some of the aspects of Johnson's visit to New York. However, Carl quite obviously did not care to discuss Johnson or his campaign against me. I could only suppose that he had heard from the legal department of CBS that he had best not get any further involved. I went in to see Henry Untermeyer, the station's sales manager, and he was even more uncommunicative than Carl. He indicated that he had heard about the matter, and he was very polite; but he made it clear that I wasn't about to get a word out of him on it. I started explaining how black-listing was carried out, and that actually the pressure brought to bear on sponsors could be met with pressure from the other direction. In about five minutes, however, I realized that I wasn't telling him anything that he didn't already know. He began to look so uncomfortable that I departed from his office.

It happened that on that very day I had a luncheon appointment with Sidney Davis, a young lawyer from Louis Nizer's office. I had met him through a mutual friend, columnist Harriet Van Horne, of the *New York World-Telegram and Sun,* who had suggested that Sidney Davis would be an excellent counsel for the union. I had arranged to meet him and discuss that matter. Now, after the shellacking I had received at the meeting, there seemed little point in having that discussion. But I had heard so much about Louis Nizer and about his spectacular victory over Westbrook Pegler, that I decided to keep the date after all.

At our luncheon I told Davis just what had happened. I explained that I was no longer in a position to influence the union to retain him as its counsel. Now, I told him, I had to fight to prevent my enemies, in the union and outside it, from cutting off my livelihood. I would not go down without a real struggle; if I could get hold of something to hit them with, I intended to let fly. I asked him if he thought Nizer would be interested in taking the case should it come to a lawsuit. He said he would discuss it with Mr. Nizer.

That evening, after my show, I had a drink with Gerald Dickler, who told me that Charles Collingwood had called him earlier, greatly alarmed at the news that Johnson and AWARE were hitting my sponsors, and had suggested we come over to his house to discuss what could be done to save my job. We found Charles at home, looking as though it was he, not I, who was about to be blacklisted. We quickly agreed that, as far as the union was concerned, our course had been run, and that we were in total defeat there. We then turned to the matter of my relations with CBS.

Charles said that he intended to do everything within his power to save my job, and that he was open to suggestion. I brought up the matter of suing AWARE. Dickler very quickly pointed out that there was no basis on which to sue. Neither Ward nor Untermeyer nor anyone else who had information would be willing to get on a stand and deliver it. Besides, their testimony would probably be only hearsay anyway—Johnson hadn't been to see them.

Then Gerry turned to me, a little impatiently and said, "Forget about suing. I want you to concentrate on holding your job."

Charles had invited a friend of his, Carl Ruff, who was in public relations for several food store chains. We sat and discussed how we could offset Johnson's pressure on my sponsors. Ruff suggested that if I knew any supermarket executives, perhaps I should go to them directly and tell them what was happening. Owners of supermarkets have a lot of power with food distributors, and food distributors were the principal sponsors on my program.

This struck us as a fine idea, and I did know such a person. As a matter of fact, he was an important figure in the chain-store business, Lansing P. Shield, president of Grand Union Supermarkets, one of the largest chains in the country.

We agreed that I should get hold of Mr. Shield the first thing next day, to see if he would give me a hand. I told them that I would still like to sue somebody, if I knew whom to sue. Gerry pointed out again, quite correctly, that I had no tangible evidence on which to sue. He also said that it was foolhardy of me to expect my employers at CBS to give testimony that would involve the sponsors who were canceling contracts with me. That would threaten CBS's relations with the sponsors, and it was more than one could expect them to do.

Gerry and Charles agreed that they would go together to see the CBS officials and try to forestall any plans to fire me. Although Charles was an employee of CBS, he said he felt duty-bound to speak to them in my behalf. It would put the CBS officials on notice that if I was fired, the reason would be obvious.

The next day, down at CBS, Carl Ward told me that they had had the affidavit that I had given him photostated, and copies distributed to their salesmen to give to any sponsors who raised an issue concerning my patriotism. He said he hoped it would work.

I was feeling so cocky at the time that I did a stupid thing. I said, "Well, you know, Carl, my attorneys tell me that I ought to sue Libby's Frozen Foods for canceling their contract with me. That would force this issue into the open, and then they would have to tell about Mr. Johnson."

Before I got the words out of my mouth, I knew I'd made a serious mistake. Carl Ward began to shake his head negatively before I finished. It startled him so that all he could say was: "No, no. No, no, no. Not that. Not that, ever." He was leaving that day for a trip to the West Coast, and during his stay on the Coast, for about a week, he called back to make sure that I would not do such a ridiculous thing as sue the Libby company.

The next afternoon I called Lansing Shield, who said he would be happy to come up to my office. I went over the bulletin with him and told him how Johnson was butchering me with my sponsors. He said he knew Laurence Johnson very well, and he was amazed to hear that Johnson would do such a thing without ever having met or confronted me. He was sure that all he had to do was call Johnson and Johnson would realize he had made a mistake. He knew that Johnson was a man with very fixed notions, but he was quite sure that Johnson would not want to do me any harm.

It turned out that he was unable to reach Johnson by telephone, so he wrote a letter. In a few days, Laurence Johnson called him. When Shield phoned me to tell me about it, he was somewhat shaken up. He reported that Johnson had said that he knew all about me, and that I was a very dangerous man. He said he would furnish Shield with proof of it. Shield advised me gravely: "John, you had better get you the best lawyer you can find, and get this thing straightened out. It's very serious."

I thanked him, and told him that I was going to do that very thing—if I could get any tangible evidence in my hands.

A couple of days later, Sam Slate came into my office. He said that Tom Murray, an account executive with the Grey advertising agency, had come over to CBS quite infuriated at having received a call from Laurence Johnson, followed by a vicious letter attacking me.

Johnson had warned Murray that unless Murray removed the Hoffman Beverage account from my program, he, Johnson, would boycott Hoffman's in his supermarkets and would sick the American Legion on them. This had made Murray so mad that he had told Johnson to go to hell. Sure enough, within a couple of days, along came a letter from an American Legion post in Syracuse. Sam had a copy of the letter and gave it to me. I knew that at last I had the goods on them. Now, for the first time, a performer had been allowed to see the charges. Tom Murray came over. I wanted to embrace him. He knew Johnson and AWARE. He said that he would not be party to any more of their character assassinations. He said, quite undramatically, that even if it cost him his job and his reputation, he intended to help stop them. I was so moved by this honest, decent man, that I almost forgot I was involved also. I thanked him over and over, to his great embarrassment.

I called Sidney Davis and told him about the letter I now had. He said that he had spoken to Nizer about the matter and that it was time for me to see Nizer myself. Mr. Nizer would see me the next day.

The offices of Phillips, Nizer, Benjamin and Krim are located high over the Times Square area of Manhattan, occupying an entire floor of the Paramount Building. The firm is so large that they have office space on several other floors of the building, too. The stained-glass doors of the reception room are bordered by two long bronze tablets bearing the names of the members of the firm. The walls of the reception room are hung with pictures of President Truman and various justices of the United States Supreme Court, each with its personal greeting to Louis Nizer.

Nizer's private office is a wide, quiet room looking out over the midtown ship piers, the Hudson River and across to New Jersey. Its décor reflects restraint and good taste. The bookshelves around the room are filled with books—not merely law books, but books whose titles suggest a wide range of interests. A number of large easy chairs and a couch area are arranged around the heavily carpeted floor. It is not an ostentatious office, but one of pleasant comfort.

As the secretary ushered me in, Louis Nizer rose from behind his wide, polished desk and came forward to meet me. He is a man of medium height and powerful build, and I was struck at once by his warmth and geniality.

He invited me to sit in one of the heavy leather chairs in front of his desk, seated himself in a high leather swivel chair behind the spacious desk, and suggested that I relate my grievances against AWARE. As I went through the recitation of the events which led up to my present situation, I was only barely aware that Nizer was quietly but firmly moving me past trivia to important points in the case. He never hurried me. He just moved me along, listening gravely and nodding.

When I had finished he asked me if I understood the implications of filing a lawsuit against a group like AWARE. I told him that I thought I did. I knew that my opponents would give me a mighty hard time, if that's what he meant. He nodded; but he said he meant more than that. He said that I should know that it might take several years to bring the case to trial. During that time, great pressure would be brought to bear on me—not only economic pressure, but subtle emotional pressures. It was quite possible that my family would suffer. He then detailed a rather black picture of legal procedures. It all added up to a grim warning.

I told him that I was prepared to go through whatever might seem necessary in order to bring this group of people to trial in a public courtroom. I felt the issues involved were vital ones.

He fell silent, reflected for a moment, and then smiled warmly. He said, "I have deliberately tried to discourage you. I don't want you to be misled that this would be an easy case. It won't be. This action will be a long one. But you will win in the end. I will represent you."

His voice did not change as he made this final statement, but it had a certain quality that caught me up, lifted my spirit and reassured me.

Involuntarily I rose to my feet and stood in front of his desk. I reached my hand out to shake his. He smiled and shook my hand—and then told me to sit down again. He pointed out that our relationship would go far beyond that of client and counsel; that it would become almost a family relationship; that as of now we were joined forever against a common foe, and that the very nature of our battle would be one that would draw us very close together.

He looked over some of the papers and documents that I had brought along. He said that he wanted me to meet Paul Martinson, a partner of his, who would prepare the necessary papers for filing the suit. His secretary took me in to meet Mr. Martinson.

Paul Martinson is a man of kindly face and thinning auburn hair. As he went through various papers, asking me questions, I began to experience the same comfortable, secure feeling that I always had with scholarly, pleasant professors at the university. By the time he had finished his questioning and had written down the information which would be the basis of our formal complaint, I knew that I was talking to a very fine legal mind. I soon conceived a great affection for him, the same kind of affection I had for J. Frank Dobie, one of deep admiration coupled with a desire to give him a hug every once in a while. His grasp of the entire case was immediate and complete. He would cluck with distress over some offensive statement made by the defendants-to-be and would shake his head in exasperation at their villainy. He had an enchanting habit of talking on the phone, speaking to a visitor in his office, and reading a paper or document, all at the same time. His visitor might not be quite sure exactly which one he was commenting to or on. *He* was always sure.

I went home, lighthearted and excited. I began flexing my muscles and fancying myself a dangerous foe indeed to all wrongdoers, especially AWARE. Now my union foes would tremble! And up and down Madison Avenue, word would go out that John Henry Faulk had Louis Nizer fighting his case.

I started calling up friends to tell them that I was going to sue AWARE, and that Louis Nizer was taking the case. I was almost manic with joy; I didn't bother to listen to their reactions. A friend of mine, Palmer Webber, came up to see me, and as we discussed the matter of Nizer taking my case, he asked me how much of a retainer Nizer was charging. I brushed his question aside with the glib statement that Nizer wasn't charging any retainer. Palmer, knowing that I could be carried away with my own enthusiasm, explained to me that Nizer's office would probably require an immense retainer to take such a prolonged litigation. After all, Nizer was a million-dollar lawyer. He handled cases for the biggest corporations in America and was considered one of the two or three finest trial lawyers in the land. I had better get ready to cough up fifty to a hundred thousand dollars as a retainer fee.

I was dumfounded. Nizer had said nothing about this. Palmer pointed out that he probably took it for granted that I knew it. Just getting Nizer to take the case was enough. But in a lawsuit such as this one promised to be, Nizer's firm would be out thousands of dollars just in expenditures. A retainer would be absolutely necessary.

I called Charles Collingwood and asked him if he'd ever heard of this retainer business. Charles said, "Yes. In all likelihood, Nizer will require a rather large retainer."

Detecting the disappointment and anxiety in my voice, Charles assured me that he would do his best to help me raise the required retainer. He thought a lawsuit was very important; he said that he thought other people along Madison Avenue would be anxious to see the matter brought to trial and would probably give me a hand financially too.

"After all," Charles commented, "this lawsuit will be a benefit to the entire radio and television industry. I think you'll find strong support amongst them."

Deciding that I had better talk to Nizer about the matter at once, I called him and asked for an appointment. The next morning I went down and asked him about the retainer. I told him what my friends had said about a fifty- to a hundred-thousand-dollar retainer. I told him candidly that it would be impossible for me to raise that kind of money. I didn't even know whether I would be working.

To my relief, Nizer told me that my friends had misinformed me. Ordinarily his firm did require a large retainer. In the instance of my suit, it would be ten thousand dollars, which was minimal for a major case. He explained that this retainer was not for legal fees, but for actual out-of-pocket expenses. I promised him that the retainer would be forthcoming shortly. I didn't tell him that my savings did not nearly amount to the money required.

During the next several days, I frantically called friends, trying to raise money. They were all willing and anxious to help, and several did. But I was far short of the whole amount when the day arrived for payment. Not everyone, by any means, felt that I was wise to sue.

Ward of CBS felt that it was a very dubious move. He felt it would call the public's attention to my troubles with AWARE. "Best to let this whole thing blow over, Johnny. Perhaps it will."

Sam Slate felt a little differently. He thought it would probably shake up Madison Avenue and raise a real question about me. However, he said that with Louis Nizer guiding my case it would very likely knock AWARE out of the pitcher's box.

Gerry Dickler was doubtful. He pointed out that his chief concern was for my career; he did not want to see me become a martyr. He also pointed out that after the suit was filed, I could be sure that the defendants would increase their pressure on the radio and television industry to starve me out. They would have real incentive now. "They don't want to be brought into court, and if they can avoid it, they're not going to be, Johnny. You'd better prepare for some real tough and rough fighting on their part." I argued that this was an opportunity of a lifetime. I could expose their fraud in open court. If no one else realized what a travesty they made of patriotism, I had to go through with it.

Gerry said that I would find few friends in the industry who would support me during the trial. "They'll be scared to death of you now. Of course, after you have won it, if you do, they will come flocking up to pat your back and shake your hand. You won't see much of them until the trial actually takes place. You can depend on that."

Several days later, Paul Martinson called me to say that he was filing the suit. He said the evidence indicated a conspiracy between AWARE, Vincent Hartnett and Laurence Johnson to carry out the blacklisting.

The day after the suit was filed, all of the New York papers carried the story. One of them, the *New York Post,* filled its entire front page with big, black headlines on the subject. It produced a widespread reaction along Madison Avenue.

I was still $7,500 short of having the amount needed for the retainer. I was embarrassed to go to Nizer and tell him that I couldn't raise it. He might get the idea that he had taken on a pauper. As I was sitting at my desk at CBS, racking my mind for someone to call and borrow money from, Edward R. Murrow called me from his office upstairs.

He said that he was terribly glad that I had filed the suit, and that Carl Sandburg had sent word: "Whatever's the matter with America, Johnny ain't." He said that he was mighty happy about the suit and that his door was always open to me.

I had known Ed Murrow for a number of years. J. Frank Dobie had become acquainted with him during the war years in Europe and had me look up Ed when I first came to New York. I told Ed that I wanted to see him at once and went up and laid the matter before him.

I told him that I lacked $7,500 of the retainer fee. He expressed surprise that CBS was not paying the expenses of the trial, since I was the one who was doing the fighting. I told him that, if anything, the executives to whom I had spoken were strongly opposed to my filing a suit. He said, "Tell Lou Nizer, Johnny, that he will have the money tomorrow."

I protested. "Look, Ed, I can't borrow seventy-five hundred dollars from you. Hell, I might lose my job. And even if I win the suit, there may be no money to repay such a sum as that."

Ed looked at me evenly and said, "Let's get this straight, Johnny, I am not making a personal loan to you of this money. I am investing this money in America. Louis Nizer *must* try this case. These people *must* be brought into court. This blacklisting racket must be exposed. This is a very important suit. I don't know whether even you realize how important it is."

And so it was that on the twenty-sixth of June, 1956, the lawsuit *Faulk v. AWARE, Laurence Johnson, and Vincent Hartnett* was filed in the New York State Supreme Court.

5

I had no illusions when I began. I knew good and well that I was putting my reputation on the block. I understood very well that the defendants had many allies throughout the country and that they would go over my background with a fine-tooth comb. Even had I not known this myself, Nizer and Martinson made this fact clear to me again and again.

Nizer had urged me to go carefully over my past life and think of anything—arrests, difficulties of any kind, bad debts, hot checks—anything that would reflect on my character.

"They are going to scrutinize your life very, very closely. Let's know ahead of time if there is anything with which they could embarrass you. Don't let them take us by surprise."

There was one area in which I was completely naïve. I thought that the radio and television industry would believe that I was taking a bold step and that they would admire me for it. I had the notion that once the news of my lawsuit got around, the radio and television executives—long oppressed by AWARE's vigilantism—would lose their timidity. I was more convinced of this than ever when, within a week after the suit was filed, I received hundreds of letters at CBS from listeners, all of whom approved and sympathized with my action. Many of them expressed outrage that such a lawsuit was necessary and that I was put to the trouble of having to defend myself.

The men who directed the affairs of Madison Avenue, however, reacted as though I had announced I had highly contagious mumps. There were some, perhaps, who sympathized with me and hoped I would win. But they remained very silent. Others regarded me as a complete fool. It wasn't long before I realized that instead of improving my employability, the lawsuit had had an adverse effect upon it; I had become more controversial than ever.

A couple of well-intentioned friends—rather important executives in network television—met me at a cocktail party shortly after the suit was filed. They were both very sympathetic with me and hoped that I would win, but they made an interesting observation. One of them asked me if I knew how Alger Hiss got into all of his trouble. I told him I thought I did, and explained why. He said, "Oh, no. Alger Hiss sued Whittaker Chambers. That is what brought about Alger Hiss's downfall. You better think about that, son."

His friend quickly put in: "And remember Oscar Wilde. Oscar Wilde was doing just fine until he sued the Marquis of Queensberry. He ended up a broken jailbird."

Few, if any, of the radio-TV fraternity believed for a moment that I would win the suit—that is, those among the impartial executives. The Susskinds, Murrows, and those of their persuasion, never doubted for a moment that I would win. They understood the nature of AWARE.

My greatest personal disappointment came with the union's lack of reaction. There was not a voice raised in my behalf in the union, save for a couple of close friends and loyal Middle-of-the-Road members. I was still a member of the local board; indeed, I was still a vice-president. However, I had had my ears whipped down so soundly that I was not much of a power in union affairs anymore.

Judge Ferdinand Pecora became the union's counsel about the same time that my suit was filed. The matter of whether to bring charges against members of the union who had defied the House Un-American Activities Committee was still being bandied about. Judge Pecora gave as his opinion that there was a case pending before the United States Supreme Court, *Watkins* v. *the United States,* which would have a profound effect upon the legality of our New York local's taking action against one of its members for having exercised his constitutional rights before a Congressional committee. He suggested that we lay aside the matter until the Supreme Court decision came down.

The defendants began to stir themselves. They did not take kindly to being sued. Godfrey Schmidt became attorney for the defendants.

He went on a radio program and declared that he was confident that AWARE was right and that obviously I was a man who could not be trusted. He said that he welcomed the opportunity to try the case in the courts of the land.

When he filed his answer, he asserted that I had no cause of action: there was nothing libelous in the AWARE bulletin. They had not called me a Communist. They had only repeated what was the public record of my past doings. If they had made a mistake, it was an honest one.

Nizer challenged these answers as unresponsive. Justice Saul Streit upheld Nizer and dismissed the defendants' answers. In fact, Justice Streit handed down a decision which was one of the cornerstones of our case. It held that the defendants had, indeed, sought to raise a question of my patriotism by innuendo, and that the bulletin was a libel per se. The only full defense was for the defendants to plead the truth of their innuendo: that I was a Communist, at least pro-Communist. They had to prove it by my acts and words. They could no longer hide behind what I was alleged to have done.

The defendants immediately gave notice of appeal to the Appellate Division of the New York State Supreme Court. They couldn't let Justice Streit's decision stand. It struck directly at the heart of McCarthy-type blacklisting—that of character assassination by innuendo.

Although literally hundreds of people had been involved in blacklisting in one form or another, locating witnesses was a tedious task. Under Paul Martinson's direction, the accumulation of evidence was begun. Dozens of performers, writers, and directors who had been damaged were contacted, but the great majority of them showed great reluctance to becoming involved in any way with my lawsuit.

John Crosby, radio and television columnist for the *New York Herald Tribune,* had for many months been writing scathing columns about the doings of AWARE and about blacklisting. AWARE, sometime prior to the filing of my suit, had sued John Crosby and the *Herald Tribune.* The *Herald Tribune*'s attorneys had wisely decided to investigate AWARE and Vincent Hartnett before they came to court, and they had accumulated a sizable library of factual material concerning Hartnett and AWARE. When we filed our suit, the *Herald Tribune*'s lawyers came forward and offered us detailed material, and it proved to be of great assistance to us in preparing the suit.

Another very interesting source of information on blacklisting became available to us at about that time. In the summer of 1956, the Fund for the Republic published an excellently documented study of blacklisting in the radio, television and motion picture industry. John Cogley, its editor, had done an exhaustive job of collecting information on the subject. The publication of his book was greeted by the newspapers with considerable interest, but it did not correct any of the injustices that were going on. For the most part, Cogley had been bound by his informants to omit their names. And while the facts that he related were accurate indeed, it was a considerable handicap not to be able to give names, places and dates.

A most interesting aspect of the publication of this book was the reaction of the House Un-American Activities Committee. They hauled Mr. Cogley down to Washington, and instead of investigating the charges he had made, they investigated Mr. Cogley. Not a single person in the radio and television industry came to Mr. Cogley's defense. He was understandably bitter about this. We made good use of his book in assembling the evidence for our case. And in no instance did we find him inaccurate.

As for my show at WCBS, it continued to be well sponsored. However, when a sponsor would cancel we would never know whether it was because of some backstairs pressure or for a wholly unrelated reason. Before long it became obvious to us that I had better be satisfied with doing that one show each day. The television field was obviously closed to me. Dickler and I discussed it many times, and he said that in spite of all his efforts to stir up interest, the doors remained closed. He suggested that I reconcile myself to the notion that until the lawsuit was over, nothing in the way of additional work would be forthcoming.

Most of the agency and network executives I met were cordial enough, but rather distant. I began to feel that they regarded me as something of a freak. I had tangled with AWARE, yet I was still working; and they didn't quite understand this. It was as though I had broken both legs and was still running footraces.

In December 1956, WCBS renewed my contract with them for another five years, and I breathed easy. Although by its terms I could be dismissed at the end of any thirteen-week cycle for certain reasons, I was confident that none of these remote reasons would arise and that WCBS was actually giving me a vote of confidence. I was making pretty good money out of that one show, and I had no reason to complain. As the spring of 1957 flowered across Central Park, I was completely resigned to forgetting about more ambitious plans for my career until the suit was brought to trial.

Charles Collingwood and I had been re-elected to the local board, but we were hopelessly outnumbered. We could do little but sit in board meetings and watch the other side have its way. The new board took office in January 1957. Their first several meetings in office consisted of rescinding nearly all of the resolutions that had been passed by our board the year before. Then, to make sure we understood that they meant it when they said "good riddance," they passed a resolution to fire Judge Pecora and hire in his place as counsel for the local, Morty Becker, a former member of Henry Jaffe's law firm. However this almost backfired: the papers got word of it, and the local board was embarrassed. But not for long. They resolutely carried through with their plan.

Then to make sure that no wild-eyed radicals like the Middle-of-the-Road people ever got a chance to win an election again, the local board introduced a resolution making it necessary for all candidates for office in the union to submit any statements they intended to mail to the membership to the local board for censorship before mailing. I stopped going to the local board meetings shortly after this.

Meanwhile, the defendants had failed to file their appeal from the ruling of Justice Streit within the proper time. They were so far behind the deadline that Nizer threatened to ask for judgment by default. Godfrey Schmidt agreed to a stipulation providing for pretrial examination—which is not mandatory in libel cases in New York State—and granting us the right to examine the defendants prior to their examining me. (New York Supreme Court procedure calls for the plaintiff to submit to pretrial examination before the defendants, unless otherwise stipulated.) This was just one of the many brilliant and valuable legal moves that Nizer accomplished before the case came to trial.

In April 1957, the Appellate Division unanimously sustained Justice Streit's decision declaring the AWARE bulletin libelous per se.

This knocked the props from under the defendants. The only complete defense in a libel suit is *truth*. The decision meant that they were going to have to come into court and prove that what they had alleged about me was the truth.

That same month a reassuring change occurred in the management of WCBS. Carl Ward was promoted to a position in the television network, and the position of general manager of WCBS was left vacant. The air was rife with rumors of who would become the new general manager. It was my conviction that Sam Slate would be the best possible choice. I discussed the matter with other agency and network executives. They all agreed. I talked it over with Lanny Ross and Bill Leonard, who were doing programs at WCBS. They agreed to go with me to see Frank Stanton and other network executives who were responsible for making the decision. Not that our opinion was of great value, but we thought at least we should make it known. To our delight, Sam Slate was appointed to the job of general manager in May.

Sam's elevation to the job, I felt, meant that I had a real ally against any sneak attacks on me from AWARE or the other defendants. Now, since I had managed to retain most of my sponsors, and with Sam Slate as the general manager of WCBS, everything seemed to be on an even keel, Lynne and I decided we would take the children for a month's vacation, my first real vacation since I joined WCBS. We looked around for a place to go to and discovered that Ocho Rios, Jamaica, filled the bill exactly. A number of our friends had places there, and they urged us to go. I discussed the matter with Sam Slate and he thought that it would be a great idea. He said that Lanny Ross wanted to take a vacation. I could record a couple of weeks of my show and Lanny Ross could do a couple of more weeks for me. When I returned in August, I could repay him by doing two weeks of Lanny's show while he took a vacation. Lanny was agreeable, and it was arranged that I should be gone for the whole month of July 1957.

In June, before we departed, I was offered a lead in a New Jersey summer stock production of *Tobacco Road*. I loved the play, particularly the long version of it, which had never before been performed. I agreed to take the part for two weeks. Although it delayed me a week in getting off to Jamaica, it was a successful and gratifying experience. And when I did depart for Jamaica the first week of July, I left in high spirits.

Our stay in Jamaica was all that one dreams a vacation should be. We had a small white cottage with tiled roof, right along the edge of the Caribbean. Tall palm trees and banana trees led down the green lawn to the crystal-clear water and the coral reefs.

During the month in Jamaica, I forgot that I was involved in a lawsuit, or, indeed, that I even made my living from radio. I went head over heels for skin diving and stayed under water most of the time. Lynne and the children were so well situated, and enjoying Jamaica life so much, that we decided that they should stay on for another week after I returned.

I got back to New York on Sunday night, August 5. After a good night's sleep, I awakened early and sat down at my desk to write a journal of my holiday. About nine o'clock in the morning the phone rang. It was Gerald Dickler. His voice carried a note of alarm. He asked me to come directly to his office. When I asked him what it was, he said that he would prefer to discuss it with me in person.

I showered and dressed quickly, figuring that Gerry was going to give me hell for spending too much money on my vacation. I was probably overdrawn at the bank.

When I reached his office, he stated at once that I had been fired while I was away. He handed me a registered letter which he had received in my absence, announcing the cancellation of my contract with WCBS. The news hit me like a bolt of lightning. I could only sit and blink. In the past year I had become overconfident. Of course, I had been expecting the news subconsciously since the AWARE bulletin had come out, but I had successfully pushed it out of my conscious mind.

I had told myself many times that if worse came to worst and I did get fired, I would be man enough to stand it. Now that that time had arrived I was not prepared for it at all. It took my breath away. Gerry said he was sure that there was only one explanation. They had taken advantage of the fact that I was several thousand miles away on vacation. He pointed out that this was really the first opportunity that WCBS had had, since the filing of my suit, to make such a move and cover it up with plausible reasons. He said, "Of course, none of their reasons really make any sense. You're doing as well as almost anybody at the station, and better than most of them. You've got a good record at WCBS as an earner."

I just sat there looking at the registered letter. "The plain facts are," Gerry said, "they don't want you there any more, Johnny. Somebody got to them. How or when, I don't know. But you became the source of embarrassment to WCBS. They picked up what excuses came to hand, took advantage of your absence to make the move. That's all there is to it."

"Well," I said finally, "now that it's done, it's done. Where do we go from here?"

Gerry looked glum, and shook his head. "Nowhere, I'm afraid."

"My God, I'd never have taken that vacation if I had known this was coming. Have we got any money left?"

Gerry nodded. "Yes, I've been working on that. I figure that if we're real cautious with what you have in the bank, you can get through for three or four months. Possibly until Christmas. But you are going to have to cut down on every expense—right to the bone."

He suggested that I go on up to see Sam Slate at once, since he had promised Sam that he would send me directly to him. He said that we would get together later that afternoon and discuss plans—if any.

I went to Sam Slate's office. I was embarrassed. I got the impression that he was too. Sam began by saying that he had made the decision entirely on his own, and that no one else was responsible. He then gave me several reasons for having reached the decision. He said that Arthur Godfrey and the network had pre-empted part of my time, that I had been in the same place too long, and that perhaps a change would do me good. He said, too, that my rating had slipped some.

I felt terribly sorry for him. I tried to reassure him that there were no hard feelings. And when I left his office I was certain, and I still am, of one thing: Sam Slate sincerely regretted having to fire me from WCBS.

Allen Ludden was program manager at WCBS at that time. I went in to see him. Allen told me that Sam Slate felt very badly about my being fired. He also told me that as program director he, Allen Ludden, took full responsibility for the decision. They were planning to change the program format of the station.

This somewhat baffled me. A few moments before, Sam Slate said that *he* took full responsibility. I left Allen's office rather confused. I went into my office and called Louis Nizer and told him what had happened. He wasn't confused at all; he was angry; he knew the ax had fallen at last.

6

At home that night, alone, I sat down and stared out over lower Manhattan. The impact of my firing hit me full force. I could not think of a single move to make. It seemed like the end of the road.

A bitter wave of self-pity swept over me. I thought of Lynne and the children having a fine time down in Jamaica. Little they cared that I was sitting alone, suffering. And Nizer and Martinson? It was fine enough for them to be reassuring about the justice of our cause, but who was bearing the brunt? Me. And Dickler? All he could do was to sit around and be glum. Telling me to face reality. Hell, what did he know about reality? What did he know about the pain and anxiety I was going through? And all my other friends who had shown such solicitude, and who had rejoiced in my fight against AWARE. Where were they? Probably home, thinking of reasons to avoid me now that I was an unemployed. They had been fine as long as I hadn't called on them for anything. Now let's see what they would do.

Now that I'd been tossed on the trash heap, my friends' true feelings would come out. J. Frank Dobie and Roy Bedichek, down in Austin, the two great souls who had been my greatest inspirations—how they had praised me and patted my back! How they had doted on my courage and fortitude in calling AWARE to account! What would their attitude be now? What if Dobie and Bedichek knew how frightened and cringing I was at this moment? What if they could see me now? Wiping my nose on my sleeve and rubbing my skinned knee, I smiled. I knew I was lying to myself. Dobie and Bedichek were the oak trees. They would never falter. Suddenly my self-pity was swept away by a wave of embarrassment. Dobie had told me at the commencement of my lawsuit that he was proud of me. He would always be at my side. Any time. Anywhere. When I remembered this, I was even more embarrassed. God, what if he could see me now going through this infantile self-pity? He would be amazed and shocked. Worse, ashamed for me. I was ashamed of myself.

What was really happening to me? Nothing that I had not anticipated. What did I really believe about my society? About America? What had Daddy really believed about our society when he'd catch a bus and ride for an entire hot summer's day to try a case for a Negro who could not even afford to pay Daddy's bus fare? What about the hundreds of men and women who had been harried from pillar to post in New York and Hollywood by these vicious elements, and what about those who had even been imprisoned, but who had refused to bow before their oppressors? What had they believed? The same thing that I did. They believed in the society that had produced them —that they had an obligation to it which transcended their own personal interest. I was allowing self-interest to become paramount, it was that simple. Good Elmer Davis had said: "America was not founded by cowards, and it will not be saved by cowards."

The society I believed in rested firmly on the bedrock of freedom. The genius that had founded our society and written into its laws: "Congress shall make no law respecting an establishment of religion, or prohibiting the free exercise thereof; or abridging the freedom of speech, or of the press, or the right of the people peaceably to assemble, and to petition the government for a redress of grievances" —that genius had placed a heavy obligation on me. I accepted it. I believed with every fiber of my being that America's greatness stemmed directly from those great dreams and ideals. The enemies of these ideals—the House Un-American Activities Committee, AWARE, Inc., the Ku Klux Klan—no matter what powers or shapes they assumed they could not change that conviction.

I pulled myself together and started to plan. The first and most obvious move, of course, would be to consult with Nizer and Dickler and assess exactly where the firing left me. I was going to find a job—that much was sure. I started going over the possibilities in my mind. I could not think of a thing. I decided to put off figuring that out until I could talk to Nizer and Dickler the next day.

Then I got to thinking about CBS. I found that when I thought about it I could not accept Dickler and Nizer's suspicion that my firing at CBS was the result of pressure from AWARE. For some reason or other, it seemed that I wouldn't mind so much if I had been fired for legitimate reasons, and I wanted to believe I had been. The more I thought about it, the more convinced I became. I managed to convince myself, before I went to sleep, that Sam Slate had given me straight dope as to the reasons for my dismissal.

The next morning, down in Louis Nizer's office, I recited at some length my conversations with Sam Slate and Allen Ludden. I added that they had more or less convinced me that AWARE was not involved in my firing. Nizer was impatient with me. He looked at me as though I were a balky child. "John, do you really believe that the sole and only reason for your dismissal at CBS was anything other than the defendants' pressure on CBS?"

"Well, yes," I began, "I just can't believe that WCBS would do anything that underhanded. They wouldn't have one reason and give me another."

"How long have you been at WCBS?"

"Since 1951. Almost six years."

"And doesn't it strike you as odd indeed, considering your six-year tenure, that they would cancel your contract while you were thousands of miles away on a vacation, giving you no notice, no warning whatever? Is that the routine way of dismissing an artist from a company after six years?"

"Well no, but—"

"John, I'm amazed. Wasn't it just two months ago, at the party you gave for Sam Slate, that he made a speech and said that as long as he was at CBS you would be there, too? I heard him, and so did everybody else there; he said it in no uncertain terms. Now, less than two months later, he tells you you're fired. Does that make sense to you?"

"Yes, but apparently there were changes in the network's plans. Arthur Godfrey is pre-empting part of my time. Sam had no control over that."

"You would still have a half hour. Besides, WCBS is on the air twenty-four hours a day, is it not?"

"Yes, Lou, but Sam Slate says my ratings. . . ."

"Sam Slate *said!* Don't *you* know for yourself whether your ratings have slipped or not?"

"Well, I never pay any attention to ratings. I've known for a long time that they are phony. They have no meaning, really, in assessing the success or failure of a show as far as I'm concerned. I know that radio and television executives use them to go through a sort of self-deluding ritual. And Sam has to abide by them."

"But John, *you* don't know whether your ratings have slipped or not?"

"No sir. I know they've gone up and down ever since I've been there. Everyone else has the same experience. Six months ago, Sam told me my ratings were the highest they had been since I came to CBS. Hell, I don't know."

Lou, I guess, took pity on my lack of sophistication. His voice lost its sharp cross-examining quality. "John, you were doing well at WCBS. You had a successful show. It was well sponsored. You were making money for yourself. More important, you were making money for CBS. Do you think for one moment that they would have taken the action that they did if they hadn't been pressured into it?"

I persisted. "But I can't believe that Sam Slate would have fired me under pressure, and then denied it. He would have told me. I know Sam."

"Yes, I'm sure you know Sam. And like him. And I'm sure he likes you, and respects you. But you do not understand his position in relation to his organization. If a decision was made to cancel your contract, and Sam Slate as an officer of the corporation was instructed to give you certain reasons for that decision, he would have no choice but to follow those instructions, or resign. It's that clear.

"Now," Nizer said, turning to another subject, "does Dickler have any plans for you?" I told him that I was going to Dickler's office as soon as I left him.

When I got there, I told Dickler about my conversation with Nizer about the firing. Gerry looked at me in astonishment. "But I thought I told you that yesterday!"

"I know, Gerry, but when I talked with Sam and Allen Ludden and then went home and thought about it, I just refused to believe that they had let me go under pressure."

Gerry gave me a despairing look and shook his head. "Well, there are a couple of things we ought to get settled at once," he said. "First of all, what kind of announcement is WCBS going to make to the press about this matter? I spoke to Sam when he told me you were being let out, and he told me that he would cooperate to do you the least harm."

"God Almighty," I said. "What can they say? Hell, if they say they let me out because I couldn't cut the mustard any more on the program, nobody will want me. On the other hand, if it gets out that I was fired because AWARE got to WCBS and pressured them into it, nobody will touch me."

We discussed the matter for a while, without reaching any definite conclusion. Gerry suggested that perhaps he should talk to Sam Slate about it. Then we turned to the matter of another job. Gerry was glum about my chances of finding anything in New York. "The way I see it, John, those boys are up to their tried and true methods. They're going to give you the old starvation routine. They don't want to go to trial. They want you to be amenable to a settlement. They figure you can't hold out forever. And they also figure that you'll be a lot easier to come to terms with if you're out of work and hungry."

"To hell with them. I'm playing for keeps."

"They've squeezed some mighty big boys in their day. Some mighty big ones. And they've made them knuckle under. You know that you're not going to knuckle under, and I know you're not going to knuckle under. But they don't know it. And they're going to pull out all the stops. If need be, they'll get the House Un-American Activities Committee to subpoena you. They're not going to let up. They're rough customers."

"What do you suggest I do? Go fishing?"

"Well—" Gerry softened—"I don't mean to paint a totally black picture. But you have a tendency to see nothing but the silver lining, and I want you to understand that there's a dark cloud up there too. Once you understand that, we can go ahead and be realistic about this. You know that I'm going to do *everything* possible, and I know you will, too."

I agreed that I would try to be more realistic about things. I knew that my situation would call for some sharp readjustments in my way of life. Then we talked about Lynne and the children. We agreed that while financially it would be better if they came home from Jamaica at once, maybe they should stay on there for a while. The dog days of August were on New York City like a smothering blanket. It would be better all around for them to be away.

That afternoon as I went up in the elevator to WCBS, I had a vague feeling of uneasiness. WCBS radio, at that time, occupied the entire ninth floor of the CBS building on Madison Avenue. I knew everyone in the organizations—the stenographers, the secretaries, the directors, the various sales folk, the sales and promotion people, everyone. When a performer was fired from the organization, the news went through the ranks like greased lightning. I had the feeling that they were all saying to themselves, "There goes poor old John being turned out to pasture."

Later, however, as I sat in my office, I realized that my feeling of discomfort was also from another cause. Actually, I was suspicious. That was it. And I didn't like being suspicious. I was suspicious of the people with whom I was working. I was scheduled to go in for a talk with Sam Slate, and I found myself resisting. I was suspicious of him. Suspicious that he wasn't shooting straight with me.

I did go in, however. I decided to be direct and candid. I said, "Sam this is very important to me personally. Is there any connection whatever between my troubles with AWARE and my dismissal from WCBS?"

I watched his reaction closely. He declared upon his solemn oath that there was no connection whatever, and then quickly turned to the matter of my having gotten into something of a rut on my program. He suggested that perhaps it would really be best for me in the long run to make a change.

I went back to my office and pondered the matter. It was all right for Dickler and Nizer to be convinced that WCBS had fired me under pressure. But I realized that neither one of them had had the long and close association that I had; I felt that it placed me under a certain obligation to accept WCBS's explanation until it was proved conclusively not to be so. On the other hand, I didn't like being considered a simple-minded fool. If I had been, I wanted to know it.

I was to do Lanny Ross's program for the next two weeks. His program was scheduled to come on from four o'clock to five, the hour before mine. One of the secretaries brought in his commercial schedule for the day. As I casually glanced over the list of commercials, I made an interesting discovery. I got out the commercial schedule for my own program and compared them. I was astonished to find that Lanny Ross had only about half as much commercial time on his program as I had on mine.

I asked the secretary to bring the past two months' schedules for Lanny's show. I compared them with mine. It turned out that he averaged about half the commercials that I did each day. Maybe I didn't understand ratings, but I understood simple arithmetic. WCBS was making twice as much income from my program as it was making from Lanny Ross's program. Now, one of the fundamental facts of life in American broadcasting is that commercials are the lifeblood of any radio station; but I was leaving and Lanny Ross was staying.

I had known for many years that there was a lot of double talk among executives in radio and advertising agencies concerning ratings, shares of audience, and such things. I had sat in at dozens of conferences and listened while the talk whirled around my head. I had heard one man taking a set of figures and proving a point conclusively—or at least to his satisfaction. The next moment another man would take the same figures and prove precisely the opposite point. I had little respect for such double talk and had long since learned to ignore it. A radio station—whatever public service posture it may strike—is in business to make money for its owners. That is fundamental. Just as a filling station is. My program was making a profit, and a handsome one, for WCBS.

I swiveled around in my chair and gazed out the window. Maybe Sam Slate had told me the honest truth as he believed it, but somewhere and somehow somebody in that vast organization had used the knife. The decision to cancel my contract had had nothing whatever to do with my ratings or with program changes at CBS. From that moment on I never believed otherwise.

7

My forty-fourth birthday arrived August 21, 1957. That evening I realized for the first time what a terrifying thing it must have been for the tens of thousands of men in their mid-forties who had suddenly lost their jcbs or had their professions swept away from them. I had never understood what a painful thing this must be. There they were—just as I was—with no takers for their particular training and experience. How could they bear it?

With this thought came the realization that it might take three or four years to bring my case to trial. I considered myself in my prime. These would, ordinarily, be my most productive years. And they were precisely the years in which I would be doing nothing.

I blocked off those thoughts. I knew that this was a sure road to despair. The next day, suddenly, the cloud rolled back and the sun broke through with a great flood of light. In the morning mail was an airmail letter from Bill Schwarz out in Minneapolis. He had just become program director for a big station there, WCCO. Bill had been a director on one of my shows at WCBS several years before, and he knew the kind of work I did well. He was an intelligent, energetic fellow and was going places in radio broadcasting. He was also a good friend, and he respected me.

His letter explained that one of WCCO's mainstay personalities, Cedric Adams, had no contract with WCCO and could quit or retire at any time. The station wanted to start developing another personality who could step into Mr. Adams' place in case he should leave the station. Bill had thought of me. He said he thought I would be a perfect candidate for the job. He said that if I should ever decide I was tired of New York and wanted a change from WCBS, I should let him know. He would be very interested in my coming to WCCO.

I went into a tailspin of excitement. In a flash, I convinced myself that my entire life had been dedicated to preparing for a career in Minneapolis radio. I knew that I would love Minneapolis and that the listeners would adore me. I jerked down an atlas to get the exact location of the city. It reminded me that Minnesota was the land of ten thousand lakes, sky-blue waters and all that sort of thing. I had an impulse to call the landlord and tell him we wouldn't be needing our apartment any more—I would be living in Minneapolis. Probably in a rather large house with a lake nearby.

I started to grab the phone and call Bill at once. Then I came to my senses. It wouldn't do to call Bill like that in response to his letter. It would sound too eager, and he would probably become suspicious that something was wrong. After all, if a fellow makes an inquiry about your selling him a horse and looks out the next morning to find the horse tied to a tree in the yard, he's likely to get the notion that you're trying to unload the horse before it dies. So I sat down and wrote Bill, tried to be subtle, saying that perhaps I could be persuaded if the climate suited me and the salary was right. But I struck that out. I knew I would have to be fair with Bill; he was a good friend. It wouldn't do to start negotiations off on a devious level, so I was candid and direct. I told him about the lawsuit and the difficulties I was having at WCBS. I wrote that perhaps his need for me at WCCO had come at precisely the right time and that I was most eager to talk about it. I sent the letter airmail.

After I mailed the letter to Bill, I went down to see Sam Slate. He knew Bill well and respected him. Sam said that he would be happy to call Bill and urge him to act at once. Sam told me also that he would be happy to make arrangements for me to go out to see Bill, if that became necessary. Sam was obviously as enthusiastic over the turn of events as I was, and wanted to lend himself to it fully.

I went down into my office and sat down to call Gerry Dickler and report the good news. At that moment, I got a call from Joe Hyman, a theatrical producer on Broadway. He said that they were producing a play called *Fair Game* and that its author had suggested me for a part. The author had in fact written the part with me in mind. Mr. Hyman wanted to send me the script to see if I'd be interested in auditioning for the part. I told him he needn't send it—I would come over immediately and get it.

Then I sat there and blinked at the wall. I called Gerry on the phone. "Listen, Gerry, you've heard that lightning never strikes twice in the same place? Well, that's nonsense. It's just done it."

Gerry grunted. "What's happened now?"

"Two bolts have just hit me."

"Good God," he gasped. "You mean they've fired you twice?"

"Nope. These were good bolts," I said. "I'm now in a state of utter confusion, however. Whether to become a major star in Minneapolis radio or to star on Broadway."

Gerry became interested right away. He told me to calm down and tell him what had happened.

When I had finished, he became almost as excited as I was. He cautioned me to take it easy: "Nothing is firm yet, Johnny. No contracts are signed. Don't get your hopes too high."

He suggested that I read the play and then wait to hear what Sam Slate reported on his conversation with Bill Schwarz.

Just before I went on the air, Sam Slate came in. He had just spoken with Schwarz in Minneapolis. He said Bill was very excited over the prospect of my coming out, and glad that I was going to be free to do so. He wanted to talk to me. I was to call him the first chance I got. Right after my show, I called Bill and he said that he'd decided to come to New York to go over the whole proposition. He was confident that we could work something out. I was too.

I went down to Hyman's office, got the play, and read it that evening. The part that they wanted me to audition for was a small one, but it was a juicy one. The play was about the garment district, and my part was to be a character, a buyer from Dallas, leering and gauche, but deliciously humorous, wheeling and dealing throughout the garment district. I knew that I could do the character up brown on stage. Before I went to sleep that night I was already thinking that being fired by WCBS had proved to be a blessing in disguise.

The next day, Gerry Dickler and I had lunch. We went over the two jobs—the two possibilities which were before me. Gerry pointed out that Broadway was a mighty risky business, the pay was far less than I could make at WCCO and plays being produced did not mean that they would be hits. "Some of them close in Philadelphia or New

Haven and never get to Broadway. And besides, remember they're only *considering* you for the part. You haven't auditioned yet; they haven't offered you a contract."

I went down to the theater to audition that very afternoon. I was delighted to discover that Moss Hart was to direct the play. He was sitting out in the theater watching the audition. I knew Moss and his wife, Kitty Carlisle. They'd been friends of mine for a number of years. In fact, we had done a couple of television shows together. He was quite surprised to see me auditioning for a play. I went through a couple of scenes, and Moss came around to tell me that he was delighted. "I had no idea you had such a flair for the stage, Johnny. Splendid. Splendid."

The next day Joe Hyman called me to say they were offering me the part.

Bill Schwarz came to New York, and we had a meeting. He had glowing accounts of the good life in Minneapolis. He also felt that my chances of cutting a wide swath in radio circles there were good indeed. I told him about the Broadway offer, and about the dilemma I was in. Bill liked me, and he said that he would not urge me in the matter; but he did hope that I would decide on Minneapolis. He had arranged to have the station manager, who was in Washington, D.C., at the time, come up to New York to meet me.

The station manager and I went to dinner and got along fine. He and Bill suggested that I bring Lynne out to Minneapolis to look the place over. They said we should plan to stay a week or so with all expenses paid. Look over the housing situation there, and the schools. I could meet all the folks at the station. I agreed to do so.

I was treading on air. In fact, I was so excited when Friday, September 13, came around that I scarcely noticed the combination. It was to be my last day at WCBS. After six years, I was to say farewell to my audience. I did so with great regret. I was very fond of my listeners. The next week Lynne and I flew out to Minneapolis.

Bill told me that he wanted to introduce me to everyone at the station, and then launch a contest around my coming to WCCO. He had me interviewed by each of the station's personalities on the air. Listeners were to write in, telling why they liked Texas and why they would like to take a trip there. The winner would be given a trip to Texas. It was a dubious prize, but it brought forth a lot of letters. I was taken around for interviews, and I met practically everyone in Minneapolis, it seemed to me, including Governor Orville L. Freeman, with whom I did an interview. He congratulated me on coming to Minneapolis, and on having been born in Texas. I congratulated him on being Governor of Minnesota.

When I wasn't whirling around the station meeting people, Lynne and I were being driven around Minneapolis looking over prospective homes. It is a beautiful town, and it does have dozens of lakes. Lynne planned to return to New York several days before I was to return. The night before she went back she called my attention to a matter which had escaped me. I had been so busy grinning and being effervescent and personable that I hadn't noticed an important detail. Nobody had actually sat down and talked contract with me. Nor had they by the time I was ready to leave town.

On the way back to New York, I became uneasy. By the time I had reached New York, I resolved that I had better get hold of Joe Hyman at once and tell him that I would take the Broadway show. I had decided that there was something amiss in Minneapolis.

Before I'd gone out to Minneapolis, I had told the producers of *Fair Game* that I had to go out and look over this job, but that I would let them know as soon as I made a decision as to whether or not I would take the part. Joe said they would hold it open as long as they could, but that they were going to have to cast it pretty soon —the play was going into rehearsal.

As soon as I got to the apartment in New York, I told Lynne that I had decided that we'd better take the play. She looked at me sadly. "I realized, Johnny, before I left Minneapolis that something was afoot there that didn't look good for us. I called the producer as soon as I got to New York. They were in Philadelphia. They have already cast that part, and have gone into rehearsal. They were terribly disappointed."

I sat down and thought, now I am really going to feel like a fool if this Minneapolis thing doesn't come through. I was almost ashamed to think about it. It was as though I had taken a week's pay and shot craps with it. I began silently to berate myself for my stupidity. However, I got hold of myself at once. I declared resolutely, "Well, the last thing that Bill Schwarz said to me was that he would let me know. And shortly. So we'll know in a short time whether or not the WCCO job is firm. Let's not sit around and wring our hands until we know for sure."

Bill was as good as his word. He let me know shortly. They didn't want me.

8

The long wait began in October 1957—the long wait to confront AWARE face to face before a bar of justice. I say it really began then, although I suppose I had been waiting since Val Adams called me about the AWARE bulletin. However, up until this time most of my concern had been with what *might* happen. (There had always been an income to lean back on.) Now unemployment had come to sit in our house like a turkey buzzard—roosting there, watching, and waiting.

Both Louis Nizer and Gerald Dickler had anticipated what waiting out the lawsuit could do to me, if I were unemployed. After I returned from Minneapolis, Lou had a long talk with me. He recommended that I not for one moment consider myself unemployable. He said that I should not regard any door as closed until I had tried it. He said that I would be surprised to know how many executives in radio and television did not even know that I'd been fired from CBS, or why. He suggested that I should certainly not take it for granted that the blacklist was airtight. I should never bring up the matter when I was dealing with a prospective employer. If the prospective employer mentioned it, I should minimize the relative importance of my lawsuit. I should present a competent and positive countenance at all times.

Then Gerry Dickler and I sat down and made plans—or at least we tried to. We started out by figuring how long I could make my bank account hold out if worse came to worst in the coming months and I did not get work immediately. The most important matter that had to be resolved was the business of getting a job. Gerry said, and

I agreed, that we should systematically explore every contact either of us had in radio or television in New York. Until we had done this, I should not consider going into another field. Gerry said that he would call every executive in the industry that he knew. I was to do the same.

I made a list of everyone I could think of who could be instrumental in getting me work in radio and television. All of the network and independent stations' executives, advertising executives, independent packagers of shows—everyone. I made a vow that I would follow each lead to its end—no matter how tenuous it seemed to be.

The first call I made was to an executive, a personal friend of mine named Bill, who headed a production company that packaged several radio and television shows. They had one show in particular that was just right for me, a panel show. When I phoned him, he seemed delighted to hear from me. I asked him if I could drop by and see him the next day at eleven o'clock. He replied, "By all means. I'll be glad to see you."

I pretended that it was a social call. I didn't mention the purpose of my visit. I intimated that I would be in the building and thought it would be great to see him again. I was greatly encouraged by his cordiality and was filled with anticipation.

Next morning the receptionist in Bill's office took my name and smiled pleasantly as she called it in on the phone to Bill's secretary. She said he had asked if I could wait. I smiled and took a seat. The office was ornately furnished. I glanced at my watch; I was three minutes early. Perhaps that was why I had been asked to wait. On the other hand, if Bill was actually as anxious to see me as he had indicated on the phone, it was strange that he was not there and ready for me. I put the thought out of my mind quickly. I tried to concentrate on the pictures of the various television personalities on the walls of the reception room. Most of them were friends of mine, smiling toothy smiles at me—secure in their jobs. Well, who knows, I thought, my picture might be up there, too, before long. I glanced at my watch again. Now it was exactly eleven o'clock. The receptionist was looking at a movie magazine. After a moment I cleared my throat, "Did you tell Mr. Bill my name—Faulk?"

She nodded. I mumbled, "Well, the appointment was at exactly eleven o'clock. I really don't have the time to waste."

The receptionist looked up. "Oh, his secretary said he was expecting you. He's not at his desk right now. She said it would only be a minute or two."

I thanked her. This was funny. What could he be doing? Perhaps he was calling around to find out where I stood in the industry. In all likelihood, he had discovered that I was in trouble, and was probably trying to figure out a gentle way to let me down. Now, that couldn't be it. He hadn't even hinted that he knew what I was coming to see him for. Nor had I. He didn't know that I was looking for work. I had pretended it was just a social visit. But why this delay?

I tried to keep from glancing at my watch, but couldn't. It was now nearly five minutes after eleven. I was seized with a strong impulse to tell the receptionist that I couldn't wait another minute. That would be a damn fool thing to do. I restrained myself. After all, Bill might have been in a meeting that had run five minutes late. It happened lots of times. I tried to compose myself and appear casual.

In another moment, Bill dashed out smiling brightly and started pumping my hand, "Sorry John, I was in the men's room. Damn ulcer's kicking up. By God, it is good to see you. How've you been?"

And with that, he escorted me into his office and, still smiling and chatting away, indicated an easy chair before his handsome desk for me to sit in. I felt reassured. It was clear that he was delighted to see me. I suddenly loved him very much. He asked if I cared for coffee, and when I said yes, he told his secretary to get some for us, and he leaned back.

"I didn't see you on Fire Island this summer, Johnny."

"No, we spent our vacation in Jamaica, Bill." I was pleased that the conversation started off so easily, and went on at some length about our vacation. Bill told me how he had become a water skier during that summer, and how fond he was of the sport. Then I launched into a lengthy description of my exploits as a skin-diver in Jamaica. Coffee came, and we settled into a conversation about the relative merits of Fire Island and Westhampton Beach as summering places. The time sped by. The visit was going very pleasantly, but I knew that I couldn't spend the whole visit on triviality. On the other hand, I couldn't bring myself to break off the conversation and declare that I'd come to see him about getting a job. After a great while Bill said, "Hey, somebody—I think it was my mother—told me you were not at CBS any more. She was sore as hell. She doted on your program, you know."

I smiled. "Well, bless her heart! No, I had to let that show go, Bill. Oh, I loved it, of course. It was like visiting with neighbors every afternoon, but I was in a rut. I had to break away somehow. I want to concentrate on television."

"Oh," he said, and he nodded. "You have a TV show now? You working with Goodson and Todman?"

I shook my head, searching frantically for a logical answer. I obviously couldn't tell him that I had dropped my CBS show and had nothing whatever to do. He would know that I was either crazy or lying. "Well, as a matter of fact," I said, "I had a big offer out in Minneapolis. A hell of a big deal offered me. Lynne and I went out and looked over it, and I almost took it, but we decided that we couldn't leave New York. Besides, I've about decided to concentrate on television, and New York's the place for that, of course."

Bill smiled agreeably. "Well, I think you might be right, but I'll tell you right now my mother's going to miss you every afternoon. She was one of your most loyal fans."

"Yeah, I know. You know, she wrote to me and I wrote to her. She wrote Mama a beautiful letter a couple of years ago when Mama was up here in New York and was on my show. But hell, Bill, I would like to get into television."

"What kind of show are you doing, John?" he asked.

"Well, I've been considering several things. As a matter of fact"—and here I tried to look and sound as though the thought had just struck me—"I like that panel show of yours. It's a hell of a good one. If you ever need a panelist, I'd like to have a go at it."

Bill nodded pleasantly. "Sure, Johnny, you're a cinch for it. In fact, I've thought of calling you several times. You'd be great on it." And then he paused. "But you know that it doesn't pay but about three hundred bucks a shot?"

I tried to remain casual. "That's not the main point at all, Bill. I really need to get with television audiences. Need exposure. Your show's popular. It would be just perfect for me there."

"I'll check into it right away," he said. I was delighted to see that he made a note of the matter on a pad. "It's a good idea. I think you'll be great. I'll have my secretary call you on Thursday. Or you can call me. Either way. About eleven. How about it?"

I told him yes. I restrained an impulse to leap up and hug and kiss him; instead I got up, saying I had to be getting on, I had taken up enough of his time. He glanced at his watch and said yep, he had a twelve o'clock appointment and that he would expect to hear from me on Thursday, if his secretary hadn't called me.

I caught a taxi home. I felt full of fire. I dashed into the apartment, jumping up and down, dancing around, caught up little Frank Dobie in my arms and did a waltz with him, kissed Lynne, and told her all the news. I rushed to the telephone and called Gerald Dickler. He was delighted too, but he said, "That's not the only fish in the sea. Keep fishing, son. Have you called Mark Goodson yet?"

"I was going to call him this afternoon, Gerry, but I'd better hold off, I guess. If I'm going to do Bill's show, and it looks like a cinch I will be doing it, I couldn't do a Goodson-Todman show too." I was feeling wolfish.

That afternoon I picked up Johanna and Evelyn after school and took all three children to the park.

At eleven o'clock on Thursday, I called Bill's office. His secretary told me that he was not in, but that she knew he wanted to speak to me. He would call me after lunch, if I would tell her where I would be. When I hung up, I had a vague feeling of uneasiness. At three o'clock, when Bill hadn't called, I called him. After much delay, he came to the phone. His voice was cheerful still, but a bit shaded, it seemed—cautious. "Johnny, I guess I should have checked before I told you that you were all set. It seems they've got things pretty well set on the panel for the next few weeks. They already have arrangements made. But stay in touch. The first opening will go to you." I guess he sensed the disappointment in my reply. Then he added, "How 'bout lunch next week? Say next Monday?"

I said that I would be delighted, but I couldn't make it on Monday.

"Then Tuesday. At one o'clock, at Louis and Armand's?"

On Tuesday morning Bill's secretary called and asked if I could come to his office. When I got there I knew that Bill had heard something unpleasant. He was cheerful enough, and full of good will, but preoccupied. "I'm in pretty much of a push for lunch," he said, "but I did want to visit with you. How about our eating up here instead of going out? That is, if you don't mind. We can talk a lot better here too."

I agreed, and sandwiches were sent up. Our conversation was of a trivial sort. He didn't mention the panel show until I was preparing to leave, and then he said, "Be sure and stay in touch with me, Johnny. I'll be on the Coast for a couple of weeks, but I'll be back. In the meanwhile, I have told them that if anything comes up they should give you a call. My secretary has your number."

In the next several weeks, each interview I arranged turned out more or less the way the one with Bill did. Dickler located an opening at WOR. It looked quite promising. After lengthy negotiation and a detailed discussion of the terms of the contract, everything fell silent. Nothing happened. A sort of macabre game started. Each day we watched our bank account dwindle, dwindle, dwindle. And each day I ran frantically about, looking for work, racing against the time when there would be no money left. It wasn't much fun to play the game, but I was terribly interested in who would win. Would I get a job before the bank account gave out? I quit debating whether to take taxis. The matter became academic.

One of the brightest spots in that dark period in the fall of 1957 was Rhodelle. Rhodelle Rogers had been our maid, our companion and our confidant for several years. She lived with us, more as a member of the family than as an employee. The children were comfortable and happy in her care. She had come to New York from Kingstree, South Carolina. A number of her brothers and sisters still lived there. They visited her in New York occasionally, and they too came and stayed with us. Rhodelle took a keen interest in everything that involved us. She didn't understand all the details of my being fired or of my lawsuit, but she understood enough to be outraged at the defendants. She had a rare gift for satire, and a nimble wit. She caught the nuances of various personalities who came to visit us, and could do little verbal caricatures which were delightful.

She and I had evolved a rather macabre, but amusing, game. She knew how keenly I felt about race relations, and like many, many Negroes of the South, she understood subtleties of the Southern problem as well, if not better, than I did. I would turn on my recording machine and pretend that I was a white sheriff who had come out to Rhodelle's house to dispossess her. I would go through a condescending, gruff speech to her, and she would reply with the mock servility that Southern Negroes frequently adopt in the presence of authority which they do not respect, but understand all too well. After she had properly made the ritual show of obsequiousness in the sheriff's presence, he would depart. Then she would record her real thoughts about him. They were hilarious and often illuminating and very, very shrewd.

Lynne never enjoyed our game; it was too real for her. But Rhodelle and I enjoyed it very much. We'd sit and play it back, and admire each other's acting.

One day, after Gerry and I had gone over the reduction of my living costs, I announced to Rhodelle that we could not afford to pay her any longer. I told her that I didn't know when I would work again. She was welcome to leave her things at our home as long as she found it necessary, but that we could no longer keep her on as an employee.

She understood perfectly and was completely sympathetic. She went away to look for work over a weekend. That Sunday night she returned and sat down with us. She said she didn't know what had possessed her. That we were her friends and she would not leave us at a time like this. It was her thought that matters would work out best if she stayed on and helped early in the mornings and in the evenings with the children, and went out and got day work. That is, if we didn't charge her rent. Perhaps, in fact, she said she might be able to contribute to the upkeep of the family.

We protested, but Rhodelle would not listen. She was going to stay. She said simply and directly, "I can't walk away from somebody just when I'm needed. That's when I ought to be there."

And so it came about that Rhodelle lived with us, went out and found work during the day, but was always home to help get supper and carry on the responsibilities of the house. It was a great comfort indeed.

As Thanksgiving time drew near, I had begun to run out of contacts—persons to call on in search of work. It was then that the "not-knowing" set in. The waiting and the "not-knowing." More and more I caught myself sitting at my desk staring at the wall in front of me. More and more I found it difficult to make calls. I tried to read. I couldn't concentrate. I tried to involve myself with the children, project myself into their lives, go more places with them, do more things.

It didn't work. I discovered that self-doubt was creeping in. I began to wonder about my talent. How did I know I was being refused employment because of the blacklist? Not a single soul had told me. No one had called me in and said, "Look here, you're blacklisted. We can't use you." So how did I know? How did I know it wasn't my own inadequacies as a performer that were keeping me out of work? A sort of ennui set in. When I looked into the mirror, I saw in my countenance something that was remotely familiar to me. I thought about it a great deal. It reminded me in a troubled way of something far away and long ago. I thought more about it. Then one morning, it came to me. By God, that was it—I was beginning to look like Pete Wesley.

Pete Wesley had lived on our place long years ago, in the early 1930s. He was a poor, East Texas farmer—a sharecropper who had finally given up the hopeless fight against unbelievable odds: a sandy, worked-out farm that wouldn't yield a decent crop, and endless debt. He had bundled up his few sorry possessions and moved with his wife, Thelma, and three small sons to Austin. Daddy had moved them out on our place, where Pete was to help me with the milking each day.

I was very fond of Pete and felt sorry for him and his family. He was in his early thirties, but he had the air of an old man. His manner was old. His face sagged. His voice sagged. His overalls, his hat, everything about him sagged. He looked defeated. But his eyes—soft-blue and gentle—told an even sadder tale than his sagging expression. There was a quiet despair in them.

I would go out and sit on his front porch with him, and try to comfort him. I would talk about the Roosevelt Administration and the coming reforms, and the fact that there would be a WPA that would enable men like him to go and find a way to earn a living. He would smile and shake his head. "Cain't quite figure it out," he said, gazing with that helpless and hopeless expression out across the fields. "I don't seem to be able to get aholt of nothin' to grip onto. Just nothin' I try to grab holt of seems to be there. Sort of like I'm driftin' down a flood river with no way to catch holt of somethin' on the bank and stop my driftin'."

Pete had worried me, and I had told him that he couldn't give up like that. He had his children to think about and his wife. Better times were coming, I knew. And he should know so too. "Don't reckon there's no way for you to understand, Johnny," he would say, not looking at me, but continuing to gaze out at nothing. "You might be right. Better times might be comin', but that ain't what's gettin' me. It's this not-knowin' that gits me down. Not-knowin' what's goin' to happen day after day. Not-knowin' whether it's me, or somethin' else that's missin' out. Just not-knowin'."

Have mercy, Lord, was I getting to be like Pete Wesley? It scared the daylights out of me. Getting to where I sat around gazing at nothing, baffled. I shook myself. I wasn't about to let that happen. There was no reason for it. I resolved then and there to get out and do something. Not just sit there drifting, but for the first time in my life, I understood fully all the sorrow that Pete Wesley's expression conveyed.

9

The second week in December 1957, I became obsessed with the idea that we were going to make this one of the merriest Christmases the Faulk family had ever had. I would refuse to think of my employment status again until after Christmas.

Gerald Dickler had estimated that my bank account would float us into the last week of January. All right, I thought, we'll end our bank account a week sooner. We scurried around making all sort of plans. The children and I went Christmas-tree picking along Amsterdam Avenue in high style, and we picked a big one. We invited a pack of friends in for rum punch and carol singing, and to help us decorate the tree. As for Christmas gifts, we went for quantity instead of quality. Maybe the children weren't going to open many very fine gifts, but they were going to open a whole lot of them.

And for Christmas dinner I cooked a very large goose. I had never cooked goose before. We'd always had a turkey. Now why in the world I chose a goose, I don't know. It wasn't until I was about to take it out of the oven that it suddenly struck me: cooked goose—how symbolic for Christmas 1957.

New Year's is a time for planning, so I proposed to plan some. Making plans can be a very powerful antidote to the kind of frustrating hopelessness and anxiety which had been assailing me recently. Not only that, but it's good for your friends, too. For instance, when a solicitous friend would ask: "How are things going, Johnny?" I could reply briskly, "Oh, very good. Very good. Got a couple of things planned. Pretty exciting ones too." This usually made the friend feel better. Ordinarily, he was too polite to ask for specifics. That way he and I both felt good about my plan.

I can think of no better way to communicate to the reader my feelings at that time than to reproduce the actual page from my journal as I set it down that day.

Goodbye 1957, the Year I Was Fired
Hello 1958, the Year I'll Be Hired

I. First order of business of 1958: Find a job.
  1. Possibilities: Radio and Television
    A. The Jack Paar Show. I must quit horsing around and get in touch with Paar. I must do it with dignity, but with a purpose.
    B. Explore the idea of a show of my own, independently packaged and sold to a sponsor.
    C. Leave no stone unturned in the radio-television field.
  2. Possibilities of work outside radio and television field.
    A. None at present.
II. Second order of business for 1958:
  1. Fight self-pity. Fight it like the plague. (Remember they can't beat you, but they can make you beat yourself.)
  2. Plan realistically
    A. Serious consideration of Lynne's going to work.
    B. Face fact that you may have to borrow money: get prepared for it.
    C. Keep that Pete Wesley look off your face.

Looking over the above now, I am not as embarrassed as I thought I would be. Actually, it was, under the circumstances, the confusion, the not knowing what was coming next, a pretty fair attempt to head into 1958 with my throttle wide open.

Shortly after New Year's, Dickler suggested I had better not wait until we had no money left in the bank whatever before I made plans to borrow some money. I had been very squeamish about this.

"What if I get a job next week, Gerry?" I argued.

"Then you could return the money and live on your earnings," Gerry replied. "What's worrying me is what if you do *not* get a job. You're going to have to have some resources."

I promised him that I would sit down at once and figure out just what to do about borrowing money. Going to a bank for the loan was out of the question; unemployed and without security as I was, that would be about as pointless as going to AWARE and asking for money enough to tide me over till the suit came to trial. I made a mental inventory of our possessions that might be hocked. There was really nothing that we owned that was worth hocking. Lynne had had one piece of valuable jewelry—an umbrella diamond ring worth several thousand dollars—but, a year or so before, our daughter Evelyn had thrown it out the window or down the toilet, we never knew which.

I knew that whatever loan I got would have to be made on exceptionally flexible terms, such as one could arrange only with a friend, and it would have to be an especially qualified friend—one who could lend me the money without having to have it back at any specific date. This sharply narrowed my field of potential lenders. I wrestled incessantly with the problem; I couldn't sleep at night trying to figure it out. I persuaded myself that my stake in the lawsuit constituted some kind of security; I could ask some of my wealthy friends to lend me money against the sum that I would recover in court. Then I realized there might not be any recovery. Nizer had told me that after years of litigation and a verdict in our favor, the jury might only award me one dollar for damages. The costs of the case were mounting astronomically. All the jockeying that was going on in the courts was expensive. There were times when there would be as many as half a dozen lawyers from Nizer's firm working on the preparation of a brief in refutation of some point that the defendants had made. The chances of having much money for the repayment of loans after the suit was over were slim indeed.

Obviously, I concluded, the only thing that I could do was to go to a prospective lender and candidly tell him the facts. If he saw fit to make the sort of gift that I needed, all right. If not, well I would take my business elsewhere.

I made a list of well-to-do friends whom I could consider as prospects. Then I started working out an appproach to them. I rationalized that in a way I was fighting the battle of all right-minded men in this country. I would not be humble and apologetic when I approached them. I would simply outline the circumstances which had landed me in my present financial state, and ask if they could lend me five hundred dollars.

Five hundred dollars! That was a big chunk of money to ask anyone for. But I realized that I would run myself ragged trying to raise the amount I needed, if I asked for fifty or a hundred dollars at a time. So I might as well start at five hundred.

The friend I selected was Herbert Steinmann. He and his wife, Anne, were generous, intelligent people, with a deep sense of social responsibility, and a great affection for me, I believed. We had been warm friends and had served together on the board of a mental health clinic. When it came to the matter of actually calling him up and asking for an appointment, however, I hesitated. What if I were being completely unrealistic about this business? What if Herb, who was a good social friend, were to feel that I had presumed on our friendship by asking him for what amounted to a gift? We would both be terribly embarrassed.

When I finally screwed up enough courage to visit Herb at his elegant town house, he was eager to know all about the progress of the lawsuit. As he fixed me a drink, I told him the latest court news. Then I began relating a little of my experiences in job hunting. He suddenly interrupted me. "Oh, by the way, Johnny. Forgive me for interrupting you, but the thought just struck me, and I might forget to mention it later. Would you consider letting me give you a check for a thousand dollars? You know, just to help you along right now? After all, this is my fight, too. I think you ought to let me participate —even if it is just in the limited way of giving money."

I don't recall what else I said during that visit, but I presume it was inspired. When I got home I rhapsodied over Herbert Steinmann's generosity. Then I got down to figuring out what I would do about making the thousand dollars stretch as far as it would go.

At that time, in early 1958, Jack Paar was going well on his NBC *Tonight* show. He had taken over the show in the summer of 1957 and had made it an immediate success. His show was now the talk of the town. Just about everybody stayed up to watch it.

I had replaced Jack on a CBS morning show back in 1955, and he had come back on the show several times to visit with me after I had taken it over. Later we had gone out to dinner with the Paars and José Melis' family back in 1956. I felt pretty sure he would give me a guest shot on his night show.

However, that was the hitch: We were friends; and I disliked the idea of calling him and asking him to give me a job. I debated the matter with myself daily and kept putting it off. Finally, I decided to write him a letter. I did so, going through a detailed preface that took a page and a half. I explained that I did not want to impose on our friendship, but that if he didn't mind, would he be so kind and just let me show him the kind of thing that I could do. After he had seen my work, if he didn't think I was up to snuff, there would be no hard feelings. After all, he was a professional and he had the professional quality of his show to think about. I didn't want him to think for a moment that he had to go around giving a fellow like me, who was unemployed, a job. If my talent didn't measure up, I certainly would understand. There would be no hard feelings. I ran on and on with this sort of nonsense for about two pages. I ended up by asking him to grant me an audience. A couple of days later, his secretary called and said that Jack wanted me on his show. She said I should come by and see his staff people about it. My excitement knew no bounds. I concentrated on getting some real juicy material up for the Paar show.

I spent all my waking hours thinking of witty repartee and grimacing into the mirror. Running under all this fever of activity was the thought—rather troublesome—that somebody might possibly call Paar about scheduling me before I had a chance to go on.

I went to see Paar's staff. They all knew me from three years before, when I took over the *Jack Paar Show*. They were delighted that Jack was having me on the program. I was scheduled for the show of March 3. For two weeks before the program went on, I alerted all of my friends down in Texas and all places in between that they should watch, because I was going to make my great comeback. I then fell to and worked up what I considered an extremely witty, original bit. It had to do with being unemployed. It started out: "Oh, it's sort of stylish being unemployed these days. Lots of folks are, Jack. Former President Truman. Former President Herbert Hoover. King Farouk and the Duke of Windsor."

On the night of the show, I went down to the theater an hour and a half early, even before the cameramen showed up. When Jack came in, he was warm and friendly. He said he was delighted to have me with him. He then said, "There'd be no point in our going over your material, Johnny. You're just as good as I am when it comes to ad libbing. Let's just keep it on a conversational level." I assured him that was just exactly what I would like to do. When Jack introduced me on the show, I went out, shook his hand, sat down, and took a seat near him.

He started talking to me. My mind went absolutely blank. Words came out of my mouth upside down and sideways. Lines that I thought would panic the audience were so indescribably twisted that they only puzzled the audience—and Jack Paar. Paar realized that I was freezing. He quickly brought out another guest, an old-time vaudevillian.

For an hour and a half, I sat there in total silence. Just sat. I felt so sick, so utterly undone by my ridiculous performance that I refused to think of it. When I got home, a group of friends who had gathered at the house with Lynne to watch the show sat about angrily, all of them uttering vindictive remarks about Paar. I was ashamed to tell them that it was entirely my fault. I kept silent. I was so traumatized that I couldn't bring myself to place the blame where it correctly belonged—on myself. I never got up the courage to call Jack for another try.

Lynne managed to find temporary employment as a saleslady with a fancy bathroom-fixture store, but her salary was scarcely sufficient to buy her the clothes necessary to go out to work.

One night shortly after the Paar debacle, I was asked to entertain at a benefit for a low-cost mental-health clinic. I did so. And at the gathering I was introduced to an affable gentleman named Louis Schweitzer. Mr. Schweitzer had recently bought Station WBAI-FM. Mr. Schweitzer told me that he would be happy to give me an hour each evening on his station. I could do any kind of program I wanted to and if it attracted sponsors (at that time WBAI accepted commercials) I could keep any of the revenue the program brought in. I knew that a small FM station had an extremely limited audience, especially a new station such as WBAI. But it was a quality audience. I decided to do the kind of program that I had always wanted to do. A program of real folk music, relating my experiences as a collector of folk material. It turned out that WBAI-FM's manager was Bert Cowlan, a stalwart AFTRA member who had supported our side in the union fight. I wrote off to the Library of Congress for tapes of material that I had sent there when I was collecting folk material on a Julius Rosenwald Fellowship in Texas. They were mostly songs that I had recorded in the early 1940s on Texas prison farms, and in rural churches. Both Bert Cowlan and Mr. Schweitzer were most anxious to see that my program—for my sake—went well. If anything, they were more anxious on my behalf than they were on the station's. And they gave me all the help that I could possibly want. It was decided that I would do a nightly broadcast over WBAI from midnight until one o'clock each morning. I began the program about the middle of April 1958; I had a fine time talking and playing recordings that had been made in remote places in the South. Presumably, so did the dozen or so listeners that I had. It was a rather esoteric program; not very commercial.

Shortly after my having started the show at WBAI-FM, I received a letter from an old friend. The letter read:

Dear Johnny:
  During the weekend I read in Variety about your joining WBAI-FM on a nighttime show. So before I do anything else, here are hearty congratulations.
  Actually the purpose of this letter is to find out a) how happy you are on the job, b) have you ever thought about San Francisco and the West Coast, and c) if you are, what kind of financial arrangements are you interested in?
  What I am thinking about is the possibility of a DJ show, five or six days a week, of possibly three-four hours duration daytime. In any event, let me hear from you.
  Best personal regards,

Sincerely   yours,
Wendell B. Campbell

It had been agreed by Bert Cowlan, Mr. Schweitzer and myself that should something of a tangible nature come along—that is, a job in commercial broadcasting—I would be free to take it. I immediately fired a letter back to Wendell Campbell saying that I had not thought of San Francisco, but that I had been thinking of it steadily since he had written. I would be very interested in the kind of show he talked about—one that would give me three or four hours a day on the air. I had been in San Francisco in 1936 for a short while and I loved the place. I was tempted to call Wendell Campbell and tell him that I was free to come at any time to San Francisco, and would do so most happily. However I refrained from calling him. I wanted to give him a chance to answer my letter.

He did so within the next week, saying that he thought I would be perfect for the job, and that he wanted to start serious negotiation with me about it. I was terribly excited about the prospect of a real paying job. Especially one on the West Coast where AWARE's cold, clammy hands could not reach me. I would not have been so sanguine had I been more perceptive about a visit I had received on April 25, several weeks before.

It was early in the morning. Lynne was away from home, the children were in school. Frank Dobie was at home with me. I was still in my bathrobe and pajamas when the doorbell rang. I opened the door a crack, and there stood a strange-looking woman with a briefcase. She announced that she was Mrs. Scotti, an investigator from the House Un-American Activities Committee, and she made a move to come in through the door. I suggested that I was not yet dressed and was not receiving company at that hour. I had been warned by Louis Nizer that I was to talk to no one, regardless of what the caller pretended to be, without informing him. I also knew that the defendants were in constant correspondence with the House Un-American Activities Committee.

Mrs. Scotti told me that she wanted to ask me some questions, and then asked rather plaintively, "Don't you want to cooperate?"

I explained to her that since I was involved with a very important piece of litigation, it would be necessary for me to talk to my attorney before I talked with her; or perhaps she would like to speak to him. She protested—in fact, she insisted—that it was me she wanted to speak to, not my attorney. I steadfastly refused to admit her, and she left.

I called Nizer later that morning and informed him of her visit. He told me that I had done exactly the right thing, and that under no circumstances should I involve myself in a conversation with any member of that committee without his knowledge. He added, however, with a chuckle, "Don't you worry a bit. You'll probably hear no more from them. They're on one of their fishing expeditions. Think no more about it."

I followed his advice and forgot the matter. I wouldn't have, had I known then what I was to find out later, and very shortly—namely, that the defendants in my suit and members of the House Un-American Activities Committee had plans for me that were considerably at variance with my own plans.

10

A few days later I called Sam Slate and told him about the San Francisco offer. He suggested that I come down to his office. There he told me that Wendell Campbell had already called him from San Francisco and had told him that he was very anxious to bring me to KFRC.

However, Sam said, Wendell was concerned over the lawsuit in which I was involved. In fact, he and Sam had discussed the matter and agreed that there would be real drawbacks to my signing a contract in San Francisco as long as I was involved in a lawsuit in New York. Sam then suggested that I should give serious consideration to dropping the suit. He pointed out that we had won our points over Hartnett and Johnson in court. He said he was sure that now the defendants would be perfectly willing to make a public apology. That is, if I would drop the suit. I asked him how he knew this, and he said it was his impression that they were very anxious to have the suit dropped.

He seemed to have information that he did not care to disclose, but kept suggesting that if I forced AWARE to fight, they would come out on top. Nevertheless, I appreciated Sam's concern and told him so. I told him that I would give his suggestion serious thought.

After leaving Sam's office I called Nizer and told him what Sam had said. Nizer wanted to call Wendell Campbell in San Francisco and assure him that the litigation would in no way interfere with my moving to San Francisco. The case would not come to trial for another year or so at the very least, and we probably could arrange matters so that I would attend the trial during a vacation period. When I asked Nizer what he made of Sam's insistence that my wisest course now would be to settle for a public apology, Nizer chuckled. He said that Sam was probably accurate, which meant that now was a propitious time to call the first of the defendants for his examination before trial. In the meantime, I should continue to push the San Francisco deal with all my power.

Papers were served on Hartnett directing him to come to Nizer's office for examination before trial, on Thursday, June 5, 1958. Paul Martinson explained to me exactly what an examination before trial, or EBT, was. New York Supreme Court procedure provides that each party to a civil suit may examine the other party before trial. The chief purpose of this is to ascertain exactly what will be at issue when the case comes to court. This narrows the area of disagreement and prevents either side from taking the other one by surprise with unexpected evidence or issues. Each side is entitled, through EBT, to discover exactly what evidence and issues the other has relied on and what will be presented for trial. The EBT is conducted in the presence of a court reporter, the witnesses are sworn, and all evidence given is part of the official court record. Martinson told me that I was perfectly welcome to be present at the Hartnett examination. Inasmuch as this was the first face-to-face confrontation, I was full of anticipation and excitement over the prospect.

About a week before the Hartnett examination, I received a subpoena to appear before the House Un-American Activities Committee. I was directed to appear on June 17, 1958. Nizer told me not to worry about it however, and to sleep soundly and forget the matter. But I couldn't go to sleep that night.

I was deeply concerned over this latest turn in events. I had no love for this particular committee and knew that Vincent Hartnett had been in communication with them quite frequently. It angered me to think that an agency of my government might join the defendants in the persecution of me. It occurred to me, as a matter of fact, that it was probably a clumsy attempt on the part of the defendants to frighten me into settling the suit. I was pretty sure that the defendants would stop at nothing to undo me. I was equally sure that the HUAC would be happy to accommodate them in any way it could.

My reasons for distrusting the HUAC ran back a number of years. I knew, for instance, that in the days before World War II the Dies Committee, as the HUAC was known at that time, had enjoyed the praise and support of some of America's most unsavory pro-Hitler groups. Names like Gerald L. K. Smith, Joseph P. Kamp, Merwin K. Hart, Gerald Winrod and other like personalities had been among the committee's earliest and stanchest supporters. The Dies Committee had made headlines in Texas papers back in 1944, by claiming that the University of Texas was a hotbed of Communists. When the president of the university, Dr. Homer Price Rainey, had demanded that Dies either put up or shut up, Dies apologized. He even declared that the University of Texas was a model American institution. But the harm had already been done, and serious harm, to the university.

Later, Representative John E. Rankin of Mississippi and Representative John S. Wood of Georgia had taken over the Committee. They were notorious for their violent anti-Semitic and anti-Negro speeches. In the late Forties, when J. Parnell Thomas was the chairman of the Committee he had been sent to prison as a common thief, but not until after his Committee had wrought havoc in Hollywood with its reckless hearings. I remembered how in his magazine *The Cross and the Flag*, Gerald L. K. Smith had boasted that his Christian Nationalist Party deserved the credit for pushing the HUAC into Hollywood investigations. The Committee had even so far overstepped itself that it subpoenaed President Harry S Truman—or attempted to. They didn't get very far. It didn't stretch my imagination much to believe that an organization like AWARE, Inc., would urge the Committee to attack me, and that the Committee would likely oblige them. I knew that the HUAC was a great favorite with most of the vigilante groups, such as AWARE, across the country. They doted on its so-called findings, but worst of all, HUAC furnished a platform and Congressional immunity to an assortment of crackpot witnesses, as unsavory and unwholesome a group as ever assembled anywhere.

The next day I went down and told Nizer exactly how I felt about the committee. I felt that he was entitled to know what my true feelings were. Nizer said that he didn't think it would be legal for them to call me at this time. I was involved in a lawsuit that involved precisely the same matters that they wanted to question me about. He said that it was clearly such an unfair thing for the HUAC to have done that he was sure that the subpoena would be lifted.

My concern over the subpoena was overshadowed by the arrival of Thursday, June 5, 1958, the date set for Vincent Hartnett's first day of EBT. My excitement was at high pitch. Nizer had explained to me the procedure. Hartnett would be examined, then Johnson, and then, perhaps, several of the directors of AWARE. Then the defendants' attorneys would examine me, and the trial date would be set. In other words, this was the beginning of the end, I thought. I could scarcely sleep the night before Hartnett was to come into Nizer's office and be examined. I was up at six o'clock and got dressed. Although the EBT was not to start till ten-thirty, I was down at Nizer's office by nine o'clock, long before he was. I went into his office and took a seat on a large sofa at one end of the room.

As I sat there in the office, alone, waiting, I reflected on the strangeness of the situation. It had been almost two years ago, to the day, that my suit had been filed. The whole course of my life had been changed, and yet I had never laid eyes on any of the men, Vincent Hartnett included, who had been most responsible for my present predicament. I had seen Godfrey Schmidt, who was president of AWARE and attorney for the defendants, once at a distance, but I had never met him.

Shortly after ten o'clock, three men entered the room. I recognized one of them as Godfrey Schmidt, and presumed another was Hartnett. They were chatting amicably and seemed very much at ease. They noticed me sitting on the sofa at the far end of the room, and they nodded curtly. Then one of them commented, "That's John Henry Faulk." Schmidt came forward and shook my hand, explaining that he had thought I was an attorney. He then introduced me to his companions, a Mr. Chalif, another lawyer for AWARE, and Vincent Hartnett. I had wondered for some time whether I would shake hands with Schmidt and Hartnett. Now I found that I could do so. I remembered that Daddy had always said that one should never refuse to shake hands with any man, no matter how strongly one disliked him, lest one proved that the other was more courteous. Vincent Hartnett was smoking a large cigar and was obviously in a pleasant frame of mind.

I was relieved to see Nizer come into the room, followed by two attorneys from his firm, Mr. Gersten and Mr. Shainswit. Before long the official court reporter came in and set up his little machine at a spot near Nizer's desk. Introductions were made all around and Nizer sat down behind his desk, flanked by Gersten and Shainswit. Hartnett was sworn by the court reporter and his EBT began.

Nizer's manner was courteous and correct. Vincent Hartnett, obviously at ease, puffed away on his big cigar, giving his answers easily and clearly. The atmosphere that was created was one of a pleasant tête-à-tête, accompanied by the tapping of the court reporter's machine. If a question was asked that Schmidt thought improper or irrelevant, he would object. The lawyers would then talk off the record, and if a colloquy between Schmidt and Nizer failed to resolve Schmidt's objection, that line of question was dropped until the record could be taken before a justice of the New York Supreme Court for his ruling on it.

The questioning went along the lines of Vincent Hartnett's background and the origins of AWARE, Inc. Outside, the June sunshine spread its wide smile down over the Hudson River and my gaze kept wandering out toward the sparkling waters and the great ships pulling in and out of the piers there. Everything seemed easy. There was no particular line or direction in the questions that Nizer was asking. At one point he asked a question about some person, and Schmidt objected on the grounds that the person and the question did not relate to John Henry Faulk's case. Nizer explained that we had charged a conspiracy. Thus he was entitled to cover a great many other matters relating to AWARE, its operations and its origins, and other persons who had been affected by its practices. Schmidt seemed surprised at this explanation, as though he had not realized before what the "conspiracy" in our original charge meant. He and Hartnett exchanged a brief whispered conversation. From the expression on his face, and his general manner, I gathered that this was the first time he really recognized the width and breadth that our lawsuit might assume.

A little later Nizer asked a question which involved an accusation against Hartnett. It was the first stinging question that had been put. It upset both Schmidt and Hartnett. There was a brief argument, off the record, between the lawyers. Hartnett was clearly annoyed. "Mr. Nizer," he snapped, "I would remind you that I'm not on the witness stand, and you're not a district attorney."

Nizer eyed him intently for a moment. Then he remarked quietly to the court reporter, "The following is on the record." Looking directly at Vincent Hartnett, his voice cold, but without rage, Nizer said, "Do I understand, sir, you presume to instruct me in the conduct of this examination? Are you, sir? How dare you impudently speak of district attorneys and witnesses! You sir, you who have sat as judge, jury, prosecuting attorney and executioner on the lives and careers of hundreds of loyal, innocent victims! You, sir, who have drawn the noose of starvation around the neck of that innocent man sitting there, seeking to starve his children and destroy his reputation. You dare, sir, instruct me in the conduct of this case?"

The eloquent outrage in Nizer's voice sent Schmidt and Hartnett reeling backward. They were startled and confused. Hartnett cleared his throat as though to reply, and Schmidt quickly put his hand on his arm and shushed him. Hartnett tried to place a cigar in his mouth and put it in his left ear instead. Schmidt protested that Nizer's remarks were unnecessarily harsh. Nizer replied to Schmidt that he needed no instruction from him, either. It was clear that both Schmidt and Hartnett were shaken not only by the sharp lash of Nizer's words, but by the abrupt awakening they had to what the future held for them in this suit.

From that point on, Hartnett answered the questions obediently, and Schmidt showed a definite reluctance and nervousness, at objecting. Nizer really opened up on the case then, and began to probe for names, names of people whom Hartnett had blacklisted, names of his colleagues in the blacklisting business. I sat on the sofa, spellbound. I was hearing things that amazed me. Hartnett named personality after personality, and described his method of informing on people, gathering information on them, et cetera, in great detail. Nizer dug deeper and deeper into the conspiracy. By the time the first session of the EBT was over, Vincent Hartnett realized that he was in for a much rougher experience than he had anticipated. He showed it, too.

Each day Nizer continued his relentless examination of Hartnett. The names of people who had been Hartnett's aides, the ones who had given him secret information, all came out and were placed on the record. The amount of money Hartnett collected for his services startled me. I had no idea he had such a lucrative business going. There it was. He was forced to turn over his income tax returns and explain the sources of his income. Most of it had been derived from furnishing information on entertainers to the various agencies, networks and sponsors. I realized that the case was going to reveal things that had never been suspected by the bitterest critics of AWARE.

I was still under subpoena by the HUAC and still directed to appear before them on June 17. About a week before I was to appear, a friend sent me an interesting printed invitation. I could scarcely believe what it said. It was an invitation to a cocktail party, to be given at the Hotel McAlpin on April 17, from five to eight o'clock, by AWARE, Inc., in honor of the members of the HUAC and its staff. Nizer had already questioned Hartnett on the subject of his relationship with the HUAC and discovered that Vincent Hartnett had a very close connection with staff members of the HUAC, and that they exchanged information. When I took Nizer the invitation he was outraged. He got busy on the matter at once. It was clear that HUAC, with its close association with AWARE, had no business calling me as a witness at this time. And they didn't.

On the following Monday, June 16, I received a telegram from Congressman Walter, continuing my subpoena from June 17 to July 17. When I showed it to Nizer he was not satisfied. He immediately fired off a letter to the counsel of HUAC pointing out that July 17 was no more desirable than June 17. He said further that obviously I could not be called before the HUAC before my EBT had taken place. He asked that the subpoena be dropped, or continued, at least until October 31.

It is an interesting coincidence that on the very next day, June 17, when I was scheduled to appear before HUAC, Hartnett, having learned that I was not going to have to appear, completely capitulated to us in his EBT. I was not present, because I had business elsewhere, but Nizer reported to me that Hartnett had not had his heart in the testimony. Then, along toward the middle of the afternoon, both Hartnett and Schmidt seemed to have given up. Nizer phoned me at once and reported that they had made very damaging admissions. They admitted on the record that they had been fed a barrel of false information about me, and had offered to make any public statement we desired them to.

Nizer was almost as excited over the surrender of Hartnett and Schmidt as I was. He had not expected them to go to such lengths in their admissions so soon, he said. Nizer told me that it would now be just a matter of time till we had completely undone them all. He said that he had scheduled a meeting with Schmidt the next day to discuss the matter. I would have turned handsprings had I been able to. I was ecstatic with joy. Now I knew that I would soon be going to San

Francisco. This cleared the way entirely. Nizer told me that he would have Schmidt's and Hartnett's testimony printed up so that I might send it to San Francisco at once. Murray Kempton, columnist on the *New York Post,* and one of the best newspapermen in town, called me and said he too had an invitation to the AWARE cocktail party that evening, and asked if Lynne and I would care to join him there. I told him I didn't think I should go, but perhaps Lynne would like to go and have a look at the members of the HUAC as well as the people of AWARE, since she had never laid eyes on any of the defendants. I invited Murray to join us for dinner after the cocktail party.

He and Lynne went. They stayed a long time, and when they joined me for dinner, they were full of stories about the chagrin that was expressed on every side at my not being called before the Committee that day. Murray Kempton said that seldom had he seen such an assortment of malcontents stirring around and mouthing such bitter predictions of doom at the hands of the Communists.

The days ahead looked bright indeed. The case was to go forward with all haste. The HUAC sent word that my hearing before them had been postponed until November 18. I went up to see Sam Slate, and ran into Jack Stirling, a former colleague of mine at WCBS. He was a friend of Wendell Campbell's, and said he knew that Wendell Campbell was most anxious to have me in San Francisco. I told them all about Hartnett's EBT. Then I began my impatient wait to hear from Wendell Campbell in San Francisco. A day or so later I was telling Lynne with great confidence that there was nothing like patience. I had been patient and seen this thing through, and now look what was happening. Now, not only were the defendants going rapidly down the drain, but I was being freed to go back to work. Our troubles were over. Of course, I had no way of knowing that they were just beginning. We really hadn't seen anything yet.

11

Though Hartnett and Schmidt had hopelessly compromised their case, there were other defendants to be examined and a great deal more information to be acquired. I was thinking about the day when we would be completely through with Mr. Hartnett and start on Mr. Johnson and the other defendants. The HUAC had continued my subpoena, so that was off my mind. The San Francisco deal seemed absolutely set. My only problem was whether or not I would take it, now that I was apparently going to be a free man and could probably find work in New York City. In the morning mail of June 28 an air-mail letter came from Wendell Campbell in San Francisco. It was filled with pleasant remarks about how well he thought I would do on the radio show. It also outlined in some detail the kind of thing Mr. Campbell had in mind for the show I would be doing. It ended with a suggestion that I go down to WOR and cut a thirty-minute audition tape so that he might play it for the other executives at the San Francisco station. He said that he had arranged with a Mr. Leder, of WOR, for me to do the audition at no cost.

I noticed another letter in the same mail addressed to me in an envelope identical with the one I had just opened. In it, however, was a letter addressed to Mr. Robert Leder, Mutual Broadcasting Company. It was an original. The thought struck me that perhaps the secretary had made a mistake and had meant to send me a copy of Mr. Leder's letter and had sent me the original instead. I started reading it; it concerned a request that Mr. Leder allow me the facilities of the studios at WOR. The bill was to be sent to Mr. Wendell Campbell. As I read on, I realized that the secretary's mistake had been a bit more serious than simply sending me the original instead of a carbon. I had an idea that neither the original nor a carbon had been intended for me. Mr. Campbell discussed my victory over AWARE and added that if it was true that I was free of controversy, "Then we will definitely be interested in having John Henry Faulk out here."

As I read the letter over, I realized that here was the first concrete evidence that had come into my hands since I had been fired that AWARE was a factor in my employability. I called Nizer at once and explained the situation to him. He told me we should put the letter in another envelope and send it on to Mr. Leder with a note that it had been sent to me by mistake. But before doing so, perhaps, I should have it photostated. I followed his suggestion.

Later in the day I was telling Sam Slate about this strange situation and the fact that Wendell Campbell wanted me to do an audition tape. Sam said I was welcome to do it right there, with my old director giving me a hand, in the WCBS studios. I accepted his gracious offer, made the tape and sent it out to Mr. Campbell.

A day or so later, Paul Martinson called me from the Nizer office to say that Godfrey Schmidt had withdrawn from the case and they were substituting another attorney. He said with a chuckle that I could never guess who this new attorney would be. As irony—or fate —would have it, the new counsel for the defense was Mr. Roy Cohn, the dauntless young man who had figured so prominently in the McCarthy investigation days. Roy Cohn, the scourge of subversives. I felt that surely Paul Martinson was pulling my leg. There was something so weirdly dramatic about this turn of events. Roy Cohn, a gentleman whom I could not have admired less, opposed by Paul Martinson and Louis Nizer.

I got on the phone and spread the glad news to all my friends. "Now you'll see the fur fly." My friends agreed, and wished they could get seats for the shindig. The next day I called Nizer and asked him when the next EBT with Vincent Hartnett was scheduled. I explained to him that I couldn't wait, that I was on tenterhooks to see Roy Cohn in action.

There was a note of chagrin in Lou's voice. "I'm afraid you're going to have to wait, John. Roy Cohn has announced that he's going abroad for a couple of months. He said he would let us know when it will be convenient for him to continue his clients' EBT. Perhaps in September or October." For a moment I was too shocked to make comment. I thought that the EBT would go right through to completion. In fact, I had rather banked on that.

"But, Lou," I said, "how can Cohn make a decision like that on his own? He can't just up and declare he will continue this case when it's convenient for him. What about us? Don't we have a right to demand that he stay here and continue right now? Hell, Hartnett's already given up."

Lou carefully explained to me that we could do nothing whatever about Mr. Cohn's decision. He counseled me to reconcile myself to the unpleasant fact that the suit was at a standstill until September, maybe even October. Even though Hartnett had admitted his error, there was yet his malice to be established. He said I should concentrate on my San Francisco job.

I called Gerry Dickler and told him I wanted to come down and talk to him about an idea I had concerning San Francisco. Actually, I wanted to find out what he thought about me trying to raise the money for a trip to San Francisco. I realized that I was going to have to have that job now. Maybe it would be best for me to go out there directly to be there in person to push the matter.

When I got down to Gerry's office, the first thing he said was, "As I understand it, the HUAC continued your subpoena until November eighteenth. They did not quash it. Is that right?"

I nodded absent-mindedly and said, "Yes. That's right. But that's no problem now."

"Have you told Wendell Campbell that you are still under subpoena, and scheduled to be called on November eighteenth for the HUAC?"

I hadn't thought of it. "Why, no," I said, "I didn't think it was important. I just sent him the audition tape. He was pretty hot on the whole thing."

"Johnny, don't you see what you're up against? They continued your subpoena. They did not cancel it. In other words you're still under subpoena by the HUAC. Don't you know why? They might have failed in their effort to call you last month, but they haven't given up. They're not going to let AWARE down. Do you think that Wendell Campbell, or any executive in radio or television in this country, is going to give a man a job who is under subpoena by the HUAC?"

I sat there dumfounded. Why hadn't I thought of that? In all likelihood, Wendell Campbell had already learned of my being subpoenaed by the HUAC. The New York papers had carried the story. But even if he were under the impression that it was over and done with, I was obligated to tell him that not only was the trial going to be stretched out further, but that I was still under subpoena. There was no point in thinking about any kind of work until that was over with. I cursed the HUAC and the defendants under my breath. They were a lot slyer and cleverer than I had given them credit for.

Nizer had warned me that I should do nothing in New York that would create unfavorable publicity. I couldn't openly attack HUAC. One night as I sat writing at my desk, I had an inspired thought. I would tell Texana about my subpoena. That was it. I would let Texana carry the ball from down in Texas. She could rally some strong protest.

Texana, my sister, is a year younger than I. In all outward appearances she is a typical Texas housewife, a devoted mother, a dedicated member of the Methodist Church, and much occupied with civic and educational affairs in the community—the same community, South Austin, where I was born and grew up and where she has lived all her life. But there is really nothing typical about Teck, as she is universally called. She combines a primitive Protestant ethic with a set of fiercely held egalitarian attitudes. More than this, she acts upon her convictions, with alacrity and dedication. She, like my family, derived her strongly held liberal opinions from our father, who spent his life as a civil-rights lawyer. As Teck puts it, "I love my government, and I love my children. But Lord have mercy, that don't mean that either of them are perfect. Just because I love 'em. It means that I've got an obligation to see that they do right. I'm not going to sit by and watch my children or my government go to the devil simply because it's too much trouble to do anything about it." Inaction and indifference to civic responsibility are deadly sins in Teck's book. She holds, as Tocqueville and James Madison did, that justice is the principal end of government. Consequently, she felt injustice is the very antithesis of good government.

I wrote to Texana and outlined exactly what had happened. I really didn't know what she could do or how she could do it. But of one thing I was certain. Texana would do something, and do it at once.

Within a week, Texana had written me a lengthy letter. In it she outlined what she had already set in motion, people she had seen and urged to do something. She also outlined what she intended to do, which concerned itself mostly with putting fire under some of the Congressmen in Washington, and calling to their attention the behavior of the HUAC. The letter was filled with expressions of indignation at the duplicity of AWARE and the HUAC. Delightful malapropisms are a hallmark of Texana's speech and her writing. Her letter stated that "some of those congressmen get too big for their breeches. They forget what the people at the grassroots are thinking. They have to be affronted [confronted] with the fact that they work for us, we don't work for them. When somebody is not being treated fair in America, it's everybody's business. But it's those congressmen's business in particular. If they think they can keep pussyfootin around that Unamerican Committee and Roy Cone, they're mistaken. They need to be told better. When I hire somebody to clean my yard and he just fiddles around at the job, I let him go and get somebody who will really do it. Well, that's the way I feel about those congressmen. If they cain't get the job done, let 'em quit, and let's get somebody that can." Texana had rounded up a number of her more conscientious church friends, a couple of labor leaders in Austin, and J. Frank Dobie, and had fired them up to take out after the HUAC. I breathed easier. Since there was little or nothing I could do at my end but wait, I once more concentrated my thoughts on trying to earn a living.

12

The most punishing aspect of being blacklisted was not the economic hardships that it worked on its victims, but the painful inability to use one's creative resources. It shuts one off from his contact with the public on the most important level of his existence, the creative level. This was the reason I had made such a sorry botch of the Jack Paar show. It was also the reason I would spend frustrating and fruitless hours trying to work on new material. New ideas simply would not take form. I could not create in a vacuum. I knew that others had overcome the difficulty of being isolated from the public, but I couldn't.

In my acute discomfiture I began to understand why some artists had capitulated to the other side—traded their integrity to Satan, as it were—in order to get back into their profession. I knew that the state of mind I was in was exactly what the defendants had planned—going into that fatuous depression, and finally saying, "To hell with it all. I'll settle this deal and get back to work." Well, I thought, if that's their game, they'll damn well be disappointed this time. I'm going to do something.

And I did. I found out that I could make a fast and vast fortune selling mutual fund shares. Some friends who sold them told me about it. I didn't even know what mutual funds were at the time. They explained that it was a very simple matter. With my connections in show business, I could not miss. They made an appointment for me with a gentleman from a firm specializing in selling shares in mutual funds. He was a splendid dynamic personality, and after an hour's talk he convinced me that I would soon be on the road to becoming a tycoon in financial circles. However, before I qualified to sell shares I had to take a course and become completely conversant with all financial details.

Stock and bond salesmen are carefully supervised by the government. They have to take a test and get a certificate. Rascals aren't tolerated. I had entered a new world, the terminology of which stopped me flat. I spent hours learning the difference between preferred and common stock, about municipal bonds, and all about the federal regulations that apply to selling them. I say I spent hours learning it. Actually, I spent hours trying to learn. Somehow or other, it wouldn't stick in my mind. However, it came time to take an examination to qualify as a bona fide stocks and bonds salesman. I took it and presumably I passed, since I was congratulated by my friend. He said I was now ready to go forth. He gave me a large packet of material, business cards with my name on them, and wished me well. I was to report to him daily on my contacts and the results that I had achieved.

One would believe that a person with a modicum of common sense and little energy could really go to town on such a deal. In the first place, I had been given a guide which told in minute detail exactly how a prospective buyer should be approached, the first thing that should be said to him, and how he should be brought into the fold step by step. It not only extolled the virtues of mutual funds, but pointed out how in the long run it was the surest way to make one's savings mount and mount. I was still hesitant on making my first contact. I figured I had better make a dry run on two faithful friends first—not only faithful, but tolerant—Doris and Eli Friedland. I told them to pretend they wanted to put away a little money each month. I would show them the advantages of putting it into mutual fund shares. I tried to sell them our five-thousand-dollar investment plan.

"Now, folks, as you can see here, we want you to invest five thousand dollars. Oh. You don't have five thousand dollars? Well, don't you worry about that. We have the perfect plan for you. That's the joy of mutual. You can put in just a little bit each month, and after a while you will have a big five-thousand-dollar investment going your direction. Now, how much can you spare every month?" They thought for a minute and said, "Oh, let's say fifty dollars a month."

"Very well then," I continued in a businesslike, stock-salesman fashion, "here's just the thing for you. You put in fifty dollars each month. That fifty dollars will be used to buy shares. At the end of one year you will have put in—now let's see, excuse me sir, how much is fifty dollars a month for one year? Oh, six hundred dollars. Gosh, is that all? Well! Very well, you will have put in six hundred dollars at the end of a year."

Doris and Eli looked at me blankly. "So?"

I smiled uncertainly. "What I mean is, you will have bought six hundred dollars' worth of shares of mutual fund."

"How many shares will I own at that time?" Doris asked.

"Well, I don't know exactly, it depends on what they are selling for. You can see that, can't you?"

"Well, now," said Eli thoughtfully, "at the end of a year I have bought six hundred dollars' worth of mutual fund shares. Correct?"

I nodded. I was bringing him around.

He continued. "But suddenly I lose my job and need that six hundred dollars. Can I sell those shares for six hundred dollars at that time, and get my money back?"

"No, I'm afraid that wouldn't work. You see—er—let me see now. Mmmm. No, I don't guess you would really have six hundred dollars' worth of shares at that time. After all, I've got to make a commission from the sale, and so has the corporation. How the hell are we going to make a commission from it and give you six hundred dollars' worth of shares at the same time?" I asked indignantly.

"Well, in that case," Doris said testily, "I'll just put my savings each month in a savings and loan association. It will draw interest there, and the whole sum, in fact more than the six hundred dollars, would be given back to me if I needed it at the end of a year—six hundred dollars plus whatever interest it had drawn."

I was stymied. I knew that I had not studied my procedure well enough. I couldn't let this sort of thing happen when I got with a real prospect. It would be disastrous to have each one end up by saying it didn't look like a very good deal, and me agreeing with them. I went back to my books and studied some more. I was required by law to tell anyone to whom I was trying to sell shares that they were investing their money and that it might be worth more and it might be worth less at the end of a given time. In other words, they were gambling. I did not like gambling with my own money, and even less did I like persuading someone to gamble with his. However, I had put so much time into learning to be a stock salesman that I felt I had to carry on. Every few days, I would call on a friend and give it a go. Several of my friends would offer to lend me money, but they would not invest in mutual funds. I would return home with my self-confidence as a salesman severely shaken. It would usually take me about forty-eight hours to overhaul my courage and get in shape to go through another sales pitch with someone. In a month's time I had managed to make two sales for five hundred dollars each. We were so hard-pressed financially that I knew that I could not afford the luxury of learning to be a bond salesman.

Things had picked up considerably about this time in the lawsuit. In the latter part of September, Roy Cohn came back from foreign shores. Paul Martinson, who had taken over the EBT, demanded that Mr. Cohn present himself and Vincent Hartnett to continue the examination.

On the day appointed for the resumption of the EBT, I went down to Paul Martinson's office to observe the proceedings. I had never had the pleasure of meeting Mr. Cohn before, and was looking forward to seeing him in operation. He came in, the very essence of freshness and briskness, along with his partner Tom Bolan. His manner was self-assured and, I might say, a bit arrogant. As the EBT began it was obvious that Mr. Cohn was going to put up with no nonsense. His objections were couched in terms like "Don't answer that!" and "You can't ask that!" As I watched his performance I began to think there was something wrong with me. Mr. Cohn had a reputation as a formidable, shrewd and able lawyer. For the life of me—and I listened very intently—I could not discover the slightest basis for such a reputation. As far as I know, that was the last EBT at which Mr. Cohn honored us with his presence. Thereafter his partner Thomas Bolan took charge.

There were several more sessions, in which the attorneys directed Hartnett to refuse to answer many of Paul Martinson's questions and to refuse to produce several documents that had been asked for; and then they indicated that they could not be bothered with more EBT for the present. Paul said that this would have to be ruled on, and he charged that the attorneys and their client were being dilatory. A number of very important issues had come up, and there was a wide difference of opinion on them. It became necessary for the matters to be resolved by the court. Briefs were filed before Justice Fine, and he was asked to make rulings on the various issues. In November, Justice Fine handed down his decision, and it was a whacking fine one for us. The defendants were directed not only to produce all the documents and letters and evidence that Paul had demanded, but also to continue the EBT on a regular schedule.

In late October, I received word that Texana's efforts had been rewarded. I got a telegram from HUAC canceling my subpoena.

Although I enjoyed a feeling of well-being on the legal front, our financial affairs were in hopeless chaos. It had become so excruciatingly painful for me to go to friends and borrow money, that I had just about stopped doing it. As a result we had slipped further and further into debt. Lynne had found a job as advertising and promotion manager with a dress-manufacturing company, but the salary was so inadequate that we were being hounded by creditors. Many of them could do nothing but demand, but some of them—like the gas and electric company, the telephone company and our landlord —*could* do something about it, and they were daily threatening to do so.

I had several suits of clothes that were durable and nice, but they were several years old and, combined with shirts of equal age, they had a slightly seedy appearance. Much worse than that, I began to *feel* seedy. Christmas was less than a month away, but celebrating it was not my chief concern; I was worried whether we would last that long.

The most deadening and at the same time painful aspect of that period was the fact that once I had failed at selling mutual funds, I didn't seem to be able to think of another thing that I could possibly do. I got to thinking of myself as a bum, as a ne'er-do-well. One Saturday evening Myrna Loy, a long-time friend, dropped by to see us. At the same time, Chris and Merle Debuskey came by. We had not seen any of them for quite a while. They were all full of excitement over the latest development in the case, Justice Fine's decision, which had been reported in the papers. The pleasantness of the gathering soon turned to gloom as they began to realize the rather desperate state that we were in. Chris and Myrna asked me if I minded if they undertook to do something about it. I laughed and said, "Hell, no." I wanted to do something myself, and anything that anybody could do would be most welcome at this point.

The first week in December Chris called me and told me that she had rounded up several of the union members who had stood firmly with me, Carl King, Craig Timberlake, Stan Burns, Del Horstmann, and they, together with Herb Steinmann and Myrna Loy and a friend, Mrs. Sophie Jacobs, were planning a huge party for me—a very exclusive one, as a matter of fact, to which even I was not invited. It turned out that they had arranged a sort of benefit for me. Mrs. Roosevelt came, as did luminaries of the show world. Each was asked to contribute some money. They did so, and generously. Gerry Dickler took charge of the funds to administer them. Max Youngstein, Sophie Jacobs and Myrna Loy were the trustees, and here, a week and a half before Christmas, the Faulk family was suddenly solvent again. I was so overcome that I scarcely knew what to do. It was as though the hand of providence had reached down and pulled me back from the brink of disaster.

I sat down with Lynne and had a long talk. We had enough money to get us by for a while. I suggested that we should turn our minds immediately to moving down to Texas, much as both of us disliked the idea of leaving New York. After all, we could live much cheaper in Texas. The children would have more space and fresh air to play in. And there was bound to be some way of earning a living in Austin.

By New Year's Day, 1959, we had our minds made up. We agreed that we should not be precipitate in our move to Austin. I would go down first, ostensibly to visit my family, but really to look around for the most promising way to make a living there, talk to my friends, see who would give me a hand and who wouldn't. And there was the matter of finding a place to live. I went down to Austin and got in touch with Cactus Pryor, who was program director of the one television station in Austin, KTBC-TV. He also did a daily radio show on KTBC. Cactus and I had been friends for a number of years. He had frequently visited us in New York. He understood the nature of my lawsuit. While he was not sure that I should have undertaken it, he was one hundred per cent for giving me all the support he could in Austin. I asked him about the other radio stations there. He said that he thought it would be a splendid idea if I looked around.

I hatched up a notion that I thought I could sell to one of the radio stations. It struck me as a handsome one. I went to see the manager of one of the smallest stations there, but one of the oldest, KNOW. It was affiliated with the ABC network. I suggested to the manager that if he would give me two hours a day to do a program on his station, with my contact with sponsors in New York and by hustling around Austin, I felt that I could earn the station some money and myself some too. He was quite agreeable to this, having known my reputation in New York. He knew nothing about my lawsuit, and I didn't mention it. As far as he was concerned, and as far as I told him, I was returning to Austin to settle down. We made an arrangement whereby, when I returned to New York, I would have promotions made by various nationally famous friends of mine, announcing the fact that I was going to be returning to Austin and start a program on KNOW. The manager thought this was a fine idea. They could play them there for several weeks before I actually started my program. We then made arrangements for me, when I returned to New York, to get in contact with their station representative. The station representative in New York and I would hustle up some business and see if I could come on the air sometime in March with a full, sold-out program.

I returned to New York and, full of enthusiasm, went to work calling on prospective advertisers. I knew the time buyers in several agencies. I really got quite carried away with the idea. Here I was in New York, shut out of radio for over a year and a half, and now I was going to go back to Austin, Texas, and make my living in radio. I realized that I could make a pretty good living through the arrangement I had made with the manager of the station. Best of all, I would still be in radio, the thing that I knew how to do best.

We were to leave New York on Saturday morning, March 14. Our belongings were to be shipped a week or so beforehand. I returned home from a busy day on Madison Avenue on Tuesday, March 3, and found an airmail special delivery letter from the manager of KNOW. It was short and to the point. It stated that the station had programming plans that made it impossible for me to be included as one of its personalities. We would "just have to forget the whole thing." As I read the letter over for the second time, I had a strange sensation of having really been expecting this letter. I sat down at my desk. I didn't want to show it to Lynne until my mind was clear. At the moment, I didn't know what to do. Would we go to Texas, now, or stay in New York? The more I thought about it, the more I realized that we would have to go to Texas. We had gathered too much impetus for the move. Besides that, we had given up our apartment, and a house was waiting for us in Texas. I gazed around me at the bundles and packing boxes all ready for shipping. The walls were bare of pictures. Everything but the beds, chairs and enough for our daily living were ready to go. I felt a sudden surge of defiant anger. "Hell," I snorted, "Don't you worry about a thing. I'm going to turn this letter over to Nizer and let him worry about it. We're going on to Texas."

I called Nizer and told him the latest development. He told me to come to his office at once. He was furious when he read the letter. I asked him if I didn't have grounds for a lawsuit against the station. He shook his head. "John, that would never do. You have enough lawsuits for a while, anyhow. But you certainly wouldn't want to start your new life in Austin with a lawsuit. No. We will have to go another route on this. This letter sounds final. It might not be, though. Maybe we can rescue the job, somehow."

I told him I didn't think there was any chance at all. He was right about a lawsuit against the station. I had long since determined that my life in Austin was going to be a quiet and unobtrusive one. I was going to do everything possible to ingratiate myself with the Austin community. Certainly a lawsuit against an Austin radio station would not fit into the picture at all. Lou suggested that we get in touch with an Austin attorney and have him make discreet inquiry around to see if he could discover the source of the trouble. Lou was convinced that AWARE had gotten to the station somehow or other. Through Cactus Pryor, I located a prominent Austin attorney and turned the whole thing over to him.

The Texas fever was on me. Although I was going back there without the slightest notion of what I was going to do when I got there, the week before we left found me eager with anticipation. I even outdid the children in excitement. A couple of days before we took off, a great snowstorm swept over New York. The children and I took their sled and went out to Central Park. I told them to belly-whop down the hills and wallow in the snow for all they were worth. It would be their last frolic in the snow for a long, long time.

On Saturday morning, March 14, just after dawn, we all loaded into the car, drove out through the Lincoln Tunnel onto the Jersey Turnpike. As we drove down the turnpike, we passed a section from which you can see the spires of lower Manhattan. I pulled over to the right and drove slowly. Lynne and I looked at it for a fleeting moment. The children were all looking down the road—ahead.

13

As we drove south, each mile found the woods and fields turning greener, as though spring were moving north to meet us. And it seemed, too, that each mile I drove toward Texas, my spirits lifted. I turned over in my mind the prospects before me. I realized that in my preoccupation with making the decision to go to Texas, I had overlooked many of the advantages of living in Austin. Austin was an interesting town. Besides, it was home. I had lived there all my life until I came to New York in 1946.

Austin is as near the dead center of the state as the founding fathers could put it. Although it's only on the western fringes of what in this country is called "the South," it is by background and social custom a Southern town. It has a large Negro population, which, until recently, was rigidly segregated by law and tradition. The University of Texas and the state capital are located there, the former lending a mild intellectual atmosphere to the town, the latter a political air. However, the predominant influence in Austin life during my childhood and youth was a sort of Bible-belt Protestantism.

Flowing down through the wooded limestone hills to the west, the Colorado River runs along the southern border of the business section of Austin. The portion of the town lying south of the river is called South Austin. That is where I grew up. The fashionable and well-to-do citizens of the town all lived north of the river. During my childhood days South Austin was a rather self-contained community, more rural than urban. Most of our neighbors maintained their own milk cows, chickens, and a garden. Churchgoing was by far the most popular activity.

In those days, the population of South Austin was about equally divided between Southern Methodists and Southern Baptists. There were a few stray Southern Presbyterians about, and among the very poor there was an exotic sect called the Holy Rollers. There was one family in South Austin known to be Catholic, the Gillises. Mr. Gillis was such a charitable and worthy citizen that he was respected and well liked by one and all. His name was seldom mentioned in conversation, however, without his being identified as a Catholic.

My family were all Methodists. Not only religious Methodists, but social Methodists. I was in my adolescence, in fact, before I came to realize that people met in social gatherings not connected in one way or another with the church. My parents were what the community called "pillars" of the Fred Allen Memorial Methodist Church in South Austin.

My childhood was that of any other churchgoing middle-class child in South Austin, with the exception that I was considered something of a sinner rather early in life. This was because I used profanity and knew the facts of life. My nearest and most constant companions from infancy to the first seven or eight years of my life were the children of a Negro family who lived on our place, the Batts. Together we frolicked about the cow lot and barn, through the woods and the fields, finding bird's nests, investigating hay stacks and cedar thickets, and climbing the live oak trees to see the world around us more clearly.

Daddy had been reared a sharecropper. However, he arranged to get an education, was graduated from the University of Texas Law School, and became a lawyer in Austin in 1900. He was a popular young lawyer and had a thriving clientele. However, he had discovered Emerson, Thoreau, and Thomas Jefferson. From them he went to Spinoza. He had long been an avid student of the Bible. His childhood experiences with poverty and deprivation weighed heavily on his mind. He began to move slowly but surely in his philosophy away from orthodoxy toward the wide world of the freethinker. Mama, who married Daddy in 1902, was a pious Methodist. She was only mildly disturbed when Daddy undertook to explain to her that he loved and believed in the teachings of Jesus Christ but did not believe in the divinity of Jesus. Mama said she accepted his opinion because she accepted Daddy completely. Daddy became concerned with matters of civil rights and social justice. He formed a friendship and correspondence with Eugene V. Debs, who strongly influenced him toward socialism. He began to envisage the unlimited joy and happiness that could come to mankind through achieving a liberated mind.

Yet Daddy identified so completely and affectionately with his Texas surroundings that he was not regarded as alien in the community. I suppose few of them understood what he really believed. He was held in respect and admiration for his ready wit and good humor. In spite of his unorthodox beliefs he was very active in the Masonic order and a faithful member of the Methodist church. In fact, for as long as I can remember, he was the teacher of the Adult Bible Class at our church. He mixed a strong brew of Spinoza and Emerson with the scriptures and served it out to his nodding listeners every Sunday morning.

By the time I was a senior in high school I had come to appreciate and listen closely to the things that Daddy said and the observations he made. He had a sure and firm grasp on the history of the United States. "We've come a long way, Johnny, and we've got a long way to go. But America has the juice and the power to get there." The "there," to Daddy's way of thinking, was a state of freedom and justice, complete democracy. He was not so vain as to regard himself as a self-made man. On the contrary, he knew that many forces in our society made it possible for him to come from the life of a sharecropper to that of a comfortable enlightened citizen, and he felt because he had been successful in his climb that he had a lifelong obligation to assist others who were less fortunate than himself. One of his favorite themes was: "Jesus said, 'As you do unto the least of these, ye do unto Me,' and in a democracy like America, Johnny, as we do unto our least privileged citizen, whether he's Catholic, Jew or Protestant, native or foreign born, Negro or white, you do unto America."

Daddy was convinced that bigotry was a two-edged sword that punished the wielder as much as it did the victim. It was during this period that I first heard from him that racial integration would be an accomplished fact, probably within my lifetime. He believed this firmly. He told me that Negroes would go to the University of Texas just as white students did. He also told me that I, as a privileged white Texan and Southerner, had a great responsibility to help in hastening that day when the terrible injustice of racial segregation would end.

It was always more or less taken for granted that I would become a lawyer. I took a prelaw course at the university. However, my chief interest had been literature. I was an avid reader and the world of books was my greatest joy. In my junior year I took J. Frank Dobie's *Life and Literature of the Southwest.* Since that time many of my interests and activities have been influenced by Dobie.

Dobie was not only a scholar, he was a humanitarian and a thinker. He gave generously of his time and thought to me. Two other men at the university shared his love for free, searching intellect: Roy Bedichek and Walter P. Webb. The three of them have been my mentors since my university days.

J. Frank Dobie, Roy Bedichek, and Walter P. Webb lived in Austin. As I drove along, a warm affectionate feeling crept over me. I would join their circle again, go out to the Webb or Dobie ranch, sit out late at night talking. Dobie and Bedichek had, perhaps, the greatest influence on my life, aside from my parents. Their conversation, their interests, their observations on the world around us had always fired my spirit, my imagination. Their respect and affection had meant a lot to me, particularly the last three years. I smiled as I recalled how Vincent Hartnett, in his EBT, had testified that he regarded me as suspect, in part, because he had read in *Newsweek* that J. Frank Dobie was a close friend of mine, and that I had been greatly influenced by him. In Hartnett's book, J. Frank Dobie was suspect.

My heart was pounding with excitement as we drove up dusty West Live Oak Street, and turned into our old home place. My sister Mary, with her husband, Chester Koock, and their seven children, were lined up, waiting for us. Texana and her husband, John T. Conn, and their three children, my niece Anne McAfee and her husband Bill and their five children, and my brother, Hamilton, and his wife, Bernice, were all on hand to greet us. My other sister, Martha, was teaching school in Houston. Their children had made "Welcome Home" signs of cardboard and brown wrapping paper, lettered in red, green, blue and yellow crayon: "Welcome New York Cousins" and "Back Home at Last." A great hugging and kissing and general jubilation took place. This was followed by a washing up and a sumptuous meal. Everybody, including the children, babbled at the same time. The scene resembled a Sunday-school picnic more than a family gathering.

In the midst of the festivities my nephew Bill Koock, a huge six-footer about eighteen years old, hopped up from the table, bounded across the wide dining room, reached under a table in the corner of the room and brought out a half-grown possum. "Gotcha, you rascal!" he said, laughing as he held the startled creature high by the tail for all to see. The New York end of the family gasped with astonishment. The others just giggled and continued eating. Bill made a speech to the possum against trespassing, admonishing him with the forefinger of his left hand while holding him aloft in his right hand. Lynne had dropped her knife and fork and was staring. Mary commented pleasantly, as she continued to eat, "An old mamma possum raised a whole brood of them under the kitchen this past month. The fool things think they own our house now. They're all over it. They act like *we're* the ones who are trespassing. Put him out in the backyard, Billy."

It had been, during my childhood there at the old home place, a standing joke that anywhere from half a dozen to a dozen guests could scarcely cause a ripple in the bedding situation at home. It was still true. The extra Faulks who had arrived from New York were stowed away with ease, in the half dozen bedrooms.

I had a long visit with J. Frank Dobie and Roy Bedichek the next day. I recounted all of my experiences with the trial up to that point. I told them just as soon as we got settled, we would resume our regular sessions. My first order of business would be, of course, to find something to do in Austin. Getting the family settled was one thing. Getting them fed was quite another. Our resources were about depleted. I had to begin making a living and quickly. Dobie and Bedichek suggested that it would be wiser for me not to explain why I had left New York and come to Austin to live. They thought it would hurt my chances of getting into a business.

I went over to see two more friends, Jerre Williams and his wife. Jerre was professor of law at the University of Texas Law School. He and his wife had followed my case avidly, not only as personal friends, but because they were interested in the issues involved. They agreed with Dobie and Bedichek. They told me that in all likelihood some of AWARE's friends, or those who would be sympathetic to AWARE's point of view, in Austin had already caused my difficulty with the Austin radio station. I was rather surprised to hear that there was any knowledge of AWARE in Austin. Jerre and Mary Pearl explained to me that there was an active group in Austin, called the Austin Anti-Communist League. They made it their business twenty-four hours a day to guard Austin against Communist subversion. They frequently brought speakers to town. In fact, they had brought Robert Welch of the John Birch Society there. They said I would stand small chance of earning a livelihood in Austin if I ever got that bunch after me. I saw their point.

So my problem was not so simple as just going out and locating some sort of work. I had to have a pretty logical reason for having moved back to Austin to live, and that was clear. I was known in Austin by a great many people, who generally assumed that I was enjoying a successful career in New York—an assumption that was helped along by the fact that several of my network shows had been broadcast in Austin. Besides, my homecomings had always been written up in the local newspapers, and often in the course of my visits I had been invited to speak before the city's various church and civic groups.

The most politic explanation for this homecoming would be that I had come to my senses and moved back to this true paradise on earth, Austin, Texas. This would be readily accepted by most Austinites, because they devoutly believed that any rational being would prefer Austin to any other spot in the universe. But if I indicated that I was broke and looking desperately for work, eyebrows would be raised. Why would I quit a thriving career to move back home and try to find work? I decided that the wisest course for me was to let it be thought that, having made some money in New York, I had now retired, as any sensible individual would, to Austin to spend the rest of my days. I would let it be known that I was very eager to become part of the community life there, and that I would be happy to take on some worth-while job.

I was asked to entertain at the Austin Lions Club, and I accepted the invitation. I worked up a wonderful speech on returning to Texas, including all sorts of anecdotes and humorous sallies. It was a great success. Within a week I had another half-dozen invitations to speak before civic and church groups there. I was convinced that in a short time something good would come along.

Sure enough, one day toward the end of March, I received a call from Buck Hood, an editor on the one Austin daily paper. He had told me, and obviously meant it, that he would help me to find something to do in Austin. He asked me to come down to his office. When I got there, he introduced me to a Joe Crow, a local real-estate man, and Pat Stanford, a young gentleman from Midland, Texas, who had just bought a huge tract of land in Austin and was planning to develop it into a housing subdivision. It was to be called University Hills. Since it was Stanford's first venture in Austin, he too wanted to become part of the community, as well as promote his new subdivision. Buck Hood had had an idea. He sold Crow and Stanford on the notion of doing a public-service film on the Salvation Army, and hiring me to direct and narrate it. I had never had the slightest connection with film production, but I kept quiet about it. Stanford went for the suggestion. And for the first time in a year and a half I had a job.

In addition to the film, which turned out pretty well, my work consisted in trying to think up ways to get University Hills depicted in the public's mind as a modern Eden. I was to use my best efforts to get newspaper, radio and television mention for the subdivision. I stayed up all night trying to think of ways of getting University Hills mentioned in the local newspaper; I spent all day trying to think of ways getting it mentioned on radio and television. It wasn't easy. But it would have been impossible had not Buck Hood and Cactus Pryor worked tirelessly with me.

From the very first week of our coming to Texas, Paul Martinson had been writing letters regularly. It was a practice which proved, for the next three years, to be one of the greatest factors in maintaining my morale. Nearly every week Paul would write to me of what was happening in the lawsuit. His letters were always filled with good humor and affectionate concern for our well-being and little asides on various personalities who were involved in the suit.

He had written that Vincent Hartnett was understandably wearing a bit thin with the EBT. Paul had managed to accumulate some 2,500 pages of testimony from him, as well as valuable documentary evidence. Roy Cohn and Thomas Bolan had protested that the long EBT was impairing Hartnett's health. They were also refusing to let him answer questions that Paul thought were highly pertinent. This would always cause considerable delay, as Paul would have to draw up briefs and apply to the court for rulings which would compel Hartnett to continue with the EBT, to produce records that had been requested, and to answer questions that had been asked. Louis Nizer, too, made it a practice to send along letters filled with encouragement and good will.

In the latter part of May 1959, Roy Bedichek died suddenly, of a heart attack that came as he was waiting for lunch, after which he had planned to go out into the Texas countryside on a bird-watching jaunt. His death caused a great melancholy to come over me for many days. Even today I never see a patch of wild flowers or hear a bird burst into song without Mr. Bedichek coming to mind.

The spring gave way to summer. New York became further and further away in my thoughts. Save for an occasional letter from a friend there, and the Martinson and Nizer letters, I seldom had occasion or time to think about it. I was too concerned about how to survive in Texas. I knew that the public-relations job with Pat Stanford was only temporary at best. Not only that, but despite our frugality we could not seem to make ends meet on what I was receiving. We began to slip further and further into debt. I had to write to friends in New York and borrow money.

Advertising and public relations seemed to be the only fields I could find work in. There are only one or two small advertising agencies in Austin. We figured that with energy and creative work we might make a niche for ourselves there at least.

One day our friend Joe Crow called me. He wanted me and Lynne to come down and meet a Mr. Berenson, at his office, at once. Mr. Berenson, who came from Boston, was a developer of huge shopping centers throughout the country. He had put up the gigantic Gulf Gate shopping center in Houston and the Gateway shopping center in Beaumont, and many more. Now, Mr. Berenson was in the process of putting up a huge shopping center, to be called Capital Plaza, in Austin.

Mr. Berenson said that in all other communities where he had built shopping centers, the radio, television and newspapers had fallen all over each other currying favor with him as the stores were being built. But in Austin, and here he shook his head sadly, there was not even a flicker of interest. The newspaper and the broadcasting station seemed hostile to his project. He then explained that the generation of public interest in such a venture was absolutely essential to its success. The shopping public had to know that they were going to have a huge regional shopping center, big airy new stores, a wide variety of goods to select from, and acres of free parking space.

He wanted to know whether Lynne and I could do something about his problem. Could we get free publicity in the newspaper, on radio and on television? He said that immediately prior to the grand opening, in March, of the two largest stores, Montgomery Ward and H. E. Butt, there would be a huge advertising campaign in the newspapers and other media; but he wanted to start the drums beating at once. He said that Joe Crow had spoken very highly of our acumen and of my good connections in Austin. If we could get publicity for him, he would hire us, not only as a public-relations firm, but also to take charge of all advertising, and there would be considerable of it. We assured him that he had called the right persons. He hired us on the spot. We were to receive a retainer each month for several months. Then, when the considerable advertising program was launched, we would have full control of that and, of course, receive the regular commissions on all advertising that we placed.

By the time Lynne and I reached home, we had already formed our advertising and public-relations firm. At least we had named it: John Henry Faulk Associates.

As luck would have it, a lifetime friend of mine, Rex Kitchens, was the contractor in charge of construction at Capital Plaza. He was actually like a member of my family. He promised he would do anything possible to help me out, so I went out to see Rex with a publicity scheme. If he would let me solicit all of his skilled workers, laborers, foremen, and so forth, for donations to the Salvation Army Christmas Shoe Fund drive, I would get Captain McClure, of the Salvation Army, to come out and receive the donations. It would make a good story; with the Salvation Army in it, the newspaper could scarcely turn it down.

For the next couple of days Lynne and I were in a whirl of activity. We were getting ready for our first big publicity break on Capital Plaza, and we wanted to make sure nothing went wrong. I called the newspaper and told them that we were going to have a real story for them. I told the paper that I would write the story and asked them to send out a photographer. Then I called the television news people and told them that it was going to be worth covering by television. I wrote the story very carefully, with only one paragraph, far down in the story, mentioning the fact that Capital Plaza, the new multi-million-dollar shopping center, would soon be in operation. Then Lynne and I went out and surveyed and resurveyed the vast acreage of half-completed buildings and construction machinery. Since the huge Montgomery Ward department store was the most imposing building in Capital Plaza, as well as the most nearly completed, we decided that the pictures should be taken in front of it. But there was no sign on it, and we realized that a news picture showing Rex Kitchens and Captain McClure and a huge brick wall would never do. The local executives of Montgomery Ward told us that they could not put up a sign unless it was authorized by the Fort Worth office, and the Fort Worth executives told us that they could not authorize a sign that carried any name other than "Montgomery Ward"; we would have to get up our own sign if we wanted "Capital Plaza" on it. We decided to do just that and to get a couple of workmen to hold it in the background.

The day for the picture taking arrived. So did a gully-washer of a rain. Lynne and I were in absolute despair. The rain stopped a couple of hours before the time appointed for the brief ceremony, but it left in its wake a cold drizzle and knee-deep mud on the construction site.

Rex Kitchens had risen to the occasion. He had rallied all of his carpenters, electricians and laborers in a great mass behind him, posed them precisely on the spot, muddy as it was, that Lynne had suggested. Captain McClure stepped forward to receive the canvas bag of money from him. TV cameras whirred, our photographer snapped away.

The next morning, there it was, the story just as I had written it, without a single deletion, the picture of Rex and Captain McClure, the workmen in the background, the Capital Plaza sign and Montgomery Ward's, all clear and bright. Capital Plaza had made the Austin paper. I switched on the TV news. In a moment, here came Rex Kitchens and Captain McClure, smiling brightly, raincoated against the drizzle, with Ward's big sign in the background, and the news commentator reading: "At Capital Plaza, Austin's great new shopping center, now hurrying toward completion, . . ." and so on. We felt like a highly successful public relations firm.

Our friend and counselor, Joe Crow, suggested that since shopping centers were proliferating over Texas in a mad tumble of construction, we should become specialists in the promotion and publicizing of shopping centers. Nobody else in Texas was doing it. We decided that it was a good idea. It was not that we liked shopping centers; we didn't. They were big headaches, particularly in dealing with fractious merchants' associations and recalcitrant owners whose respective interests in the shopping center frequently conflicted. But it was the only thing we had experience in. So we went busily about trying to scrape up clients in Texas. We put out word that we were available to promote and advertise shopping centers; we were specialists in that field, as a matter of fact. As we came to find out, it was not a very wise field to go into.

While we were waiting for shopping-center business to flow in, we searched for other clients. I would go out to talk to a promising, enterprising business. We would prepare a presentation of the kind of services we would render them, and then sit down and talk the matter over. We didn't make much headway. We did gain several small, temporary accounts this way. Lynne was far more adequate at talking advertising business than I was. She seemed to make real sense when she talked. I didn't. Practically every hour of every business day I was reminded in one uncomfortable way or another of my inadequacy in the business world. Although I flung myself into the activity with a zest, I had a profound sense of insecurity. I would go whizzing around town trying to look like a dynamic, self-assured public-relations man. When I sat down to talk over a business proposition, it would not be five minutes before the gentleman with whom I was talking realized I was not much of an expert. I simply did not understand figures and the like. Worse than that, though, I found it very difficult to adjust to the business of having to curry favor, to be constantly a hail-fellow-well-met, and to do all the other things that a public-relations man is required to do.

It was a far cry from all my days on WCBS in New York. There I had been invited to supermarket openings and public affairs of that sort. The sponsor would send a car for me, have me driven out, and I was one of the celebrities posing for pictures, signing autographs, cutting ribbons, and so forth. Now the matter was reversed. It was my job to plan and execute such affairs, to wheedle prominent city and state dignitaries to attend, to make sure that reporters and newscasters and photographers were on hand, to try frantically to get a story in the papers or on the air. And all this activity had to be accompanied by a state of chronic good humor and good will. I was required to put up with all sorts of rudeness and petty politics.

Austin was not an advertising- nor a public-relations-conscious town. Most of its business, both civic and public, was conducted in a very low key. Arrangements were made behind closed doors. For all of my forced grinning and my affected good will, I made small impression indeed. I didn't mind the hard work and the long hours. I was rather gratified to have my mind occupied with business, and I was desperately anxious to learn the ropes. It was just when I paused long enough to realize how inadequate I was as a businessman that I was deeply pained. Our business was always in the red. We borrowed more money—money to live on and keep our business going. It was during this period, too, that I became conscious of a discomforting fact.

I hoped that the time would come when I would get another shot at my profession. I wanted to keep my hand in by working on new material and developing new ideas. When I would sit down to work over some material, I would discover to my dismay that nothing would happen. My creative juices refused to flow. In my public appearances before civic and business groups, I was forced to fall back on old tried-and-true material from the years past. I simply could not make anything come out right that was new. This was frustrating and painful. The more I thought it over, the more I realized that time was slipping away from me, counting against me. I knew that if I had to wait long enough for my case to come to trial, I would be virtually unknown as an entertainer. When you're in the latter part of your forties, this is a depressing thought. The realization that I would have to begin my career all over again brought on cold sweat.

It also prompted me to redouble my efforts at establishing our advertising business. Nizer had told me many times that while we might win the suit, there might be no damages awarded, and if they were awarded, there might be nothing to collect. The better part of wisdom suggested that I had better have a well-established business to fall back on. But at this point it seemed that my business refused to become well established. At times I almost longed for the days when I was blacklisted in New York. At least there, when I suffered a rebuff and hostility, I could salve my ego with the knowledge that the matter did not relate to me personally, it was the blacklist. But in Austin, I did not have even that thin satisfaction. It was not rebuff and hostility I had to contend with. It was loss of status and, more discomforting than that, indifference.

In May we were called by a huge shopping center which was under construction in San Antonio, Texas. I went down and talked to the owners and merchants. We signed a contract. John Henry Faulk Associates was to handle the grand opening, and all the pre-grand opening affairs. Now, we had two important clients: Capital Plaza and the San Antonio shopping center.

14

In the early part of 1960, Paul Martinson wrote to me that he had completed Vincent Hartnett's EBT. There had been "nothing spectacular in his testimony, although it did contain a few bits of the mosaic that we have constructed." In the spring he conducted the EBT of Paul Milton, an officer of AWARE and a collaborator on the libelous publication about me. After they completed Milton's EBT, they began on Laurence Johnson; he, of course, was a key witness, since he supposedly was a multimillionaire and, should we win a judgment, would be solvent enough to pay it off. However, he was an elderly man, and Paul wrote to me that he was having great difficulty in getting Johnson to answer questions. As he wrote, "Johnson's almost universal answer to everything is 'I don't recollect,' and only when confronted with documents will he remember."

Paul's letters also contained a detailed account of his efforts to obtain information from the agencies and networks on the matter of blacklisting. He was refused repeatedly and got very little cooperation from any of them. He wrote me that Charles Collingwood and Tom Murray, who had given us our documentary evidence of Johnson's activities against me, were not only willing but eager to help in any way that they could. Collingwood lent his prestige to the attempt to persuade witnesses to come forward and help us. However, for the most part, those who had any association with AWARE, or Mr. Johnson, or Mr. Hartnett, were in no mood to get involved with them again. Although Paul tirelessly and patiently followed out each lead to its end, accumulating a little evidence here and there, with his unbelievable persistence, he was almost bitter in his condemnation of those in the agencies and networks who refused to cooperate.

He reminded me, in one of his letters in the fall of 1960, that when the EBT of Johnson was completed, it would then be my turn to be examined by the defendants. After my EBT was completed, a trial date would be set. I was waiting.

As 1961 rolled around, John Henry Faulk Associates found themselves with but one small client. The shopping centers had opened, so our business had disappeared. We had many bright prospects, but nothing seemed to materialize. Our overhead had grown considerably, since we had moved into larger quarters back in the summer of 1960 and had taken on a regular stenographer and an art director—both, incidentally, loyal and fine people. After four years, I had grown accustomed to wheedling, borrowing and what not, enough for my family to get by on; now I had to do the same thing to support an expensive office.

At about this time, I had a lengthy, reassuring letter from Louis Nizer, examining the various factors that were causing delays and prolonging our litigation. First the defendants were waging a deliberate campaign of obstruction, and this necessitated time-consuming recourse to the court; second, the business of gathering evidence from the uncooperative and overcautious radio and television industry was a long and tedious one. But, he added in his letter, "rest assured that there will be a judgment day in court. We are determined to bring your cause to fruition, and time, instead of dulling the sword, will only make it sharper when the trial date comes. After all, we went through the same procedure of about five years' delay in the Pegler case. There must have been the same feeling on the part of the defendants that their cause was growing stale. They woke up to learn that our outrage at their conduct had merely accumulated ferocity through the years. So, with deep apology for the delayed trial date, but with renewed assurance of our continued vigor, I send this word to bolster your patience—which fortunately has been robust without these explanations."

Nizer's good letter seemed to change our fortunes. Shortly afterward we got as a client the prize advertiser of Austin, the Austin Savings and Loan Association. Then in July, Paul Martinson sent me the long-awaited word that I should come to New York for my EBT.

I got back to New York early on a gray, rainy morning, August 24,

1961. As I walked with my suitcase from the West Side Airlines Terminal in Manhattan toward Broadway, the peculiarity of the town enthralled me. The taxis, buses, trucks, Con Edison tearing up a street—a discordant rhapsody, but it was New York. I wanted to reach out and hug the town. I had to restrain myself from shouting out loud, "I'm back, New York; you can rest easy now." Actually until that moment, I hadn't realized how very much I loved the town, how congenial it was, and how much at home I felt there.

Paul Martinson was waiting for me when I walked into Nizer's offices. He introduced me to George Berger, his assistant in the case. George had been working with Paul on the suit for more than a year, and I was pleased to discover that he was as familiar with every detail of the lawsuit and the personalities involved as I was.

Louis Nizer and I walked over to the Algonquin Hotel for lunch at the Round Table. In his discussion with me he was a kind of combination of spiritual adviser and football coach.

"Remember at all times during this examination," he said, "you have right and justice on your side. Keep that in your mind. Answer all questions honestly and straightforwardly. But do not volunteer information, and do not be evasive. Be direct and succinct. Above all"—and here he looked at me sharply—"do not try to be clever and witty in your answers. Never try to match wits with Cohn or Bolan, or whoever is conducting the EBT. When a witness does that, the results are usually disastrous."

Roy Cohn's office was on a high floor in one of the tall buildings down near Wall Street. Its windows commanded a view of the East River and New York Harbor, including the Statue of Liberty. It was a spacious, comfortable office, the desks were covered with mementos and knickknacks. The walls were adorned with plaques and pictures of Mr. Cohn with various dignitaries and public figures. Squeezed between these on the walls were citations and letters from various superpatriotic organizations praising Mr. Cohn's services. Hung on one wall was a huge photograph of Roy Cohn leaning over the shoulder of the late Senator McCarthy whispering in his ear. It symbolized the McCarthy era to me, Roy Cohn whispering to McCarthy. Paul Martinson whispered in my ear, as we stood gazing at it, "I would keep that in the basement bathroom if it were mine."

Thomas Bolan, a partner of Cohn's, conducted the examination.

At his side, at all times, was Vincent Hartnett, who had brought a huge package of material from his files, and now and again passed along a piece of material to Bolan for my questioning. The court reporter sat between us. By my side sat Paul Martinson and George Berger.

The first day of the examination was taken up with questions of a rather cursory sort about my background. The court reporter, unused to my Texas accent, often asked me to repeat each answer several times, while he wrestled to get it straight. Bolan's manner was both pleasant and courteous, and the examination went along very well. At one point he asked me if I had any records, written or printed material, on speeches I had made, any evidence of places where I had spoken. I answered, yes, I believed that I did, and would try to locate them. He asked me to bring them in the next day, as he would want them for evidence.

Paul Martinson immediately discerned that this was a rare chance indeed. That evening, I collected all of the plaques, awards, letters of praise, et cetera, that I had received for the six or seven years I had been in New York. They represented citations from appearances before every imaginable church, civic, patriotic and educational institution. There were two bulky packages of them. We were pretty sure that Mr. Bolan was not searching for such evidence, but he had requested it, and we knew that when we submitted it, it would become part of the record. We turned the materials over to him and they were properly marked as exhibits in the case. There were several citations that must have stung Mr. Bolan rather sharply. One plaque, from a Jewish congregation in New Jersey, lauded me as "the man who best exemplified the American way of life in the Community." Another, from the D.A.R., cited me for patriotic services in my broadcasts.

The EBT in some respects resembled a chess game. I was playing Bolan. He was trying to checkmate me. Paul Martinson and George Berger were my expert advisers, listening intently to every question, watching every move. At times Paul would object so strenuously that a lengthy wrangle would ensue, off the record. During these times, I would gaze out the window over New York Harbor and the Statue of Liberty. At one point, Mr. Bolan confided to me that his wife had been a listener of mine years before.

During my stay in New York, I kept running into acquaintances from earlier days. We greeted each other warmly, and of course I expected them to express surprise and delight that I was back in New York and to make anxious inquiry about my lawsuit. On the contrary, although most of them were pleasant enough and asked me about my health, they apparently didn't know that I had ever left the city. Only one or two of them inquired about my lawsuit; and these inquiries were something like "How did that lawsuit that you were in come out?" It seemed that the vast majority of people in radio and television had either entirely forgotten that I had ever been involved in a lawsuit, or remembered it only in terms of my having sued somebody, or somebody having sued me, once in the distant past. This was something of a comedown for me. I had to face the fact that most of the people in the radio and television industry neither knew nor cared about what had happened to me, and would have very little interest in the lawsuit or its outcome. I realized, with a chilly feeling, that they would care a lot less about my efforts to get back into the industry after the suit. I was a kind of forgotten man.

My emotions seesawed from ebullient self-confidence to depressed anxiety. At times I would fancy that the networks and sponsors, freed from the horror of enforced blacklisting, would take me up on their shoulders and bear me down Madison Avenue amid loud hurrahs. Within an hour I would nose-dive in the opposite direction. What if the awful fear was still over the land? What if we won, but I got only a dollar as damages? What if the radio and television industry couldn't quite recall my name, and I remained unemployable?

In any case, I thought it was the better part of wisdom if I had a business to come back to in Austin after the trial, so I redoubled my efforts to make our agency a success. I got back to Austin, in the middle of September, with the news that the end of the long wait was in sight. Paul had told me that they would very soon have information on when the case would go on the court calendar. Difficult as it was to concentrate on anything but the imminent trial, I pitched into business again.

Shortly after this, Louis Nizer's book, *My Life in Court,* was published. It immediately went to the top of the best-seller list. Friends who knew that Louis Nizer was soon to represent me in my lawsuit in New York treated me with new respect. I was feeling a great deal like crowing, but my experiences from the past several years had taught me caution. I tempered my tendency to exult with a conscious effort to remain calm and collected.

On March 16, 1962, the long-awaited call came. Paul Martinson phoned to say that the case was scheduled to begin on April 3. He and Nizer wanted me to be in New York not later than March 28, in order to be fully prepared when we went into court. He told me that I should plan to spend at least six weeks in court. This meant I would be away from home for nearly two months. From the moment of his call, my world in Austin turned topsy-turvy. I began to pack my gear and dashed about kissing loved ones goodbye. Since we had no cash at all on hand, we decided that I would drive to New York; driving was cheaper than flying, and it would enable me to carry along enough gear to last me for the two months that I would be away.

Just before I left, I suddenly remembered something: I didn't know where I was going to stay in New York; I did not have the wherewithal to stay in a hotel. I called Chris and Merle Debuskey. I asked them if they could put me up for a couple of weeks. They said they would be happy to put me up in their extra bedroom for the entire duration of the trial. I told them it would probably take six weeks, maybe two months. It didn't seem to faze them. They said that was perfectly all right with them, they would be honored to have me. I loaded my clothes and all the documents and letters that I had on the case into my car. On Wednesday, March 21, as the sun came up over Travis Heights, I drove out of Austin toward New York on the last lap of a six-year journey.

15

I've been lucky all my life in having kindly friends who have been ready to reach out a hand and help me. Such friends are Chris and Merle Debuskey. They had prepared a room in their not spacious, but comfortable, book-lined apartment for me and were waiting for my arrival. Since the inception of my lawsuit, both Chris and Merle had stood steadfastly by me. Chris is a modern dancer, and a very fine one. Merle is a press representative for several Broadway shows. They are both literate and well informed, and good conversationalists. For the duration of my trial these two dedicated their entire time to me.

The following morning, as I walked through the bright March sunlight across town to Nizer's office, I kept wanting to reach out and pat the buildings as I passed and tell them, "It's mighty nice to see you all again. I'm glad to be back." Louis Nizer, Paul Martinson and George Berger were waiting for me in Nizer's office when I arrived. After a warm and cordial greeting, I detected a strange note, in Lou's voice. The same warmth, hospitality and concern were there, but there was something new.

"We have no time to waste," he said. "We have an entire case to prepare." I was surprised. I had had the notion that the case was fully prepared, and that we could start trying it that very day if necessary. After all, it had been six years in preparation. Scarcely a week of those six years had passed without something being done on it. I would have thought that it had been fully prepared by this time. As a matter of fact, I was under the impression that I would have little to do upon arriving in New York but sit back and watch the lawyers have at it.

I found out mighty soon how wrong my impression had been. Lou began by outlining the hundreds of things that had to be done. Then I got the impression that we would never be prepared. He told me that my first task was to review my EBT until I was familiar with every aspect of it. When I allowed I thought I knew pretty well what I had said to Bolan six months before, he cut me off short and said that wasn't sufficient. I had to know exactly how I had answered each question. He didn't want me to be tripped up on some triviality when I got on the stand. He ended up by announcing that we would all go to his house for dinner that night. I interjected, "By the way, Lou, I won't be able to dine with you tonight. I'll have to meet you later. I promised—" He cut me off kindly but sharply. "You'll have to cancel any dinner engagement you have made. We're going to work on this case. And incidentally, I would suggest that you make no other engagements at any time. From now on, until the verdict is in, your entire concentration must be on this case. I want you to take good care of yourself, get plenty of sleep, eat well and be in perfect trim. You've got the ordeal of your life before you."

I took my EBT, went to an office and started looking through it. I grumbled to myself some at having such a mountainous lot of work loaded on me. After all, what did I have lawyers for if I was going to have to work up the case? I got over my bad temper quickly. I had seen the huge stacks of exhibits, briefs and EBT transcripts that were in Paul Martinson's office, the accumulation of six years' work done by Louis Nizer and Paul Martinson and George Berger. I had little room to complain, and I knew it. I plowed into the EBT.

I spent the entire day digging through it. It was a terrible bore, reading what Bolan had asked me and how I had answered six months before. But I read it all, down to the tiniest detail. That evening Paul, George, Lou and I took a taxi up to Lou's home. George had three overstuffed briefcases full of notes, briefs and exhibits. That evening's program was a pattern of each evening we spent for the next three months. I later came to regard it as a ritual. We were greeted fondly and graciously at the door by Mildred Nizer, who invited us to sit down in the side living room and asked us if we wouldn't have a drink. Lou declined, saying no, we are going to have to work later, and drinks might slow down our work. After chatting a bit we adjourned to the dinner table. There, Lou sat at one end of the table and Mildred at the other, while dinner was served. Paul and George sat on one side, and I sat on the other. The conversation was light, pitched on the news of the day and matters not connected with my lawsuit. We ate in a casual, unhurried fashion, with much jesting and light conversation, for all the world like a social evening. When we had had coffee, Lou arose from the table and said, "Well, are we ready?" And we all went into the living room again. Mildred asked if there was anything that she could get or do to make us comfortable. After being told no, she retired. Lou, Paul and George all slipped off their jackets and rolled up their sleeves, each took a handful of sharpened yellow pencils in one hand and a long yellow legal pad in the other, and from that moment on the evening was devoted to The Lawsuit.

As the evening ran on I got the idea that this was an old procedure with Martinson and the Nizers. It had been followed in dozens of cases before.

The first thing on the evening's agenda was a discussion and speculation on Bolan's petition to the court to delay the start of the trial from April 3 to some future date. It seemed that Mr. Bolan found it necessary to go to Egypt with a prizefighter with whom he had a business association. Lou said he felt confident that the court would not grant Bolan more than two week's delay, and he added that we could make good use of that time in better preparing the case.

I then brought up the matter of the several calls that I had received that day from the New York newspapers; I had put the newspapermen off so that I might be able to find out what I was supposed to say—or, more important, what I was supposed to *not* say to newspapermen. Lou jumped on that like a duck on a June bug. "You're not to say anything at all! Be courteous but firm, explain that you have no statement whatsoever. We're going to try this case in the courts, not in the newspapers." Paul Martinson then brought up the matter of CBS and what its role in the lawsuit would be. Both Lou and Paul had serious misgivings about CBS and its declared neutrality in the case. They felt that CBS, by its refusal to aid me in the past, had indicated that they would not in any way give me any aid in the actual trial.

"Just a minute," I said, "do you mean that CBS is not going to be on our side in this case?"

"They certainly haven't been on your side so far," Lou said.

"Yes, but now the chips are down," I protested. "CBS loathes AWARE and the defendants. They'll be glad to testify for us. They are not about to support the defendants. And it would be absurd to think so."

Lou explained patiently that I had better be prepared for some pretty grotesque absurdities in the coming days. He said CBS would do whatever it thought served its interest best.

"Yes," I said, "but both Sam Slate and Carl Ward know exactly what happened, they know that Johnson attacked me, they know about the AWARE bulletin, they know all the problems that I had, and if we call them on the stand under oath, they would never lie. They would tell the truth."

"You'd be surprised how much they could forget on the witness stand. They just wouldn't remember," George Berger commented.

"Hell, I was thinking we should call them and get them to testify for us," I said somewhat lamely. "Now it seems that you are all worried about whether they are going to testify on the other side."

Lou nodded. "If CBS joins the defendants in this matter and comes down to court and testifies for AWARE, it could hurt us very badly."

I was troubled by their cynicism—that's how I regarded their attitude. I was convinced that their fears were not real. CBS would never lend support to the defendants in this case.

A discussion arose over the witnesses we would be able to get for the trial. Lou said that we would have to bring in two or three character witnesses. These should be persons of impressive and unimpeachable character, who had known me over a period of years, and who could vouch for my good name and reputation.

It was agreed that I should get in touch with several distinguished professors and ministers who knew me well. I was sure that this would be easy, for I had dozens of friends in these groups who had already asked me how they could help out. In addition, there were other witnesses we would have to get who would be crucial to the case, persons who had had experience with blacklisting. They would have to have had firsthand knowledge to qualify as witnesses. We would have to get people who had actually been blacklisted, as well as radio and television executives and agency executives, and if possible, sponsors who had been pressured by defendants in one way or another and could testify to that effect.

Paul Martinson said that it was going to be very difficult. Over the past six years he had been able to persuade only one or two to come forth. Of course, Charles Collingwood said that he would be more than willing—in fact he was anxious to come and help in every way. He would be a very important witness. And then there was Tom Murray. Paul said that he had talked to a number of network and agency executives who had admitted that they knew a great deal about the matter but were not going to get on the witness stand; they were concerned with their own reputations and their own safety. Lou thought that if I made a direct approach to them, indicating how strong our position was, perhaps they would consent to come. He said I should spend the next week doing nothing but making appointments and sitting down with prospective witnesses and seeing if I could not persuade them to come and testify.

The first name he gave me was that of David Susskind. I knew that this would be easy, for David Susskind had taken a strong position in my behalf and had expressed a thorough dislike for the defendants. He had valuable information to give, too, for he had lots of experience with blacklisting. I was given a dozen or so names to contact. Lou said that he wanted George Berger and me to sit down at the very earliest moment and make a comprehensive list of all of my citations and plaques beyond the ones I had produced for my EBT, the circumstances under which I had received them, and what they dealt with. I told him I thought this would take at least a month. He said, "You'll have to get it done in a couple of days."

I made bold, a little later, to ask if this evening was to be typical of all of the evenings, or could we consider ourselves prepared after I had done the things assigned to me. Lou said we were really only beginning, that we were only deciding what had to be done. He said that when we really got down to work, I would discover that this had been a very easy and sociable evening. Once or twice I had told an anecdote that had nothing whatever to do with the trial. In the future there was to be no discussion, apparently, that was not directly related to the trial. Along about two o'clock in the morning we broke up. My mind was reeling with the mass of things that I had to do.

As I rode home in the taxi, I was uneasy. It seemed that we would be working twenty-four hours a day for the next two months, if we were to accomplish even a third of what Lou had outlined. Lou had cautioned me, as I left him that evening, that he wanted me to get plenty of sleep and retain a clear and placid mind. He wanted me to put aside all social gatherings and to concentrate my entire energies on the case. I began to feel something like a fighter in training. I had planned to make an outline, before I went to sleep that night, of the things that I had to do, but by the time I got home I literally fell into bed exhausted.

The first thing the next morning I called David Susskind. Reaching him by telephone was like trying to reach the President in the White House. At that time he had a half dozen different projects going full tilt. He was not only producing motion pictures and programs for television, but presiding over a two-hour television discussion program, *Open End,* each week. However, when I finally persuaded a secretary to tell him that I was trying to reach him, he got on the phone at once. He said he would cancel everything and see me right away. The moment I arrived in his office, the receptionist announced me and I was ushered through the maze of offices to his sanctum sanctorum. His hospitality made me comfortable the moment we shook hands. He wanted to know all about the case and how far it had developed. I told him that we were about set and that I had come to see him about being a witness. He said that he was ready and willing. He said he had been looking forward to the day when he could go on the stand and tell about blacklisting, because his experience with it had been not only lengthy, but horrible. He had produced hundreds of television shows during the Fifties and had had to have the talent for these shows cleared by the defendants, before he was allowed to use them as performers on his programs. He said that he could give first-hand testimony on the blacklisting apparatus and exactly how it worked.

He asked me how I was making out since I had come to New York. I told him that I was fairly broke but had a place to live. He immediately called in his secretary and said, "Write Johnny a check for a thousand dollars." I told him I didn't need that much, but he said, "You might need it. What you don't need, send down to Texas to help your family out." He seemed so overjoyed and enthusiastic that I was infected by it. He said that all the records in his office were open to us for our use in the case. Then he asked me what date I thought he would be needed. I told him that the opening of the trial had been delayed, so we would probably not be able to use him as a witness before the early part of May. His face fell. He said that he was scheduled to be in London for the entire month of May and perhaps for some time after that. He was going over to film a television spectacular. I was alarmed to learn this. In a moment, however, his face brightened; he thought of a solution. "I'll tell you what I can do," he said, "I can fly back from London for the days that I will be needed in court."

I called Tony Randall. Tony had helped me organize the Middle-of-the-Road slate back in 1955. He had been a conscientious union member and had been very articulate in his opposition to blacklisting. Since that time he had become a highly paid, very popular star, not only on television but in the movies and on Broadway. When I reached him on the phone, he too was enthusiastic, and said that he would give all help possible. He came bouncing down to Nizer's office looking about fifteen years younger than when I had seen him five years before. He declared he would be delighted to get on the stand and tell what he knew and what he thought about AWARE and its associates. However, he too was preparing to leave the country. He had to go to Turkey to do a movie and would be there for several months.

Lou said that he thought that he could arrange for Tony to be taken out of turn as a witness.

The willingness and enthusiasm of Susskind and Randall misled me: I got the idea that getting witnesses to come would be the easiest thing in the world. But I soon discovered that this wasn't the case. The very next man that I called—a very important witness—was a highly paid, successful and talented director who had been much misused by the defendants in the past and had had direct and excruciating experiences with them. However, he made it clear at once that he did not even want to discuss the matter with me. He told me to discuss the matter with his agent. I called his agent and got about the same results that I would have gotten had I called upon Governor Barnett of Mississippi to be a speaker at an NAACP convention.

The following day I approached another important witness, the vice-president of an advertising agency. This man too had had direct and unpleasant experiences with AWARE and with Hartnett; he had been forced to reject certain artists who had not been approved by Mr. Hartnett. When I went up to see him, he was very direct. He said that I was a fool for having become involved with the case, and that he would have nothing whatever to do with the case. He said this with finality that left no room for further discussion of the matter.

The next three agency people whom I approached responded in a similar fashion. At the end of a week, I still had only two witnesses. I became embarrassed at having to report failure each evening. However, Lou didn't seem to mind; he would instruct me to go back and try again.

Things changed when I reached Garry Moore the following week. Of course, Garry had a backbreaking schedule of work in radio and television, but he wanted to know only when I would need him and where; he would be delighted to testify. To us he was a very important witness—not only for his prestige, but for the fact that as a member of the Middle-of-the-Road slate he and I had been closely associated in the union, even when I was getting licked.

Walter Cronkite called me when he learned that I was in town. We had been good friends and had done several shows together. He was acquainted with my fight in the union. He told me that CBS had assigned him to go down to Cape Canaveral, and he might be gone during my trial, but if he was in New York, he would be delighted to appear as a witness.

One of the allegations that the defendants had lodged against me was that I had entertained for an organization called the Southern Conference for Human Welfare back in the late 1940s. When I had been questioned about this on my pretrial examination, I said that I not only had entertained for the organization but also had been a proud member of it, especially since Mrs. Roosevelt had been very active in the organization—had been, in fact, one of its founders back in 1938. Mrs. Roosevelt had corresponded with me several times on the matter of my lawsuit, and she had encouraged me to carry on; now Mr. Nizer felt that it would be excellent if she would give testimony on the Southern Conference. I called Myrna Loy, who was a close friend of Mrs. Roosevelt's, and asked her if she would find out whether Mrs. Roosevelt would be willing to come. Unfortunately Mrs. Roosevelt was in bad health and felt that unless her testimony was crucial, she would prefer to avoid going on the witness stand. But she made it clear that if she were needed, she would certainly be on hand. We did not ask her to come.

Lou and Paul felt that we should get as a witness some executive, from an advertising agency or from one of the networks, who had had direct experience with the defendants. I suggested Mark Goodson. Mark Goodson and Bill Todman owned the Goodson-Todman office, which produced many of the best quiz shows on the air and was by far the most successful company of its kind in the country. I had known both men personally from the time of their first radio quiz show, back in the late Forties. Mark and I had become personal friends when I was a regular panelist on one of their network television shows, *It's News to Me.* Many times in the early Fifties he had told me how various pressure groups had sought to make him drop certain individuals from his shows and how he had resisted them as a matter of principle. Nevertheless, there had been times when he was forced to drop artists; and I remembered Mark telling me of a considerable struggle that he had had with Laurence Johnson over the employment of an artist of whom Johnson did not approve. When I related this to Nizer, he said, "Get hold of him at once. Go and see him. He's our man."

I was becoming callous to the imposition on the time of busy and important persons in the radio and television industry. However, I did try to make my visits short. When I saw Mark I prepared to come directly to the point, but he insisted that I tell him of my experiences over the past several years. Only after that did we get down to talking about the case. I told him how important it was that we have him as a witness. He pointed out that he had no direct experience with my being blacklisted. He was, however, very conversant with the blacklisting of other artists. He didn't like it at all; he felt it was a disgrace that the industry itself had not done more to rid itself of this curse. He assured me that if Nizer and I thought it would be of value, he would gladly come and tell all he knew about the ugly business. I felt triumphant as I left. Nizer and Martinson were delighted when I told them the news.

That evening, Paul and Lou told me that if I could get two more witnesses, they would give me a rest. The two witnesses that they wanted me to talk to were Kenneth Roberts, a popular and important announcer, and Kim Hunter, an actress. Vincent Hartnett had given both of them a hard time, and they had very important testimony that they could give.

I knew Ken well and gave him a call. He came down and had lunch with Paul Martinson and me. He said that he would be delighted to come and testify. He was working for one sponsor at the time. It was a highly paid job, but in spite of any embarrassment that might result, he felt it was very important that he put himself on record in this case. It turned out that his sponsor was cooperative and gave his blessings when Ken announced that he intended to testify.

Paul told me that he thought Kim Hunter was one of the most important witnesses that we could possibly get, if we could get her. I had known Kim and her husband, Bob Emmett, for a number of years. In the early days of my lawsuit, we had discussed its implications at some length. She had won an Academy Award and had been very popular and in great demand until she crossed swords with Vincent Hartnett and his associates. Their attack on her had had a dismal effect on her career. It had been such a shaking experience that she could scarcely discuss it without breaking into tears. Paul said he had talked to her several times in the past six years and that she had indicated that she would not want to testify or get mixed up in the suit at all. She had re-established herself and was enjoying great success. While she knew and disliked the defendants, she felt she owed it to her career to stand clear of any further involvements. At this time she was doing a Broadway play called *Write Me a Murder.*

I got in touch with her and told her that the suit was about to go to trial. She said that Vincent Hartnett and AWARE had been such grim experiences for her that it was traumatic to even discuss it, let alone take a public position in opposition to them. That evening I told Nizer and Paul about my talk with her. I said that I felt that since her experiences with the defendants had left such deep scars, that I did not want to persuade her to come. Lou was sympathetic but suggested that Paul and I have lunch with her and discuss the matter. Several days later we went to Sardi's.

Kim is not only a beautiful but a very talented actress. Paul outlined to her what we would want her to testify on. She gave every indication that she wanted desperately to help us. Her eyes filled with tears as Paul related to her my years of unemployment. When we got down to discussing whether or not she would testify, she pointed out to us that Bob Emmett, her husband, was now a promising playwright and she wouldn't want to do anything to harm his career. She told us that her public-relations man and her attorney would have to be consulted in the matter. She felt she could get them all to come up to Paul's office in a day or so and talk the whole thing out. Before we parted I explained to Kim that I had taken on this case of my own free will and that I did not expect to involve those to whom it would bring hurt or harm.

A couple of days later Kim, Bob, her attorney and her public-relations man, all came up to Paul Martinson's office. We discussed the whole thing extensively. I explained that nothing which had happened to me in the last six years in any way entitled me to say that there was no risk involved. It was a very great risk, especially to one who earned his living before the public. As Kim's public-relations man pointed out, there were not only some newspapers, but also a large segment of the American public, who still held a person suspect for simply opposing organizations such as AWARE; it was a hangover from the McCarthy days. Kim's attorney pointed out that while she might come and testify for me and I might win the case, her career could still suffer later. Paul Martinson did not agree. He said that we were going to have a sweeping victory, and that it would redound to Kim's credit that she participated. He pointed out also that justice was on our side, and that the other side deserved to be soundly trounced. It would be a great satisfaction to Kim in coming years to know that she had been one of those who had made their trouncing possible. The discussion went on pro and con for some time. Kim and I remained pretty much silent as Bob Emmett, her husband, her attorney, her public-relations man and Paul Martinson discussed all aspects of the case.

When the discussion ended we all sat looking at one another. There was nothing more to say. Then Kim very deliberately got up from her chair across the office and came walking toward me. From the expression on her face, I was sure she was going to apologize, wish me well, and say that she thought it best to stay out of the case. Instead, she placed her arms around my neck and kissed me, and said quite solemnly, "I have decided I'm going to testify. I want to be part of this trial. I'm going to do it for your sake, Johnny, because I admire you. But most of all I'm going to do it for my own sake and in behalf of my children and my profession and my country."

That evening when we gathered at Lou's house for dinner, I boasted to Mildred that I felt that I'd about completed my job of rounding up witnesses. I had just about depleted my energy, too. It had been a nerve-wracking, emotional experience. I said jokingly that I thought I was due for a vacation. Lou smiled broadly and said, "Not a vacation, John, but I'll tell you what—you can have a drink tonight. Mildred, fix him a gin and tonic. That's what you like, isn't it, John?" I felt shortchanged, but settled for the gin and tonic. I had long since found out that Louis Nizer's concept of preparing a case didn't mean working just five days a week on it; it meant working seven days a week, and not one of the twenty-four hours of any day was considered an inappropriate time for working like hell. I had begun to notice each evening—or rather, morning; sometimes as late as three o'clock—that Nizer was always as bright-eyed and energetic at the end of our session as he was at the beginning, while Paul and George and I could scarcely grope our way to the door. I really had been rather lucky, I guessed, to get a drink.

16

The several weeks preceding the opening of the trial are interesting to reflect on, but they were hell to live through.

The days and nights of that period ran together in one long, grueling session of feverish preparation. During the day at the office, Paul and George gathered the voluminous records, documents, exhibits, examination-before-trial testimony, information on prospective witnesses, and the multitude of other matters related to the case. Each night was spent going over it all, sorting it out, examining every detail of the battle strategy, and fitting the evidence into each planned maneuver of the coming battle. Our strategy called for going on the offensive and staying there. However, no item of our defenses was overlooked. Nizer did not intend to let a surprise flank attack or diversionary maneuver take him off guard, if backbreaking preparation could prevent it.

It was awesome to behold Lou in full command. Every ounce of his prodigious energy and brilliant intelligence was concentrated on the coming fray, as though it were to be the crucial battle of all time. He was a master of self-discipline, and he demanded complete discipline from all of us. Any matter that did not substantially pertain to the destruction of the enemy was arbitrarily dismissed from his mind and conversation.

I quickly learned that a peculiar psychological attitude prevailed in the thinking of Lou, Paul and George. There were no neutrals for them. Ordinarily, they were kindly and tolerant toward differences of opinion, but not where my case was concerned. Persons who possessed information that would aid our cause either made it available to us or were lumped in with the enemy. Paul Martinson directed me to contact an executive in an agency about some evidence he was thought to possess. The executive explained that he had the information and wished he could supply it to us, but hesitated to do so for fear of reprisals from the defendants and their allies. He sought to soften his refusal by explaining to me that he was on our side and hoped we won the case. When I reported the incident and said that I sympathized with the man's dilemma, Paul snapped: "He's a jerk and a coward. Whether he knows it or not, he's helping AWARE."

Another time, a CBS executive was in a position to do our case a great service, but refused to do so, for no other reason than that he preferred to be neutral in the case. Nizer courteously and patiently reasoned with him for nearly half an hour on the telephone; then, as the man remained adamant in his neutrality, Nizer's voice took on the deadly tone of outrage. With cold precision, he said, "I do not understand your position. We have spent six years and many thousands of dollars to cleanse your industry of these racketeers. Faulk has placed his career on the line. And you smugly sit there cowering behind a nonpartisan position! You are neither a good citizen nor a good executive." And he clapped the phone down.

Our night sessions were the roughest for me. Lou, ensconced in a great reclining chair that hoisted his heels up to the level of his nose, would have on one side of him a jar filled with sharpened soft-lead pencils; on the other side, a great stack of long yellow legal-size pads. Paul Martinson would sit erect in a straight chair, like a learned professor at a seminar. George Berger presided over the contents of the four bulging briefcases, which he knew in fantastic detail. I would shift from chair to chair, struggling to keep my mind on the business at hand. Lou would ride his chair, for all the world like a man napping in a canoe, questioning, writing, suggesting, questioning, and writing, writing, writing, for hours on end. He seemed incapable of fatigue. It was almost scary the way his alertness and enthusiasm seemed to increase as the evening wore on.

Lou is an absolute master of writing on a pad in his lap or propped against one knee. It was a sight to behold, the way he went scrawling through the pages of yellow pads, his pencil flashing like summer lightning playing along the horizon. As soon as he used up one pad, he would drop it aside and seize another one. An editor of Thomas

Wolfe's said that Wolfe used to stand at a tall desk, pour a Niagara of words onto sheets of paper as fast as he could write, and fling each page into a handy packing box, and reach for a fresh one at the same time. I would have matched Louis Nizer against Wolfe any day. Ben Bodne, a long-time friend of Lou's, told me that when Lou was writing *My Life in Court,* the Bodnes and the Nizers took a trip to Florida. Ben, Mary, Mildred and Lou would play gin rummy as they drove along in Ben's Rolls Royce. When Lou was not playing a hand, he would have a yellow pad across his knees writing on his book.

Shortly after our intense preparations had begun, the Elizabeth Taylor–Eddie Fisher difficulties hit the front pages of all the papers in this country and, apparently, the rest of the world. They were in Rome, where Miss Taylor was completing the film *Cleopatra.* Nizer represented them both. Reporters were constantly after Lou for statements, but he brushed them aside. Each day, there were more headlines and newsprint devoted to the matter, both in the United States and in Europe, it seemed, than to all other national and international news combined. Miss Taylor would call Lou from Rome for counsel almost every evening. He would suspend our work and go into the next room long enough to talk to her, then emerge and go on with the preparation. It was rather exciting for me, being on the inside of an international event. Although Lou never disclosed the nature of his conversations with her, I could at least boast to Chris and Merle that "Liz called us last night," and pretend to have the inside dope on the affair.

One morning in early April I was walking along the street toward the office, and a *New York Post* headline caught my eye. It ran, "LIZ CALLS LAWYER, COME TO ROME AT ONCE." A subhead read, "Wants Nizer; Says It's ALL Over." I snatched the paper from the stand and found it was a special by-line story by Earl Wilson. It reported that although Nizer was preparing to go into court with the *John Henry Faulk* v. *AWARE* case, he might have to delay the trial and rush to Rome. I had left Lou's apartment at about three o'clock that morning and, at that time, he had not even hinted that such a thing was contemplated. I figured that something had come up that made it imperative that he get to Rome right away. I suddenly resented Miss Taylor's imposition on my attorney. I headed for Lou's office thinking of arguments to use with him—"Hell, my suit was filed before those two were even married. Now they can just hold still until I get my divorce from AWARE!" I announced to Miss McHugh, Lou's private secretary, that I had to see him at once. She called Lou on the intercom. Her voice conveyed alarm. She nodded to me, and I bolted into his office waving the paper. Lou glanced at it, smiled, and looked up at me. "What's happened, John?"

"This story says that you're going to Rome," I blurted out.

He laughed as he understood the source of my agitation. "Oh, I see. Well, I'm *not* going to Rome. That's a newspaper story, and it's nonsense. Elizabeth is anxious for me to come over, but she also understands that we have this case to try. However, I'm glad you came in. I wanted to ask you about your plaques and citations. Did you bring all of them up from Texas with you?" I told him I had, and I attempted to apologize for my unnecessary alarm over the newspaper story. He looked at me sharply. "I've told you several times, John, not to concern yourself with what you read in the papers—about your case or about anything else. You just concentrate on this lawsuit. Now, I want you to bring in all of your citations and honors, and go over them with George Berger this afternoon." I left, feeling a little silly, but considerably relieved.

I went back to the apartment and got the two packing cases which were filled with various plaques, citations, and pictures of me receiving awards. George Berger and I sat down in his office, he on one side of the desk, me across from him, with a dictaphone between us. George would hold up a plaque or a picture and say into the microphone, "I ask you what this is." I would reply, "That is a plaque I received in 1953 for my work with an organization called Help for Mentally Retarded Children." George would mark the exhibit, reach for another and repeat the process. This was not only boring and tedious, but it made me uncomfortable to sit there reciting examples of my sweetness and goodness over and over. Since there were more than a hundred such items, I told George that it seemed to me we would be gilding the lily to dump them all into the record. I suggested that if I were on the jury and somebody took up several hours of my time exhibiting his citations to me, I would probably work up such a distaste for him I would come to loathe him. George would listen politely to my discourse, then go right on, as Nizer had instructed us to do.

That evening I told Lou that the recitation and public exhibition of my virtues ran contrary to everything I had ever been taught about modesty being a virtue.

"This is no time for false modesty, John," he replied emphatically. "These exhibits will help give the jury a full-scale picture of a responsible, conscientious citizen, and that's what I want them to see." That ended the discussion.

As April 16 drew near, it seemed to me that we had more preparation still to be done than we had when we started, two weeks before. However, on Sunday evening, a few hours before we were to be in court for the first time, Lou announced that we were in good shape and ready for the first skirmish—the selection of a jury.

The next morning I joined Lou, Paul and George at their office, and we all went down to Foley Square by taxi. The New York State Supreme Court Building stands beside the United States Court House, and is somewhat dwarfed by the great Federal edifice. Perhaps, that is why it didn't look very imposing to me.

As we got out on the sidewalk in front, I studied the building. It was huge and grimy. Across the front was the legend, "THE TRUE ADMINISTRATION OF JUSTICE IS THE FIRMEST PILLAR OF GOOD GOVERNMENT," supported by huge, Greek columns. The wide steps leading up to the entrance resembled those leading up to the Roman Forum. I was disappointed. I had somehow fancied that the New York State Supreme Court Building would be a handsome contemporary building. We entered its vast portals and walked down the hall toward the rotunda. On each floor a circular corridor runs around the rotunda, and from it radiate several shorter but wider corridors, each leading to two courtrooms.

We went up to the second floor and made our way to Room 252. As we pushed through the green-leather-covered doors, I was amazed by the smallness of the courtroom. It was plain and rather barren. Its beige walls were bare of any adornment save the inscription "IN GOD WE TRUST" over the judge's bench. There were three or four rows of pewlike benches for spectators, then a railing, beyond which was the long counsel table, to the right the jury box, to the left the desks for the bailiffs. Several uniformed court attendants were lolling about, chatting. Through the tall windows along one side of the courtroom came the sounds of New York going about its noisy business.

We took our seats along one side of the long counsel table. George explained to me that the defense attorneys would sit at the same table, directly across from us. And soon they came—Mr. Bolan and an assistant, Mr. Lang—and took their places there. I hadn't realized that we would be so close to them; for some reason, I had thought we would have separate tables.

As I sat down in my chair, I had to remind myself that this was all real—not just a dream. The jury box and witness stand stood empty, as did the judge's bench. An atmosphere of waiting hung over the room. I tried to appear relaxed and familiar with all this, but became even more tense trying to do so.

Before long, a uniformed attendant shepherded in a group of some fifty well-dressed people, who took seats in the spectators' benches. Each one, it seemed, immediately whipped out a newspaper, opened it and began to read. Had I not known they were all New Yorkers, this would have proved it—a New Yorker never pauses more than thirty seconds anywhere without starting to read a newspaper. I was mildly distressed. Not a single one of the prospective jurors, or veniremen, as they are called, seemed to know that I existed. I felt that they should be giving their attention to me. Yet, they seemed wholly indifferent to my presence in the courtroom. Most of them seemed indifferent to the fact that they were there.

At that moment, the court clerk, standing beside the judge's bench, cried: "The Justice of the Court! All rise!" We all stood, as Justice Abraham Geller, a graying, handsome man about six feet tall, with a stern but pleasant expression, entered in his legal robes. He thanked the veniremen for coming, and then made a statement to the effect that this would be an unusual case, involving some issues that would require rather a long trial. He told the veniremen that those who felt that for substantial reasons they could not serve for as much as a month or perhaps six weeks should come forward and give their excuses. I was shocked to see that over half of the veniremen arose and lined up to go by the judge's bench. I felt somewhat like a performer with half of the audience getting up to leave. As each one in the line came up to the bench he and the judge held a whispered conference. The judge either accepted the applicant's reasons for not serving and directed him to inform the attendant, or did not accept them and directed him to take his seat again. Two or three of them, as they briefly whispered to the judge, turned and looked in my direction. The judge nodded and excused them. They were persons who knew me too well to qualify as unbiased jurors.

After all the veniremen who wished to be excused had been heard and everyone was seated again, two court attendants went over to the brass drum into which slips of paper containing the names of the prospective jurors had been placed. One of the attendants would give the drum a crank and the other would run his hand into it, pull out a slip of paper and hand it to the first, who would call out the name of one of the veniremen and direct him to take a specific seat in the jury box. Twelve names were chosen and twelve people sat in the jury box. The rest of the veniremen were directed to remain seated in the spectators' benches.

At a signal from the judge, Lou arose and addressed the tentative jury, briefly stating the nature of the case, identifying the plaintiff, the defendants, and the attorneys for each side, and asking whether any of the twelve had any acquaintance with the participants in the case, or any opinions on the issues involved, that would make it impossible for him to render an unbiased verdict. He called their attention to the fact that Roy Cohn was the attorney of record for the defendants, though his partner, Mr. Bolan, would be trying the case. I saw Bolan wince. Several weeks before, Roy Cohn had been involved in a dispute involving the Fifth Avenue Coach Company, which he represented, and the Transport Workers Union and the City of New York, and his role in the affair had brought him a good deal of public criticism. He was not, therefore, an unqualified asset as an advocate in court. In fact, I noticed several of the prospective jurymen smirk when Nizer mentioned Cohn.

Then began the process of "challenging" individual prospective jurors. A challenge is, of course, an exception taken by either of the attorneys to any of the jurors. It may be a challenge for cause—as, for example, when the venireman is somehow related to one of the parties to the present suit and thus is likely to be prejudiced one way or the other. Or it may be a peremptory challenge, for which the lawyer is not required to state any reason at all. There is no limit to the number of challenges that may be made for cause; but the number of peremptory challenges is limited, usually by agreement between the two sides. In our case, Nizer and Bolan stipulated that each side would have a maximum of eight such challenges.

I had heard Paul and Lou discuss the selection of the jury at some length, but I had not given it much thought. It turned out to be a fascinating sort of guessing game. Nizer and Bolan both had to decide from a group composed of complete strangers how each would feel about the issues of the case. At one point, a juryman was asked if he had any knowledge of any members of the Nizer firm, and the entire list was read. Then he was asked if he had any knowledge of members of Bolan's and Cohn's firm, and that list was read. The juryman said that while he didn't personally know Roy Cohn, he felt it only fair to admit that he could not give an unprejudiced judgment in a case in which Cohn was even indirectly a participant. He was, of course, dismissed.

One of Nizer's questions to each prospective juryman was whether he had any mental reservations that would make it impossible for him to grant damages amounting to a million dollars or more. One prospective juror said he didn't think that even the President could be libeled a million dollars' worth. Lou thanked him kindly and had him dismissed. As each venireman was dismissed, his place was promptly filled by another, whose name was selected from the drum. Toward the middle of the afternoon, Lou suggested to the judge that it would take another day to complete the selection of the jury. It was agreed to adjourn until the next day. Then, when the jurors and veniremen had left the courtroom, Lou asked for a conference in the judge's chambers. He and Martinson and Berger, joined by Bolan and Lang, went in together.

Our suit as we filed it in 1956 asked for half a million dollars compensatory damages. Now Nizer submitted briefs and arguments to support the position that, since I had been unemployed for six years as a direct result of the defendants' acts, the original claim was insufficient and that our complaint should be amended to ask for one million dollars. Bolan vigorously opposed the motion, but Judge Geller sustained it.

The next day, the selection of the jury continued. At one point, George Berger scribbled something on a scrap of paper and passed it along to Lou, who looked at it, glanced at George, and nodded. He then turned and said, "We excuse juror number six," thus using up one of our peremptory challenges. George leaned over to me and explained that he had discovered that that juror had been reading the *National Review,* a magazine whose political orientation was similar to that of AWARE. "If she reads that kind of magazine, we have an idea of how she would feel before the case even starts," George said.

After twelve jurors had been selected, two alternate jurors were selected; they would sit in chairs near the jury each day and listen to the entire trial; then, if one of the regular jurors became ill or for some reason could not continue, one of the alternates would take his place. One of the veniremen who was called up as a prospective alternate juror said that he belonged to AFTRA. This wasn't necessarily favorable to me, since there was in AFTRA a faction which was completely unsympathetic to me, and I had no way of knowing whether the gentleman belonged to that faction of the union or not. However, the fact that he was a member of AFTRA caused Bolan to ask whether he knew me. The juror said No, he'd never heard of me before. Then Bolan asked him if he knew anything about blacklisting. The gentleman leaned forward and said, "I know enough about it to hate it. It's an abomination to our industry, and I hope something is done to wipe it out." Bolan immediately used up one of his peremptory challenges.

The selection of the jury was completed a half hour or so before noon recess. Judge Geller made a rather lengthy speech to the jury. He pointed out that they were to be judges in this case, just as he was, but they would judge the facts, while he would judge the law; it was their business to arrive at a just decision in the case. He cautioned them sternly about discussing the case with one another or with anyone during the trial. He suggested that the newspapers would be carrying accounts of the case, and that they were to avoid reading any of them. As he spoke to them, I studied each juror. Each appeared to be intelligent and alert. Their occupations and their backgrounds were varied. Not one of them looked at me even once. Nor was there a clue on a single face to indicate what we might expect from him. As I looked at them I thought, Well, this is it. My entire future is in the hands of twelve complete strangers. Twelve people, each of whom had said he or she had never heard my name, knew nothing about me. I wanted to jump up and shout, "Look here, you needn't bother to hear the evidence. I'm completely right, and the defendants are completely wrong! We could save a lot of trouble if you would just render your decision now."

Sitting four feet from me at that moment, Vincent Hartnett probably was thinking precisely the same thing, with the exception that in his opinion it was he who was completely right. Each of us would regard any decision contrary to him a grave miscarriage of justice. As I looked at him, his mouth was a tight, thin line, and his eyes, slightly bulging, gazed unblinking at the jury. His face was a blank mask. I felt a sudden compassion for him. I had heard he had a number of children, and I wondered whether his wife and children were waiting anxiously to learn how he had fared that day. Were they as convinced of the complete correctness of his position and my villainy, as my friends and family were of my complete correctness and his villainy? What a strange thing Justice is! It is well that she is blind. For justice, seen through my eyes, would be the opposite seen through Hartnett's eyes. Or, perhaps, it is only injustice that is blind.

As I studied Hartnett's expression further, the set line of the mouth, the unyielding expression on his face, I realized that whatever the outcome of this case, his complete and total conviction that he was right and that we were wrong would remain unchanged. I realized at the same time that in all likelihood, Vincent Hartnett had never felt the slightest twinge of conscience for the great number of careers he had wrecked. Whatever evidence we might present of blighted careers, anguish and suffering, his self-righteousness would protect him from a feeling of guilt for his acts.

When the judge finished his speech to the jury, he dismissed us all and adjourned court till the following Monday, April 23.

We had lunch at the Algonquin Round Table. Raoul, the maitre de, had become interested in our case. He hovered over us, making sure that everything was just right. It was a leisurely lunch to celebrate the completion of the first stage of our trial—the selection of the jury. The conversation revolved entirely around speculation on what sort of person each of the jurors was. Lou summed up his attitude: "They're a group of typical Americans, and I like that. Actually, those twelve people are the American public in miniature. That's good. I trust the American people, especially when the whole truth is presented to them—all the pros and cons of a situation. They will reach a fair and just verdict." After lunch, we went directly back to the office to work.

17

About five o'clock that afternoon, we got a call to come into Lou's office at once; an emergency had occurred. We went in to find Lou sitting behind his desk and George Berger standing beside him, both looking grim. George had just returned from CBS and reported that when he had gone to the legal department of CBS with the subpoena to get any records they might have of me, he had been told by the CBS lawyers in charge that Roy Cohn's office had come with a subpoena a couple of weeks before and had taken the records. One of the CBS lawyers then explained to George that they had turned over the original records and had no copies. George had replied that this was unbelievable. It was shocking enough that CBS was obviously cooperating with Cohn's office by making the records available to them, but it was unthinkable that they would give Cohn the originals and not even retain a copy of the records. In fact, George commented, a CBS lawyer had told him that they did not even have a record of which documents had been turned over to Cohn.

I asked Lou what this meant. He was clearly angry. "It means, John, that someone at CBS is incredibly stupid, or that they are openly cooperating with Roy Cohn. I'm afraid it's the latter."

I found this hard to believe. "But if Cohn's office got out a subpoena for the documents, CBS didn't have any choice, did they?"

Lou replied impatiently, "Oh, yes, they did. A very great choice. A *subpoena duces tecum* means that the corporation is directed to present the papers in court at the time of the trial. The procedure ordinarily is simple. On an appointed day, an officer of the corporation or some other authorized person from the corporation goes down to the court with the papers subpoenaed. They are turned over and entered as exhibits. The person in charge of them waits until the operation is completed and then takes the papers back to his company's files."

Paul nodded. "No corporation turns over original records without even keeping a copy of them, especially to a party in a lawsuit—unless the corporation favors that party against the other."

"When I talked to the attorneys at CBS," George said, "they pretended they didn't even know who Vincent Hartnett and AWARE were. They were very evasive." George said the CBS lawyers told him they would try to get the records back immediately, and they promised to call him as soon as they did. It simply didn't make sense to me. Certainly none of my friends at CBS, and I had many there, would have been sympathetic to such a thing. And I couldn't believe that Frank Stanton, the president of CBS, would condone it.

Lou, with his customary matter-of-factness, said, "Well, we'll see what happens tomorrow. We've got a lot of work ahead of us tonight. Let's get to it." And we all went up to the Nizer apartment for our evening ritual.

The following day, George Berger received a call from the CBS lawyers. Cohn's office had returned the documents. We could have photostatic copies of them if we desired. *We desired!* George went bounding over to CBS to get them.

When we got the copies of my records, George and Paul went through them very carefully. They were looking for documents which could help our cause. At the same time, they were looking for documents which might possibly, in Cohn's hands, do our cause harm. We knew that Cohn had seen everything in the records, thanks to CBS. Actually, the records turned up very little that was significant one way or the other.

That morning *The New York Times* carried a story which was headed "Jury Picked in TV Libel Suit; Faulk Seeks Several Million." It was a two-column story under the by-line of John Sibley. He gave an account of the couple of days proceedings down at the court, how the jury had been chosen and how Nizer had asked them if they would be willing to give as much as a million dollars if the damages were proven. That evening as we dined together, I commented: "You know, that *Times* story is pretty good. Somebody told me that John Sibley would be there every day. He's been assigned to cover the case."

"Yes, and there will be other newspaper men there, too," Lou replied, "when we get well into the trial. But I want you to keep your mind strictly on the case. Conserve your energy. That's the main thing now. You are the center of this trial and I want you to be in the peak of condition. Forget about news stories or whether this trial is covered at all in the newspapers or anywhere else. Concentrate on the trial."

The next several days dragged along in a never-ending series of exercises in the preparation for my direct examination. On Easter Sunday, April 22, Lou made a special concession. He announced that we would not start to work until about two in the afternoon. But when we did meet, he made up for lost time. Along about midnight, I became so numb and irritable that I could scarcely sit still. Paul and Lou and George were plugging away. I hated to throw in the towel, but I finally said, "Gentlemen, I'm out of gas. My engine won't run. I'm going to have to drop out."

Lou looked at me, first with surprise, then compassion. "John, you do look tired," he said, as though he were noticing something about me that was strange and new. "I want you to feel rested and relaxed tomorrow. You'd better go home at once and get some sleep." Then, thoughtfully, he added, "In fact, Paul, you and George had better go now, too. I want to work on my opening speech for tomorrow. I haven't started on it yet." As fresh and vigorous as ever, he settled back into his big reclining chair, his feet hoisted toward the ceiling, with a new supply of sharpened pencils and a stack of yellow pads within reach. He had already launched into his opening speech and was writing furiously by the time we went out the door.

Nizer made it a strict rule, on that first day and throughout the entire trial, that we be seated at the counsel table at least ten minutes before the appointed time for the court session to start. He felt that to arrive late, even by a minute, was an imposition on the court. I got there thirty minutes early. Fifteen minutes later, George Berger and two clerks from the Nizer office arrived, with four crammed briefcases. Paul and Lou followed, greeted me affectionately, and took their places at the table. After a while, the defense lawyers entered, Mr. Bolan carrying a small briefcase, and Mr. Lang and Mr. Hartnett carrying two heavy suitcases full of papers. They took their places, and nodded a curt greeting in our general direction.

Word that Louis Nizer was delivering his opening speech that day brought out a raft of spectators. There were fans of Louis Nizer and a goodly number of friends of mine. It was a standing-room-only crowd. Soon the bailiff called out his "Hear ye! Hear ye!" and we all stood as Justice Geller, in his judicial robe, came in and took his seat. He announced that he would have additional benches brought in and would have a table set up for the members of the press that were there. He then turned his attention to the jury. He pointed out to them again that each of them would be a judge in this case, just as if he or she was in judicial robes, and that it would be the task of each to judge the facts as they were presented. It was his task to judge the law. He and they were to be something like partners in judging and making sure justice was done. Though he spoke for only a few minutes, I became impatient for him to stop and let Nizer get started. I thought to myself, The law's delay. The law's delay. It hasn't changed one bit since Hamlet's day.

Suddenly, I was overwhelmed by the realization that *the trial has started!* The trial of John Henry Faulk versus AWARE, Vincent Hartnett and Laurence Johnson has actually started! However costly and unpleasant those months and years of preparation had been, I knew now, with quiet certainty, that it had been a small price to pay for this moment.

My God, this is America! Here I sit, a onetime cow-milking South Austin boy who came to New York, felt an injustice had been done him, and demanded satisfaction. The American people have done the rest—provided all this: a courtroom, a jury, a judge, court attendants, the free press to report the proceedings, and the opportunity to present my complaint and have its merits argued fully. The thought awed me. Everybody in that courtroom—everybody—was there because I, a citizen, felt I had been unjustly treated! I knew that whatever the outcome of the trial, the meaning and impact of this great truth would never escape me again.

As these thoughts raced through my mind, Justice Geller completed his remarks to the jury and nodded to Lou. A hush settled over the courtroom as Lou rose from the table and moved in front of the jury. His easy, poised manner in no way betrayed the exhausting hours of preparation he had given to the case. He appeared quiet and sure as he began to speak. Every eye in the courtroom was fixed on him.

NIZER: May it please your Honor, Miss Tindale, Madame Forelady, and ladies and gentlemen of the jury: As his Honor has already indicated to you, . . . the law, in its wisdom, permits the lawyer on each side to tell you the entire case from his viewpoint, so that when you hear a bit of testimony you know that it relates to the rest of the proof, why it has some relevance to the entire case.

I avail myself, with his Honor's permission, and so will my learned adversary, of that privilege now, the purpose being for me to attempt to explain to you what this suit is about, what we claim in this litigation, what our position is with respect to certain positions taken by the defendants, and they will do the same with respect to us, and then, having a larger perspective of the entire controversy, you will be able to follow particular pieces of testimony a little more clearly. . . .

First, the parties. Who are they? The man who brings this suit is John Henry Faulk. He has sat there from the beginning of the selection of the jury, the third gentleman on that side (indicating).

Lou then went over my entire history, how I had been born in Austin, had been educated in the schools of Texas, and had received my degrees from the University of Texas. He dwelt at some length on the graduate work that I had done in Negro folklore, on my background as a teacher, and on the fellowship that I had received. He outlined my career during the war, how I had tried to get into the army and had been prevented because of blindness in one eye, had gone into the Merchant Marine and had later become an assistant field director for the American Red Cross in Cairo, Egypt. He told how later I had joined the Army and been assigned to rehabilitation work at an Army hospital. Then he outlined for the court and the jury my career as a radio and televsion performer. He went over this in some detail and very effectively.

As he was telling this, I studied the faces of the jurors. Each was listening intently, his eyes following Lou as he moved about. I glanced across the table from time to time at the faces of Bolan, Lang and Hartnett. Their faces were blank; their thoughts seemed far away. It was as though they were not listening to what was being said at all. Nizer summed up my career in radio and television.

. . . So here was a man who was rising as one of the great stars in radio and later television . . . when a certain situation arose in a dispute in which he was charged with being either Communist or pro-Communist, and just cut off his career sharply as if with a knife.

Lou then turned his attention to the defendants.

Who are the defendants in this case? One of them is Vincent Hartnett. He is this gentleman here, seated here, third in this row (indicating).

We will show you about Mr. Hartnett's career. He was a man who
earned some sixty dollars to seventy-five dollars a week in radio in
some script department. Then he was out of work for a considerable
time, but then fell upon the idea which brought him a great deal of
prosperity. That was the idea of collecting data, becoming a so-called
consultant on radio artists and television artists, and informing the radio
companies and the television companies, the sponsors, the people who
advertised, or the agencies who placed these programs, informing them
of the records of those artists, the so-called records, their affiliation with
questionable causes. He was the principal author of "Red Channels," a
book which made these listings of people on the air. He thereafter
continued this work, charging sponsors five dollars a throw, to put it
bluntly, to investigate somebody.

He would decide whether a certain performer was a good American, what his alleged record was, and we will show you how this worked.

If a name came back after a couple of weeks, if the same actor
had a second show on radio or television, why, then Hartnett charged
less . . . he charged two dollars, for original performances five dollars to check, and in some cases twenty dollars, and if it was a little
more important for some reason, fifty dollars, and we will show you
that these payments were made to him, and that a man who had
earned sixty dollars to seventy-five dollars a week was earning twenty-
six thousand dollars a year collecting these payments as an alleged
consultant.

BOLAN: I object, your Honor.

THE COURT: Overruled as long as he abstains from making comments,
but of course the jury has fully in mind, and I will not repeat it
again, that this does not constitute evidence whatever. This is merely
what counsel intends to prove. Bearing that admonition in mind, just
indicate what you intend to prove but make no comments or arguments with respect to what you intend to prove.

BOLAN: Thank you.

NIZER: Thank you, sir. I realize that the argument will be made in summation. I am trying to limit myself to what we intend to prove from that witness stand, with documents and evidence.

Then, after outlining for some time the methods used by Mr. Hartnett, Mr. Johnson, and AWARE in achieving the blacklisting of artists, and describing how they had worked on me, Lou said:

> Let me call your attention to one other thing we will prove. Aware, Inc., is not an organization that has any authority from the government of the United States. It is a private organization. . . . So Aware, Inc., has no standing except as a private individual, with Mr. Hartnett cashing in.
>
> Second, we will show you that Mr. Johnson has not been designated. He is self-appointed and self-anointed. He has no authority of any governmental authority to pass upon the lives of American citizens, economically, patriotically, or any other way.

Lou then launched into a lengthy and detailed account of how the quarrel arose between me and the defendants. He went into the union fight, describing it at length (over many objections from Bolan). The judge quite often sustained Bolan's objections when he felt that Lou was violating his direction to stick strictly to what he intended to prove, not to go into argument.

Nizer then took up the allegations in the AWARE bulletin about me, and went over them in great detail. From time to time Justice Geller would interrupt him.

THE COURT: Mr. Nizer, when you go over those items, indicate what you intend to prove without commenting on it, and save your comments for summation.

Lou outlined the manner in which AWARE, Hartnett and Johnson, with the cooperation of an American Legion post in Syracuse, had used the AWARE bulletin to get me completely blacklisted, he described the industry's reaction to their efforts, and told how ultimately I came to be fired by CBS. He then dwelt at some length on my efforts to find employment after I was fired. He described it so effectively and heartbreakingly that I found myself about to cry. The jury was watching very closely, listening to every word he said.

At one point he summed up the issues as he saw them from our position:

> What we have brought, for the first time so far as I know, is an issue before this court, whether an American court of justice is going to approve the kind of blacklisting that went on in this case for all artists, and which John Henry Faulk makes a test of in his own case, and we're going to bring other evidence to you as to how this operated on famous artists.
>
> What we are bringing to this court is a question as to whether private organizations, or as I would call them, vigilantes, can exist in this nation, when we have a court of law by which we can obtain relief.

He then spent some time on the damages that he intended to prove. I noted, or thought I did, Mr. Bolan wincing as he mentioned huge sums of money exceeding a million dollars. Lou pointed out that the defendants would certainly try to minimize the damages they had done me. He concluded his opening statement to the jury by saying:

> And now I shall conclude with one final observation. Mr. Faulk will take the stand, and others will follow for the plaintiff. I know that you will observe him closely because, as his Honor has instructed you, that is the genius of our system, that they watch witnesses for credibility.
>
> I plead with you particularly to observe Mr. Hartnett when the time comes for him to take the stand, and Mr. Laurence A. Johnson, when the time comes for him to take the stand. I plead with you to watch them closely and listen to their answers and observe their mannerisms, and see who it was, as we charge, intimidating the entire television industry.
>
> I want you to follow their answers closely. I plead with you in this particular case to take particular note of Mr. Hartnett and Mr. Johnson under oath and under cross-examination, and when you do I have no doubt that, in what we consider a great cause, Justice will be done not only for this plaintiff but for a great American cause as well.

When Lou finished speaking, Justice Geller declared a recess for lunch. He cautioned the jury not to discuss the case with anyone else or with each other. He further cautioned them not to read the news-papers. As the spectators rose to leave the room, a number of them pressed forward to shake Lou's hand. Smiling and courteous, he moved them aside and called on Paul, George and me to go with him directly to Gasner's Restaurant; he was anxious to discuss the jury's reactions. On our way out of the courthouse, people continued to step forward to greet him. He smiled warmly, but resolutely marched along, obviously preoccupied with our conference at Gasner's.

Gasner's is located in the vicinity of Foley Square, and at lunchtime it is filled with lawyers and judges; it almost seemed that the clientele consisted exclusively of members of the legal profession. The manage-ment had reserved a table for us; and this same table would be reserved for us every day the court was in session during our trial.

As soon as we were seated and had placed our orders, Lou asked each of us for our impressions of the jury's reaction to his speech. I tossed out brightly, "Well, I'll say this; they all stayed awake." Lou wasn't amused; this was a deadly serious matter. George and Paul dis-cussed the jurors, one by one, and the facial expressions of each when Lou had been addressing them. I was fascinated with this minute attention to detail. Paul would say, "Juror number X seemed to be deeply interested when you mentioned such and such." George would check his notes, and observe, "When you said such and such, I noticed juror number Y seemed indifferent. His eyes wandered and he looked at the ceiling once or twice." I realized now why Lou had been indifferent to the spectators and his admirers in court. He was interested in the reactions of but twelve people for the duration of this trial. Other attorneys in the restaurant stopped by our table to speak to Lou. He would nod warmly, but indicate by his manner that he was involved in a business conversation and could not be disturbed.

After lunch, when the court reconvened, I noticed that only about half of the spectators present had been on hand that morning. There were some new ones. And some of the benches were empty. It puzzled me and I asked George about it. He smiled and nodded toward Lou. The morning crowd had come to hear Nizer's opening speech. Mr. Bolan's opening speech, to come next, apparently did not have the same appeal.

The judge indicated to Bolan that he could begin. Bolan rose and went before the jury. He was a well-built young man and rather handsome, dressed in the Ivy League fashion. As he began to speak, the jury again gave their full attention.

BOLAN: May it please the court, Miss Tindale, ladies and gentlemen of the jury:

As you probably know, my name is Thomas Bolan and I am the attorney for each of the three defendants in this case. I am assisted by Mr. John Lang, an associate in my office. The three defendants are, as you know, Aware, Inc. In case there is some confusion in your mind as to the "Inc.," that is simply an abbreviation for "incorporated." Aware is a New York corporation.

The other two defendants are individuals. Mr. Vincent Hartnett, who lives in Scarsdale, New York and Mr. Laurence Johnson, who lives in Syracuse, New York.

Now, before discussing the complaint, I would like to just speak a few words on the background of the individual defendants. Before I do that, too, I would like to say that my duty is rather a solemn one, because this is not an ordinary case. It is not just a simple case where one party is seeking to get money from another party.

The plaintiff, John Henry Faulk, in support of his complaint, has charged that the defendants have conspired against him. He has libeled the defendants, and Mr. Nizer did not bring this out. He has libeled them as extortionists, as racketeers, and as intimidators, as terrorists.

So, therefore, in this case there is more than money involved as far as my clients are concerned. Their reputations are at stake, and, in the case of Aware, its powerful existence is at stake.

Now, the charges that I have read to you, or have mentioned to you are surely all very serious. It is a very serious charge to call someone an extortionist or racketeer, but I assure you those charges, like the other charges, in this complaint, are absolutely without foundation. By the end of this trial I am convinced that you will agree that the plaintiff has failed to sustain those charges.

Now, as to the background of the individuals, first of all, Aware is a New York corporation. It is a membership corporation, formed under the laws of the State of New York. It was formed in 1953.

It describes itself as an organization to combat the Communist conspiracy in the entertainment and communications field. Among its dedicated purposes are to disseminate information and material concerning the Communist Party, the Communist fronts, and similar areas.

Also among its purposes is to expose situations where known Communists or even strong anti-Communists have unwittingly or unknowingly given their support to either the Communist Party or Communist front groups. That is one of its purposes.

It is a nonprofit corporation: that is, it is not in the business of making money. None of its officers receive any salary or any other sort of remuneration. It relies solely on the dues it collects from its members, and contributions from friends.

It has never received any money for any of its anti-Communist activities. Its members are decent, honorable, and respectable people. They are not extortionists. They are not racketeers. Mr. Alexander Dick is the Chairman of the Board of Aware. He sits there now at the end of the counsel table.

Seated next to Mr. Dick, on his left, is Mr. Vincent Hartnett, who is one of the individual defendants. In a few words as to Mr. Hartnett, Mr. Hartnett is a vice-president of Aware, and is one of its founders. Aware was founded as a corporation in 1953. It had been active as an unincorporated group for about a year prior to that.

Mr. Hartnett is forty-six years of age. He has six children. He attended the University of Notre Dame, where he received two degrees, a B.A. degree and an M.A. degree, both with highest honors, both *maxima cum laude*. He graduated with highest honors in both instances.

Bolan then went into Hartnett's background in the radio and television field and his having been an assistant producer in radio. He outlined at some length Mr. Hartnett's service in the United States Navy as an intelligence officer. After this, he stated:

. . . Mr. Hartnett is an expert and a specialist in the field of Communism, the Communist Party front groups. He spent many years of study, read many articles, has written many articles, and has accumulated enormous files on the workings of the Communist Party, and the Communist front groups in particular.

In the course of time many organizations and groups requested Mr. Hartnett to do special work into the backgrounds of prospective actors or entertainers in radio and television, and other related fields.

These people, the producers or sponsors, did not want to take the risk of hiring somebody who either had been identified as a member of the Communist Party or who had a significant record of affiliation with organizations closely tied in with the Communist Party, and they wanted a check made, and Mr. Hartnett was an expert in the field, and he was called upon to do that work.

In the course of time, Mr. Hartnett devoted all of his time, all of his efforts, which were considerable, in this field. He was paid for his services in this area.

He was called on several occasions as an expert witness on Communism, once by the House Un-American Activities Committee, and on another occasion by the Senate Internal Security Committee. He was recognized as an expert in this field. He was a researcher into Communism and the Communist Party, and I may say J. Edgar Hoover sent Mr. Hartnett a letter.

NIZER: I object.

THE COURT: I will have to sustain the objection to that. Let us await the offer of testimony on that, and whether it is receivable.

BOLAN: As this trial will show, Mr. Hartnett is not a terrorist. He was a sincere dedicated man, who was painstaking in his research, and, as you will see, he is scrupulously honest, perhaps more so, I was going to say, than anyone I have encountered, but I objected to a similar statement by Mr. Nizer as to his experience, so I will not say it.

THE COURT: Mr. Bolan, please keep your voice up. I want to hear every word that is said. You dropped your voice.

NIZER: He just announced, your Honor, that he was not going to make a statement, which he then made.

Bolan then described at some length Laurence Johnson—who he was and how he was connected with the case. Bolan pointed out what he considered his main task.

My main job here now is to discuss with you what this case is all about. I submit to you, what the case is all about is right here in the complaint, and the case is about this one simple issue: Did the defendants damage the reputation and professional career of John Henry Faulk? That is the only issue in this case. Did these defendants damage Mr. Faulk's reputation and professional career?

Mr. Faulk said they entered into a conspiracy to do this. He said that the three of them, the three defendants, got together in February 1956, and at that time they entered into an illegal agreement in which they in a sense said, "Let's destroy the reputation and career of Mr. John Henry Faulk."

I submit to you that the evidence will show no such agreement was made, no such effort was ever made by any of the defendants.

Before going into more detail as to what the case is about, let me say what it is not about.

Most of what Mr. Nizer said had nothing to do with this case, nothing to do with the charge that these defendants damaged the reputation and career of Mr. Faulk. This case is not a great cause, a great case to expose—

NIZER: Your Honor, I object.

THE COURT: Sustained.

BOLAN: That is what Mr. Nizer said, your Honor, and I am answering.

THE COURT: Mr. Bolan, I understand what you said. I have been paying strict attention. Save your summation for later on. That is all I am trying to say. You just indicate what you intend to prove.

BOLAN: This case is not a case which has for its main issue the popularity of John Henry Faulk. It is not a case to show how many friends Mr. Faulk has, or how many friends he has in the entertainment field; how many witnesses will come here and say, "Mr. Faulk is a great man."

This case has one issue: Did the defendants damage the reputation and career of Mr. Faulk? All other issues are irrelevant. It is not an issue in this case—

NIZER: Your Honor, I submit—

THE COURT: Sustained. That is a question of law for the court to determine. What evidence may or may not be introduced in connection with the plaintiff's complaint and the defenses that are offered. Let the court make that determination at the proper time.

BOLAN: It has been stated that the AFTRA union, the American Federation of Television and Radio Artists, condemned Aware by resolution. Mr. Nizer read parts of it to you. I say to you it will be shown at this trial that that resolution has nothing to do with the issue in this case, namely, whether or not Mr. Faulk's reputation was damaged by the defendants.

NIZER: Your Honor, this is a charge to the jury by Mr. Bolan.

THE COURT: I think, Mr. Bolan, I made it perfectly clear that I want you to leave legal questions to me. It is my responsibility, Mr. Bolan.

BOLAN: I am stating a fact, your Honor.

THE COURT: No, you are not. You are making a legal argument. Mr. Bolan, limit yourself to the opening.

BOLAN: May I be heard on that, your Honor?

THE COURT: No, it is not necessary. It is evident to me that you were endeavoring to cover some legal problems on the question of whether evidence is admissible. I will pass upon that and the legal effect of that evidence. That is my responsibility. Proceed, Mr. Bolan.

Bolan then launched into a lengthy and detailed account of the allegations which AWARE had made against me. He went over Bulletin 16 in great detail. This gave rise to a number of objections by Nizer, most of which were overruled by the court. Bolan stated quite candidly that AWARE and the other defendants had always been opposed to having identified Communist members, persons who had used the Fifth Amendment or any other amendment, or who had significant Communist-front records, employed in the television and radio industry. He claimed that AWARE had support of the House Un-American Activities Committee in this regard. Nizer objected vigorously to this. Bolan proceeded to claim that AWARE and the other defendants had relied on the very highest quality sources for their information. He listed among these sources the House Un-American Activities Committee and the Senate Subcommittee on Internal Security. He said that he intended to prove that after AWARE's attack upon me in February 1956 my popularity as a radio entertainer went up and up, that in December 1956 CBS hired me for a new five-year contract and gave me a big raise, after which my rating went "down, down, down, down." He closed by saying:

And we will show that beyond any doubt, too, Mr. Faulk's earnings were not affected by anything that Aware did and nobody of the defendants, either Aware, Johnson or Hartnett, or anybody else, ever went to any of Faulk's sponsors to request that his services be terminated. Nobody in any of the defendants ever collected one cent for the activities with respect to Mr. Faulk, and we will prove that beyond any doubt.

And that is about all I have to say, with the exception that I will not be speaking to you again until the end of the trial. As I said at the beginning, this is an extremely serious matter so far as my clients are concerned, and I urge you to pay careful attention to the defendants.

Mr. Nizer said to pay attention to Mr. Hartnett and Mr. Johnson on the stand. Of course, you should pay attention. Pay attention to Mr. Faulk, too. Mr. Faulk by profession is an actor. Keep that in mind, too.

Above all, I do urge you to give your most careful attention to all of the evidence, and I am sure that when all the evidence is in you will find that the defendants did nothing which in any way damaged the reputation or professional career of the plaintiff. Thank you for your attention.

As Mr. Bolan finished his speech, I could not escape the feeling that perhaps I had taken the matter of my blacklisting too seriously. Bolan managed to make it all sound trivial.

The court adjourned and we went back uptown. We went over each point of Bolan's opening speech. Lou said that it was clear that the defendants were going to try to minimize the damages. That was to be their angle. There was, of course, a chance that they might seek to prove I was a Communist. But nothing Bolan had said indicated that they believed such a thing. Their main emphasis would be their contention that I had not been damaged. "They might spring some surprise witnesses on us," Lou said, "and we want to be ready in case they try to prove the truth of their allegations. In a lawsuit such as this, one must be prepared at all times for the unexpected as well as the expected." However, it was agreed that we had best concentrate on establishing our claim for damages. An important concern was whether or not CBS would come into court on the side of the defendants. I still found it unbelievable that CBS would follow such a course.

We didn't work late that night. After we had gone over my direct testimony for the following morning, Lou suggested that I go home and get a good night's sleep. He repeated, for the thousandth time, that he wanted me to be completely rested. I was in bed by midnight.

18

When I reached the courtroom the next morning no one was around. It was too early—by more than an hour. I went in and took my seat at the counsel table. I had the whole room to myself. A lone attendant wandered in, looked around for a while, and wandered out again. As I sat there, waiting and thinking, I looked at the empty witness stand and tried to picture myself sitting there. Should I fold my arms and look solemn? Or sit relaxed and look benign? Should I lean forward eagerly? Or lean back calmly? Lou had advised over and over again that I should simply be myself. I wondered how the hell a man could know whether he was being himself, sitting there between the judge and the jury, his every word and gesture being observed by the jury and recorded by a stenographer. Then an interesting new thought occurred to me: It was only under such circumstances that I could really be myself; only under pressure, every fiber in my body being put to the test, could I really find out what there was to me. Then, and only then, did I clearly see that this would not be an ordeal; it would be an opportunity to prove to myself what I honestly believed about myself. A glorious opportunity!

After a while, several court attendants drifted in, and a few spectators arrived. Then the Nizer entourage came in. Lou, Paul, George and two clerks from Nizer's office with the inevitable heavily laden briefcases. They greeted me and took their seats. George started laying out material on the table from the briefcases. I eyed the three men who were absorbed in my welfare, spending their days and nights working to achieve a just hearing for me. These three sharply intelligent men were wholeheartedly devoted to my cause; and knowing this, I was deeply moved. The words "Thy rod and thy staff, they comfort me" came back into my mind, and I felt a lump in my throat. This trio of tireless souls were more than my rod and my staff. They were my sword and shield.

I was a little surprised that there were not more spectators present. When I thought of it, the explanation was easy to come by. Yesterday the benches had been crowded with Nizer's admirers who had come to hear his opening speech. Obviously, the prospect of hearing my opening testimony didn't have the same strong appeal to the public. I thought about the origins of my troubles, the union fights, and noticed with a pang of resentment that not a single member of AFTRA was present, save Chris who was there as a friend, not as a union member.

After what seemed an eternity, it was ten-thirty—the time for court to convene. Nothing happened. I glanced at my watch and at the clock on the wall. The minutes were ticking by. Bolan, Lang and Hartnett came in, carrying their battered suitcases, and took their places. The court attendants continued to chat in low tones. Finally, the jury filed into the jury box and took their seats. There they sat, gazing without expression, straight ahead. After another endless spell of waiting the bailiff came forward and announced the judge. We got to our feet and Justice Geller entered. "At long last," I breathed. I looked at the clock on the wall; it was exactly ten forty-five.

As we all sat down again, I fell to musing, waiting for the judge to call out: "We will now hear from John Henry Faulk." Nothing happened. There wasn't a sound in the courtroom. I looked expectantly at the judge. He was looking back at me—expectantly. After a while, I became aware of George nudging me. I leaned my ear over toward him and he said, "Get up, John. Can't you see Nizer is waiting?" I was startled. Glancing around I saw Lou nodding at me and repeating softly, "Will you take the witness stand, Mr. Faulk?" Self-consciously, I got up and walked toward the stand, repressing the desire to explain to the judge and the jury that I was sorry I had caused a delay, but that I had expected the judge to instruct me to take the stand. The bailiff swore me in, and I stepped into the witness box and took my seat. Lou smiled at me, meaning to reassure me. "Will you please state your name and address?" At that point, my life as a witness began.

I have a conviction about witnesses: One who has never sat in a witness chair cannot possibly conceive of what the experience is like.

You sit there, with twelve pairs of jurors' eyes fixed upon you, with a judge who is listening to every word, and a courtroom full of spectators and reporters watching your every gesture. If you blink your eyes, scratch your nose, frown, smile, nod your head, or react with any expression whatever, it is observed. The slightest shift in position is noticed. One might think a performer, used to audiences, would be at home, but this is nothing like being on the stage before an audience. An entertainer has some control over himself and the audience. His training, experience and skill in his craft give him some control over the feelings he engenders in his observers. He knows what to expect of himself in his performance. However, a witness whose function is to supply information which will affect the outcome of a lawsuit is something of a tool or a pawn. He speaks only when he is asked a question, and he'd better not try to do more. He is completely under the control of the lawyer questioning him. To make matters worse, there is a court reporter about three feet below him taking down every syllable uttered. One might achieve some degree of comfort in a witness stand, but I doubt if anyone ever gets sufficiently used to it to enjoy it.

Lou's questions led me through an account of my early life—family, schools, churches, and all sorts of related trivia. He kept me lively in my answers by his tone of voice. He cleverly had me dwell at length on the thesis I had written for my M.A. degree, the first of its kind ever accepted at the University of Texas. It consisted of ten sermons that I had transcribed as they were preached by ten Negro ministers. When I related this, Lou questioned me at length how I came to write it. I told him of my consuming interest in the folklore of the Southwest, how I had been attracted by the epic quality of the Negro sermons, an art form rapidly disappearing at the time I started transcribing them. I described the imagery and the grandeur of the Negro folk sermon. I told him how I had received a Julius Rosenwald Fellowship to record these sermons for the Library of Congress.

Lou had pressed me so hard to give full and in some ways immodest answers that I discovered myself several times becoming fulsome in my answers. Lou would ask a question, Bolan would object, but I would have answered the question before Mr. Bolan objected. At one point Justice Geller said, "Mr. Faulk, I know you are not familiar with this. When counsel rises to object give him a chance to object so that I can make a ruling." Thereafter I started keeping my eye on Mr. Bolan more closely. When I would see him rise I would halt my testimony. He would crouch in his chair, like a rooster fixing to fly off the roost. This would cause Nizer to urge me to proceed. At one point, when I saw Mr. Bolan start to rise, I paused, and Nizer told me to go ahead. I explained that I thought Mr. Bolan was going to object. The judge commented, "If he did not rise in time, we will not hold it against you."

By the time Justice Geller adjourned the court for lunch, I was feeling confident, if not comfortable. As we went down the corridor, several reporters eased along beside me, but Lou hurried me along. He was absolutely firm about my not talking about my case to reporters. Murray Kempton, of the *New York Post,* came up and we pumped hands enthusiastically. He is one of the most skillful columnists in New York and an old friend, and I felt that I had to chat with him. We talked as we walked along. When we parted, I explained to Lou that we had talked only of matters unrelated to the case. Lou commented knowingly, "You'll see whether it's related to the case or not in tomorrow's column."

As Paul, Lou, George and I sat down to lunch at Gasner's, Lou patted my shoulder. "You did fine as a start, John. But remember, no false modesty this afternoon when we get into the awards you've received. If you received them, you've a right to be proud of them. Now, you speak right up about them on the stand."

And that afternoon I did exactly that, for almost the entire session. I warmed up to the subject with vigor as I went along. By the time court adjourned at four o'clock, I figured the judge and jury were quite relieved to have me shut up.

That evening I bounced over to Lou's apartment feeling quite refreshed. However, about one o'clock that morning I was numb again. My ears refused to communicate the sounds to my brain. Lou decided I'd had all I could take for the night, and sympathetically he suggested I go home. "I want you to get a good night's sleep and be well rested for tomorrow." For some reason, he would repeat this every night, although it was sometimes as late as four o'clock in the morning when he'd say it. A good night's sleep between four and eight o'clock?

The next day, Lou succeeded in getting the court's consent to introduce an astonishing amount of material that CBS had published on me, that is, promotional material, which was very effusive indeed.

Each time he had to wrestle it in over Bolan's objection. The question of what was hearsay evidence and what was not began to confuse the jury, and the judge had to explain it to them at length.

At lunch recess, we got a copy of the *New York Post*. It carried Murray Kempton's first article on the trial. It was entitled "The Return," and Murray seemed to give the whole posture of the case in that one succinct article, which read in part:

> Judge Abraham Geller's courtroom was crowded yesterday, as it is likely to be for the next six weeks, because Louis Nizer will be practicing surgery there.
>
> Nizer, of course, was the chief attraction; but, once there, it was surprising how glad many of the spectators were to see John Henry Faulk again. He sat yesterday, still with the wit disguised as country foolishness, as though the business that had stopped his career was faintly comic. He will be sparing and therefore more terrible in his moments of rage. He returns unchanged and intact, the most immensely formidable kind of witness, the one who can laugh at himself. He will take his vengeance without rancor. There is a sense that when this one is over, Aware will never be able to hurt anyone else again

I discovered that I was getting rather used to being on the witness stand. It was like riding a stiff-legged horse; it's never comfortable, but once you get used to it, you don't notice how rough it is. I had plenty of time for reflection, for Bolan was constantly objecting and setting off whispered wrangles at the bench between him and Nizer. These discussions were conducted in such low tones that I could hear only the mumble of their voices. So, I would sit there thinking about various things, like getting hung in a barbed-wire fence one time while I was rabbit hunting; or falling down and skinning my knees while flying a kite. Sometimes, my thoughts would wander so far from the courtroom, that I wouldn't notice that the conference at the bench was over and that Lou was poised to continue questioning me. I would come back with a start.

It was with real pleasure that I heard Lou request the court's permission to suspend my direct examination and to put David Susskind on the stand the following day, Friday. Susskind's testimony would be the jury's first taste of the bitter facts of blacklisting. Indeed, it would be the first time ever that such testimony had been given in a court. And it would be given by a person whose name was news in itself.

A ripple of excitement ran through the spectator section and the jury box when Susskind was sworn in and took the witness chair. It was obvious that every one of the jurors recognized him. Susskind, volatile and creative, had, for a number of years, been unusually outspoken in his opinions. This had won him as many detractors as admirers. My personal experience with him had been a happy one. Since I had first known him, in the mid-Fifties, he had always been considerate and generous with me. Never once had he wavered or equivocated in his position of strong support for our cause.

Bolan objected to the court's ruling that Susskind could be presented as a witness out of order, on the grounds that the defendants had gotten absolutely no advance notice of the fact that Susskind was going to be on. He claimed that Susskind was a surprise witness, in that the defense counsel had not been told that Susskind might have to go off on a trip on short notice. The court overruled him. Susskind began his direct testimony by telling of his background, how he attended schools in Brookline, Massachusetts, later went to the University of Wisconsin, and was graduated from Harvard University in 1942 with a Bachelor of Science degree *cum laude*. Susskind told of his work during the war with the National Labor Board in Washington and then of having joined the Navy in September 1942. After the war he joined the New York office of Warner Brothers motion picture company, in the advertising and publicity department. He told of how he got into the television in 1948. He and one of the men in Century Artists Ltd. formed Talent Associates Ltd. The purpose of the organization was twofold: managing creative personnel, not performers, but writers, directors and producers, and the creation of new programs, selling them and putting them on the air. Talent Associates Ltd., as Susskind described it, was one of the oldest television program packaging companies in New York. In 1952, according to his testimony, his company abandoned the management of talent and devoted itself exclusively to creating new television programs, selling them and producing them. They had started, in the fall of 1948, producing a program called *Philco Television Playhouse,* a program which ran once a week, fifty-two weeks a year, for six years. As Lou had Susskind testify to the stars that he had hired in the past, Mr. Bolan became impatient.

BOLAN: I will concede that this witness is an expert TV producer or anything of that sort without the necessity of going into detail.

THE COURT: Mr. Bolan, he is not required to do so. He can if he wants to accept your concession. Do you accept the concession?

NIZER: No, I do not, sir. There are certain aspects of this, your Honor—

THE COURT: Then he is entitled to establish it to a certain degree.

The court permitted Susskind to testify at length about the number of stars that had been on his program, their names, as well as the directors and writers on the programs. After Lou had established clearly through David's direct testimony that he had had vast experience as a producer of innumerable dramatic shows on television for various sponsors, he took up a copy of the examination before trial of Mr. Hartnett. Bolan objected strenuously, but the court overruled him, pointing out that both attorneys were permitted to read from the EBT of any witness. Lou proceeded to read direct testimony of Mr. Hartnett given several years previously at his EBT. His purpose became very apparent as he read the questions and Hartnett's answers that dealt with Hartnett's arrangement with the Young & Rubicam advertising agency. As everyone in the courtroom listened, Lou read Hartnett's account of how he charged Young & Rubicam for clearing talent for one of Y & R's clients, the Lorillard Company. Hartnett had testified that he had received nine thousand dollars in equal installments for clearing talent on a program sponsored by Lorillard. His agreement was that for a particular period, the first report he would give on talent was five dollars, for a longer report it might be twenty dollars or more, and for a repeat on a name it was ordinarily two dollars. The name of the program for which Hartnett cleared the names was *Appointment with Adventure*. Lou laid aside the EBT and turned to the witness.

NIZER: Mr. Susskind, I will interrupt at this point in the reading to ask you what was the program "Appointment with Adventure."

SUSSKIND [after the Judge had overruled several objections from Mr. Bolan]: "Appointment with Adventure" was a half-hour dramatic program conceived by my company and sold to Young & Rubicam on behalf of the Lorillard Company and it was on, I believe, in March 1955, Sunday nights 10 P.M. and stayed for 50 weeks every Sunday night.

NIZER: And the Young & Rubicam Company, which is the agency you mentioned, is the same agency as the one I have referred to as dealing with this program?

SUSSKIND: Yes, sir, the same.

Lou then took up Hartnett's EBT again and read his testimony on his dealings with Young & Rubicam in clearing names for the Lorillard program. Hartnett had told how one of the people at the agency would call him almost daily on the telephone, read off a list of names of actors and actresses, directors, producers, supervisors, technicians, and all persons connected with the show. He had testified that he had been given the names of assistant stage directors and other peripheral workers to clear, even lighting technicians. After Lou had read at considerable length from Hartnett's EBT concerning the clearing of talent and others connected with *Appointment with Adventure,* he turned again to Susskind on the witness stand.

NIZER: Mr. Susskind, I have read certain passages about a program called "Appointment with Adventure," and you have already told us that you were packager, the producer of that program for the Lorillard Company. Is that right?

SUSSKIND: Yes, sir. We created that program. We sold it to Young & Rubicam for Lorillard, and I personally produced the program.

NIZER: When you say you sold it to Young & Rubicam, that was an advertising agency that represented the sponsor of the cigarettes, Lorillard, is that the sequence of it?

SUSSKIND: Yes, sir.

NIZER: Now, did you when you selected various actors and actresses and even the names of technicians or the director or the assistant director, did you submit those names to anyone?

BOLAN: I object, your Honor.

THE COURT: Overruled.

BOLAN: He is here as an expert witness. That has nothing to do with his background.

THE COURT: I understand him to say he produced the witness as an expert witness and for other purposes.

NIZER: That is right.

THE COURT: That is what he said.

SUSSKIND: Yes, sir, I had to submit the names of everybody on every show in every category to an executive of Young & Rubicam, and nobody could be engaged by me finally or a deal made and consummated, before a clearance or acceptance came back from Young & Rubicam.

NIZER: Did that acceptance deal with the quality of the actor or the technician or the director?

BOLAN: I object, your Honor.

THE COURT: Sustained. Reframe your question.

NIZER: When you submitted these names what was the purpose of submission.

BOLAN: I object, your Honor.

THE COURT: Overruled.

SUSSKIND: When I sold the program to the advertising agency, Young & Rubicam, for Lorillard cigarettes, the condition of the sale was that all names of all personnel in all categories on every program were to be submitted for political clearance by Young & Rubicam, and nobody was to be hired until they approved and said, "All right, hire such a person."

NIZER: These names were submitted on the telephone?

SUSSKIND: All the names were submitted by me or members of my organization to an executive of Young & Rubicam or his secretary, over the telephone.

NIZER: How long did it take before the approval or disapproval came back?

BOLAN: I object, your Honor.

THE COURT: Overruled.

SUSSKIND: It generally took forty-eight hours. I was told that I should always anticipate a forty-eight-hour delay on the approval or rejection of any name.

. . . .

NIZER: Can you estimate how many names on this one program over the year that it ran that you submitted in this way for political approval?

BOLAN: I object, your Honor.

THE COURT: Overruled.

SUSSKIND: I must have submitted over the period of time about five thousand names, I would guess.

THE COURT: For this one program?

SUSSKIND: For this one program.

THE COURT: Did you state the period of time this program . . .

SUSSKIND: This program was on the air for fifty consecutive weeks.

THE COURT: From when to when?

SUSSKIND: From April 3, 1955 to March 11, 1956.

NIZER: Can you give us the estimate of how many of the names that you submitted came back rejected.

SUSSKIND: I would guess approximately 33 1/3%, perhaps a little higher, came back politically rejected.

NIZER: What was the practice with respect to inquiring about a particular name? Describe it in your own way.

SUSSKIND: The practice was that I would telephone the executive at Young & Rubicam. I would have had previously made tentative commitments to actors, writers, producers, directors, everybody on the program, telling them, "We think we want you on this program. We will advise you on this soon definitely one way or another." I would then call the advertising agency executive. I would submit the names. He would, as I say, reject or approve them in terms of their political acceptability.

THE COURT: Can you indicate who you spoke to, Mr. Susskind?

SUSSKIND: If you want me to. . . .

THE COURT: Yes.

SUSSKIND: The executive in charge of this particular program for Lorillard Company was David Levy. He was assisted by other men, but he was the primary executive.

. . . .

NIZER: Tell us what was said?

SUSSKIND: I said to Mr. Levy that it is extraordinarily difficult to find the right actors for the right parts, the right writers for the right scripts, and the right directors for the right stories, that his rejections were making the program almost unworkable and impossible artistically, and that I could not accept the responsibility for the steady deterioration of the program when this practice was in vogue. I said, "If you reject somebody, let me get that somebody and ask him. In many cases I know these people and they are fine people, and I know that they are acceptable. You only say no or yes to me about them, but you never give me any substantiation." He said, "I can't give you any. I deplore this practice as much as you do. We're caught in a trap. I have no alternative."

. . . .

I said, "The production of the program is being seriously impaired. Human beings are suffering loss of employment without any substantiation, without any charges, without even their knowing that they can't be hired, and I am being embarrassed constantly with the agents and the lawyers of the actors and the writers and the directors by saying 'I am sorry we cannot hire you on the fact of political rejection.'

"I know a great number of the people you have rejected. I know them socially and professionally and there is no question about their political reliability or their good citizenship or their loyalty to this country, and on all these grounds I beg you to let me confront these people with whatever you have on them and let them answer and you will find that they will be all right and you will have a much better show." And he (Mr. Levy) said, "I am helpless. We are helpless. This is the practice. We have no choice, and we have to pay $5 for every clearance and $2 for every recheck. Do you think we like it? It's costing us a bloody fortune." And I believe he said, "Cut down the number of actors you submit, cut down the number of directors and the number of writers, because you are breaking us. It's $5 a throw, and $2 a throw, and you give us eight actors for each role and then you give us three writers for each script, and then you give us four directors for each show. Somebody is getting rich. We're growing broke. Stop it. Narrow it down."

I said, "I can't narrow it down, because I have learned that your percentage of rejections is so high I have to have alternative choices to be prepared when you reject them politically." And he said, "I am helpless. Stop this talk. Get on with it. Do the best you can." I said, "If this continues I will withdraw personally as producer of the show."

NIZER: What was Mr. Levy's position in Young & Rubicam?

SUSSKIND: He was vice-president, and he was specifically assigned to certain accounts, Borden, Lorillard, and so forth.

NIZER: Did he ever send you any list himself?

SUSSKIND: Yes, sir.

NIZER: Were they sent in writing? Were they written communications, is what I mean?

SUSSKIND: Yes, sir. When I sold the Borden Company, Young & Rubicam, a program, television program for the Borden Milk Company, the program was called "Justice," a half-hour weekly series on NBC Thursday nights, based on cases from the Legal Aid Society. A condition of the sale was that a list of the actors would be given me which numbered roughly 150, and that all roles on all programs in this series were to be billed from these politically cleared actors' names, and only such actors could be employed.

NIZER: What took place on this occasion when this happened?

SUSSKIND: I said to Mr. Levy, I mean the executive in charge of account . . .

I said, "It's impossible to cast a program from a list of a hundred and fifty-odd names. There are three thousand actors in the AFTRA union in New York. There are ten thousand actors in the Screen Actors Guild. I can't anticipate every script that will be written, but surely this hundred and fifty names will never permit me to do a program of any quality or any workability. It's impossible." He (Levy) said, "The Borden Company in its previous program had so much trouble with politically unreliable actors and pro-Communist sympathizers that they had made up this list." He said, "This white list is the only useful actors list for this program. Take it or leave it. If you don't want to use this list, you don't have the sale. If you will use this list, you can have the sale."

I took the program, commenting at the time, "This list will have to be enlarged and you will be forced to enlarge it. You will come to understand that, and incidentally this list is the most humdrum list of dead-beat, untalented actors I have ever seen."

Nizer then introduced into evidence a letter from Levy, on Young & Rubicam's stationery, to David Susskind, which Susskind testified had accompanied the list of 150 names of usable and approved actors and actresses. Lou also produced receipts that we had obtained from Hartnett at his EBT, and he read Hartnett's EBT testimony to the effect that he had received from the Borden Company $6,905 in 1954, and in 1955 he received $10,000 from them. Lou then asked Susskind:

When these names came back not approved, rejected for political reasons, what was your practice in dealing with the actors and actresses
or director who was not approved? What happened then?

SUSSKIND: Because of the necessity of political clearance we always
booked actors on what we called a hold. That's a technical phrase in
the business.

NIZER: Hold?

SUSSKIND: Yes. You say, "We would like Kim Stanley for this part, but
we are not quite sure. Will you, her agent, please make her available
for a forty-eight-hour period and not let her take another engagement
while we make up our minds? We will get back to you." In the meantime, we establish together that her price will be such and such and
that she will be available during the period of time for rehearsals and
the program. That was a hold, or a tentative, or an option on her
services. I only use her as an illustration.

THE COURT: Whom would you say this to?

SUSSKIND: I would say this to the talent agent who represented that client,
or the person or management, or in some cases these people are represented by attorney. Then I would put the names in for clearance. When
they came back rejected, part of my instruction at the beginning of the
program when I made the sale of "Appointment with Adventure" and
subsequently "Justice" and many other programs, it was stipulated that
I was never to tell any rejectee why he was rejected.

Susskind explained at some length how the agency executives had
instructed him never to allow any actor or actress to know that they
were being rejected for political reasons. Nizer elicited from him that
this was the general practice in all television and radio during that
period. Bolan objected that none of Susskind's testimony had anything to do with me—that the real issue was whether or not John
Faulk had been damaged. But Judge Geller overruled Bolan; he also
said that he, the judge, would make the rulings as to what was admissible and what wasn't admissible, and that Bolan need not make
speeches to the jury about it. Susskind then told how, after getting
an actor cleared, if he chose to use him on a program some weeks
later it was necessary to get his name cleared all over again.

The spectators and the members of the press, as well as the jury,
seemed appalled at the whole clearance business. A kind of tension
seemed to be growing in the courtroom. Then Lou asked:

Did you also submit the names even of children on this program? Could you put a child on without getting clearance?

SUSSKIND: Even children.

. . . .

NIZER: Will you give us an illustration or instance on this program if that occurred for a child?

SUSSKIND: Every one had to be cleared politically, including children.

BOLAN: May I ask this witness be responsive? He was asked for an illustration.

SUSSKIND: I will give you an illustration. In the course of "Appointment with Adventure," sponsored by Lorillard at Young & Rubicam Agency, we required the services of a, I believe, at least a seven- or eight-year-old girl actress, child actress. It was a backbreaking assignment to find a child who could act well enough to be in a professional program coast to coast. We went to all the established sources, the talent agencies. They did not represent children.

BOLAN: Your Honor, he was asked to give an illustration, and not a case history on a search for an actor or actress. Give us the illustration, not the whole story.

THE COURT: Overruled. I will allow it.

SUSSKIND: It was an extraordinarily difficult search involving going to the public-schools system, the United Nations schools. We finally found a child, an American child eight years old, female. I put her name in along with some other names. That child's name came back unacceptable, politically unreliable.

That did it. The whole courtroom, spectators and jurors alike gave way to an audible gasp. Justice Geller looked the courtroom over sternly and said, "I will not tolerate any outburst of that kind, or I will order the courtroom cleared. This is not a show. This is a courtroom."

There was a continued stirring among the spectators as Susskind continued to testify how he had urged that he be given a reason that he could not use this eight-year-old child; she surely couldn't be political. The agency finally told him that it was because the child's father was suspect. Bolan, of course, was furious at this testimony being allowed to go on record. His protest to the court was so persistent that Lou finally said, "All right, I will connect it to page 847 of Mr. Hartnett's examination before trial."

He then read from Hartnett's own statement that he did check children and charged a fee for them. When Hartnett had been asked why he checked on children, he explained that there were two reasons: some children's parents had left-wing tendencies, and that would make them objectionable or the child suspect, and the other reason was that some children start in on Communist activities on their own. As Hartnett had said, "They are rather enterprising."

Nizer then had Susskind describe in great detail the types of personalities who earn large salaries in television, men like Arthur Godfrey, Garry Moore, Steve Allen, and others. Finally he asked:

Can you state with reasonable certainty into what category Mr. John Henry Faulk would have fitted into the television broadcasting profession?

BOLAN: I object.

THE COURT: Overruled.

SUSSKIND: In my very considered opinion John Henry Faulk, had he been allowed to continue as a performer on television, would have become a star of the first magnitude, and would have enjoyed an income and reputation in the company of the stars we previously mentioned.

THE COURT: You say that with a reasonable degree of certainty?

SUSSKIND: Yes, sir.

NIZER: Your witness.

The court then declared a short recess before Mr. Bolan was to begin his cross-examination of Susskind. Mr. Bolan announced that he wanted to make a motion, but not in the presence of the jury. The judge excused the jury and asked whether Bolan would like to go into chambers. Mr. Bolan then stated that he would like to move for a mistrial on the ground that the testimony of Susskind was inadmissible.

BOLAN: It is completely inflammatory. He has spent most of his time talking about blacklisting, relating conversations that he had with some third party, with no relationship to any of the defendants.

The jury has been given the impression that the issue here is whether the defendants have been guilty of blacklisting certain other performers and in particular in the television and radio industry, and I submit that the testimony of this witness has not been directed against the defendants, and has been completely prejudicial, and I believe of the nature that does warrant a mistrial.

Justice Geller did not concur with Mr. Bolan's interpretation of Susskind's testimony, and overruled his motion for a mistrial.

After lunch, Susskind went on the stand for his cross-examination. Bolan approached him the way Mama used to approach a chicken snake in a hen nest. Within a matter of moments they were crossing swords, with Lou popping up full of objections, and Justice Geller trying to hold the fort, with observations like:

> Just a minute. Let us get a bit organized here. Mr. Susskind, you answer the questions just to the extent that the questions call for. Do not respond beyond that, but you, Mr. Bolan, give the witness an opportunity to complete his answer.

. . . .

BOLAN: Did you ever have any discussion with these people as to what was meant by a political rejection or political clearance or political approval?

THE COURT: These people mean who?

BOLAN: The people in the advertising agencies that you say you had these conversations with, particularly, for instance, Mr. Levy.

SUSSKIND: I endeavored over and over again to find out what the charges were so that I could investigate the charges or apprise the actor and give him the opportunity to face the accusation and discover whether it was true and, if it was true, whether it was sufficient to bar him from employment. This opportunity was never granted me by the advertising agency or firms or anybody else who made the final determination.

BOLAN: Do you have any idea that these charges related to Communist Party membership or Communist Party front group membership?

SUSSKIND: I know of specific instances where I do know things about the charges, in the case of a particular actor. She was unemployable because her husband was deemed to have pro-Communist organization sympathy. She herself was clear and clean politically.

A little later, Bolan asked Susskind if by blacklisting he meant that practice that prevented artists from appearing on television and radio who had been identified as Communist Party members. Nizer objected to the question.

THE COURT: Overruled. I will let him answer that. He can take care of himself.

.   .   .   .

SUSSKIND: I don't know the theory of blacklisting except that it is a private vigilanteism calculated to keep people off—

BOLAN: Mr. Susskind—

SUSSKIND: —off television.

BOLAN: Mr. Susskind, I remind you to please answer my question, and yes or no would be sufficient.

SUSSKIND: I have answered, sir.

BOLAN: Yes or no would be sufficient.

SUSSKIND: I can't answer that yes or no.

BOLAN: Then you may say that you cannot answer it.

THE COURT: No. That question did not call for a yes or no answer, if the witness could not give it.

BOLAN: You stated that a whisper as to a man's political reliability would cut off his employment automatically in television. Is that correct?

SUSSKIND: I so stated.

BOLAN: Would you so state the fact that a man identified as a member of the Communist Party by sworn testimony—would that be sufficient a whisper as to cut off his employment?

SUSSKIND: A man identified as a Communist Party member?

BOLAN: Yes.

SUSSKIND: He would be dead as a duck and should be.

BOLAN: Haven't you yourself employed a number of people who have been identified by sworn testimony as members of the Communist Party?

SUSSKIND: I am not aware that I have ever employed a member of the Communist Party, and if that ever happened, I was unaware of such evidence.

BOLAN: I did not ask you whether you ever employed a member of the

Communist Party, Mr. Susskind. I am asking you, did you ever employ a man who had been identified as a member of the Communist Party, identified by sworn testimony under oath?

THE COURT: You mean his sworn testimony?

BOLAN: Identified probably by sworn testimony as a member of the Communist Party.

SUSSKIND: Identified by whom?

THE COURT: Wait a minute.

NIZER: I object to that, your Honor.

THE COURT: Sustained. Vague.

BOLAN: Your Honor, it is not vague. I am trying to find out—

THE COURT: That is my ruling. If you want you can state within the argument, your legal position.

BOLAN: My legal position is this: I am testing the credibility of this witness. He stated a short time ago—

NIZER: I object.

THE COURT: This is the argument. I want your legal position. So I will sustain the objection as put as being vague and indefinite. Put a different question.

BOLAN: Will you say the fact that a man has been identified as a member of the Communist Party under sworn testimony would be equivalent to a whisper that you had described this morning?

NIZER: The same objection.

THE COURT: I will let him answer that. Go ahead.

SUSSKIND: If Harvey Matusow identified such a man, no. That is not a whisper, that is a lie, because he is a proven liar before a Congressional committee. It depends on who identified him, and how was that man faced with his accuser. Was he allowed to bring counsel? If they indict him, official agencies of our government, the Attorney General's office, the district attorney of New York?

The heated exchange continued. Lou, Judge Geller, Bolan and Susskind, all participated. Bolan seemed most eager to establish the fact that Susskind would regard it as blacklisting if an artist were barred from the air simply because he had pleaded the Fifth Amendment. They went backward and forward over that. Finally Lou asked Bolan on the record:

In this cross-examination, may I ask of counsel [Bolan] respectfully is it intended to justify the practice of blacklisting if somebody did testify about somebody and that person never had an opportunity to face his accuser, are you trying to justify that practice in this question?

BOLAN: I am trying to justify, Mr. Nizer, the right of a private group to advocate that people who take the Fifth when questioned on Communist Party membership need not or should not be employed on television. . . .

A moment later Bolan asked, rather sarcastically, if Susskind had not taken strenuous exception to advertising agencies who kept artists from appearing on his program for political reasons:

SUSSKIND: I took strenuous exception.

BOLAN: Fine. That's an answer.

THE COURT: Let him finish his answer.

SUSSKIND: Mr. Bolan, I haven't finished.

THE COURT: I will decide, Mr. Susskind. I am the moderator here. I know you on your program will decide how far they can go. I will decide that here. You may complete your answer.

.   .   .   .

SUSSKIND: I took strenuous exception to the whole system of blacklisting of everything decent and moral and American, and in principle I did not think that that was the advertising agency's function, or anybody's function, except law enforcement agencies and authorized elements of our government.

When Bolan pressed Susskind for an answer as to whether he would consider it blacklisting if a person who had taken the Fifth Amendment was barred from performing or holding a job in radio and television, Susskind answered:

SUSSKIND: Yes, I would consider that blacklisting. The Fifth Amendment is a constitutional privilege and he was never faced with the charge. He had no counsel, no opportunity to answer, and the Fifth Amendment is part of our Bill of Rights. It is not against the law. It is not a crime. It is a constitutional privilege that I subscribe to with all my might.

When Bolan pressed Susskind to say whether he would consider it blacklisting if an actor who had been identified by sworn testimony as a Communist Party member were barred, Mr. Nizer objected and the court sustained it.

THE COURT: That was put before. The objection was sustained and sustained again. If you put the proper question, I will permit it. Sworn testimony but of what? By whom? By what? An examination by whom? . . .

Are you contending, Mr. Bolan, because somebody comes before the House Un-American Activities Committee and swears to something about somebody, that that establishes a fact?

BOLAN: I am not seeking to establish the fact. I am seeking to establish the right of the advertiser to consider that a man who has been identified under sworn testimony as a Communist Party member—that is all I'm trying. I am trying to find out if that is part of blacklisting.

THE COURT: Put another question. If you want to put to him questions based on judicial determination, you may put that.

Bolan continued to press the matter of an actor or actress identified before a committee of Congress in sworn testimony as a Communist, what would Susskind do about that? Justice Geller was becoming impatient with Bolan.

THE COURT: . . . A committee's report of Congress does not constitute an adjudication.

Later on, in a heated exchange between the judge and Bolan over the significance of sworn testimony before Congressional committees, the judge said, "Somebody that is thoroughly irresponsible can state something under oath. Does that make it valid?"

Bolan, after trying unsuccessfully to get Susskind to testify that he really did not know too much about my professional career and had not seen me often, finally gave up and court was adjourned for the weekend.

We had to rush uptown after court adjourned, for Lou was scheduled to catch a plane almost immediately. He had to fly to Florida and address the Florida Bar Association that Saturday. He had declined all such engagements for the duration of the trial, although he was in constant demand as a speaker, but he felt, he told us, that he was obligated to fulfill this engagement before the Florida Bar Association, since it was of such long standing, and it would be unfair to cancel it. He spent a fast hour giving directions to us for the work to be done in his absence. From the amount he outlined, I would have sworn he was going to be gone for six months rather than forty-eight hours. Then he took off for Florida, and David Susskind departed for England.

The second week of my direct examination started off on the subject of my role in the union elections. Bolan strove mightily, through objections, to keep me from testifying on what was said at the two union meetings in the spring of 1955. They were the meetings at which the resolution to condemn AWARE, Inc. had been discussed. He was successful, too, for much of my testimony was pure hearsay, consequently inadmissible. As will be seen later, during my cross-examination he was eventually responsible for this very evidence getting into the records.

My direct examination would have been completed in two or three days, perhaps, had it not been for the interminable arguments over the admission of evidence and exhibits. Lou wanted me to give full and detailed accounts of each item. He would start in on a line of questioning, for instance, about the period when I first learned that Laurence Johnson had come to New York and was knocking sponsors off my show in April 1956. This involved my testifying about conversations I had with Carl Ward and Sam Slate. I would start to relate a conversation between Ward and myself by saying, "I went into Ward's office. He was very upset." Bolan would object. The court would warn me not to characterize Mr. Ward's state of mind, just to repeat his direct words to me. Then I would undertake to explain that Ward had told me that somebody had told him, objection again, pure hearsay. Then a lengthy argument at the bench between Bolan and Nizer, out of hearing of the jury, with the judge ruling that I should stick strictly to the facts. I tried to do that, but at the same time follow Nizer's instruction to get in a full account of everything.

Ben Bodne, a South Carolina gentleman, had come to New York just after the war and had purchased the Algonquin Hotel. He was a devoted friend and admirer of Nizer's and came to court nearly every day, arriving there in a chauffeur-driven Rolls-Royce which would also come down and meet him each afternoon after court. Early in my second week of testimony, Lou had me describe what had happened after I had been blacklisted and gone broke. He urged me to describe in detail the hardships and deprivations my family and I had suffered, ending up on the note that I was still broke and heavily in debt. That day at lunch, Ben Bodne approached me and said that he wanted me to do him a favor. Since I was broke, he knew the matter of supporting myself during the trial was of great concern to me, and he wanted me to be his guest at the Algonquin for the duration of the trial. He pointed out that it would be his way of helping to fight the battle we were waging. The atmosphere of the Algonquin was genteel and literary. I loved the place. Knowing I had imposed on Chris and Merle long enough, I accepted gratefully. That afternoon after court, Ben and I sallied down to the street and prepared to climb into his waiting Rolls-Royce. George Berger came dashing up to me and said Lou wanted to see me immediately. I went over to where he was standing, some hundred feet away. "Don't get into a Rolls-Royce in front of the courthouse; some of the jurors might see you! You're supposed to be an unemployed victim of the blacklist. If you're going to ride home with Ben, walk up the street a couple of blocks and let him pick you up out of sight of the jurors." That was the procedure I followed each afternoon thereafter.

19

My direct examination lasted almost two weeks. On Thursday of the second week, Lou announced he was turning me over to Bolan for cross-examination. However, Bolan was absent that day—probably preparing for my cross-examination—and Mr. Lang requested that the court adjourn until the next morning, at which time Bolan would begin to cross-examine me.

Although I considered myself something of a veteran on the witness stand, by the time Bolan was ready to cross-examine me, I was uncontrollably tense and anxious. In spite of every effort, including prayer, I could not seem to calm my apprehensions.

First off, Bolan wanted to show I was never anything but a minor figure in broadcasting—a mere disc jockey.

BOLAN: Were you a disc jockey on CBS?
FAULK: I didn't regard myself as one nor did CBS regard me as one.
BOLAN: They did not?
FAULK: No.
BOLAN: Did the profession regard you as a disk jockey?
FAULK: I don't know how to answer that. Never was I included as a disc jockey in common parlance.

. . . .

BOLAN: I have noticed that Mr. Nizer and yourself have not used the term disc jockey at all up to this point.
NIZER: I object to that, sir.

THE COURT: Sustained.

BOLAN: Do you have any aversion to being described as a disc jockey?

NIZER: Objection, sir.

THE COURT: Overruled.

FAULK: Not in the least, sir. I—

BOLAN: That is an answer. You said before that you were not regarded as a disc jockey in the profession.

FAULK: I was not.

BOLAN: I show you defendant's Exhibit A for identification and ask if that refreshes your recollection in any way?

FAULK: I don't know what you mean by refreshing my recollection.

BOLAN: Weren't you a member of Fresh Air Disc Jockey Committee for the Herald Tribune Fresh Air Fund at one time?

FAULK: That is perfectly correct, sir.

BOLAN: Haven't you always been referred to in reviews as a disc jockey?

FAULK: No. I was not.

BOLAN: Have you ever been referred to in reviews as a disc jockey?

FAULK: I don't remember any specific instance, but in all likelihood I have been, yes, sir.

BOLAN: You do not remember any specific instance? You are not sure you have ever been referred to as a disc jockey?

FAULK: I said I didn't remember any specific instance of being referred to.

BOLAN: But I ask you the question, have you ever been referred to as a disc jockey in the reviews?

FAULK: I say that, in all likelihood, yes.

After considerable wrangling between Nizer and Bolan over whether or not I was going to be allowed to explain what I was talking about when I said I did not regard myself a disc jockey and that CBS did not regard me as one, Judge Geller permitted me to testify.

FAULK: The reason I said that in all likelihood is at the time my contract was signed, the one to which you just referred, it was that they did not know how to describe me, describe the kind of program I was going to do, because I was employed primarily for the kind of stories and comments that I made. It was understood that I knew nothing about music. A disc jockey is an authority on music.

It was clear that Mr. Bolan wanted to derogate my abilities as a performer as much as possible. A little later he asked:

Did you ever hear the term "professional Texan"?

FAULK: Oh, yes indeed.

BOLAN: Did you ever hear it in reference to you?

FAULK: I think that I have, yes.

BOLAN: What does the term mean?

FAULK: I think in one instance someone writing a review of me, and I don't even recall who it was because it stung. It's very uncomplimentary as far as I'm concerned.

It means one that is pompous and inflated and goes about boasting of Texas being the biggest and the best and the finest, and that the sun rises and sets there; that the first law of gravity was passed by the Texas state legislature.

THE COURT: Aren't the Texans proud of being the biggest and the best?

FAULK: I'm infinitely proud. I am trying to characterize a pompous humbug who gives Texas a black eye. By the way, it's one of the points I made quite frequently on my program, of these Texas oil men who say they could buy Russia. They would lease it back to Khrushchev, that sort of thing.

. . . .

It is part and parcel of that.

BOLAN: Isn't it part of your performance as a disc jockey, Mr. Faulk, to exaggerate your Texas accent and to exaggerate your background in Texas?

NIZER: Objection.

THE COURT: Sustained.

. . . .

BOLAN: Isn't it a part of your act as a disc jockey, as a person from Texas, to underplay your intelligence?

NIZER: Objection.

THE COURT: Sustained.

. . . .

BOLAN: Isn't it a part of your act, or wasn't it a part of your act on CBS to act the part of an ignorant person rather than an intelligent one?

NIZER: Objection as incompetent, irrelevant and immaterial.

THE COURT: I'm going to allow that.

FAULK: It certainly was not. It's far from it.

BOLAN: Did you—

THE COURT: Let him finish.

BOLAN: That is an answer.

THE COURT: I'm going to let him finish.

FAULK: I referred frequently to my lectures at Yale University. I quoted Shakespeare quite frequently, and John Milton quite frequently over the air. I do it on a folk level, that is quite true, but that's very different from conducting myself like a country bumpkin. I imagine that that is what you are suggesting I did.

I had a rather wide listening audience among university people, Princeton and Columbia Universities.

Bolan finally gave up on that and wanted to know what I thought of Mr. Ward and Mr. Slate.

BOLAN: Mr. Slate was a very close friend of yours?

FAULK: Yes, I so regarded him.

BOLAN: Did you regard Mr. Slate and Mr. Ward as truthful and honest persons?

. . . .

FAULK: Within the limitations of an executive in a radio and television business, I would say yes, but there are limitations, you see, . . .

BOLAN: Mr. Slate, does that statement apply to him?

THE COURT: Whether he is truthful and honest?

BOLAN: Yes.

FAULK: Mr. Slate is a truthful and honest man, but in . . . I don't want to go the whole hog there, and I'll tell you why. This is no reflection on the man's character at all, but executives, as we have heard testimony in this court, executives who are very honest men and are very good men, quite frequently are impelled to take actions and positions that could be described as less than candid, let us say.

BOLAN: They were compelled not to tell the truth?

FAULK: Let us say withhold the truth.

BOLAN: Did you just testify that because of his executive position, Mr. Slate was compelled to withhold the truth?

FAULK: I did not, and if I did, I certainly should have not said such a thing.

Mr. Bolan then turned his attention to the schedule of commercial spots on my program during the year 1956, subsequent to the attack by AWARE. This proved to be the grimmest time I had on the witness stand. For a couple of days we labored back and forth over the tedious and extremely technical matter of my rotating commercial schedule involving some two dozen sponsors. I tried desperately to remember when and under what circumstances I had which spots, and Bolan tried, with considerable success at times, to trip me up. The wonder is he did not do it more often.

When he got around to the period of my dismissal from WCBS in August 1957, he went over and over the reasons that Sam Slate had given me at the time for my firing. He was very careful to establish through my testimony that Sam Slate had never once said that I was being fired because AWARE was using pressure on him. When I had finally testified to the several reasons that Sam Slate had given me, such as changing the programming at WCBS, my having been on the same show too long, and several others, Bolan asked:

Did you consider Mr. Slate to be a truthful man, this very close friend of yours, when he made these statements to you as to why you had lost your job?

FAULK: I considered Mr. Slate to be a man under very profound emotional stress, sir, that he had to take an action that he abominated.

BOLAN: Now will you answer the question? Did you consider him to be a truthful man?

FAULK: Under those circumstances, sir, Mr. Slate was neither truthful nor dishonest. Mr. Slate was acting at the direction of the corporation for which he worked.

Mr. Bolan had subpoenaed William B. Greene, an attorney at WCBS, to bring down records he wanted to use in my cross-examination. It was necessary to put Mr. Greene on the witness stand while I stood aside for a while, to testify that these were authentic records from CBS. To the considerable astonishment of Mr. Bolan, after Mr. Greene had identified the records as being authentic and from CBS, Mr. Nizer asked to cross-examine him—Mr. Greene was the lawyer that had been at CBS several months before, when the Roy Cohn office came and got the original records on me.

NIZER: Was any associate of Mr. Roy Cohn, on behalf of the defendants, in your office with respect to these records, some months ago?

GREENE: Yes sir. Mr. Lang.

NIZER: And were the original records delivered to Mr. Lang at that time?

GREENE: Certain of the original records were delivered to him, yes, sir.

NIZER: And he had those for how long, sir, in his own office?

GREENE: To the best of my knowledge, sir, I would say two weeks.

NIZER: And did you have a copy of these original records made before they were delivered to Mr. Cohn?

GREENE: A copy of those which are now in Mr. Bolan's hands, no, sir.

NIZER: So that Mr.—

THE COURT: Now, wait, let me understand that. You say "a copy of those which are now in Mr. Bolan's hand" did you not make that statement? Did you make a copy of any which were delivered to Mr. Cohn?

GREENE: No, sir, the reason I answered it that way, your Honor, there may have been copies of other papers that are in the files spread in other files within the company. I don't know that.

NIZER: I understand, in other words, sir, the records which you delivered to the defendants' counsel were the original records of CBS, of which no copy was kept in your office?

GREENE: That is correct.

Nizer turned on his heel, commenting, "That's all."

At one point, Bolan handed me an article which had appeared about a year before in *The Nation* magazine, entitled "Disc Jockey Fights the Blacklist." Nizer was on his feet at once, demanding that the entire article be admitted as evidence. The article was highly favorable to me, and it mentioned certain things about the defendants and my fight with them that could not have been put into evidence by us. However, as Bolan had presented the article in an attempt to establish that I was merely a disc jockey, the court ruled the article in its entirety be admitted into the record.

The high point of my cross-examination occurred toward its end. It happened one day when Bolan sought to prove that the anti-AWARE resolution, which had been passed by the membership of AFTRA in 1955, was actually Communist-inspired. Since my activities on the Middle-of-the-Road slate had grown directly out of this anti-AWARE resolution, Bolan obviously wanted to connect the beginnings of the Middle-of-the-Road slate, at least my participation in it, with what he considered the sinister forces in the union who had promulgated the anti-AWARE resolution. His determination to do this led him, I believe, into a couple of the most costly mistakes of the entire trial.

He set out, through his questioning of me, to establish the names of those who had introduced and supported the anti-AWARE resolution. He wanted to prove that they all were of questionable patriotism; they had been charged with various Communist and pro-Communist proclivities. He also wanted to get into the record the names of prominent personalities, like Bud Collyer, Vicki Cummings and Alan Bunce, who had supported AWARE with strong statements at the time of the voting. On my direct examination, I had testified at length (or in as much detail as possible over Bolan's objections) on what various persons had said at the two meetings, the one in March and May 1955, of AFTRA. I had also testified that I had received two statements in the mail with my ballot in June 1955, one statement supporting AWARE and urging me not to vote for the condemnation of same, and the other for condemning AWARE and giving the reasons for it. Bolan, of course, was allowed to introduce these statements into evidence since I had testified about them. He was particularly anxious to get the pro-AWARE statement in. No sooner was it admitted in evidence than he read it with relish to the jury.

BOLAN [From the pro-AWARE statement]: "The issue is not, as the proponents of the misleading resolution would have us believe, the organization called Aware. So far, the only thing most of us know about Aware is what we are told by its enemies. But we can be sure of one thing, if what Aware said about certain AFTRA members had not been true, if it had not, if it had really been smear and inference and innuendo, these members would have challenged their exposures instead of coming crying to AFTRA. Here is the real issue. An insignificant number of AFTRANs, who have been identified under oath as Communist Party members, or who have identified themselves with Communist front organizations, have been trying for years, unsuccessfully to gain power and leadership in our union, and they have now seized upon Aware's exposure of their activities as a means of trying to gain AFTRA's sympathy and support. In this effort they have hidden behind the skirts of a few misguided AFTRANs innocently involved in left-wing affiliations hoping thereby to make themselves appear equally innocent. They tell us that an outside organization has been interfering in the internal affairs of our union, but they conveniently neglect to mention that Aware's comments about their own unsavory outside activities were made nearly a month after AFTRA elections were over. Furthermore, they hoped we will forget that their Communist fronts which they do not ask us to condemn, are quite definitely outside organizations, outside not only of our union but of our country."

Bolan had apparently forgotten all about, or had never read the anti-AWARE statement on the other side that had been sent to the membership at the same time. It had now become part of the record. Nizer reminded him of this fact. He hesitated a moment, then asked, with noticeable lack of enthusiasm:

Did you want the other side read, Mr. Nizer?

NIZER: I would like to read it, if you're not going to. I would like to read all of it.

BOLAN: These are for the resolution: "If you read the papers you know that the New York AFTRA membership voted 'Yes' to condemn the action of Aware, Inc. at the largest meeting in AFTRA's history. Actors Equity membership voted yes to condemn the actions of Aware in their last—

NIZER: May I read it please? May I have the privilege of reading the section, so that it is not read with less emphasis than the other side?

THE COURT: That statement is stricken out. Mr. Bolan, would you read it—maybe we're all getting hungry—read it a little louder and a little slower.

BOLAN: "Actors Equity Council unanimously voted yes to condemn the actions of Aware, Inc.

"The New York Times said 'Aware, Inc. condemned. Local members of the federation have scored Aware for promulgating smear tactics or lists in interfering in the internal affairs of the union.' Variety said, 'The resolution against Aware for adopting smear methods and blacklisting was passed on Tuesday. By Friday of the week three persons, one of whom had not acted on radio or TV for two years, was hired by an ad agency for a network show.' "

THE COURT: You'd better speak up a little bit.

NIZER: I would like to read this.

THE COURT: The last sentence I hardly got.

BOLAN: "By Friday of the week three persons, one of whom had not acted in radio and television for two years, was hired by an ad agency for a network show."

As I listened to Bolan reading the anti-AWARE statement, I could not for the life of me figure out why on earth he had ever allowed such a thing to get into evidence, let alone introduce it himself and stand up and read it.

Bolan then sought to introduce portions of the minutes of the two AFTRA meetings in 1955. These minutes contained charges by pro-AWARE members against the advocates of the resolution to the effect that an anti-AWARE vote would be serving the cause of international Communism. Nizer indicated that he would not object to the admission of the minutes into the record if Mr. Bolan would agree to our looking them over during the lunch hour. During lunch we went over them and realized that the contents of the minutes would serve our interests far better than those of the defendants. Bolan had overlooked the fact that these same minutes also contained some inspired invective against AWARE. These were speeches made by anti-AWARE union members at the two meetings. When court reconvened that afternoon, Nizer, with calculated casualness so as not to arouse Bolan's suspicions, told the court that so far as he was concerned, the minutes could be admitted since it would save the court's time by avoiding an argument over them. Bolan looked downright grateful for Nizer's accommodating gesture.

Bolan started off by reading from the minutes of the March 1955 meeting of AFTRA. He read a speech by Godfrey Schmidt, at that time president of AWARE, Inc., and a member of AFTRA. Schmidt had spoken at the meeting defending AWARE and its bulletin attacking AFTRA members who had been candidates against the AWARE-supported slate the year before.

BOLAN [reading from Schmidt's speech]: " . . . There is a clear intent expressed here in the anti-Aware resolution that another type of activity should be denominated blacklisting. That is to say, to tell the truth about candidates . . . The truth, ladies and gentlemen: Every single line in this is the unchallengeable truth, and the best proof of it that none of you will dare, if you feel aggrieved, bring it to court, as you could . . . I submit that Aware, which is also the recipient of some of these aspersions, can take care of itself. It has a fine set of principles and a good program, but it is the kind of thing that I need not bring here unless you want to. Thank you."

NIZER: May I read something from this same exhibit?

THE COURT: Yes.

BOLAN: I must finish it, your Honor. Your Honor, I will let Mr. Nizer read while I check my notes as to the pages.

NIZER: Thank you.

Lou then proceeded to read excerpts from the speeches of Miss Elaine Eldridge, an actress and member of AFTRA who said among other things:

NIZER [reading from Eldridge speech]: "I had no idea that Mr. Schmidt was here to espouse the cause of Aware, or what he calls the opposition to his sentiments as being necessarily Communistic, which I think is most unfair labeling anyone who opposes you . . . Forgive me, if I appear a little emotional about it, but I was one of the people named because I had accepted two years ago a telephone call which came to me from the National Committee of Arts, Sciences and Professions, asking me if I would be willing to teach on their staff. I said yes, and I went to one meeting at which the program was to be organized, and it fell through. I never heard anything further from it. That was two years ago, and today that organization is still not on the Attorney General's list. So I think it is a little presumptuous and perhaps a little premature on the part of Mr. Schmidt to consider all these people as dangerous and menaces to our society. I assure you that I don't think I am. I will let you be judge. Thank you." (Applause)

Lou then read portions of a speech by Miss Lee Grant, an actress.

NIZER [reading Miss Grant's speech]: "Miss Grant: I think Mr. Schmidt, in using the sentiments of anti-Communism which is nationally felt today, is covering the real purpose of Aware, Inc. It has been used by Mr. McCarthy, whom I do not agree with, but who Mr. Schmidt does agree with. He spoke at his rally in Madison Square Garden. . . . I think the fact that our board members [board members of AFTRA] are sitting with a man, Vincent Hartnett, who is the author of Red Channels and helped to put out lists is a shameful, shameful thing, and should not be tolerated in our union." (Applause)

Lou then read the entire statement of Leslie Barrett. It was a heartbreaking story of the punishment he received at the hands of Vincent Hartnett, who was attempting to connect him with a Communist May Day parade. Hartnett had written to Barrett saying he had a picture of Barrett marching in a May Day parade in 1951. Barrett, as it turned out, had never marched in any May Day parade at any time, but he had plenty of misery from Hartnett's charges. The jury leaned forward eagerly. Lou read on and on. From the speech of Mr. Harold Gary, Lou read:

". . . he [Schmidt] frequently uses the term 'Americanism' . . . I would like to know where Mr. Schmidt has learned his Americanism. When I learned about Americanism—and I like to think myself as a pretty good American—I learned nobody can appoint himself as a self-constituted judge and jury of his fellow man." (Applause) "I don't know how long you have been an actor, Mr. Schmidt, if you are one, but I want you to know that you're playing with dynamite, and only people who are duly authorized and licensed should be permitted to play with dynamite.

"An actor's career is very precariously perched. I have been an actor long enough to know that. The least bit of censure, whether justified or unjustified can ruin him, whether it is on moral, political or other grounds, and I think it is a horrendous thing, a criminal thing, for you to toy with other people's careers that they have given all their lives and emotions and study to. And the point is that not only are they involved, but also their families. This is a very dangerous business."

Bolan, of course, realized his mistake too late. I was still on the stand and he came at me.

BOLAN: Mr. Faulk, was the Lee Grant whose statement Mr. Nizer read the same Lee Grant who a few months ago took the Fifth Amendment—

NIZER: I object to that.

BOLAN: —when questioned as to whether she was a member of the Communist Party?

THE COURT: Mr. Bolan, that is sustained and in light of our discussion in the robing room, you should have understood not to put that question.

BOLAN: Your Honor, I take exception.

THE COURT: You cannot impute to the plaintiff the fact that somebody else took the Fifth Amendment.

BOLAN: I am not imputing to the plaintiff the fact that somebody else took the Fifth Amendment. The issue here is blacklisting, and I submit I am entitled to find out the background of the people who made the statements at the meetings.

THE COURT: No inferences are to be drawn from that question and I am now going to give the jury instructions about this Fifth Amendment business.

It has been held by our highest court that a person has the right to refuse to answer questions by pleading the Fifth Amendment, which is part of the Bill of Rights of our Constitution.

The Supreme Court of the United States has said, and I quote: "We must condemn the practice of imputing a sinister meaning to the exercise of a person's constitutional right under the Fifth Amendment."

The Supreme Court has also held that no inference of Communistic Party membership or of any subversive nature may be drawn from the exercise of the constitutional protection of the Fifth Amendment. Accordingly, no imputation may be drawn solely and in itself from the fact that a person has pleaded the Fifth Amendment and refused on that ground to answer questions by any congressional committee, meaning the Senate or the House of Representatives, and, obviously, this question was not even put with respect to the plaintiff, but somebody else.

Mr. Bolan, in a rather futile effort to undo some of the harm done by Nizer's reading, undertook to read some more of the pro-AWARE speeches. He read one by Rex Marshall, an announcer and a defender of AWARE. Marshall made some rather astonishing statements.

BOLAN [reading Marshall's speech]: "It seems to me that we're indebted to a group [Aware, Inc.] that gives its time freely to expose elements that are dangerous to this country and to this union. I don't think you can condemn a vigilante committee for being vigilant, but if it is accused of being a lynching committee, I think the accusation should be made properly by the persons who considered themselves in danger of lynching."

Marshall then made this breathtaking observation:

BOLAN [reading from Marshall's speech]: ". . . Until proper charges have been brought by those accused [referring to the people named and attacked by Aware in its bulletin] we can only assume that the accusations are justified and we should thank the people who are interested enough to give their time to look for our interest."

I noticed that the jury listened with considerable interest as Mr. Bolan read Marshall's observation that an accused person should be considered guilty until he had proved himself innocent. Bolan read the speeches of several others, including one by Mr. Vinton Hayworth, who at that time had been president of AFTRA and also a member of the board of AWARE. The reading of excerpts of Hayworth's speech seemed to affect the jury somewhat the way the reading of Marshall's speech had.

There were certain areas in which Mr. Bolan was not allowed to question me. The court's rules are such that a question may not be asked which implies something discreditable to the witness, unless there is substantiation for such a question. Despite this, during the next to the last day of my cross-examination (which had already lasted nearly two weeks), Bolan suddenly backed off across the courtroom and started firing a series of questions at me, very much in the manner of a prosecuting attorney. He was anxious to establish that I had talked with an investigator for the House Un-American Activities Committee in July 1955. Nizer was objecting all over the place lest the questions themselves imply to the jury that I had made admissions to the investigator that might be harmful to me. He made no effort to conceal his anger as Bolan persisted. Bolan's efforts backfired on him, though. Judge Geller interrupted with a statement that not only the jury, but the whole country needed to hear.

THE COURT: . . . As I have stated to you [the jury], the listing of any organization as an allegedly subversive or Communist front by a Congressional committee, and this applies also to any listing by the Attorney General of the United States, is simply an accusation, which is not a judicial determination and is not the result of a due process, by law.

The evidence to prove that it is a Communist front and subversive, not the mere fact that it was listed as such anywhere, must come forward here before you can find that it was a Communist-front organization. The fact that the listing is allowed into evidence for the limited purpose of the defendants' partial claim in mitigation of punitive damages, if there is such proof, that they relied on sources in making the charges against the plaintiff. Such listing does not go to the truth of the charge, but only as evidence offered by the defendants, if offered, with regard to their claim that if the charge is found to be false, they should not be found to have made it without an investigation or foundation, and that this should be taken into consideration, if you reach that point in fixing the amount, if any, of punitive damages against those defendants who are held liable by you.

So keep in mind as to the proof being offered concerning plaintiff's alleged participation in Communist front organizations, that proof satisfactory to you must be offered to show, (1) that he actually attended, entertained or contributed material, and not merely that it was advertised that he would so participate, or was reported that he would or did so participate, and if such actual attendance by plaintiff is not shown, then no further evidence may come, of course, may be given as to the function or organization, because it is plaintiff's knowing participation which is of vital importance to inquiry; and (2) that such organization is proved by proper proof to be a Communist front or subversive organization; and (3) that you must find from all the evidence direct or circumstantial, that plaintiff at the time of such participation had knowledge of such organization being a Communist front and subversive, and intended to aid it.

All these elements would have to be established before you may consider whether the charges that plaintiff was a pro-Communist with Communist affiliations and sympathies have been proved.

As we left the court that afternoon, Nizer commented to me, "Bolan used McCarthy tactics today; they will cost him dearly. He just ran the judgment up another million dollars with that vicious gambit."

Word came to us from Texas that Roy Cohn's office had contacted persons in Austin and that he himself was going down there to do a bit of investigating of me on his own. Actually it was Mr. Lang who went. Lou suggested that this was an act of desperation on their part, and that I should contact friends in Austin at once and find out as much as possible about Mr. Lang's activities there. It was possible he would find some shady character who would be willing to lend himself to the charge that I tried to persuade him to join the Communist Party, or had belonged to it with him, or something of the sort. During the 1950s the country had been treated to an endless parade of such witnesses before various committees. Nizer asked me to check with my contacts in the state and local police in Texas to discover if there were any professional informers to whom the defendants could go. I called a state official connected with the anti-subversive section of the state government in Austin and asked him if he knew of any Communists or ex-Communists in the vicinity. He thought for a long moment, and replied in his soft Texas accent, "Sure don't, Johnny. Know a couple of crackpot professors at the university, but they're harmless. About the nearest thing to a Communist we know anything about is a fellow down near Port Arthur, Texas, I reckon we could get in touch with him for you, if it's important." I thanked my friend and told him I didn't think it was that important. It turned out that Mr. Lang's trip to Austin was fruitless.

The cross-examination had begun to pall on me terribly. I had been subjected to Bolan for nearly two weeks and had reached the point where I did not sleep well at night, but I would lie in a semi-conscious state, fantasying sharp questions and feeble, vague answers. When, on Friday, May 11, Bolan announced he had completed his cross-examination of me, it was as though I had suddenly come to the surface after being under water for a long time.

Nizer, who I sometimes felt seemed unaware of the pressures I was under, patted my shoulder as we left the court and said, "I'm very proud of you, John. You have stood this ordeal with real honor. My secretary has bought a ticket for you on a plane to Texas tonight. I think you should go down there, relax with your family and friends, and forget all about this suit for the next two days." A number of times since, Nizer has done things like this. That weekend with my family and friends in Austin was so completely restful and rewarding that by Monday morning I felt as though I were going to the trial for the first time.

20

I got back to New York feeling refreshed. I was looking forward to getting down to the courthouse now that I could sit as a spectator, rather than as a witness.

I knew that we had lined up a formidable battery of witnesses who would take the stand and drive our case home. I intended to savor every moment of it. My active participation was over—or so I thought; it turned out that I was to be as involved as ever. I found out pretty soon that getting people to consent to appear as witnesses was just the first, and by far the least complicated, part of getting them on the stand. In the first place, there was the matter of preparing a witness, discovering exactly what information he could give and, just as important, what he would be allowed to say and how he would handle his cross-examination by Bolan. This preparation required infinite care. There was also a limit to the number of witnesses we would be allowed to call. This made it necessary to choose very carefully the ones we would use; they must be those who would lend the greatest possible weight to our cause.

Perhaps the roughest aspect of our witness problem was that of time. Most of the witnesses we planned to call were highly successful and enormously busy personalities. Their time was at a premium; they couldn't come down to the court and hang around the corridors outside the courtroom waiting to be called. It was necessary to time their arrival at the courthouse as nearly as possible with the moment they would be called to the stand. Lou could estimate fairly accurately the time a witness would require for direct examination, but only Bolan could know how much time he would devote to cross-examination.

When I got into court that morning, Charles Collingwood had just been sworn in. Paul Martinson and George Berger were in a sweat. Our next witness was supposed to be Tony Randall. He was flying to Greece early the following morning to work in a film. Collingwood was one of our key witnesses, and we knew his testimony would be lengthy. Whether Bolan would finish his cross-examination in time for us to put Tony Randall on the stand that afternoon was the problem. Tony, too, was an important witness, and we didn't want to lose the benefit of his testimony. Of course, all we could do was sit there and hope.

Charles Collingwood cut a fine figure on the stand. His distinguished and gentlemanly bearing, and his quiet, self-assured manner created a good impression, not only on the jury, but on everyone in the room with the possible exception of the defendants and their attorneys. I felt a surge of warm gratitude and pride as he testified in my behalf. Nizer carried him through an accounting of his days as a Rhodes scholar, a war correspondent and a serious student of international affairs. He had received countless awards for his distinguished broadcasts. He was solidly established as an expert witness qualified to estimate the damage my career had suffered. When Nizer got around to the affairs of AFTRA, the jury seemed to lean forward.

NIZER: You were a director and president of the union [AFTRA] from December 1955 until December 1956, is that right?

COLLINGWOOD: I was president of the New York local of AFTRA from December 1955 until the end of a one-year term.

NIZER: And you have continued as a member of the board until 1957.

COLLINGWOOD: Yes, when I left to take up my duties in London.

NIZER: Now, in the latter part of 1955, did you participate in the formation of what is called the Middle-of-the-Road slate of candidates of the New York local of AFTRA?

COLLINGWOOD: I certainly did.

NIZER: Were you the head of that slate?

COLLINGWOOD: I became the head of the slate after we had been elected.

NIZER: Were you elected by a large majority in the union?

COLLINGWOOD: The slate was elected by a very large majority, as is shown by the fact that out of 35 members of the board who were elected, 27 belonged to the Middle-of-the-Road slate.

NIZER: You were familiar with the program on which the Middle-of-the-Road slate ran and the principles which it announced?

COLLINGWOOD: Yes, I was.

NIZER: What was the occasion of the organization of the Middle-of-the-Road slate?

COLLINGWOOD: Well, as you may imagine, like most political processes, this didn't suddenly arise full bloom, and I think to explain that I must give a little bit of history of the union, if I may.

NIZER: Yes.

BOLAN: I object, your Honor.

THE COURT: Overruled.

COLLINGWOOD: During the 1950's the union membership became dominated by a self-perpetuating group who, among other things, made common cause with the various organizations who were interested in fighting, in their way, Communism in the entertainment industry, and this resulted in a process which is usually called blacklisting, in which the union was rather deeply involved.

Collingwood then related how the New York local of the union had in 1955 voted overwhelmingly to condemn AWARE, and that he and several others of us in the union had felt that with the election coming up in the fall, we should challenge the leadership of the union who had sided with AWARE.

COLLINGWOOD: . . . The vote of the referendum condemning Aware had strongly shown that the climate of opinion in the union was opposed not only to Aware, but to the leadership of the union and its close entanglements with the Aware group. It was a little difficult to round up a slate because in those days the penalties visited upon those who took issue with the leadership were very strong. They amounted to blacklisting, or at least they amounted to the threat of blacklisting. People in the union were afraid to run. They were afraid and concerned, and it was, as I said earlier, with some difficulty that we secured a full slate to run against the existing leadership of the union.

Over Bolan's objection, Lou was able to get Collingwood's testimony on the practices in the industry, when rumors or accusations brought a performer's patriotism into question.

COLLINGWOOD: It was very difficult at that time for anyone who had been charged by a private organization . . . such as Aware, or by important figures in the industry with some sort of Communist intent, however vague, it was very difficult for them to get employment, and there were many cases in which people did not know what had happened to them.

When Nizer got around to my reputation, Collingwood testified, again over Bolan's objections:

COLLINGWOOD: His reputation was very good. Although his main work had been done in radio, he had done a number of television programs, one of them was "It's News to Me," on which he was a panel member and was very good.

I have mentioned earlier my association with him on the "Morning Show," which was presided over by Jack Paar. He told the jokes and I told the news and sometimes we would have guests. Mr. Faulk was a guest, and, indeed, he substituted for Mr. Paar for a period of at least two weeks, in which he told the jokes and I told the news, and I may say that Mr. Paar is a very difficult man to follow. Mr. Faulk followed him admirably.

He then testified that my reputation for patriotism, loyalty and integrity was very high. He told how in April of 1956, after I had been attacked by Johnson and had begun to lose sponsors, he had asked for an appointment with Arthur Hull Hayes, who was at the time vice-president of CBS radio and general manager of CBS. He was presently president of CBS radio. Judge Geller allowed him to tell of his conversation with Mr. Hayes; but the judge first explained to the jury that neither Mr. Collingwood's opinion nor Arthur Hull Hayes's on what the damages done to me personally had been could be testified to.

COLLINGWOOD: There had been reports that as a result of the Aware bulletin, Mr. Faulk was in some trouble at CBS. So I asked for an appointment with Mr. Hayes. I was motivated not only by my friendship with Faulk, but as president of the New York local.

I went to see him for two reasons, one, to find out whether this was indeed the case, and, number two, to acquaint him with the attitude of the union.

I said that the union would take a very dim view indeed if, as the result of these allegations in the Aware bulletin, Faulk was severed from his employment with CBS. As far as I could see, the only reason that this might have happened was that he ran for and was elected an officer of the union, brought down Aware on his head, and if that were to happen to the first vice-president of the union, we would take a very strong view on it, that I would have to hold hearings because this would be a clear-cut case of blacklisting, to which the leadership of the union was opposed. . . . Mr. Hayes said that he was not about to be influenced by this kind of statement, that he felt that he was qualified to run his station and pick his performers without outside advice, and as long as Mr. Faulk's programs were good and as long as his sponsors stayed on, he would continue him in the capacity in which he was employed.

Nizer later asked him if Ed Murrow of CBS had conversations with executives of CBS in respect to my continued employment. Over violent objections, the court ruled that Charles could testify.

COLLINGWOOD: Mr. Murrow was active in Mr. Faulk's behalf, and I remember a conversation with Mr. Slate, who was the program manager of WCBS at the time, in which both Mr. Murrow and I urged that Mr. Faulk not be victimized because of these allegations in the Aware bulletin.

One of Collingwood's strongest bits of testimony came when Lou asked him:

What is the employment practice with respect to an artist who becomes involved in a controversy with respect to his loyalty?
BOLAN: I object.
THE COURT: Overruled.
COLLINGWOOD: Well, it really depends, Mr. Nizer, on how much guts the sponsor has, the network and the station, whether they have got enough guts to stand up to the pressures which are brought against them, or whether they don't. The time of which we are speaking, in most cases they didn't have very much guts.

Collingwood's testimony on the relationships between sponsors, advertising agencies, and performers was particularly persuasive.

COLLINGWOOD: Quite often performers were denied employment when it later turned out that the charges against them were unfounded. Therefore, it would appear to be pretty clear that actual guilt or innocence was not the controlling factor in the decisions that were made. . . . There were instances in which an actor, either because he was well connected or for some other reason, was brought before one of these persons charged by the organization for whom he worked for clearing of people. He was brought before them to explain. This was by no means, however, the universal practice. . . .

He [the accused actor] was not usually informed of the source of the charges, if they had not been made public.

By the time Collingwood's direct examination was completed, it was apparent from the faces of the jurors that he had scored heavily for us.

After lunch, when Bolan started his cross-examination of Charles, he apparently wanted to cast doubt on the relationship that Collingwood and I had had.

BOLAN: Now you have testified that you have been a friend of Mr. Faulk?

COLLINGWOOD: Yes.

BOLAN: Since when?

COLLINGWOOD: Since, oh, well, about ten years, I think, 1952, 1953, it must have been.

BOLAN: Have you ever been in his home?

COLLINGWOOD: Yes, sir.

BOLAN: How often?

COLLINGWOOD: Well, I suppose four, five times, in that order.

BOLAN: Has he been in your home?

COLLINGWOOD: Yes, he has.

BOLAN: About how often?

COLLINGWOOD: I should say three or four times, four or five, in that order.

BOLAN: Have you attended social functions with him, other than being in each other's home?

COLLINGWOOD: We found ourselves guests at the same social function, yes.

Bolan then tried to shake Collingwood's testimony as an expert witness on my abilities as a performer, but seemingly failed to do so. He then turned to the subject of other organizations than AWARE which had been engaged in blacklisting in the industry.

COLLINGWOOD: I am not aware of the whole spectrum, but there were people who organized themselves and presented information. There were letters from the American Legion and other groups referring to performers. There was an apparatus of pressure upon the network and the stations relating to their performers.

Bolan continued to press him to name other organizations aside from the American Legion. He did this, obviously, to discredit Collingwood's rather broad statement. This brought forth the following:

COLLINGWOOD: The principal one [blacklisting organization] from the point of view of the union, which was my immediate concern, was Aware, which had become an issue within the union. That there were others I had reason to believe, although I can't identify them for you, due to the inadequacy of my recollection.

Bolan then turned to the matter of Collingwood's testimony that morning on the subject of artists who had been discharged on unsubstantiated charges of disloyalty. He asked Collingwood if he could name one such artist.

COLLINGWOOD: I can certainly name one.
BOLAN: What was the name of the performer involved?
COLLINGWOOD: The performer was Mr. Leslie Barrett.
BOLAN: And is it your testimony that Mr. Barrett was discharged by reason of charges brought by the defendant Aware?
COLLINGWOOD: Discharged or had difficulty in gaining employment as a result.

And so it was that all the testimony on Barrett, which certainly was not flattering to the defendants, was reintroduced into the record.

Bolan then sought to establish through Collingwood's testimony that actually the main purpose of the Middle-of-the-Road slate had been to oppose AWARE.

COLLINGWOOD: Mr. Bolan, the union had been torn asunder. This local union of performers in radio and television had been torn asunder by a controversy over Aware, about issues involving the blacklisting, the supposed blacklisting, the fear of blacklisting, the union wasn't getting work done, it wasn't performing the functions which we felt a union should perform. We hoped that by this Middle-of-the-Road slate, a plague on both your houses, we would be able to clear the air for the resumption of normal trade union activities.

Late in Charles Collingwood's cross-examination, Bolan did a rather peculiar thing, which I still do not fully understand. He took the AWARE bulletin which had attacked me, Collingwood and Bean, and read what it said about Collingwood.

BOLAN (reading): "Will middler Charles Collingwood, new president of AFTRA New York, discharge his responsibility to enforce AFTRA's Constitution and National Rule? In a public statement of January 22, 1956, Collingwood did not show any knowledge that 12 members of his local had been identified as Communist Party members, and that 15, in all, had refused to answer when asked by the House Committee on Un-American Activities that they were Communists. Collingwood belittled the document findings of the House Committee, 1955 Annual Report, that there was a 'militant Communist faction in the New York local of AFTRA.'

"He stated, 'The blacklist is dying and the present officers of the majority of the New York local Board of AFTRA intend to do everything they can to assist the process.' "

BOLAN: Now, Mr. Collingwood, did you make a public statement on January 22, 1956?

COLLINGWOOD: Yes.

. . . .

It will be remembered that back in January 1956, shortly after the Middle-of-the-Road slate had taken over as officers of the New York

local, the House Un-American Activities Committee, in its annual
report, attacked our slate, and that Collingwood, on January 22,
1956, wrote a letter to the Committee repudiating its statements. For
some reason or other, Bolan wanted to get this letter into evidence. I
still don't know why in the world he wanted to do this. The letter
could certainly do no harm to our side. If anything, it would increase
Collingwood's stature in the eyes of the jury. I watched the jurors'
faces as Mr. Bolan read the letter. Several of them were gazing at
Collingwood on the witness stand with admiration.

BOLAN [reading Collingwood's letter of January 22, 1956]: "I have read
with amazement the quotations from the Annual Report of the House
Committee on Un-American Activities which deal with alleged Communism in the radio and television industry, with special reference to
conditions within the New York Local of the American Federation of
Television and Radio Artists.

"With the air of omniscience which has become traditional with
such documents, the report states that 'An investigation uncovered a
militant faction within the local, New York City, affiliate of the
American Federation of Television and Radio Artists.'

. . . .

"It is possible, of course, that the Committee has sources not available to the union. In that case it would seem to be the Committee's
duty to communicate to the union information that it 'uncovered.'
It is curious that, to the best of my knowledge the Committee in its
researches made no attempt to seek information from the officers or
paid executives of the New York Local of AFTRA. In its annual
report the Committee on Un-American Activities further states that
'The principal activity of Communists within AFTRA was against so-
called blacklisting. Through their campaign these Communists have
falsely convinced many fellow artists that they are denied employment if they at one time innocently supported a cause supported by
the Communist Party.'

"Now if the Committee on Un-American Activities really thinks
that the only people in the entertainment industry who are disturbed

by the excesses of blacklisting system are Communists or their dupes, then it is laboring under a misapprehension.

"Concern over the manifest inequities of the blacklist—"

NIZER: Iniquities.

BOLAN: "Inequities." Oh excuse me. "Iniquities of the blacklist is shared by the overwhelming majority of the performers and by, one suspects, a large proportion of the employers as well.

"No one in the industry wishes to have the Communist Party derive benefits from the employment in radio and television of actual dues-paying Communists, or desires to aid it or defend anyone who has been duly proven to be subversive. The New York Local of AFTRA has just elected, with the largest vote in its history, a slate of 27 officers and 27 board members, who ran as unequivocally opposed to the indiscriminate blacklisting as it now exists. There were no Communists among these elected, nor any dupes, either, and surely the electorate which swept them into office with an unprecedented large vote cannot be exclusively composed of Communists or deluded pawns, either.

"The Committee's report deplores indications that the blacklisting machinery of the industry is losing some of its force.

"It is my belief and fervent hope that this is indeed the case. The climate of opinion within the industry is changing. Perspective is returning. The blacklist is dying, and the present officers and the majority of the New York Local Board of AFTRA intend to do everything that they can do to assist the process.

"Now that people are beginning to look at these matters dispassionately, it is clear that the degree of Communist infiltration in radio and television was exaggerated from the beginning. This is not to say that the problem was not a real problem and may not be again.

"The safeguards which exist in our union's constitution in the normal management practices are more than sufficient to deal with the situation. It is regrettable that the Committee on Un-American Activities has painted a picture of the industry which is not only inaccurate, but tends to perpetuate rather than eliminate the abuses of the recent past."

BOLAN: Now, Mr. Collingwood, were you severely rebuked by the National Board of AFTRA for making such a statement?

NIZER: Objection, sir, both as to the characterization—
THE COURT: Reframe your question.
NIZER: And also because it is irrelevant.

After much wrangling between the lawyers, Bolan finally got a chance to read into the record for the jury's benefit the statement in the AWARE bulletin:

BOLAN (reading): "In public reply January 31, 1956, House Committee Un-American Activities Counsel Frank S. Tavenner told Collingwood the Committee's New York City hearings had 'established beyond any doubt the scope and the nature of concerted Communist activities in the entertainment industry and within the professional union.' He [Tavenner] continued:

"'The hearings leave no doubt as to the existence of such Communist Party faction and the recent election battle within your local further corroborates these findings.'

"Tavenner further states that 'There's no blacklisting at all . . .' "'It is significant to note that the election of the so-called anti-blacklist candidates in the recent AFTRA election (the middlers) has been greeted enthusiastically by the Communist front.'"

THE COURT: All right, now. The jury will also recall my extended remarks with respect to the Fifth Amendment and with respect to the accusations before the House Un-American Activities Committee. I don't have to go into it extensively at this point.

Luck was with us. Collingwood was dismissed from the stand in plenty of time for Tony Randall to testify. Tony was enjoying the success of a multitalented star of stage, screen and television. However, despite his considerable experience before audiences, it was quite obvious that he was nervous. Tony's testimony was brief but cogent. He told how he had been an active member of AFTRA, until AWARE became so dominant in its affairs, that he was afraid to attend meetings. As he put it, he "crawled under a rock and stayed there." Stayed there until AFTRA voted to condemn AWARE in 1955. After that he helped us organize the Middle-of-the-Road slate. His powerful voice impressed the jurors, as he testified. They liked him. Bolan, after a vain attempt to ridicule his "crawling under a rock," wisely dropped the cross-examination.

We spent that entire evening with Kim Hunter at Nizer's apartment. She said she was extremely nervous and looked on her forthcoming session on the stand with dread. All the same, she was determined to go through with it. Her anxiety seemed to stem, in good part, from the fact that she would be publicly testifying to having given way under Hartnett's threats, which placed her in an embarrassing position. Nizer assured her that the great courage and integrity she would display by her willingness to testify would win the warm approval of both the jury and the public.

When I arrived at the courthouse the next morning, the corridors were full of photographers waiting for Kim to appear; apparently it had leaked out that she would take the stand that day. As Nizer and Kim came down the hall, Lou refused firmly the photographers' requests for them to pose for pictures.

Our first witness that day obviously caught the defendants off guard. He was Tom Murray, the account executive at the Grey advertising agency. He had vital testimony to give. Throughout the trial, Mr. Bolan had been maintaining that Laurence Johnson had nothing to do with my being blacklisted and that we had no evidence connecting him directly with my case. Tom Murray was prepared to establish that connecting link. Murray had placed his career in the advertising industry at stake by coming forward as a witness. He was a gentle and quiet man, with a deep conviction, which became evident as he testified.

After giving his background and telling of his placing of Coca-Cola advertising on my program, he stated:

Mr. Faulk got more laudatory mail from listeners to the program than all other performers combined.

THE COURT: When you say Mr. Faulk got that, did he get it directly, or did you and Coca-Cola, the vice-president, get it, or both, or what?

MURRAY: It came to me, but it referred to Mr. Faulk.

Murray then told how he listened to my broadcasts regularly. Later, when he became an account executive in charge of the Hoffman Beverage account at the Grey advertising agency, he discovered that

I was advertising Hoffman beverages too. Nizer asked whether my performance for Hoffman beverages account was satisfactory.

MURRAY: It was more than satisfactory. It was as good for Hoffman as it had been for Coca-Cola.

NIZER: Now in March 1956 did you receive a communication from one Laurence Johnson?

MURRAY: Yes, I did.

NIZER: Tell us about it.

This was crucial testimony that was about to be given, and Bolan recognized it as such. He effectively and persistently objected as Nizer questioned Murray about the important facts of his conversations with Laurence Johnson. Murray testified that his conversations had taken place by telephone and in person. The court refused to allow Murray to testify as to the telephone conversation until Nizer elicited from him the fact that he could positively identify the voice on the telephone as Mr. Johnson's.

NIZER: Did you when you met Mr. Johnson subsequently refer to the telephone conversation? Did your conversation relate to it?

MURRAY: It did.

NIZER: Did Mr. Johnson, when you met with him identify himself as Laurence Johnson, the man who had called you?

MURRAY: Yes he did.

NIZER: Now will you tell us, please, on the first occasion when he telephoned you, what he said to you and what you said to him?

MURRAY: On the first occasion when I spoke to Mr. Johnson by telephone, he did not telephone me. I telephoned him in response to a message I received in my office saying that Mr. Johnson had called me while I was out of my office and would I please call him back at his hotel.

NIZER: Which you did?

MURRAY: I did, sir.

NIZER: All right, now will you tell us the conversation.

. . . .

MURRAY: First Mr. Johnson identified himself as Larry Johnson of Syracuse. He said that he owned several supermarkets and had influence over a number of others in central New York State. He gave me an indication of the total gross volume of food business that was done in the area and it was most impressive. It ran into the millions. I believe the figure was eighteen to twenty million dollars annually.

He then said, Mr. Johnson then said that he felt that it was a disgrace that our company was using a Communist, John Henry Faulk, to advertise its products.

I replied that I had no such knowledge about Mr. Faulk. And he said, "Well you had better get in line because a lot of people along Madison Avenue are getting in line and the display space which the Pabst Brewing Company has in the stores that I either own or control" is what he called "hard-won space."

THE COURT: What do you mean by "hard-won"—w-o-n, or o-n-e?

MURRAY: W-o-n. In other words, it had been difficult to achieve status that Pabst Brewing Company had in a display sense within his stores. That happens to be a very accurate statement, by the way.

NIZER: Now we will come back to what hard-won space is, but would you be good enough to finish the conversation for us.

MURRAY: I will. I said that I could not accept a telephone implication of this kind. I felt that there were legal ways of establishing whether or not Mr. Faulk—Mr. Faulk or for that matter, anyone else—was a Communist, and that I had no intention of firing or recommending the firing of a man who was a first-rate salesman for our product. Then he (Johnson) said, "How would you like it if your client were to receive a letter from an American Legion Post up here?"

And I said that I was a veteran myself and that I could not believe that the American Legion would lend itself to what I considered to be an obvious blackmail attempt, and he said, "Well, you will find out."

. . . .

NIZER: Now, what did you do immediately after you received this telephone call?

MURRAY: I went to my superior, Mr. Dalsimer. And I told him of this conversation. Mr. Dalsimer said to me, "This could be very serious. You had better get on it fast and do something about it."

NIZER: What did you do then?

MURRAY: I called the hotel again and asked to talk to Mr. Johnson.

There was no answer in his room. Then, because of the fact that it had been stated to me that this was indeed a serious matter, I think Mr. Dalsimer's phrase was . . . "This could be dynamite," and that was my cue to get on it and try to solve it. I got into a cab. I went to Mr. Johnson's hotel. I picked up the house phone in the lobby and asked to speak to him.

Again, no answer in Mr. Johnson's room. Then because, frankly I was very upset, I ran over to the desk clerk and said, "Can you help me find Mr. Larry Johnson. I have to find him." Then the clerk said, "He is standing right over there in the lobby with that other gentleman."

So I went over and I introduced myself to Mr. Johnson. I said, "I am the Tom Murray you talked to on the phone a while ago, Mr. Johnson, and I would like to discuss the matter with you further, the one that we talked about on the phone."

And Mr. Johnson said, "After the way you spoke to me, I want nothing further to do with you" and he turned and with his companion left the hotel.

.   .   .   .

NIZER: After your conversation with Mr. Johnson did your client, to your knowledge, the Pabst Brewing Company, receive a letter from an American Legion post in Syracuse?

MURRAY: It did.

NIZER: Was there attached to that letter a bulletin from Aware, Inc., which in this case has been marked Exhibit 41, but I show it to you to ask whether this is the original document that was received?

THE COURT: This very one? This is the original?

NIZER: This very one. This is the original.

THE COURT: All right.

NIZER: The letter of the American Legion and the annexed document as it was received, is this the original document that your client Pabst Blue Ribbon Company got?

MURRAY: Yes, it is.

.   .   .   .

NIZER: Did you show this letter to Mr. Dalsimer?

MURRAY: I most certainly did. As a matter of fact, we discussed it at some length.

. . . .

NIZER: What did your superior Mr. Dalsimer tell you to do?

BOLAN: I object your Honor.

THE COURT: Overruled.

MURRAY: He said that this was now even more serious than the situation had been before and that we would have to get an answer.

NIZER: An answer to?

MURRAY: An answer to the charges contained in the attached material.

NIZER: And did you take this letter to CBS?

MURRAY: I did.

NIZER: Did you personally deliver this original document, Exhibit 35, with the annexed Aware bulletin to anyone in CBS?

MURRAY: Yes, I did, to Mr. Sam Slate, who was manager of WCBS Radio.

Bolan, in his cross-examination, was most anxious to minimize the effect that Johnson had had on my loss of sponsors.

BOLAN: When Mr. Johnson said to you that Mr. Faulk was a Communist, didn't you ask him what the basis of his statement was?

MURRAY: I said I had no knowledge myself of Mr. Faulk being a Communist.

BOLAN: But you didn't ask Mr. Johnson what the basis—

MURRAY: Mr. Johnson had not qualified himself as an authority on such subjects. I thought he should be back wherever he comes from, selling baked beans, to tell you the truth. By what right does a grocer call me up and tell me so and so is a Communist, "get rid of him." I don't mind admitting I was kind of sore.

BOLAN: Then do you think Mr. Johnson was justified in not speaking to you when you saw him at the hotel?

NIZER: Objection, sir.

MURRAY: I can't characterize Mr. Johnson.

THE COURT: Sustained.

BOLAN: Did you insult Mr. Johnson during this telephone conversation?

MURRAY: That again would be a matter of interpretation. I don't think I did.

BOLAN: Did you tell him he should go back to sell baked beans?

MURRAY: No, I certainly did not.

BOLAN: Did you tell him that there were courts of law to determine whether a person was a Communist?

MURRAY: I did.

BOLAN: You didn't ask him what the basis of his information was?

MURRAY: No, I did not. He volunteered that Mr. Faulk had been written up in, I think, the "Daily Worker," or something like that, but that also cut no ice with me because Franklin D. Roosevelt was praised in the "Daily Worker."

After several more attempts to shake Murray's testimony, Bolan gave up, and Tom was dismissed from the stand.

Lou called another witness that the defendants did not expect, Samuel Dalsimer, Executive Vice-President of the Grey Advertising agency, and Tom Murray's immediate superior at the Grey Advertising Agency during the period about which Murray testified. He verified everything that Murray had said concerning Johnson's attempt to get the Hoffman Beverage account knocked off my show. It seemed that Dalsimer also had had a previous experience with Johnson, in 1952, when he was an account executive on the Block Drug Company account. Lou managed to introduce a letter which had been written in 1952 by Johnson to the Block Drug Company, and had Mr. Dalsimer identify it as one that he had read at that time. In the letter Johnson had threatened the Block Drug Company, producers of Ammnident tooth paste, which was advertised over a television program called *Danger*. The program had employed persons that Mr. Johnson described as "Stalin's little creatures." In the letter, Mr. Johnson suggested that perhaps he would get the veterans groups in Syracuse to conduct a poll in his supermarkets by placing a sign over the Ammnident display in the stores, asking the public if they wanted to buy products whose purchase price went to the international Communist conspiracy. On his cross-examination, Dalsimer readily admitted to Mr. Bolan that he did not care at all for Laurence Johnson.

Lou then called Kim Hunter to the stand. She was so nervous that

I became nervous myself. However, Judge Geller was very sympathetic. He understood that she was under a strain, and he said to her, "Miss Hunter, even though you are in a courtroom you can relax. Just assume that we are all in the living room. Just take it easy." Kim flashed him a gracious smile and somewhat more calmly testified to the innumerable Broadway plays, television shows and movies she had been in. She testified that she had appeared in the Broadway play *A Streetcar Named Desire,* which later earned her an Oscar for her performance in the screen version. This was in 1949. Nizer then asked her if she began to find that she was unable to obtain television appearances thereafter.

MISS HUNTER: It was a gradual awareness. It started in 1950.

BOLAN: Your Honor, I'm going to object to any testimony in this case long before any of the defendants were on the scene at all.

THE COURT: I am going to receive subject to connection and as indicated, subject to connection with defendants or a defendant with the same admonition that I made before with respect to the background material. I don't have to repeat it, but I made it just before when we had some other testimony through the last witness.

NIZER: You may finish your answer. You were saying there was a gradual awareness?

MISS HUNTER: Awareness of difficulties in getting employment from 1950 until 1953. There was, as I recall, a firm bit of awareness during 1952 when I was on a television program. I think it was the Celanese Theatre. I know the name of the play. It was "Petrified Forest." There were objections. From what? where? how? I don't know. I was never told. All I know is that my agent came to me and said—

BOLAN: I object, your Honor.

THE COURT: Sustained.

NIZER: Did your former employers report to you why they did not employ you during this period?

Kim did not want to discuss her former employer, or tell his name in open court. Bolan wanted the name. The court ruled that Nizer could not pursue the line of questioning unless Miss Hunter stated the name, and so that line of questioning was dropped.

The next day, however, Nizer asked the same question again, for during the evening Kim had had an opportunity to consult someone and she readily gave the name of the gentleman to whom she had talked about her being blacklisted, as William Dolger, at that time a top executive at CBS. Lou then elicited from her that she had gone to Dolger about getting work, and the court allowed her to tell about the conversation.

MISS HUNTER: I went to Mr. Dolger's office at CBS and talked to him. I can't remember the exact conversation but the substance of it was this, I am having difficulty getting employed, are you aware of that? And he said, "Yes, I am." And I said, because I didn't know who to go to—I wanted to know whether it was possible in any way for him to help me or advise me what I might do to clear away this fog.

THE COURT: What was his position at WCBS?

MISS HUNTER: At CBS he was an executive producer. I cannot remember the exact position.

NIZER: Producer of television shows?

MISS HUNTER: Yes.

NIZER: Go ahead, finish your answer.

MISS HUNTER: He said, "I am not sure that there is anything I can do, but if I possibly can do something, I will."

She then related how some months later Mr. Dolger had called her and given her one spot on a television drama. That was the only television work she had for the entire year of 1954. Lou then had her testify how, in 1953, her position against blacklisting had been well known, and further, that she had contributed to the fight against blacklisting. Then, after she had been completely blacklisted, her public-relations man, Arthur P. Jacobs, had written to Vincent Hartnett on May 12, 1953, trying to make some arrangement with Hartnett to let up on Miss Hunter, and as it turned out, Mr. Hartnett wrote back to Mr. Jacobs saying that he would investigate Miss Hunter, but there would be a fee of two hundred dollars connected with the investigation.

NIZER: Was Mr. Hartnett's request for $200 conveyed to you, Miss Hunter, at any time?

BOLAN: I object, your Honor.

THE COURT: Overruled.
MISS HUNTER: Yes, sir, it was.

. . . .

NIZER: What did you do with respect to that request?
BOLAN: I object, your Honor.
THE COURT: Overruled.
MISS HUNTER: May I explain that Mr. Jacobs called me on the telephone. We had a phone conversation in which he explained to me about the correspondence . . . and asked if I were willing to pay the $200 for information from Mr. Hartnett. I said that I would not, that my life is absolutely an open book, and I did not feel I needed Mr. Hartnett's information or investigation and I certainly wasn't going to pay $200 for it.
NIZER: And you did not?
MISS HUNTER: And I did not. However, Mr. Jacobs said "Please—"
BOLAN: I object, your Honor.
THE COURT: No, that is an answer.

Lou managed to get permission to read to the jury a letter which Mr. Hartnett had written to a Miss Geraldine B. Zorbaugh, general counsel for the American Broadcasting Company, on October 7, 1953.

NIZER (reading): "Dear Gerry, On October 2 (1953), I received from you the enclosed list of names for the purpose of evaluation. To keep my own records straight I note that on the list appeared the following names . . . and one of these names is Kim Hunter. . . . "In my opinion, finally, you would run a serious risk of adverse public opinion by featuring on your network Kim Hunter."
NIZER: Miss Hunter, had you known that Mr. Hartnett had written to the American Broadcasting Company to this effect? That they would have a serious risk if they ran you on their show?
MISS HUNTER: No sir, I did not know it.

Kim later testified that when the resolution to condemn AWARE had come up before the membership of AFTRA, Mr. Hartnett had called her and she had called him back late at night.

NIZER: Will you give us the substance as well as you recall and take it easy, Miss Hunter. Give us the substance of that conversation.

MISS HUNTER: The substance of it was that he said to show—kind of show my good faith, that I was truly a loyal American and not pro-Communist, that affidavits were not sufficient that I should by all rights do something actively anti-Communist and did I object to do any such thing, and I said, "No, certainly not."

He asked me then if I knew about the Aware resolution, the resolution to condemn Aware that was pending within our television union at AFTRA, and I said yes, I know about it.

And he said, well one way that I could show a strong anti-Communist stand would be to go to that meeting and speak up in support of Aware, publicly, in front of everybody.

I said, "Mr. Hartnett, it would be very difficult for me to speak in support of Aware because I am not in support of Aware, Incorporated."

He said, "Well, it wouldn't be necessary to support Aware, Incorporated, as such, and, in fact it wouldn't even really be necessary for you to go to the meeting, if you would be willing to send a telegram that could be read before the meeting publicly, speaking, saying in so many words that you are against this resolution to condemn Aware."

I said, "Mr. Hartnett, I will do my best to form a telegram."

NIZER: This was the time that you were having these difficulties getting employment?

BOLAN: I object, your Honor.

THE COURT: Sustained.

NIZER: I read from Mr. Hartnett's deposition [opening examination before trial] page 362, this question to Mr. Hartnett on the examination before trial: "Q. Did you ever ask an actor who was trying to clear himself from an accusation of pro-Communist affiliation and you were guiding him, did you ever ask him to demonstrate his reversal of view—"

THE COURT: We will have to have quiet. The people in the back of the room will have to be quiet.

NIZER: Excuse me, I will just pick this up. "Did you ever ask an actor who was trying to clear himself from an accusation of pro-Communist affiliation and you were guiding him, did you ever ask him to demonstrate his reversal of view, his patriotism, by voting a certain way in

AFTRA, in other words voting for an Aware group in AFTRA?"

BOLAN: I object, your Honor.

THE COURT: Overruled. You have a line of objection to this whole line of testimony, so we can move forward without interruption.

BOLAN: All right.

NIZER: "Q. Did you ever ask him to vote a certain way in AFTRA, in other words, voting for an Aware group in AFTRA? A. Yes I did. Q. Did you ever ask him to make certain speeches for the Aware group in AFTRA? A. On at least one occasion I did. Q. Who was that one occasion? A. Kim Hunter. Q. Did you do so as making that one of the tests of their clearing themselves, in other words, seeing the light of anti-Communism? A. I did."

NIZER: Now, Miss Hunter, did you thereafter send a telegram to the union?

MISS HUNTER: Yes, sir.

NIZER: Was there annexed, did you annex to a copy of that telegram a note to Mr. Hartnett?

This was objected to. However, Lou managed to get into the record a copy of the telegram Kim had sent to the membership of AFTRA. He read it aloud to the jury.

NIZER (reading): "To the membership: For your union to condemn Aware, Inc. shouldn't it also bring suit against Aware for libel and defamation of character? Is AFTRA prepared to follow this through to its logical conclusion? And what earthly good do we hope to accomplish for the union or its members by passing this resolution?

"I'm neither a member of Aware, Inc. nor a friend, nor am I in sympathy with any of its methods, but I urge you all to think very carefully indeed before voting for this resolution. The individuals hurt by Bulletin No. 12 have recourse to right any wrong that may have been committed, but AFTRA will have no recourse whatsoever if it places itself on record as protesting and aiding the Communist conspiracy, even if this action is taken in the noble desire to aid and protect the innocent. Signed, Kim Hunter."

And annexed to it, this is from Mr. Hartnett's files, May 25, 1955: "Dear Mr. Hartnett. Enclosed is a copy of the wire I sent to the AFTRA membership meeting last night. I was unable to attend the meeting so I have no idea whether it was read or not. Signed, Kim Hunter."

NIZER: After this date, did you get television appearances?

BOLAN: I object, your Honor.

THE COURT: Overruled.

MISS HUNTER: Yes, Mr. Nizer, I worked.

THE COURT: I didn't hear that. Did you finish your answer?

MISS HUNTER: I worked quite frequently after that and to the present date.

Kim's voice trembled as she gave this last testimony. The entire courtroom, including the jury, gasped. Lou then followed this by reading a letter from Hartnett to Laurence Johnson dated May 23, 1955, which ran:

NIZER (reading): "Dear Larry, Confidentially, I had a good telephone conversation this morning with Kim Hunter who just returned to New York from the Bucks County Playhouse. I stressed to Miss Hunter that she had [and "had" is underlined] to take a public stand against Communism. She assured me that she would do so and if she comes through tomorrow night at the AFTRA meeting as she promised she would do, you will hear the comrades shrieking all the way from New York to Syracuse.

　"The Kraft situation seems to me to be very much improved, thanks to you know who! Keep up the fight, Larry. You and your associates have done wonders. Sincerely, Hartnett."

After reading this, Nizer turned to Bolan and said, "Your witness."

Bolan, realizing what harm Kim's testimony had done in reference to the telegram Hartnett had forced her to send to the union, started his cross-examination of her on that subject.

BOLAN: Did Mr. Hartnett ask you to do anything you did not wish to do?

MISS HUNTER: Yes.

BOLAN: What was that?

MISS HUNTER: I did not really wish to go on record in my union as opposing the resolution.

Bolan then wanted to introduce an affidavit that Miss Hunter had given to Mr. Hartnett in 1955. Nizer objected to this unless a whole series of affidavits, the first in 1952 made by Miss Hunter, could be introduced in evidence. Bolan had not anticipated this. A Mr. Roy Brewer (whom Mr. Nizer described as "another Hartnett on the West Coast; he does the clearance and he tries to pass people, and he worked with Hartnett") and Hartnett had gotten together and obtained from Miss Hunter the series of affidavits. As Lou explained to Judge Geller outside the hearing of the jury, "In the endeavor to get Miss Hunter to comply with what they demanded as a clearance for her, she had to make a whole series of affidavits. I have them here, all sworn to. They have tried to present the last one that they accepted from her. I say that it is incomplete under the context of the circumstances, and that either they offer all of them to show how she was squeezed, otherwise I object to the whole thing."

Kim testified that back in 1953 a Roy Brewer out in Hollywood had suggested that she work with him on an affidavit that would meet Mr. Hartnett's specification and remove her from the blacklist.

Bolan read her affidavit to the jury. It was a lengthy, grim recital, obviously written under great stress. In it she protested her patriotism and stated her loathing of Communism. She told how she had lent her name to several causes, back in 1949 through 1952, which were of dubious nature in the eyes of AWARE and like folk. She had endorsed a couple of peace conferences and had signed a petition asking clemency for a condemned Negro in Mississippi, Willie McGee. She told how she had committed the grievous error of not realizing how sinister the Communist influence was and that she hoped that she could be forgiven and thenceforth would never again be duped. During Bolan's reading of the long, long affidavit, Kim dropped her eyes and seemingly had to restrain herself to keep from weeping. When Bolan had finished cross-examining Kim, Lou took over her redirect examination. He went directly to the matter of the series of written statements that Kim had given under pressure, starting back in 1953. She testified that Roy Brewer of Hollywood had assisted her in these statements. He would consult with Hartnett and then advise her on what she would have to say in each succeeding statement to meet Hartnett's requirements. The affidavits were not introduced, but

Kim's testimony about each revealed how, in each succeeding one, she had to bow a little lower to Brewer and Hartnett's demands.

During her entire ordeal upon the witness stand, Kim had fought back tears as her testimony and the documents introduced revealed how she had been punished in the past years. She was excused from the witness stand late in the afternoon and came over to me at the counsel table, and embraced me warmly.

Murray Kempton was impressed with Kim Hunter's testimony, as well as Tom Murray's. Of Kim's, he wrote, in his *New York Post* column:

WONDERS . . . Beating proud and defenseless women to their knees. Extorting confessions from people who know they have done no wrong. It is our saving grace that there is something in the Kim Hunters and the Johnny Faulks that such wonders can sometimes bend but never break. She sat there yesterday, in a place which could hardly be convenient to her yet, and Louis Nizer asked if she regretted signing a petition for Willie McGee. All our saving grace came strong and clear in her answer, "I certainly do not."

On Tom Murray's trenchant comment on Johnson, "I don't want a grocer calling me up and telling me someone is a Communist," Kempton wrote:

Thomas D. Murray exists as proof that no one can draw an indictment against an entire profession. He is a short and pleasant man, but there are refreshing traces on his person and in his voice of a capacity for indignation unadjusted to the rules of his calling. There are few heroic trades, and advertising is hardly one of them. Still, advertising can be proud of Tom Murray. Yesterday, he stood up in court and testified against a blacklister, and one brave man per profession is not so far below the national average.

21

The newspaper accounts of the trial were stirring up widespread interest in the case. Nizer's office began to get calls from people volunteering information, many anxious to come as witnesses. It was our strategy to ring the defendants round with an iron band of vital testimony by impressive witnesses. This called for great care and discretion in the selection of witnesses. Each must be able to contribute something new and important. So, for the most part, Lou concentrated on those witnesses we had already lined up.

One caller was Harvey Matusow, who suggested that while he would not be a suitable witness—he had been jailed on a perjury charge—he could direct us to a witness who would be very valuable. In the early 1950s, he had been an informer for the F.B.I.; later a professional witness for the HUAC and for cases involving persons charged with subversive activities. He had worked closely with Senator McCarthy and with Roy Cohn, and he had later become a close friend of Laurence Johnson. Johnson had insisted that a certain advertising agency employ Matusow for the purpose of checking on the patriotism of performers before they were employed on its radio and television shows. Matusow had long since repented his part as an informer. As part of his recantation, he alleged that Roy Cohn, while an assistant United States Attorney, had suborned him to testify falsely in a pending criminal action. Matusow was charged with perjury and convicted, and he spent three years in prison. Now he told us of one particular case involving a Frank Barton, of the Lennen & Newell advertising agency, and he gave a detailed account of a luncheon meeting at which he and Barton and Johnson came to an agreement on a procedure for dealing with performers whom Johnson found undesirable. It Matusow's account of the meeting with Johnson was accurate, Barton certainly could be an important witness. We reached him at his agency. He was a vice president, a conservative gentleman, and a man of unimpeachable integrity. But he did not want to become involved; it seemed unlikely that we could get him to testify.

While Lou was trying to persuade Mr. Barton, he put other witnesses on the stand who had had experience with Johnson and blacklisting. One was Himan Brown, a very successful producer and director and packager of shows. He had produced or directed such shows as *Inner Sanctum, The Thin Man, Bulldog Drummond,* and many, many more. He testified that back in 1952 he was producing and directing a radio series called *The Private Files of Matthew Bell.* The series was sponsored by the Seabrook Farms, and the advertising agency that represented Seabrook Farms was Hilton & Riggio. Brown told how in 1952 he had received a telephone call from Harvey Matusow, who invited him to a conference with Mr. Johnson to discuss some important business. Brown met Johnson and Matusow at a midtown hotel.

BROWN: Mr. Johnson told me that I was using the wrong people, actors, who were Communist-fronters, actors with Communist affiliations, and that unless I used the right actors by his lights, meaning people with other affiliations, as he described them, I would be very much in danger of losing sponsorship and losing my position with this particular client.

NIZER: Which client is this?

BROWN: The Seabrook Farms people. He had already written to them and threatened them to take all of their display of his merchandise out of his markets.

. . . .

NIZER: What markets are you referring to?

BROWN: In Syracuse, he [Johnson] had several supermarkets in Syracuse. He further went ahead to tell me that there are other supermarkets because there were some affiliations and associations where he carried a great deal of weight, that these people would listen to him, and the third thing which he stressed to me was that the American Legion Post in Syracuse would also flood the sponsor with letters to let them know that I was out of line or that I was doing the wrong thing using Communist front actors.

Brown testified that Laurence Johnson was not only *against* certain people, he was *for* some people too. For instance, he suggested that Brown should hire actors like Frank Pulaski, Vinton Hayworth and Ned Weaver. On his cross-examination, Bolan asked Brown if he had been listed by Hartnett in *Red Channels*. Brown said that he had, that one of the charges that had been listed against him was that he had sponsored a dinner for Governor Lehman and Senator Mead of New York in 1947.

BOLAN: Well, do you have a personal hatred of Mr. Hartnett?
BROWN: I have.

Peter Hilton, president of the advertising agency, Kastor-Hilton, was then called to the stand. He testified that he had been an advertising man for thirty-one years on Madison Avenue and that he had been the Hilton of Hilton & Riggio, the agency which had the Seabrook Farms account in 1952. Mr. Hilton was a personable and handsome advertising executive, and he seemed to be at ease on the witness stand. One felt that he was almost eager to give the testimony that Nizer was asking him to give. He too had met Laurence Johnson in connection with the Seabrook Farms account.

HILTON: After the program was on the air for three weeks I received a telephone call from C. F. Seabrook, who was the president of Seabrook Farms, advising me that he had received a letter from Laurence Johnson on the letterhead of the American Legion Post in Syracuse, raising the question as to whether or not Seabrook was aware that it was sponsoring a program featuring Joe Cotton [Joseph Cotten] and produced by Himan Brown. They were advancing the cause of Stalin's little creatures, as he quoted.

. . . .

Johnson indicated that if Seabrook was aware of what it was doing that he, operating supermarkets in Syracuse, would see fit to boycott

Seabrook Farms products and, furthermore, would make other supermarket operators aware of what he was doing and the reasons for doing
it. This, naturally perturbed Seabrook very much and he looked to me,
since I had recommended the program, to determine what it was all
about.

Mr. Hilton then testified that he had gone to M.C.A., who had
booked the program and who represented Joseph Cotten. Mr. Cotten had come to New York and, with Mr. Hilton, Mr. Seabrook and
an attorney for Seabrook, flew up to Syracuse to see Mr. Johnson in a
Seabrook Farms plane.

HILTON: We proceeded from the airport in Syracuse to Johnson's office,
which was in the rear of one of his supermarkets. When we arrived,
after some very stiff formalities, since it was almost noon we adjourned
to a nearby restaurant, and at that time Mr. Seabrook took the initiative and indicated to Mr. Johnson that he, personally, was very much
against anything that might be tinged with Communism. He cited the
record of Seabrook Farms throughout the war and indicated that he
would not knowingly support anything that might foster or help a
known Communist. On that occasion, as a peace offering and as an
indication of good faith I suggested that one of the commercials of the
three commercials we had on our Sunday afternoon program be devoted
to an institutional message indicating the bounty of America, the need
for protecting its free institutions.
     Mr. Johnson felt that that was a very good idea and it lessened the
tension.
NIZER: Now, before you made this suggestion, this compromise or resolution, did Mr. Johnson indicate that he would let up in his boycott,
as you call it, against Mr. Cotten?

Hilton said that Johnson had not been so easily persuaded about
Cotten, saying that Mr. Cotten's record spoke for itself.

NIZER: Did Mr. Cotten speak up in his defense, as to his Americanism?
HILTON: Mr. Cotten protested vehemently.

. . . .

Cotten went on at length to cite the work he had done during the war, and he had come prepared for that meeting with letters attesting to that fact and detailing trips that he had made entertaining the troops and engaging in war bond drives and the like.

He also related—there was an organization in California—the name of which I didn't remember, which he had been identified with some years before and it was this organization that was cited by the Un-American Activities Committee and with which he was identified. He explained his membership in that as long predating the period when it was cited.

NIZER: Did Mr. Johnson when he referred to the record testify anything particularly?

HILTON: No he did not.

NIZER: He just referred to the record?

HILTON: That is right.

. . . .

NIZER: After he [Cotten] made his reply did Mr. Johnson make any statement accepting that reply or rejecting it?

HILTON: Again, in the same spirit, he said that he had only the record to go by and he had to make his judgment as to who was American and who was not American by the record.

. . . .

NIZER: Did you leave immediately for the airport to go back?

HILTON: We left shortly after lunch and on the way to the airport passed a Johnson supermarket. Mr. Johnson asked if we would be interested in seeing it. We did. We stopped. We toured the supermarket, met his managers, and Joseph Cotten autographed some, gave some signatures to customers.

Johnson had agreed to let the program stay on as long as it included the patriotic commercial. Nizer now asked Hilton how the program fared after the attack.

NIZER: Did you have any conversations with the sponsor concerning the continuation of the program?

HILTON: Yes.

NIZER: What were they?

HILTON: In view of the problems that had arisen with it the sponsor indicated very clearly that he had no interest in continuing beyond the thirteen weeks that we were committed to.

Mr. Hilton testified then that somewhat later the series was canceled, and his agency lost the Seabrook Farms account. He attributed this to the attack by Laurence Johnson.

Our next witness was Richard Allen, former assistant business manager of the Metropolitan Opera. He testified that he had received threatening letters from the American Legion Post in Syracuse concerning Jack Gilford, and that Johnson himself had stormed into his office in 1951 and demanded that Mr. Gilford be dropped from the Met production of *Die Fledermaus* before it came to Syracuse. Mr. Johnson claimed to be deeply concerned about the welfare of his daughter, whose husband was in Korea at the time.

ALLEN: He dwelt a great deal on the emotional aspects of the position this woman was in, with her husband overseas, fighting against Communism, and we were importing Jack Gilford to Syracuse with this alleged Communistic taint. . . .

When Bolan asked if the Met considered a man's invoking the Fifth Amendment as a factor in hiring him, Mr. Allen replied without hesitation:

There was never any experience in this at all. The Metropolitan Opera in casting for any given season would be guided, first, of course, by artistic standards and then by the fact that an artist would be a member in good standing of one or more unions.

Mark Goodson was one of our star witnesses. He was one of the most distinguished producers in TV, and he had employed me a number of times over the years. Mark testified that he was the president of Goodson-Todman Productions, and told of his long-time experience in the field of quiz and panel shows: his company had produced such TV landmarks as *What's My Line, I've Got a Secret,*

The Price Is Right, and *To Tell the Truth,* and many other shows. Nizer was eager to have the jury get the full impact of Mark's eminence in the field of television, but he hurried through his direct testimony. He wanted to leave Bolan plenty of time in which to complete his cross-examination, for he had promised Mark he could leave that evening for Hollywood. After getting from Mark some of the dozens of awards he had received, Nizer started on Mark's experience as an employer of performers.

Mark testified that he had possibly hired more performers in his years as a producer than had Susskind. He confirmed Susskind's testimony by describing the system of "clearance" in greater detail. Lou asked him to elaborate on the television industry's practice of having producers submit, for approval, or clearance, names of performers to be used. After Mark had explained that the names of everyone he used had to be submitted to the network upon which his show was appearing or to the agency that represented the sponsor, he said:

> . . . Actually, no one ever went into the specific details and openly called it what it was, but before people were used they would be called on the phone, either to the network or the advertising agency, or a general list would be submitted, and then if there were objections to any of the people on the list there would come back either a phone call, more often a phone call, or another list written, and a notation would be made that these people are unacceptable. No great conversation was gone into as to why they were unacceptable, but it was understood that it was because of political reasons.

. . . .

> Let me give you a couple of examples of how it might be done. I will not mention names but assume that a certain week was coming up on a program and a new panelist or a mystery guest was going to be put on. A phone call would be made by one of the [Goodson-Todman] staff and say "Is this person all right?" And the answer might come back, "Yes, fine," or "We will have to check into it further," and, perhaps, an answer would come back in a couple of days, "Forget it. Don't use that person."

In certain instances we found this was very difficult to work with, and so a long list might be submitted and say "Just go down this list and let us know who we can work with or not," and back would come four or five checks and perhaps on the phone they would say, "The following five people should be eliminated from your consideration."

It was well known to the jurors, as well as to everyone else in the courtroom, that most of the Goodson-Todman shows were on CBS network, so there could be little doubt that Mark was making a rather vital point for us. CBS had engaged in the practice of blacklisting artists. Mark then made another important point:

NIZER: Was it the general practice for the producer or packager to be informed as to the specific grounds on which an artist was not passed?
GOODSON: It was not.

Nizer then produced a letter written by Laurence Johnson to Gilbert Swanson, of C. A. Swanson and Company, dated December 26, 1953. The Swanson company was at that time sponsor of the Goodson-Todman television panel show *The Name's the Same*. The letter from Johnson protested the appearance of Miss Judy Holliday on the program as a guest celebrity.

GOODSON: After Miss Holliday was used we were rebuked for the use of Miss Holliday by the advertising agency, who thought that we had made a serious mistake.

. . . .

NIZER: Mr. Goodson, was Miss Holliday used again on this program?
BOLAN: I object.
THE COURT: Overruled.
GOODSON: She was not.

Lou then turned his attention to the unemployability of an uncleared performer.

NIZER: Can you state with reasonable certainty whether, if a performer becomes controversial in the sense of his or her patriotism being involved, such performer—can you state with reasonable certainty the general practice as to whether such performer can obtain employment in the television and radio industry, generally, as a trade practice.

. . . .

GOODSON: Yes, I would say in general that nonclearability meant unemployability.

NIZER: Does it matter, in giving your answer—can you state with reasonable certainty what the practice was whether the innocence or guilt of that performer were established or not?

. . . .

GOODSON: Well, the innocence or guilt was never brought up, Mr. Nizer, because the facts of the matter were never discussed. When a name was not cleared it was difficult to get further information. We tried on occasions and in certain instances were able by virtue—

BOLAN: I object.

THE COURT: Overruled.

BOLAN: Not responsive.

NIZER: I submit he should finish his answer.

THE COURT: Let him answer.

GOODSON: And in certain instances were able by virtue of pressure and argument to convince the network or agency that the person should be permitted to go on.

Nizer then had Mark testify as to the difficulties they had with Abe Burrows when he was a panelist on *The Name's the Same.*

GOODSON: Starting in December 1951 we began to get mail protesting his appearance and it seemed to us to be what I would call organized mail, that is, you could tell by the quality of the postcards addressed to you that the phrasing is generally similar, so it looks as if the mail is organized as opposed to individuals writing on their own. As this mail grew I talked to our people about this and I brought Abe in.

NIZER: Abe Burrows?

GOODSON: Abe Burrows in, and I said, "We're getting a lot of mail on you. What does this mean? What is the story on it?"

Mark told how Abe had answered all his questions to his own satisfaction and that they had put up a battle for him. However, the mail continued to pour in.

GOODSON: Mr. Swanson then called me on the phone and said, "I would like to come into New York and see you about this Abe Burrows matter because we are getting mail here too." So I met with Clark Swanson. He came to see me, and Clark Swanson, who was the president of the company, discussed this with me. The advertising agency was not present, and we agreed together—as a matter of fact he said, "I think that Abe—I have to say—I think that Burrows is O.K. as far as I am concerned, and I think I'm going to ignore this mail. I think he is all right. Let's continue to use him."

About three months after that he called me from Omaha and he said, "I have just received a call from a Laurence Johnson, Syracuse, New York. Do you know him?" I said, "No, I don't. I have heard about him." And he said—

At this point Judge Geller cut Mark off, saying that he could not testify as to what Johnson had told Clark Swanson, nor what Clark Swanson had said to Johnson. However, he was allowed to continue with his firsthand testimony.

GOODSON: I will only say then, if I have to eliminate what he told me, that Mr. Johnson told him, that the net result was that Clark Swanson regrettably felt that he had now to accede to the pressure, that we would have to drop Abe Burrows, and I came to Burrows and I told him the full facts and he agreed that in the light of the pressure which was being threatened that I agreed that Swanson, who had been very decent up to this point, could not stand up under it.

NIZER: And did Mr. Burrows still state that he was innocent of any Communist affiliations?

GOODSON: Yes he did.

NIZER: Was the pressure, without giving us the conversation, did it involve the taking off of the goods of the Swanson products?

GOODSON: It was precisely the same as you read in your letter about Judy Holliday.

Mark then testified as to the sensitivity of the networks and agencies to protest mail and to pressures generally. He summed the whole thing up for the jury and the court.

GOODSON: A sponsor is in business to sell his goods. He has no interest in being involved in causes. He does not want controversy.

NIZER: He does not want what?

GOODSON: Controversy. The favorite slogan along Madison Avenue is "Why buy yourself a headache?" The advertising agency's job is to see to it that the products are sold but that the sponsor keeps out of trouble, and an advertising agency can lose a great deal, it can lose the account. The sponsor can lose a little bit of business, but he still can recoup it. The agency can lose the account and I would say that a great portion of an agency's job is concerned with the pleasing and taking care and serving a client.

So I think in many instances, the clients were perhaps even less aware of all this than the advertising agency, which considered one of its principal jobs keeping out of trouble, just keep out of trouble. I don't think that they took a political position. I think it was apolitical. It was just anti-controversial.

. . . .

Given the choice between performer A who is noncontroversial, and performer B, about whom there is any kind of a cloud whatsoever, the natural instinct on a common-sense business basis is to use the non-controversial personality. Again, a favorite saying is, "There are a lot of other actors, a lot of other performers. Why bother with this one? Why buy this headache?"

Mark was now at ease, speaking as an expert, and Nizer took advantage of the favorable impression he was making on the jury to drive home a strong point as to my capabilities as a panelist. Bolan had, of course, been playing down my television performances. So it was with considerable satisfaction that I heard Mark tell the jury how I had been a regular panelist along with Quentin Reynolds, Anna Lee, Kitty Carlisle, and at times Nina Foch, Moss Hart, Russel Crouse, on a Goodson-Todman show *It's News to Me,* which had been on CBS network from 1951 to 1954, with John Daly as the moderator.

GOODSON: I think that Johnny Faulk was a very good performer. He falls into the classification of what I would call a talker. There are actors and there are singers and there are what Fred Allen once called "pointers" like Ed Sullivan and there are talkers.

Now the talker was a type of personality who developed in the early fifties in television, who could play games, who could ad-lib and who had a definite personality, and Faulk's capabilities were in all these areas. He was a good talker. He had a capacity to play our games and he was what I would call a country-style personality. He was a Will Rogers, Herb Shriner, rural-boy type. He was like a country boy lost in New York, surrounded by the city folks and with it a certain kind of urbanity that came through because Johnny had been a teacher and knew what he was talking about, and this is what made up the particular things that Faulk delivered.

Nizer then established that a panelist on a network show was receiving several times as much today as he was in the early Fifties. Moreover, a panelist on a network show usually had many other sources of income. Mark testified, for instance, that Tom Poston, who was on *To Tell the Truth,* made much larger amounts of money making pictures and acting in summer stock; Arlene Francis made a movie in Munich; and most of the Goodson-Todman panelists were engaged in many other activities, which brought them huge incomes. Then Nizer asked him a question which elicited an effective answer, but which somewhat chilled my blood.

NIZER: You have told us about marquee value. Suppose a performer like John Faulk ceases to appear on television, beginning on February 10, 1956, and hasn't had any television appearances, assume this, with the exception of one Jack Paar appearance at night, between 1956 and th/t date, and assume further, sir, that—

THE COURT: 1956 and this date?

NIZER: To this date—leave out other assumptions for a moment and assume that he wanted to or could pick up, assume that whatever difficulty there existed was cleared away and that he could pick up his employment again, that he could be employed in television, could he start where he left off—

BOLAN: I object.

NIZER: Or can you state with reasonable certainty on that assumption whether the general practice in the industry is that having been off for these years there is an effect upon him?

BOLAN: I object.

THE COURT: Overruled.

GOODSON: You will agree, Mr. Nizer, that that is a difficult question, but I would be able to state that if a person has not been exposed for any substantial period of time his value is definitely diminished. He becomes, in effect, an unknown all over again, and it is harder today to start an unknown than it was back in the 1950s when prices were lower, how he would be able to start again, he would certainly not be able to pick up where he left off. Possibly he could pick up—No, I can't even say he could pick up with the original salary, because those payments would not be appropriate today, but he would certainly have lost because of the lack of exposure over the years.

This testimony was helping to establish my damages, of course, but it was something of an emotional bump for me to sit there and hear stated aloud from an authority what I had secretly been fearing to face myself. The next was a key question:

NIZER: At the present time, and limiting yourself for the purposes of this question, to television performers who were talkers, as you put it, the same kind of talent, can you state with reasonable certainty, based upon your knowledge and experience in the industry, what the earning capacities, men similar to these talents, what they earn in television work?

BOLAN: I object.

THE COURT: Overruled. Talking generally now, talkers. We are not talking of anyone in particular.

GOODSON: Yes, I am not giving away any trade secrets about any particular performer, although the figures I will talk about are actually earned by various people. I would say that somebody in Faulk's—

THE COURT: No, no, that is not the question.

GOODSON: You don't want that?

NIZER: That would be the next question.

GOODSON: You want Faulk out of this?

THE COURT: We want areas of earnings.

NIZER: Areas of earnings for similar kind of performers in television.

BOLAN: I object.

THE COURT: Overruled.

GOODSON: Anywhere from—

NIZER: Yes?

GOODSON: One hundred thousand dollars up to a million dollars a year if you're talking areas.

NIZER: In your opinion does Mr. John Henry Faulk fall into the category which you have generally described with these wide limits of potential earnings?

BOLAN: I object.

THE COURT: Overruled.

GOODSON: I would say that, if I can say it, that Faulk would have fallen probably between the $150,000 and $500,000 mark if he had continued as he was.

NIZER: A year?

GOODSON: A year.

NIZER: Annual earnings?

GOODSON: A year.

NIZER: Your witness.

BOLAN: Your Honor, if there is going to be a recess I would like to, before we have a recess—

THE COURT: No, we are not. It is Friday and I want to keep my promise to the jury, particularly on Friday, if I can.

Lou had told us the night before that Mark Goodson was going to be one of our most effective witnesses, and Mark was certainly proving that prediction correct. Lou had commented, too, that Bolan, probably realizing that Mark was outstanding in his field, would not undertake to discredit him on cross-examination. It would be too dangerous. Mark was quick and completely sure of himself in the matters on which he was giving testimony, and Lou speculated that Bolan would in all likelihood back away from him. However, as it came time for the cross-examination, it was obvious that the testimony Mark had just completed had cut too deeply into the defendants' case. Bolan, being the able lawyer that he is, knew that he would have to mitigate its effects on the jury, if possible. He went about the job with a will, hitting Mark with such questions as:

BOLAN: With respect to the panelists on "What's My Line," they earn from that show between one hundred fifty thousand and a million, each of them?

GOODSON: No they do not, I didn't understand that was the question directed to me.

BOLAN: Just answer my question.

GOODSON: The answer is no, they do not indeed.

And shortly afterward:

BOLAN: You mentioned one of these talkers. Herb Shriner was a talker?

GOODSON: Yes.

BOLAN: Is he active in television today?

GOODSON: To my knowledge—

NIZER: I object to that as immaterial. There may be many reasons—

THE COURT: I will allow it.

GOODSON: To my knowledge he is not active in television today, for the moment.

Then, with what I knew was a reference to the defendants' contention that my alleged falling ratings had caused my dismissal from CBS, he asked if Mark put much store by ratings.

GOODSON: If we don't, the sponsor certainly does, and the network does —yes, the ratings are of concern.

BOLAN: Would you say they are a very important fact with respect to the continuance of a television or radio program?

GOODSON: Yes they are.

Bolan ventured into the area of blacklisting, and at this point Mark came back with some stinging answers. It seemed to me that Bolan was getting the worst of the exchange, for his questions were eliciting answers from Mark which re-emphasized our position. When asked again about the practice in the radio and television industry, Mark answered sharply:

> The practice in the industry, sir, was that people were not cleared and that nobody ever said why. Now, if you asked what the general understanding was as to why this was going on—it was because we knew that there were organizations that were listing these people as having left-wing or, if you will, left-wing and Communist associations.

. . . .

BOLAN: . . . Was it the practice of the industry to reject a performer who had invoked the Fifth Amendment when questioned on Communist Party membership?

GOODSON: I really must say, again, Mr. Bolan, that we were not told what the criteria were, nor were we told when a man had taken the Fifth Amendment. I cannot say what the backstage, inner workings of the little committees that made these decisions were.

. . . .

BOLAN: Just so I am clear, are you saying then that you don't know exactly what this blacklisting procedure was?

GOODSON: The procedure?

BOLAN: You weren't told why?

GOODSON: What the criteria were?

BOLAN: Yes?

GOODSON: No, we were not told.

BOLAN: Is your objection that you weren't told?

GOODSON: My objection, sir, is to the fact that we were on several grounds, which is what I started to answer a while ago.

BOLAN: Yes.

GOODSON: My objection is one, to the fact that there was a handing down of a decision without any right of the person accused to answer back;

two, there was no differentiation, in my opinion, made between what might have turned out to be a real and genuine Communist Party affiliation and a vague association, so much so, as a matter of fact, that there were even times, as I have said, where the blacklist contained the names of people merely because they were similar to others who were apparently members of the Communist Party and, finally, I am not so sure that I would have objected to a list handed to me, for my personal decision to make. I certainly would object to a forced procedure, procedure of force, whereby pressure is applied against a performer in what I would call a nonsensitive area. For example, if we cleared a list of cowboys on "The Rebel." I was not really concerned too much about what that man's affiliations were. He was not in any position that I could see to do us or the country any harm.

If he were going to be examined for a position as an engineer in master control or as a teacher in a high school or if he were going to be editing a newscast on the Columbia network, I would probably, I would undoubtedly take a much greater interest. Whether a chorus boy on Broadway required that kind of clearance is a philosophical question and it would seem to me that one of the basic differences between our country and the Communist countries is the fact that we, perhaps, will give the opposition that right.

BOLAN: You mentioned that about chorus boys on Broadway, they don't need or require clearance?

GOODSON: They do not need or require clearance, but if they were on television, they would.

I was worrying about Bolan's conducting a lengthy cross-examination—which, of course, was his privilege—because I knew that Mark was scheduled to fly to Hollywood that night. When Judge Geller announced that he was going to suspend for the day, Lou protested. "It is only five minutes after four," he said. But Judge Geller ruled: "We will have to bring him back. It is Friday afternoon and enough of the jurors feel that they want to go away. I will respect that. Ten o'clock promptly Monday morning. I am sorry."

I had a distinct feeling that Mark really didn't mind very much his being held over by the trial. He was back in court Monday morning, looking poised and cool. Again, his testimony was most helpful to our side; his answers to the questions put by Mr. Bolan invariably included items that the defense counsel would just as soon not have had on the record. For example, Bolan took the whole list of Goodson-Todman productions and asked which of the shows had required clearances of performers. He obviously hoped that somewhere along the line Mark would trip up on one. But not once did he do so.

Mark went on to testify as to the various lists, which were being circulated on Madison Avenue, of performers who were barred from appearing on network programs.

GOODSON: The sponsors of "The Rebel" were Procter & Gamble. I am not certain whether the Procter & Gamble people got their particular clearance list from Mr. Hartnett. I cannot say. Therefore, I wouldn't know directly. There was a very strict rule that the agencies and the networks would never tell us the source of the list, but it was common knowledge where they came from. I will say that on "The Rebel" we did have a problem and the problem consisted, your Honor—

NIZER: Let him answer.

BOLAN: I didn't ask him if there was a problem.

THE COURT: Let him answer.

GOODSON: The problem concerned the fact that we apparently violated one of the clearances because of the fact that we used an author who was on the list and it turned out he was really not on it. His name was merely similar to one. But we were asked to drop him, anyway, because of the controversy.

BOLAN: Did anyone from Aware make any complaint to the producers of "Jefferson Drum"?

GOODSON: No, there would have been no reason to, since the list [blacklist] was strictly adhered to in West Coast filmed shows.

BOLAN: Whose list?

GOODSON: The list, in this particular case, of NBC, and the two agencies —I would have to check and see what those agencies were.

. . . .

BOLAN: Is it your testimony that the defendants, to your knowledge, had no connection with these practices [blacklisting].

GOODSON: Well, I was aware of the fact of the existence of Aware and the blacklisting practices of Aware although we had no direct dealings with them, and I had indirect dealings with Mr. Johnson.

BOLAN: Yes, well, now, this was all based, as far as Mr. Hartnett and Aware are concerned, based on what people told you, is that right?

GOODSON: Based on the understanding that was well known throughout the industry.

.   .   .   .

BOLAN: Did anyone ever tell you that they saw a list which Aware furnished?

.   .   .   .

GOODSON: I was told that the William Esty agency submitted names and received back clearances or lack of clearances. Now, I never saw such a list.

THE COURT: From whom did they say, did they say from whom?

GOODSON: They said, I thought they said, from Aware. Now perhaps they were giving me the technically incorrect name for the organization, your Honor.

Bolan asked if any of the defendants, to Mark Goodson's certain knowledge, had lodged complaints against *I've Got a Secret,* and *Make the Connection.* Then:

BOLAN: Now, you have testified with respect to "What's My Line," I believe.

GOODSON: But not with respect to "Name's the Same," Mr. Bolan. You did not ask me about that one.

BOLAN: We will get to it, Mr. Goodson. Just be patient, please. With respect to "What's My Line," was there any complaint there? I think you have testified that there was?

GOODSON: No, we had a regular clearance practice with "What's My Line," but I cannot say against which list CBS was doing its checking. I really can't say.

Bolan continued to press Mark for his direct knowledge of actors blacklisted from shows at the insistence of any of the defendants.

GOODSON: Every actor including every extra was cleared with CBS.

BOLAN: CBS cleared them?

GOODSON: CBS did, yes.

BOLAN: When CBS cleared a person was that a guarantee that there would be no complaint?

GOODSON: We never found a situation, with one exception, where the network cleared somebody and we later got a complaint from another organization.

BOLAN: What was the exception?

GOODSON: That was the situation where CBS cleared Judy Holliday for an appearance on "What's My Line." We used her and then used her in a subsequent week on "The Name's the Same," and Mr. Swanson was called by Mr. Johnson and told that if he didn't get her off they would boycott his goods.

Bolan then made the mistake of asking Mark what problem he had had with *The Name's the Same,* which appeared on the ABC network.

GOODSON: Yes, "The Name's the Same" did not have a clearance system, although I pretty much followed the CBS policy. So if somebody were not cleared by CBS I would tend to avoid using that person on "The Name's the Same" on ABC, just because I wanted to keep our company out of trouble, I suppose.

In the case of Judy Holliday, which was the incident that we discussed, I had tried for some time to persuade CBS that Judy Holliday should be used. They said their list indicated that she had a questionable background and that they would not go into it. Then we were approached by her agent, William Morris, and were told that George Sokolsky, a political writer, had been meeting with Miss Holliday and had determined in his judgment that she was a good American and had done some other behind-the-scenes business of which I was not aware, and they asked whether we would be willing to use Miss Holliday on "What's My Line." I said we would be very happy to, but they had to check with CBS. They went to CBS. CBS looked at the various documents and they said "Go ahead and use her," which we did.

So, just a few weeks later—we had no reaction from that at all from Mr. Johnson or from anybody. A few weeks later we decided to use Miss Holliday on "The Name's the Same," but in that particular show we billboarded it in advance. The guest star on "What's My Line," as you know, because of the fact that it is a mystery, the person comes on as a surprise. If there is going to be any protest it is after the fact. In this particular case we announced Miss Holliday in advance and we began to get mail very quickly and after this performance of Miss Holliday, which was practically a duplicate of what she had done on CBS, we got a call from Clark Swanson who said we could never use Miss Holliday again because "we have been threatened by the Laurence Johnson organization."

. . . .

Now, since they [CBS] had also rejected Oscar Hammerstein, Richard Rodgers, Moss Hart, Jerome Robbins, and an entire list of other famous people, we figured we ought to come back and find out why—

. . . .

They said we could not clear Miss Holliday and I said, "Why?" I got on the phone personally on this one and I said, "Will you please tell me why we can't use Judy Holliday?" And he [the CBS executive] said, "She is just a bad actor." That was one of the standard phrases at that time to indicate, to give you the word that this person was on a blacklist. And I said, "But can't you tell me why?" He said, "I don't want to go into it but she has a questionable background and we just can't clear her now." That was where I heard "questionable background."

As for the reason for people being on the network blacklist, Mark said:

Mr. Bolan, all I can say is there were no differentiations made between Communists, Communist sympathizers, those who had lunch with Communist sympathizers, those who knew somebody who had lunch with Communist sympathizers, and so forth, but there was one over-all list and the differentiation was not made for us.

At a later point Mark summed up the prevailing attitude among the network, agency and sponsor people:

Sponsors and their agencies wanted to keep out of trouble with the public and, therefore, wanted to eliminate anybody that might be accused of anything which could involve the sponsor in controversy, including things that you mention, but also those lists could easily also include someone who had nothing to do with it.

.   .   .   .

It [the reasons for blacklisting] also included various forms of associations that were much narrower, much further apart than that. It included general controversy of any kind and in certain cases it even— I'm ashamed to say—included the elimination of people from shows because they had the same name as members of the Communist Party.
BOLAN: Can you give us an illustration of this situation where you said it included some form of association further apart than association with the Communist Party?
GOODSON: John Henry Faulk.

.   .   .   .

BOLAN: Apart from that illustration, Mr. Goodson, can you give us another illustration?
GOODSON: Bennett Cerf.
BOLAN: And Bennett Cerf was kept off a program?
GOODSON: No, but he was put on a list.
BOLAN: Whose list, you never saw a list, did you?
GOODSON: Yes, I saw this particular list.
BOLAN: You did, you remember now that you saw a list?
GOODSON: Yes.
BOLAN: Where did you see this list or is this one in your head?
GOODSON: No, this is not in my head, this was a very tiny pamphlet and I am not sure who put it out, but it was sort—I think it was called—I

think he was put on that list because he attended some kind of a meeting, I am not sure what it was, to make some sort of protest about something, and I'm not even sure what that was.

BOLAN: Let's get what you are sure of.

GOODSON: I can assure you that I am sure about Mr. Cerf. He is not a Communist—

BOLAN: I know Mr. Cerf.

GOODSON: —or a Communist sympathizer, and he was on a list.

BOLAN: Has anyone said he was Communist?

GOODSON: He didn't have to be, because if I hadn't stood up and fought for him he might have been thrown off.

BOLAN: Who made the objection to Mr. Cerf's appearance?

GOODSON: A certain amount of mail that came in together with the little pamphlet.

BOLAN: Aren't there a lot of crank letters received, Mr. Goodson?

GOODSON: I can't define what a crank is any more, Mr. Bolan.

. . . .

BOLAN: Didn't you say?

GOODSON: Yes, there was a group of people listed on this and I think, by the way, in this list there were such names as Leopold Stokowski, Leonard Bernstein, possibly Dwight Eisenhower, and he was listed on this list.

Several jurors commented, after the case was completed, that Mark Goodson's testimony had been the most effective heard on the subject of my damages, the activities of AWARE and Johnson and the CBS policy of forbidding certain performers to appear.

Ken Roberts had been asked to come as a witness and tell of his experiences; he had suffered great hardships after his listing in *Red Channels* and had finally worked his way back into a secure position in broadcasting. When he took the stand, he revealed how hellish the life of a performer could become for having done nothing more than exercise a sense of civic responsibility. Hartnett had charged in *Red Channels* that Roberts, in 1946, had participated in a big meeting, under sponsorship of the Independent Citizens Committee of the Arts,

Sciences and Professions, for Governor Lehman and Senator Mead of New York.

Ken had suggested that we should get in touch with his friend Everett Sloan, who is considered one of the finest character actors in the profession. Sloan was willing and able to give testimony. As he sat on the stand testifying, he would frequently glance with contempt toward Mr. Hartnett at the counsel table. He told how his career as an actor had gone steadily forward from 1930. He listed the motion pictures that he had been in, the radio work that he had done, and how he had gotten into television in the late 1940s. Then suddenly, after 1952, he could not find any work. Prior to that time he had not been able to take all of the jobs that had been offered him. He looked frantically for work, and then one day in early 1953, he ran into a man he knew, a writer, who told him that he had submitted Sloan's name for a part in a play that he had just written for television. Sloan testified:

He [the friend] said, "I recommended you yesterday for a part in the Ford Theatre that I just wrote," and he said, "They turned you down." I said, "Why?" He said, "Because you are in 'Red Channels.'" I said, "I am not in 'Red Channels.'" He said, "I wasn't aware of that. They told me you were." I said, "You'd better go back and tell them that I am not." And so I called him the following day, he gave me his phone number. I called him the following day and he said, "You were right," which of course I knew I was, "you are not in 'Red Channels,' but they say they must have confused you with Alan Sloane."

NIZER: What is your first name?
SLOAN: Everett.

Clearing this matter up did not help Sloan. He still could not get work, and Lou produced a letter that Sloan had never seen and did not know existed until that moment. It was a letter that Hartnett had written to Johnson in November 1952.

NIZER (reading): "Dear Larry: Enclosed is data on Everett Sloan. You will have to be careful about the item from the Hubert Diary, as it is not privileged. If Sloan challenged it, it would be his word against Hubert's."

Lou then asked Sloan what he had done about getting himself cleared so that he could work in television again.

SLOAN: I found out by inquiring that if you work for the UN Radio more than twice, that the third time you work for them you are required to obtain the same status as a permanent employee, and that included submitting to an F.B.I. check.

NIZER: What did you do then?

SLOAN: And so, having already worked for the UN Radio twice, I sought a third employment from them, which I received.

NIZER: Was there an F.B.I. check made of your record because of that third employment for the UN?

BOLAN: I object.

THE COURT: Overruled.

SLOAN: Yes there was.

NIZER: And did you thereafter receive a writing from the United States Civil Service Commission of Washington, D. C., concerning your status?

. . . .

SLOAN: Yes I did.

Then an odd thing happened in a case that was full of odd things. Bolan revealed how little he knew of his own client's connections.

NIZER: Did you thereafter meet one Paul Milton, whom you now know as a director of Aware, Incorporated?

BOLAN: Your Honor, I object to such statements. Mr. Milton is not a director of Aware and I object to such statement.

THE COURT: Sustained, assuming—I don't have to state the reason.

BOLAN: He may have been at one time. I'm not sure of that.

NIZER: We will read it from the deposition.

Lou then took Milton's examination before trial and read Milton's testimony to the effect that he was a member of the board of directors of AWARE, Incorporated. Mr. Bolan admitted that he had not known this fact. Lou asked Sloan what he had done with the document that he had received giving him a clean bill of political health. Sloan said that a friend of his, a writer, Stanley Niss, suggested that he should see Mr. Milton. Sloan met with Milton and told him that he had the clearance from the F.B.I. as to his loyalty and asked Milton what was the best procedure to follow to re-establish himself in television. Milton read the document.

SLOAN: [Milton said] "Well, I take this with a grain of salt." Then I said, "What do you mean by that?" He said, "Well, we don't put much stock in it." And I said, "Who is we?" He said, "Aware, Incorporated." And that was the first time that he represented Aware in any way. I said, "I wasn't aware of the fact that you were a member or a director of Aware or represented them in any way." I said, "If I had known that, I certainly wouldn't have come to see you." I said, "But aside from that, what is your objection to this document, now that you have seen it?" He said, "Well, we at Aware had different standards of clearance than the United States Government's agencies. We are a little more stringent. We feel they are a little too lenient." And I said, "You mean to say that you set yourselves up as opposed to the United States Government in the matter of loyalty, which is, indeed, I would say, their province?" He said, "Yes, we do." I said, "Well, what would Aware, Inc. suggest that I do, then, in view of the fact that this document doesn't seem to mean much to them?"

And he said, "I suggest that you let me arrange a meeting for you with Mr. Hartnett, at which meeting perhaps you and he can evolve some statement that you can make that will be satisfactory to Mr. Hartnett and will also prove satisfactory to, perhaps, the people who are not presently hiring you."

NIZER: What did you say to that?

SLOAN: I said, "Go fly a kite." I told Mr. Milton that as far as I was concerned I was much more interested in the opinion of the United States Government than of Mr. Milton of Aware or of Vincent Hartnett, and that as far as I was concerned both their purpose and methods as I could gather were immoral and illegal and that I would have nothing to do with them whatsoever, and I hoped that soon that this, my feeling about their—

BOLAN: Your Honor—

NIZER: This is conversation.

THE COURT: This is part of the conversation. He may finish it.

SLOAN: I hoped that very soon the fact that they were conducting their business in a way that I considered immoral and illegal would be proven and come to light, and I walked out of the restaurant.

22

As I sat there listening to witness after witness tell of the weird, punishing effects of blacklisting, I thought of the leadership of AFTRA, the performers' union. It had been charged with protecting the members from such abuses; yet the leadership had turned a deaf ear and looked the other way. In fact, when an attempt had been made to censure AWARE, Inc., the officers of the union had violently opposed it. Later, when my Middle-of-the-Road slate had attempted to take action against blacklisting, the opposition had been solid and violent. How, I thought, could the officers have been so callous, so indifferent, to the suffering of the members? But, as I reflected on this, I realized that the union leadership had not been alone; the responsible persons in the industry had capitulated with equal indifference. Carrying the thought further, I had to admit that the citizens of the country had been equally susceptible to fear and the dread disease of passive indifference to injustice.

Lou wanted to use Gerald Dickler as a witness in a dual capacity— as my business manager who could give firsthand testimony about what exactly had happened to me at WCBS and afterward; and as an expert in the television and radio industry. This would enable Gerry to testify as to what my probable earnings might have been had I not been blacklisted. Lou wanted the impact of Gerry's testimony to be felt by the jury; he wanted to give the jury a full-length picture of a man who had been very closely associated with the inner workings of the radio and television industry from the 1930s on. But, with the trial stretching into the second month, Judge Geller hurried him along. After Gerry had testified that he represented H. V. Kaltenborn, Lowell

Thomas, and Pauline Frederick, he gave a detailed analysis of the factors that went into the making of a successful performer.

Then, having testified and retestified to his experience in the field of radio and television, Gerry proceeded to describe what an enormous success I would have been had I not been blacklisted. He did this in great detail. The defendants and their attorneys could only sit and listen.

DICKLER: He [John Henry Faulk] is one of the best storytellers I know. He is extremely inventive and ingenious in that area, particularly again, in his specialized area of folk stories.

He is a first-rate talent, I think a talent of the first class, and I think that if his career had continued and had not been interrupted, as it was, that he would be in the top rank in radio and television.

Gerry testified in some detail about how Sam Slate had called him in April 1956 and reported that Laurence Johnson was in New York, knocking sponsors off my show. Slate had asked Gerry to help him stop Johnson. Then Gerry told how he and Collingwood had gone to a meeting with Arthur Hull Hayes, manager of the CBS radio network.

DICKLER: Mr. Collingwood said he had known Johnny for a long time and felt completely confident of Mr. Faulk's patriotism and his loyalty to the country, and Mr. Hayes brushed that aside and said, "Of course, we have never had any doubt of that ourselves, but this thing came along and we have to deal with it. It is a damn nuisance and it is a kind of blackmail, and this man Johnson has done it before and he is probably going to do it again, but nobody seems to have figured out how to stop him."

Gerry testified that while I was away on vacation in July 1957 Sam Slate had called him to tell him that I was being fired. They had a meeting in the Men's Bar at the Waldorf-Astoria about it.

DICKLER: . . . He said, "We are going to have to let him [Faulk] go and I am sending you a letter, it has already been prepared. I haven't sent it out yet. I wanted to talk to you first. I am sending you a letter of termination."

. . . .

I said to Sam, "Before Johnny went away you told him that he had nothing to worry about except that there was a possibility, a probability that the Godfrey Show for Ford was likely to come in and pick up a half hour of this time, but that would not affect his relationship with the network, and he could go away with a perfectly free mind." And I said, "Why the sudden switch?" "Well," said Sam, "his ratings have been dropping and his share has been off," meaning share of audience, as used in the trade.

. . . .

And I said to him at that point, "It is not worse than it was at the time that you renewed his contract," and indeed, the whole network was off considerably, and if he was off . . . and I really don't think it was off . . . I said, "Sam, this doesn't make sense." He said, "Well, there is nothing I can do about it. The decision has been made. I have had it up with the people upstairs and Johnny is through. I feel terrible about it, but he is through."

And I said, "He is through in more ways than one. He is through in the game if this gets around."

. . . .

I said that with what has happened to Johnny in the past, if CBS won't stand by him, he won't get a job anywhere else.

Gerry then testified to the details of my efforts to find a job and his efforts to help me during 1957. Lou asked him to give, as an expert, his estimate of what I would be earning per year now. Gerry put the figure at somewhere between two hundred fifty thousand and five hundred thousand dollars. He and Nizer then went over the total earnings of my show for WCBS from the time it first went on the air in 1951 until I left the show in 1957. They went through all sorts of mathematical gymnastics, and Gerry ended up with an estimate that I had earned during that period for WCBS in the vicinity of one million dollars. I don't know about the jury, but I was very impressed with the figure.

No other performer in the country has an off-stage personality that so nearly parallels his on-stage personality as Garry Moore. He is a sincere, affable soul at all times. It is small wonder that he has become a household word in the homes of millions of Americans. His interest in me and my struggle had not diminished a bit since he joined me in my AFTRA fight. He now willingly came forward as a witness in my behalf.

On Tuesday, May 22, 1962, Garry was awarded an Emmy for his distinguished performance in television, and that night his friends and associates gave him a big party (or he had given them one, I forget which) to celebrate. It lasted very late. Yet, the next morning he was in court looking fresh and relaxed as he took the stand, his affability not diminished in the least. Justice Geller and the jury seemed pleased to have him there.

Garry gave his background in radio and television, which dated back to the mid-1930s. He testified that since 1950 he had been an actor-producer. His eminence in the field made it unnecessary to qualify him further as an expert; it was accepted as a fact by judge, jury and Mr. Bolan. Asked to tell how he came to join our Middle-of-the-Road slate, he said it was because he felt our union deserved a change in leadership and that something should be done about blacklisting. Lou then produced and read aloud into evidence a statement that Garry had made on November 23, 1955, while we were running for office in AFTRA. It was a statement made to Joe Coppola, who was writing a column at that time.

NIZER [reading]: "Garry Moore, when asked what a victory for the Middle-of-the-Road slate would mean in eliminating blacklisting, had this to say: 'I don't think anything revolutionary is going to happen, but the greatest thing in the world is human dignity. We have all been scattered in fear. I had the occasion to hire an aerialist whose name was on the blacklist. I was told he was unacceptable. I accepted the precept that if you pay a Communist it is a bad deal because while he doesn't editorialize on the air the money may go back to the Communist Party. But I insisted that they check on the aerialist. It turned out that he had the same name as a blacklisted performer, but he wasn't the same man. When a patently unproven case arises you must force it to be proved. This is the first thing I have ever joined.' " [He was referring to the Middle-of-the-Road slate.]

NIZER: Did you have that experience with the aerialist which you refer to here?

MOORE: Yes I did.

. . . .

NIZER: Did you engage this aerialist for one of your shows?

MOORE: Yes, sir, I did.

NIZER: And you submitted his name, as you did all other performers [to the network for clearance]?

MOORE: And all other performers, yes.

. . . .

NIZER: Were you familiar with Mr. Faulk's reputation for loyalty and patriotism in the industry?

MOORE: Certainly, I would never have joined the slate had I not been aware of his reputation.

NIZER: What was it?

MOORE: The reputation for being a fine man, fine citizen, absolutely anti-Communist.

Lou then had him testify as to the extent of his experience as a producer of television shows, the hundreds of artists that he had hired, and his complete familiarity with the radio and television industry. Garry stated that he knew the general salary range of artists in various categories, such as dancers, singers, emcees, et cetera. It was his business to know them well, since he produced shows. Lou then asked him:

In what category of performer would you place John Henry Faulk?

BOLAN: I object, your Honor.

THE COURT: Well then you object to the witness's qualifications?

BOLAN: No, your Honor. I object to the question, to its form particularly.

MOORE: John Henry Faulk has a rare sort of talent. There are only a handful of people in the business who function the way John Henry Faulk is capable of functioning. These are generally referred to, I suppose, as personalities, because it is hard to pinpoint the kind of talent, as opposed to dancer, or singer, or acrobat. It is a kind of talent which has a great sustaining quality, because you may have a different singer each week or a different dancer, a different actor, but the host, master of ceremonies personality is a continuing job. He is there every week. His employment is far steadier than that of people in other categories. It is a talent that is very hard to duplicate. As I say, there are a handful, Arthur Godfrey, Art Linkletter, Dave Garroway.

THE COURT: How about Garry Moore?

MOORE: No opinion, sir. (laughter)

. . . .

NIZER: Can you state, with reasonable certainty, the range of earnings that Mr. Faulk would have earned in the years I have indicated [years 1956 to 1962]?

MOORE: I can state with reasonable certainty that Mr. Faulk would have fallen within the category of a performer that I have discussed . . . His earnings would have, of course, been commensurate anywhere between two hundred thousand and upward to conceivably a million dollars.

NIZER: That testimony is, with reasonable certainty, limited to earnings from general television performance, is that not your testimony?

MOORE: Yes sir.

David Susskind, Mark Goodson, Gerald Dickler and others had given it as their opinion, "with reasonable certainty," that I would have probably been earning a minimum of two hundred thousand dollars a year had I not been blacklisted. Garry was the first one who had run my maximum earnings up to a million dollars a year. I was considerably impressed; so was Mr. Bolan, but in a rather different way. From his very first question on cross-examination of Garry

Moore, it was obvious that he wanted to discredit the million-dollar estimate.

BOLAN: Mr. Moore, you have testified, have you not, that you can state with reasonable certainty that Mr. Faulk's income from television between the years of 1956 and 1962 would have been in the range of two hundred thousand . . . up to a million dollars a year?

MOORE: Yes sir.

THE COURT: Keep your voice up, Mr. Bolan.

BOLAN: Isn't it a fact that you are not able to state with reasonable certainty what your own income might be next year?

MOORE: No, my contract's all signed up for next year. I know exactly what it's going to be.

BOLAN: Did you state earlier this month that you might have been out of a job next year?

MOORE: Yes, but this was figure of speech. It means only that I don't know the future of my present show beyond the near future.

BOLAN: And isn't it a fact that the television industry is a rather hazardous industry?

MOORE: Not for the durable people in it.

NIZER: And you are one of the durable people, is that right?

MOORE: I hope.

A little later, Mr. Bolan, still cutting away at Garry's testimony, asked:

Do you know what Mr. Faulk's plus ratings were, for example, in 1957 on radio?

MOORE: No, sir, I do not. I pay no attention to the ratings. I never have.

Garry seemed to be actually enjoying his session with Mr. Bolan. He answered each question quickly and brightly, often to the amusement of the jurors as well as the judge. For instance, when Bolan asked him about his programs:

BOLAN: Has Mr. Faulk appeared on any of these with you?

. . . .

MOORE: John Henry Faulk is not the type of talent that I would hire to be on a show that I am on because he does the same thing that I do and there isn't room for the two of us on one show.

It was clear to me that Garry was running up our scoring points. In answer to a question of Bolan's as to why he had participated in the Middle-of-the-Road slate's campaign for officers, he stated:

. . . I was terribly frightened by what was happening to people, being blacklisted, suddenly becoming unemployable, for what reason they knew not, not even being confronted or told why they were unemployable. It was a little bit like fighting with six men in a closet with the light out, and you can't tell who is hitting you.

And as Bolan pressed him harder for his definition of blacklisting, he was very explicit in his answers. At one point he said:

. . . I am speaking of cases where I hired people for jobs because they were good, because they were fine performers, gave their names to the network [CBS], as I was required to do, and the message would come back to me that such and such person is "unacceptable," and if you would say, "Why?" they would not say "It is incompetence," they would say, "He is unacceptable."

When Bolan wanted to know whether it was the sponsors or the network who blacklisted people, Garry answered:

It could come from almost any direction. The networks had a clearance board which functioned. Sponsors, too, would come to you and say, "So and so is unacceptable because he is in 'Red Channels,'" or something of that nature. But most of the time the word came 'way round about, you never quite knew who was making the decision about this man's livelihood.

When Garry Moore was dismissed from the witness stand, I figured that what with his and Mark Goodson's direct testimony on how they had been required to have performers on their shows cleared by the network, the defense would surely not put on any witnesses who would undertake to contradict them. Their testimony had been too persuasive to be successfully contradicted. I was wrong about this, however, as I was to find out later. The defendants did produce such a witness, one from the very same network that Mr. Moore and Mr. Goodson worked for.

Lou had at last succeeded in persuading Frank Barton to appear and testify on the Johnson-Matusow episode. As he took the stand, he looked every bit the successful Madison Avenue advertising executive—self-assured and intelligent. He testified that he was vice-president and general manager of the Lennen & Newell advertising agency and went on to tell how in 1952 his agency had handled the Schlitz Beer account and produced a television show *The Schlitz Playhouse of Stars*. At this point Lou read a portion of the examination before trial of Laurence Johnson, wherein Johnson admitted sending a telegram to E. C. Eihlein of the Schlitz Brewing Company protesting the use of Frank Silvera on the program. The matter had been passed from the brewery executives on to the executives of the agency to look into. A short time later Johnson called Barton and asked that they have a meeting to discuss the matter. Barton met with Johnson and Harvey Matusow at the Hampshire House, and Barton described what happened at the meeting:

BARTON: . . . Mr. Johnson made a long patriotic speech about Communists and what they were doing and how we should fight them and they shouldn't be appearing on programs where they were before the public.

I assured him that we were just as patriotic as he was, and that we and our client had no more desire to have Communists on our show than he did, or any other good American did, but the question was, who were Communists? We had no knowledge in this field. He claimed that he did have knowledge and that a lot of other people had knowledge, and if we would take the trouble, make the effort, we could gain such knowledge and know who was and who wasn't.

Then he raised the specific issue with regard to certain programs that he knew about, he said, where he had gotten the cast lists somehow, and claimed certain people were Communists, and he wanted those programs off the air.

Barton then went on to describe how, as he sat discussing the matter at lunch with Johnson:

He got fairly angry with me and started to pound the table and raise his voice sufficiently to attract attention around the dining room, then he calmed down.

The matter was resolved by an agreement, suggested by Mr. Johnson, that in the future Mr. Barton's agency would use the services of Mr. Matusow to discover who was Communist or pro-Communist and who was not, so far as the programs were concerned. Lou then asked him:

Was there any discussion with respect to what Mr. Matusow would be and any financial arrangements?

BOLAN: I object.

THE COURT: Overruled.

BARTON: Yes, we agreed to pay Mr. Matusow the sum of a hundred and fifty dollars, I think it was, in return for which he supplied us with two years' back issues of a publication called "Counterattack," which listed information, or reported information, about a great many people many of which were in our field of entertainment, of the entertainment business, and from these lists Mr. Matusow showed us how to set up a card index where we could find references.

Bolan, on his cross-examination, did not make much headway, but he tried. On the subject of those persons about whom Johnson had protested appearing on the *Schlitz Playhouse of Stars,* Bolan asked:

Did Mr. Johnson state to you why he considered these individuals to be Communist-fronters?

BARTON: Merely that he had information that they were.

BOLAN: Did you ask him what his information was?

BARTON: That is one of the points we had a big argument on, we wanted to know how he set himself up as an authority, how he would know this. We didn't have such knowledge. He merely told us that if we took the trouble we could get it. He had gotten it.

Lou then called up Harry J. Blackburn, an executive in the Rhein-
gold Brewery, who testified that Laurence Johnson had phoned him
in 1956 and told him that I was a Communist. After that, Lou called
up Lester Wolff, an advertising executive and television program
operator, who testified that I came to him, sometime in late 1957 or
early 1958, looking for work. He wanted to use me on a program,
but on investigation he discovered that there was too much controversy raging around me, and consequently he didn't use me.

Our case had been nailed down very securely by our witnesses.
However, Lou had wanted to bring in several character witnesses for
me. A week before, a perfect one had come along, out of the blue, as
it were. Henry Nash Smith, a professor at the University of California,
and one of the most distinguished scholars in the field of American
letters, had flown to New York to attend a meeting of the American
Council of Learned Societies. He called me to find out how the case
was progressing, and I realized at once that here was an ideal character witness, impressive, and distinguished, who had known me for over
twenty years. Henry said that he would be delighted to come and
testify. I relayed the glad tidings to Lou, pointing out that surely the
angels were working with us for here was the best possible witness
and we wouldn't even have to pay his travel expenses. However, he
would have to be called at once as he had to return to California.

Nizer was delighted. He, Paul, and George were engrossed in other
preparation, so he suggested that I prepare his questions for Smith's
testimony from Who's Who in America, which contained a lengthy
entry on Henry Nash Smith. The testimony of a character witness is a
rather perfunctory business. He simply gives his background, an account of how long and how well he has known the individual about
whose reputation he is testifying, and then his estimate of the person's
reputation for patriotism and loyalty. I prepared the questions as
Nizer had instructed from Who's Who, and Nizer put Henry on the
stand. He pointed out to us that Smith would only be on the stand for
a few moments, since the direct was probably all there would be to
his testimony. Bolan in all likelihood would not attempt to cross-
examine such a distinguished witness. As Henry took his seat, he
looked exactly the role he filled in life, a mild-mannered scholar and
gentleman.

Henry testified that he had received his Ph.D. at Harvard University in the field of the history of American civilization and was presently a professor of English at the University of California, in Berkeley. He had written *The Virgin Land: The American West as Symbol and Myth,* which was published by the Harvard University Press, and which won for him the John H. Dunning Prize of the American Historical Association and the Bancroft Award in American History. He cited half a dozen other distinguished awards and positions that he held, and then told how we had become acquainted in 1940, how he frequently visited in my home and I in his, how J. Frank Dobie and Dr. Walter Webb and Roy Bedichek and he had joined me on jaunts about once a month down there. We had become very good friends and he was very well acquainted with me. My reputation for patriotism and loyalty in the community was of the very highest.

To our astonishment, Bolan announced that he would cross-examine the witness. During Henry's direct examination, I noticed Vincent Hartnett slip out of the courtroom and return some moments later and pass a note to Bolan, smiling triumphantly the while. Bolan's cross-examination of Henry seemed pointless for a few minutes. Then his purpose was revealed:

BOLAN: Have you signed a petition to have the House Un-American Activities Committee abolished?

NIZER: Objection.

THE COURT: Sustained. This is the type of question that I have indicated before, where from the question alone no inference of any kind must be drawn.

BOLAN: May I approach the bench, your Honor, on the record?

Of course, to Bolan and Hartnett the fact that a citizen dared object to the HUAC cast some question on his patriotism. Bolan apparently figured that the jury would feel the same way. After a lengthy wrangle at the bench, which resulted in a heated exchange between Justice Geller and Bolan, the objection was sustained and Henry was promptly dismissed from the stand.

Ed Murrow had suggested that J. Frank Dobie should be brought up as a character witness for me. Murrow was so anxious to have Dobie's strong personality come before the jury in the case that he offered to pay Dobie's expenses to New York from Texas. Mr. Dobie had told me that he would gladly come and pay his own way if it would help our case. At the time of the trial, however, he was in poor health and I was afraid that his coming would tax his waning strength too much. I told Lou that we should get another friend of mine, Dr. Erwin R. Goodenough, of Yale University. Dr. Goodenough had known me for twenty years; we were intimate friends. He too was one of the most distinguished scholars in his field, that of the history of religion.

However, Justice Geller ruled that he was calling a halt to our parade of witnesses. Lou argued the matter with him, and Justice Geller consented to let us present one final witness, if he was not merely a character witness. Lou explained that he was a very important one, Fred Mitchell, vice-president of Norman, Craig & Kummel, a large advertising agency on Madison Avenue. As a witness Fred Mitchell was of great value to us from three directions. As a character witness he could say that he had known me for many years, since the early Forties in Texas. Further, he qualified as an expert on damages since he had supervised the television advertising of some of his agencies' biggest accounts. A third value to us lay in the fact that he could give testimony on my unemployability, for he had tried to help me get work during the time when I was blacklisted.

Lou on direct examination had Fred Mitchell tell of his impressive background as an advertising executive on Madison Avenue, that he had supervised forty million dollars' worth of television and radio advertising for various accounts, and that he was vice-president at Norman, Craig & Kummel, and senior account executive of a huge account there. After this, Lou led him through his experiences with me, and how he had first met me at the University of Texas in 1941 when I was teaching there and he was a student. Fred testified that he had heard me speak on a number of occasions, that I was very popular and impressive, that my reputation for loyalty and patriotism was of the very highest. He also told of our friendship since 1951 in New York and how he had nominated me and I had been elected president of the University of Texas Ex-Students Association in New York, and served in that capacity for two terms. Lou asked him if in 1957 and 1958 I had come to him to get work.

MITCHELL: I told Mr. Faulk that he was virtually unemployable and he better get the charges removed if he was going to continue to earn a livelihood.

NIZER: Did he at any time seek employment from you without the use of his name? Was that ever suggested?

MITCHELL: Well, Mr. Faulk suggested it to me when I told him that he was going to have difficulty in television, that he would be very happy to use his voice alone and do radio commercials, and I am sorry I laughed at him because his voice is so unique, there was no possibility of there being any disguise of the voice.

When Fred had been dismissed from the witness box, just before noon on Friday, May 25, more than a month after the trial had begun, Lou announced: "The plaintiff rests."

23

We had presented our side of the case. Now the time had come for the defendants to present theirs. Bolan called only two witnesses during the afternoon after Nizer rested our case; the defendants' presentation would start in earnest on the following Monday morning. These first witnesses were both functionaries of CBS, and they had brought in voluminous financial records and the day-by-day F.C.C. logs of my program. They were there merely to identify the items that they had brought.

"The plaintiff rests" is strictly a legal term. The verb "rests" was not even remotely related to the reality of the activities that we had in store for us in the days ahead—particularly that weekend; it was a feverish one.

We had speculated at length on what witness Bolan would put on the stand first. This was not idle speculation. It was of utmost importance that we know, in order to be prepared to cross-examine him. Both Lou and Paul were sure that it would be Hartnett. They hoped that it would be, because they were fully prepared for Hartnett's testimony. However, Nizer didn't trust them to do what they were expected to do. He prepared for four or five different possible witnesses, just in case they led off with someone other than Hartnett. One of the four or five was Paul Milton, who had been in on the founding of AWARE, was long associated with Mr. Hartnett, and did most of the writing on the bulletins which AWARE circulated. It was Mr. Milton who took the stand as the first major witness for the defense, and Nizer was well prepared.

As Milton settled into the witness chair he looked as calm and as composed as a dignified businessman taking his place in a church pew on Sunday. He was balding and gray, with a neatly trimmed gray mustache. His expression was that of a pleasant but serious responsible citizen performing a civic duty which neither pleased nor displeased him. It gave me something of a start to realize that I had never laid eyes on Paul Milton until the moment he took the witness stand. Goodness knows, I had heard enough about him to feel that I knew him well. He had been one of the chief factors in AWARE. His fame as a hyperactive, self-appointed guardian of other writers' political morals and his tireless activities as an informer before Congressional committees had earned him quite a reputation.

Answering Bolan's questions with apparent candor and diffidence, he was the very picture of respectable cooperation. His expression was almost pious as he raised his eyes ceilingward during the frequent and heated wrangles between Bolan and Nizer over objections. I was uneasy at seeing him making such a fine impression on the jury. As a matter of fact, he was making a pretty good impression on me, as his answers came, even and direct, without a hint of guile. His testimony revealed that he had been graduated from Cornell in 1926, had become a writer, then an editor, and then had moved into the field of script-writing for radio and television. He described in detail the origins of AWARE in the early 1950s and how he had participated actively in that organization. For some years he had been chairman of AWARE's Information Committee. As such he was responsible for the preparation of the bulletins and other written information that AWARE put out.

At several points in Milton's direct testimony that day, he said things that rather amazed me. For instance:

BOLAN: You stated that AWARE's membership at one point was 350 members, is that correct?

MILTON: Yes.

BOLAN: Were there some members of AWARE who were also members of the American Federation of Radio and Television Artists?

MILTON: Yes, there were.

BOLAN: And at its peak of 350 members, approximately how many members were members of AFTRA?

MILTON: I would say from 75 to 100.

.   .   .   .

THE COURT: Were you a member of AFTRA at that time?
MILTON: No, sir, never.

Bolan got testimony from Milton to the effect that he and other members of the board of directors of AWARE had relied on Vincent Hartnett for their information, which went into Bulletin 16, the one libeling me, and to build this up, he wanted Milton to testify as to Hartnett's reputation as a researcher. Nizer objected to this, and the court sustained Nizer's objection. A very interesting colloquy took place outside the hearing of the jury but on the record, before Judge Geller. Bolan argued:

I'm entitled to show that the board of directors of AWARE had considered Hartnett's reputation to be one of the finest as a researcher, and that they were confidently relying on the material which he supplied for the publication of their bulletins. It is a pure question of reliance. . . . They relied on Hartnett and I have a right to show, I submit, why they relied and placed so much reliance upon Hartnett.

Nizer replied:

In other words, Milton can say that he relied on Hartnett, and Hartnett can say that he relied on Milton, and this is internal reliance testimony on reputation, and Milton is going to say Hartnett had a good reputation as a researcher. Do you think that is the reliance proof that is submitted by courts with respect to libels?

Judge Geller sustained Lou's position. A little later in court, Bolan asked Milton:

Well, with respect to the allegations of Bulletin 16 concerning Mr. Faulk, did you have any personal knowledge on which you relied with respect to the allegations concerning Mr. Faulk? . . .
MILTON: As an individual, no.

That evening, when we gathered at Nizer's apartment, I mentioned the fact that I was uneasy about the good impression that Milton was making as a witness. I pointed out that I had thought that Milton would be one of our prize exhibits of the defendants' evil doings, and instead he was coming off like a genial Baptist deacon. I knew, of course, that he was on his direct testimony and was more or less paddling downstream; he would naturally look good. But I hadn't planned on his looking that good. Lou observed, "He's on his direct now. Wait until we get him on cross." Paul and George had already contacted what turned out to be an invaluable source of information on Mr. Milton's career. Robert Cenedella and Philo Higley were both writers who had some firsthand knowledge of Mr. Milton. In fact, they had so much documented evidence of his reckless and pitiless destruction of his fellow writers' careers in the early Fifties that we had to omit a good deal of it.

The next day Milton began testifying under cross-examination by Nizer. Within a matter of minutes, his pious self-composure evaporated. He began to look shopworn and gray. He was clearly shaken by the turn his life as a witness had taken. His work with AWARE and Hartnett did not seem as selfless and noble under Nizer's questions as it had appeared under Bolan's.

Nizer was allowed to ask Milton if he had relied on a citation in the House Un-American Activities Committee report on People's Songs when he described the organization as a Communist-front organization in the AWARE bulletin. Milton replied that he had indeed relied on the HUAC report.

NIZER: You have just testified, Mr. Milton, that you relied on this paragraph in the House Un-American Activities Committee Guide which has a quote, "All of the productions of People's Songs follow the Communist party line as assiduously as do the people behind the organization," and at the end of the quote, the source of that quote is given as the "California Committee on Un-American Activities report 1948, page 302." You so testified a moment ago, did you?

MILTON: Yes.

NIZER: And the California Committee on Un-American Activities is also called the Tenney Committee?

MILTON: It was, yes.

NIZER: Have you not testified that the Tenney Committee, the California Committee, was unreliable?

MILTON: I don't think I said that, sir.

NIZER: You don't? Page 162, were you asked the following question on your examination before trial under oath:

"Question: You knew that the citations by the California Committee are not reliable necessarily?

"Answer: That's right."

Did you make that answer to that question [in 1960]?

MILTON: Yes.

Nizer established on cross-examination once and for all that it was the purpose of AWARE Inc. bulletins to influence AFTRA's affairs.

NIZER: And have you also testified that, broadly speaking, you intended to influence the AFTRA members' conduct even in their own elections?

MILTON: Broadly speaking, yes.

NIZER: At the very time that Exhibit was published by you . . .

THE COURT: "You," meaning AWARE.

NIZER: AWARE, Inc. You knew, did you not, that there was going to be a national election a few months later?

MILTON: Yes.

NIZER: And Exhibit 41 [AWARE bulletin attacking the Middle-of-the-Road slate], of course, is not a private publication, that is the one that went out to thousands, right?

MILTON: About two thousand.

NIZER: You knew that there was a national election coming up that year, in 1956, didn't you?

MILTON: I think in the summer.

NIZER: And you also knew that there would be another annual local election in the fall of 1956, didn't you?

MILTON: Yes.

NIZER: And you also knew that AWARE members who were officers of AFTRA ran repeatedly, that is, they ran in succession for re-election—you knew that, too, didn't you?

MILTON: That's my impression. I'd have to look at the names to see exactly who did what . . .

NIZER: And those same AWARE members who were members of AFTRA were active in election disputes in AFTRA, weren't they?

MILTON: I assume they were, yes.

Lou then took the libelous Bulletin 16 and turned to a statement in it that Milton admitted having written—namely, "The Middle-of-the-Road ticket was first reported by the *Daily Worker* on November 15, 1955."

NIZER: Now I ask you isn't it a fact that in addition to the "Times" and the "Tribune" there were other publications which, prior to the "Daily Worker," discussed the Middle-of-the-Road slate?

. . . .

MILTON: All that our files show now is "Variety" and straight news reports.

. . . .

NIZER: And "Variety" is the trade publication for the entertainment industry; isn't it a leading one, right?

MILTON: Yes.

NIZER: And a reliable one?

MILTON: Yes, sir.

NIZER: You didn't mention the fact that there was one report prior to the "Daily Worker"; you said the first one was the "Daily Worker," didn't you, at that point?

. . . .

MILTON: Yes, there are some other references, however.

. . . .

NIZER: And you knew that was incorrect at the time you wrote this, didn't you?

MILTON: Yes.

NIZER: As a matter of fact, as far back as July 11, 1955, not November, I show you Exhibit 52 in evidence, the "New York Times," "More about AWARE" and refers to the Middle—

BOLAN: Your Honor, the Middle-of-the-Road slate, the testimony has been—

THE COURT: No, Mr. Bolan.

BOLAN: May I approach the bench, your Honor?

THE COURT: No, not necessary. Just give the legal objections, no argument.

BOLAN: The legal objection is, your Honor, that this document couldn't possibly have any relevancy to what is now being questioned.

THE COURT: You object to it on the ground that it is irrelevant?

BOLAN: Yes, sir.

THE COURT: Objection overruled. You may answer the question.

MILTON: This dealt with the previous condemnation, had nothing to do with the Middle-of-the-Road slate, which didn't even exist then, as far as the public knew.

NIZER: I call your attention to Exhibit 52 . . . and ask you if this language didn't mean to you that the "New York Times" article as far back as July 1955 was suggesting a middle position between the AWARE blacklisting and the Communist issue? Doesn't that mean that to you?

MILTON: That was Mr. Gould's [Jack Gould of *The New York Times*] opinion.

NIZER: Yes. I am not asking you—

MILTON: I do not recognize the use of the word "blacklisting" in connection with AWARE.

THE COURT: That isn't the question.

MILTON: I don't recognize that statement to mean anything whatsoever except Mr. Jack Gould's opinion.

Lou then took each one of the specifications in Bulletin 16 that Milton had written against me and went down them one by one. He established that Milton did not even know what organization it was that I was supposed to have appeared before at Club 65 back in 1946. It turned out to be the Newspaper Guild unit from the *Amsterdam News,* a Harlem newspaper.

NIZER: Do you consider the "Amsterdam News" in any way a pro-Communist newspaper?

MILTON: Not to my knowledge, no, sir.

NIZER: Do you consider the "Amsterdam News" unit of the Newspaper Guild of New York a pro-Communist organization?

. . . .

MILTON: I don't know anything about it.

NIZER: ... Have you not testified that the only thing was the "Daily Worker" that you relied upon?

MILTON: As you read my statement, yes.

. . . .

NIZER: And you never inquired of Mr. Hartnett as to what organization was meeting at Club 65?

. . . .

MILTON: I don't recall that I did. I hope that I did.

NIZER: Now that you see that it is the Newspaper Guild function which took place at Club 65, you should know that that organization and that meeting so far as that function was concerned, was a legitimate, non-Communist function of professional newspaper men, wouldn't you?

BOLAN: I object, your Honor.

THE COURT: Overruled.

MILTON: I don't know what kind of meeting it was.

. . . .

NIZER: I am asking you now. I just read to you what was in the bulletin. I am asking you, didn't you know at the time that you published this that Club 65 was a site for non-Communist affairs?

MILTON: It may have been.

NIZER: And didn't you also testify that Club 65 was not subversive?

. . . .

MILTON: The place itself may well not have been subversive.

Lou then elicited from Milton a rather fascinating statement.

NIZER: And as a writer, did you consider this item, which omitted the meeting that took place, omitted the Newspaper Guild that was supposed to meet there, you have stated that this is a favorite pro-Communist site, did you consider this a fair report based upon a full investigation?

MILTON: In the light of what we were doing, yes.

NIZER: In the light of what you were doing, which was to injure Mr. Faulk, you mean, don't you?

MILTON: No, the bulletin says what we were doing.

NIZER: Haven't you testified that what you were doing was trying to bring out everything adverse to Mr. Faulk that you could in this bulletin?

MILTON: That was an incidental purpose. The main purpose was the union question.

Milton had been mighty chary about using the term "blacklisting" in connection with his or any of the other defendants' activities. He preferred to call it "screening." On the last day of his cross-examination, I suppose, Nizer had punched so hard that Milton didn't have his wits about him. Nizer asked about the days immediately before AWARE was organized.

NIZER: Haven't you testified that Johnson, Laurence Johnson, and his Syracuse friends were active in the work of, as you put it, "screening" or blacklisting performers, before AWARE, Inc. was organized? Haven't you so testified?

MILTON: That's right.

Milton had belonged to a faction of the Radio Writers Guild that called themselves We, The Undersigned. Lou sought to have Milton admit that We, The Undersigned was really the forerunner of AWARE, Inc. . . .

NIZER: Is it not a fact that you and other leading members of We, The Undersigned, joined AWARE, Inc.? Is that a fact?

BOLAN: I object.

THE COURT: Overruled.

MILTON: I believe four persons that were in the Radio Writers Guild, We, The Undersigned, joined AWARE. . . .

NIZER: We, The Undersigned, including yourself, signed a statement making pro-Communist charges against certain members of your union, the Radio Writers Guild, is that right? . . .

MILTON: I would have to see the documents again, Mr. Nizer, to know if we used the term "pro-Communist." . . .

NIZER: . . . You knew that Harvey Matusow was working with Laurence Johnson, giving him assistance in this work which you have called screening? . . .

MILTON: I think that was later.

NIZER: How much later?

MILTON: A year or more. I don't know.

NIZER: Isn't it a fact that at that time you knew that Matusow was working with Mr. Johnson?

MILTON: My impression is, when he did, it was later than 1952. . . .

NIZER: Did you also ask Mr. Matusow for information at about that time in connection with pro-Communist—alleged pro-Communist activities of various others? . . .

MILTON: I don't remember any formal request. I had some social conversations with him, very brief.

NIZER: I show you this envelope and ask you if you addressed this envelope to Mr. Matusow?

MILTON: Yes.

NIZER: And I show you these enclosures and ask you if those are your typewritten sheets that you put into that envelope? . . .

MILTON: Yes. On this occasion, apparently I did.

NIZER: Does that refresh your recollection, sir, if you did communicate with Mr. Matusow to give you aid on alleged pro-Communist activities of various others? . . .

MILTON: Yes, on that occasion. . . .

NIZER: The people that you wrote to Matusow about for information, were they all writers of the Radio Writers Guild? . . .

MILTON: What names were there?

Lou did not want to put the writers' names before the public, so the judge ruled that Milton could look at them and see if they were the right names. He did and agreed.

NIZER: These writers, the names you looked at a few moments ago, which I will mark for identification on three yellow sheets—were writers who opposed the slate that you supported in the Writers Guild, were they not?

MILTON: Yes, they were the administration slate, so-called.

NIZER: And you charged these writers with having pro-Communist affiliations, isn't that it?

MILTON: I won't adopt that language, Mr. Nizer, until I could look at the bulletins, or the publications, releases that We, The Undersigned issued.

Milton was at great pains to explain that he had never intended to charge any individual with pro-Communism. Simply, the groups to which they belonged would be pro-Communist. As he testified:

. . . If that appeared in a public statement we made I will have to stand by it. I would hope we did not use it. The organizations, yes. I am talking about attribution of personal pro-Communism to the individual involved.

NIZER: In other words, as I understand you, Mr. Milton, if a person belongs to an organization that is pro-Communist, that does not make him pro-Communist, is that right?

MILTON: Not automatically.

NIZER: Certainly, if he doesn't belong to it but he just attends a function, even of a pro-Communist organization, that doesn't make him pro-Communist, does it?

MILTON: I said the other day, not automatically.

THE COURT: That, in and of itself, does not make him a pro-Communist?

MILTON: I said no, not automatically.

THE COURT: I don't know what you mean, not automatically, to that question. Will you explain?

MILTON: I do not deduce personal pro-Communism from—

THE COURT: Mere attendance in an organization?

MILTON: Or even membership, depending of course what the organization is. . . .

NIZER: Some of these writers lost their jobs, didn't they?

MILTON: I suppose so. All writers lose jobs.

NIZER: No, after your criticism under the We, The Undersigned statement I am talking about, some of these writers lost their jobs, didn't they?

MILTON: One man told us he was in danger of losing his job.

NIZER: Some of them actually did lose their jobs, didn't they, as a result of this?

MILTON: I don't know.

NIZER: You don't know. Was there a man by the name of Sheldon Stark who, prior to your criticism and testimony about him, was employed in "Treasury Men in Action"?

MILTON: He was employed at the producing office. I can't tell you whether it was that program or another they produced. I am not certain now.

NIZER: Was it Mr. Hartnett the gentleman who acted as a consultant, as you call it, through that program, "Treasury Men in Action"?

MILTON: I am not sure.

NIZER: Didn't you obtain a job on "Treasury Men in Action" after Mr. Stark lost his job?

MILTON: Yes.

NIZER: Wasn't this program sponsored by the Borden Milk Company?

MILTON: I think so, yes.

Nizer read aloud one of the allegations which Milton had written against me in the AWARE bulletin: "According to the *Daily Worker,* of April 17, 1947, 'Johnny Faulk' was to appear as an entertainer at the opening of 'Headline Cabaret,' sponsored by Stage for Action (officially designated a Communist front). The late Philip Loeb was billed as emcee."

NIZER: Had you ever heard of Headline Cabaret at the time you wrote this?

MILTON: Prior to—no, I think it was just a one-time show or something.

NIZER: Did you know at that time that that particular show, "Headline Cabaret" show, had been approved by the Theatre Authority?

MILTON: No, I don't think so.

He gave this answer in spite of the fact that the "Approved by Theatre Authority" was clearly printed on the exhibit or advertisement from which he had taken his information about me. It turned out that Milton was not even sure of what the Theatre Authority was. He asked Nizer what it was. Nizer said it was an agency set up by four unions in the entertainment field—Equity, AFTRA, AGVA, and the Screen Actors Guild—to protect the interests of the unions and their members in relation to performances at benefit shows. Members of these unions are forbidden to perform at any benefit production that has not been approved by the Authority. Milton expressed some surprise to learn this. Also, he was surprised to learn that the Theatre Authority had approved the entertainment that I was said to have attended.

NIZER: Did you deliberately and purposefully omit that statement ["approved by the Theatre Authority"] from your paragraph in Exhibit 41?

MILTON: Yes, we omitted it.

NIZER: Is the answer to my question, "Yes, you deliberately and purposefully omitted it?"

MILTON: Yes.

NIZER: Did you put in the fact that the late Philip Loeb was billed as M.C.? Did you also notice that Art Carney was one of the entertainers at this function?

MILTON: Yes.

NIZER: Did you deliberately and purposefully omit the name of Art Carney from this item?

MILTON: Yes. . . .

NIZER: You were the head of what committee? What was it called, your committee [in AWARE]?

MILTON: Information.

NIZER: Did you ask for information about a program of this event before you wrote this charge in Exhibit 41? Did you or did you not?

MILTON: I said I don't recall specifically the same program.

NIZER: I would like a direct answer, Mr. Milton. I don't mean specifically in any way. Did you make any inquiries to see the document of the printed program for this occasion before you made this charge?

MILTON: I have to say no as you phrased it . . .

NIZER: To this day, have you any information that John Henry Faulk appeared at the "Headline Cabaret"?

MILTON: In my possession, no.

Lou took up the matter of Milton's charge that I had entertained for a Henry A. Wallace benefit under the auspices of the Progressive Citizens of America. He asked Milton if he wrote the paragraph charging me with doing so. Milton answered, "Yes, sir." He then elicited from Milton the information that he had relied on the House Un-American Activities Committee's guide as a source for the allegation that the Progressive Citizens of America was pro-Communist. Nizer then got him to admit that any mention of any organization whatever before the House Un-American Activities Committee ended up in the guide. There was a House Un-American Activities Committee Guide and a House Un-American Activities Committee Cumulative Index that just contained every name that was ever mentioned before it.

NIZER: Take the cumulative index of names. You know that President Eisenhower's name appears in that cumulative index, don't you, from our own experience?

MILTON: The index, as I understand it, lists everyone who testified regardless of the nature of their testimony.

NIZER: It also lists anybody who was mentioned by some witness having, say, sent greetings to the Russian Relief or something like that; you would have President Eisenhower on that if he were mentioned? . . . The index would mention the name of any individual who was mentioned by some witness in connection with any activity that he claimed was pro-Communist, right?

MILTON: I'd have to look at that again. I haven't seen that publication for some time. I am not sure. My impression was that it lists only witnesses. Whether it also mentions people who were mentioned by other witnesses I couldn't say now.

NIZER: You don't know that?

MILTON: Not without looking at the publication again.

NIZER: Going back to organizations now, if, for example, Harvey Matusow testified that a certain organization in his opinion was questionable, that organization would appear on this guide index, wouldn't it?

MILTON: Some, yes.

NIZER: And individuals that you have mentioned have appeared on the cumulative index, haven't they?

MILTON: I believe so, yes.

NIZER: Did the House Un-American Activities Guide that you referred to cite solely this California Un-American Activities Committee item, their citation, as a sole basis for calling the Progressive Citizens of America pro-Communists?

MILTON: Talking from recollection, yes.

NIZER: And you have already testified that the California Un-American Activities Committee was unreliable in many respects?

MILTON: In some, yes. I don't know if I said many.

Lou continued to take up each of the charges one by one that Milton had made against me in the AWARE bulletin. Under Lou's merciless cross-examination, Milton admitted that he had no knowledge of the truth of a single one of the charges. But Lou went further. He had Milton admit that he did not even believe in the reliability of many of the sources which he used.

NIZER: My question is, haven't you testified that you had heard, before you wrote Exhibit 41, that the Progressive Citizens of America was simply a liberal organization, not a Communist-front organization, that you had heard that and you had no reason to disbelieve that?

MILTON: The record shows that I did.

NIZER: Nevertheless, you still wrote in Exhibit 41, "Progressive Citizens of America officially designated as a Communist front," didn't you?

MILTON: Yes.

Lou then made Milton admit in each case where he had used the term "officially designated Communist front," it was a calculated misuse of such term. Actually, it had no meaning whatever, since there had been no official finding on any of the so-called Communist-front groups. After getting from Milton an admission that he knew before he wrote the bulletin that I was not a member of any one of the organizations that he mentioned in the bulletin and for which I allegedly entertained, Milton admitted one of the principal points of our charges against the defendant, namely, that the entire problem grew out of my activity in the union. AWARE had attacked me only because I had taken part in the union election.

MILTON: The entire purpose of the entire bulletin was to illuminate a controversy in AFTRA, and another purpose was to draw attention to Mr. Faulk and several other individuals in relation to that question.

Lou drove the point home even more strongly:

NIZER: Isn't it a fact that at this time in July of 1955, the chief officers of AFTRA were either members of AWARE or strong supporters of AWARE?

MILTON: I have to see the list of officers.

Lou then read off a number of names of AFTRA officers who had opposed us most violently: Ned Weaver, Vinton Hayworth, Alan Bunce, Bud Collyer. Milton admitted that they were all either active members or former members of AWARE. He further got Milton to admit that AWARE had become interested in the Middle-of-the-Road slate shortly after we had announced we were running for office in the fall of 1955.

Lou then read from the minutes of a board meeting of AWARE in December 1955, in which the officers of AWARE had discussed preparing a run-down of those who had won on the Middle-of-the Road slate, with particular emphasis on what they called the "worst people on the slate."

NIZER: And the special people that were singled out in Exhibit 41, a Mr. Collingwood, a Mr. Faulk and a Mr. Bean, right, those three?

MILTON: Of the slate, that's right.

It was actually on the fourth item that had been alleged against me in the AWARE bulletin that Mr. Nizer made his strongest case against Milton.

NIZER: The fourth item that you alleged against Mr. Faulk reads as follows: "A program dated April 25, 1946, named 'John Faulk' as a scheduled entertainer (with identified Communist Earl Robinson and two non-Communists) under the auspices of the Independent Citizens Committee of the Arts, Sciences and Professions (officially designated a Communist front, and predecessor of the Progressive Citizens of America)."

Did you write that item, sir?

MILTON: I wrote it or rewrote it.

NIZER: Did you see that program before you wrote Exhibit 41?

MILTON: I believe I did.

NIZER: And you read it, did you not?

MILTON: Yes.

NIZER: You know, therefore, you knew before you wrote Exhibit 41, this charge, that this event was a first-year salute to the United Nations; you knew that, didn't you?

MILTON: Yes, sir. . . .

NIZER: And you deliberately and purposefully omitted the fact that this occasion was a United Nations' salute on the first-year anniversary of the United Nations when you wrote this article that I have read to you from Exhibit 41, didn't you?

MILTON: Yes. . . .

NIZER: You also knew before you wrote Exhibit 41, this item in which you referred to simply Mr. Faulk as an entertainer "with identified Communist Earl Robinson," you also knew at that time that on this occasion the Secretary of State of the United States at that time, Edward Stettinius, was a speaker? You knew that too didn't you?

MILTON: Yes.

NIZER: And you deliberately and purposefully omitted that from this item, didn't you?

MILTON: That's right. . . .

NIZER: You observed from looking at Exhibit 53 that the Columbia Broadcasting System broadcast this event on a network? Do you see that? Not only do you see it, didn't you notice that before you wrote your item in Exhibit 41?

MILTON: Yes, yes. . . .

NIZER: You also saw by looking at Exhibit 53, which you say you read before you published this, that Trygve Lie of the United Nations also was there and presided in a way over that part of the program? You noticed that, didn't you?

MILTON: Yes, sir.

NIZER: And you purposefully and deliberately omitted that fact in describing the occasion which you said Mr. Faulk attended, didn't you?

MILTON: That's right. . . .

NIZER: And you noticed and knew before you wrote Exhibit 41 that among the sponsors of this event which you accused Mr. Faulk of attending was the American Association of the United Nations, right? You noticed that?

MILTON: Yes.

NIZER: And the American Association of University Women?

MILTON: Yes, the whole list.

NIZER: And the American Bar Association?

MILTON: Yes.

NIZER: And the Young Men's Christian Association?

MILTON: Yes.

And then Nizer moving close up before Milton looked him in the eye and demanded:

NIZER: . . . Wasn't it your purpose when you wrote this item in the way you did to give the impression to the sponsors, the advertising agency, the newspapers to whom you mailed this Exhibit 41, that Mr. Faulk had attended a pro-Communist function? Wasn't that your purpose?

MILTON: I said so, didn't I?

Every now and then I would glance back into the spectators' section during the grilling that Lou was giving Milton. Bob Cenedella, Philo Higley and their wives and several other writers who had had unhappy experiences as a result of Mr. Milton's maneuverings in the years past sat with expressions of grim satisfaction as he squirmed and floundered before Lou's relentless cross-examination. It was interesting to note that none of the writers wore expressions of vengeance. They were not unkind men. Rather, they seemed to be feeling that at long last the world was being told something that they had known for many years—a shabby hoax had been perpetrated on the television industry and the American public. Now, it was being revealed for what it really was. When Milton was finally dismissed from the witness stand, he did not look like a very fearsome fellow, nor did the cause of the defendants seem very much improved.

24

The last week in May, Lou suggested that I take a couple of days off to visit friends, relax, and get my mind completely off the case. For two months I had chafed because I'd been unable to visit with long-time friends. I had promised many of them that we would get together the first chance I got. The chance seemed to have arrived. Forty-eight hours of complete freedom! When Lou announced that I would be free to make plans I desired, I sat down at the phone to start calling. I couldn't decide whom to call first.

I called Chris and Merle to tell them the good news. Chris said she just that moment finished talking with Myrna Loy about the case. Myrna was rehearsing for a play and had been able to get to court only a couple of times. I remembered with a pang of guilt that I had failed to call Myrna regularly and report as I had promised to do. Myrna had been a good and faithful friend and I knew how interested she was in the developments. Chris said Merle wanted us to go down to "Second City" and catch a new show they were having and then have dinner in Greenwich Village. "Fine," I said, "and I'll call Myrna and see if she would like to join us." Myrna went along and it was a fine evening, full of animated talk. But I discovered an uncomfortable fact as the evening progressed. No matter what was going on on the stage or what subject was being discussed, I unconsciously but persistently turned the conversation back to the trial. Not only that, but I found myself thinking of excuses for not seeing friends that weekend. By the time the evening was over I had made a firm decision: I would call no one. Instead, I would go up to the Bronx Zoo the following day, alone, and I would start seeing friends the following night.

After a happy day at the zoo, wandering about and procrastinating about making phone calls, I remembered that Lou had subpoenaed the entire set of minutes of AWARE, Inc.'s board meetings. I had only got to glance at them. I went down to the office and got them from George Berger. I spent the rest of my brief vacation going through the minutes and making notes. They were instructive reading. They faithfully reported each board meeting of AWARE; who was present; what was discussed; and who said what, about what. Lou, of course, had subpoenaed them for use as evidence of the defendants' deliberate plan to destroy my career, and they had it all there, all right, in black and white. I got a kind of behind-the-scenes look at exactly what AWARE's reaction had been to the announcement, made back in November 1955, of our running for office in the union. They had been pretty unhappy about it. A month later, after our slate had been elected in the AFTRA election AWARE's minutes reported the following:

> AFTRA election. General discussion of attack on AWARE by John Henry Faulk. Mr. Keene spoke for getting background on all those who won from the other slate, while Mr. Weaver spoke for concentrating only on the bad ones. It was generally decided that AWARE should not make a statement at this time. Mr. Hartnett suggested reprinting two columns from the Daily Worker with a few comments by AWARE and then send the copies to the agencies. He is to prepare a run-down on the worst people on the slate and a special board meeting will be held to approve it.

There were many other interesting items in the AWARE minutes. Those that interested me most, however, were the several references to Henry Jaffe. The minutes reported that AWARE's members went to Jaffe (at that time he was counsel for AFTRA) during the spring and summer of 1955 while AWARE had been under attack in the union. Jaffe had suggested strategy for their attacks on other union members. This was a matter that Mr. Jaffe never thought to mention during the unhappy period of our association with him back in '56.

On June 6, the day Vincent Hartnett followed Paul Milton to the witness stand, a heat wave was settling over New York. The courtroom was getting uncomfortably warm and Justice Geller directed attendants to put up tall electric fans near the jury to keep jurors as comfortable as possible. He suggested that the men on the jury might remove their jackets but cautioned that none of the spectators in the courtroom might do so.

As I watched Hartnett being sworn in and taking his seat in the witness chair, I had the feeling that had it been sweltering hot or icy cold in the courtroom, Hartnett's precise proper manner would have been the same, unaffected by any outside influence.

Sitting there neat and prim, his mouth a thin straight line, his eyes straight ahead, he gave the appearance of a well-disciplined little soldier, awaiting orders, which he would carry out to the minutest detail. It touched me somehow, to see that he wore a military decoration in the lapel of his neat blue jacket. For some reason I felt terribly sorry for him at that moment. My own direct testimony had taken a week, two full days of which had been spent reciting my virtues and accomplishments in open court. I assumed that Hartnett would take at least that much time, perhaps more, so I settled back into my chair as Bolan began Hartnett's direct examination. As a matter of fact I was eager to hear about Hartnett's background. I knew very little about it, since our researches and examinations of him had been confined to his doings subsequent to 1950. Bolan seemed to be just as eager to have Hartnett go into his background as I was to hear about it. Mr. Hartnett, it turned out, was even born on a patriotic note.

BOLAN: Mr. Hartnett, when and where were you born?

HARTNETT: I was born in St. Louis, Missouri, on July 4, 1916.

. . . .

BOLAN: What colleges did you attend?

HARTNETT: I attended Fordham University for my freshman year, 1933 to 1934; and I transferred to the University of Notre Dame, where I studied from 1934 to 1937, when I got my B.A. degree.

BOLAN: Was that with honors?

HARTNETT: Yes, maxima cum laude.

NIZER: I object to this, Your Honor. The character and reputation of the defendant are not in issue.

THE COURT: That is correct, but I will allow a certain degree of background, a limited amount, Mr. Bolan, because it is Mr. Faulk that is suing, and the defendant's reputation is not involved in this case.

BOLAN: What other degree did you receive?

HARTNETT: I received also my M.A. degree in 1939, also maxima cum laude, with highest honors.

. . . .

BOLAN: In connection with obtaining your Master's degree at Notre Dame, did you take any courses dealing with Communism?

HARTNETT: Yes. . . .

BOLAN: What were those courses?

NIZER: Objection.

THE COURT: Sustained.

BOLAN: I am trying to line up a foundation to establish Mr. Hartnett as an expert in the field of Communism and Communist infiltration of the radio and television industry.

THE COURT: I will let you—on the question of Communism, I don't understand the concept of an expert on Communism. An expert has to be an expert on a scientific subject or something of that character. You may qualify him, if you intend to use him as an expert, in the practices of the radio and television industry. That you may do, but on the question of Communism, you may elicit any facts that he has, but the jury is the one that will have to judge that, Mr. Bolan.

Bolan continued to try to get testimony of Hartnett's background into the record, especially that of his background in the Navy during the war. He was allowed to tell how he had been commissioned an ensign in the United States Navy in 1942 and that he had gone thereafter on active duty.

Bolan followed what I considered a rather odd course in his direct examination of Hartnett. It seemed to me that he was having Hartnett describe his occupation exactly as we had described it—that of a private vigilante.

BOLAN: Mr. Hartnett, beginning in August 1952, what was your occupation?

HARTNETT: A professional consultant on the Communist and/or Communist-front records of persons working in the entertainment industry, particularly radio and television.

BOLAN: Did you continue in that occupation through and until 1956?

HARTNETT: I did.

BOLAN: Was that a full-time job?

HARTNETT: Yes.

BOLAN: Mr. Hartnett, you testified that you began accumulating files [reports on entertainers] particularly in 1949, you started to build up files concerning the Communist infiltration of the radio and television industry. Did you use those files in connection with your work as a researcher?

HARTNETT: Yes.

BOLAN: Will you tell us briefly what your files consisted of?

HARTNETT: First, a virtually complete file of all the published hearings and reports of the Special Committee on Un-American Activities of the United States House of Representatives and of the successor committee, the Standing House Committee on Un-American Activities of the House of Representatives.

Secondly, all the relevant published hearings and reports of the Senate Internal Security Subcommittee.

Thirdly, all the relevant published hearings and reports of the Senate Permanent Subcommittee on Government Operations, some incidental reports and other Congressional investigating committees.

A file of Communist publications, particularly of the "Daily Worker," official organ of the Communist Party. A file of "Masses and Mainstream," monthly Communist magazine, and its successor, "Mainstream." A file of "Sing Out," a publication of People's Artists, successor to People's Songs. Some early Communist theatrical literature such as "Tack Magazine," "Theatre Arts Committee Magazine," "New Theatre Magazine," a Communist monthly publication in the theatre. A file of the "Daily Compass," a party-line newspaper, a daily newspaper. A file of show business, "Actor's Cues," which at a certain period contained a good many items about Communist-front activities in entertainment.

NIZER: I object to these conclusions as to what these publications contained. He was asked to give the names of the publications.

HARTNETT: A collection of what we term primary source material, that is, letterheads, circulars, programs and announcements of various Communist-front organizations.

NIZER: I object to that phrase, "Communist-front organizations" as a conclusion of this witness.

THE COURT: Yes, strike that out.

Hartnett testified that what he didn't have in his own files he could usually find over in the theatre collection at the New York Public Library, the place he frequently went to for further information on artists. Having described his mighty files of gossip, Hartnett then began to testify on the happy days back in 1952 when he went into business.

BOLAN: Mr. Hartnett, after you went into this research business in 1952, did you obtain any clients on a regular basis?

HARTNETT: Yes.

BOLAN: Who was your first client?

HARTNETT: The Borden Company.

BOLAN: When did you obtain that client?

HARTNETT: In August 1952.

BOLAN: Did you have any discussion with any official of Borden's prior to your being engaged?

HARTNETT: Yes.

BOLAN: With whom?

HARTNETT: Stuart Peabody.

BOLAN: What was his position with Borden's?

HARTNETT: In general, over-all charge of their advertising program.

BOLAN: What duties did you perform for Borden's after you were retained?

NIZER: Objection, your Honor.

THE COURT: I will allow it. You may answer. Don't give us conversations. Just indicate the services and duties you performed.

HARTNETT: I checked the names of prospective employees on their television program for any known Communist Party or Communist-front records.

NIZER: I object to the word "known" as a characterization.

THE COURT: Right, strike it out. Bear in mind what I said before, Mr. Hartnett. It is for the jury to make determinations, so that if you refer to them, don't characterize it as "known." That is for the jury to determine, not your conclusion. . . .

BOLAN: What was your financial arrangement with Borden's, Mr. Hartnett?

HARTNETT: Initially, a fee of $20 for each name checked.

BOLAN: Did the arrangement change subsequent to that?

HARTNETT: Yes, as the volume of names increased, by mutual agreement, we set a fee of $5.00 per name checked, and later, of $2.00 if a name was repeated, came back a second or third time.

BOLAN: Were you later paid a flat fee by Borden's?

HARTNETT: I was.

He continued—proudly, I thought—to list the names of clients he had. There were Lever Brothers, the American Broadcasting Company, Young & Rubicam advertising agency, the Kudner Agency. I was particularly interested in the American Broadcasting Company being one of Mr. Hartnett's clients at that time. For Hartnett testified that prior to being retained by the American Broadcasting Company, he had discussed his being hired, with one of the officials of the company, Miss Geraldine B. Zorbaugh, who was General Counsel for ABC. This same Miss Geraldine B. Zorbaugh was in the Legal Department of CBS at the time, a couple of months earlier, when we were trying to get records which had been turned over to Roy Cohn. Hartnett sought to relate how he had furnished information to various government agencies including the F.B.I., but this was not permitted by Judge Geller, who said, "Obviously, anybody can supply information to any governmental authority, if they ask for it, or voluntarily they can appear before it. That doesn't add anything to the issues in this case."

As Hartnett reeled off the names of the big companies that had done business with him, I wondered if the jury was thinking the same thing that I was at that moment about the so-called responsible American companies who hired Mr. Hartnett.

I was somehow impressed with the sincerity with which Hartnett was testifying. I was convinced that he really didn't know what his testimony sounded like to a nonbeliever. There I sat listening—I who had been unemployed for the last five years, largely through the doings of Mr. Hartnett—scarcely able to keep from laughing out loud at such testimony as:

BOLAN: Did you, when you rendered any reports, indicate whether the performer, artist, or who it may be, should or should not be employed?
HARTNETT: In my reports? My reports were always strictly objective, sir.

Or when Hartnett made reference to instances wherein his compassionate understanding impelled him to leniency:

> I recollect in a couple of cases where an individual—several cases where individuals had been involved in the Communist Party or seriously considered Communist-front groups, that I felt that there had been a repudiation of such, and a positive favorable information; and in such cases, for example, Lee J. Cobb, Frank Maxwell, and a few others—I did there recommend that the person be given a break, yes.

Or when Hartnett was testifying as to the methods he followed in giving his reports to his clients:

> Well, the initial report would be almost always by telephone, and then there would be a written report where there was information to be reported. However, I want to make this point, that I was generally— such a volume that I could often be behind in the written reports.

Bolan and Hartnett ran into a real problem. For years, Hartnett, AWARE and others had been citing the House Un-American Activities Committee as their authority for allegations of Communism or pro-Communism. For years Mr. Hartnett had been selling such information to sponsors, networks, agencies and the general public. Now Mr. Hartnett was in a court of law; and each time he applied the term "Communist or pro-Communist" to an individual or an organization Judge Geller informed him that in a court of law such characterizations are not admissible unless their truth is established. Hartnett would fall back on the citations of the House Un-American Activities Committee. Repeatedly, Judge Geller would state that these citations of the House Un-American Activities Committee had no legal standing as truth:

> . . . those citations, as I have already told the jury, are not binding and do not constitute a finding—a proper finding. It must be a judicial finding, and those statements of citations by the House Committee and

the Attorney General's list do not constitute truth, or that this organization is such a Communist-character organization.

That will be for the jury to determine, as I have already said, based on all the facts addressed to this particular organization.

Mr. Bolan seemed somewhat surprised by the judge's ruling.

BOLAN: Your Honor, unless I misunderstand, and I would like some clarification, in other words, unless it can be established that this organization by judicial process was designated and found to be a Communist-front, no testimony on that area is permitted.

THE COURT: No, I didn't say that, Mr. Bolan. I did not say it. I said that the jury will make the determination based on the evidence that you offered. I did say that the House Un-American Activities Committee citation, the Attorney General's list citation, do not constitute proof that these organizations—that this organization—is a Communist-front or a Communist or a pro-Communist organization; and I elaborated on that fully. Such citations or listings by the House Committee or Attorney General do not constitute a judicial finding that an organization is a Communistic or pro-Communistic front organization.

So it came about that the only thing that Mr. Hartnett could do was to attempt, by testifying that he had relied on the House Un-American Activities Committee reports in good faith, to mitigate the damages that might be assessed. That was at least a partial defense, but it had nothing whatever to do with *truth,* which would have been a complete defense.

By the end of the second day of Hartnett's direct testimony, when I was beginning to be terribly bored with it, Bolan announced that he had completed his direct examination. Word went out from spectators to friends outside that Nizer was about to start his cross-examination. As Lou stood up, I knew that my prolonged experience with the defendants had reached a stage that was in a way the most dramatic of the whole affair. But it was about three-thirty in the afternoon, and I supposed that Lou wouldn't get really warmed up on Hartnett in the short time before court adjourned. I was mistaken. Lou plunged right in, hitting Hartnett where he lived—in the House Un-American Activities Committee reports.

NIZER: Now, sir, we have had all these booklets and citations offered on the subject of reliance all day today. You realize that citations of the House Un-American Activities Committee are not official designations; isn't that so? . . .

HARTNETT: Yes, in the legal sense. . . .

NIZER: None of the people who employed you to give them data about professional artists who were going to appear on radio and television, none of those ever made an inquiry to you about Mr. John Henry Faulk, did they?

HARTNETT: No.

NIZER: Did you ever, in the case of John Henry Faulk, write to employers of John Henry Faulk citing anything against his record so far as patriotism and loyalty are concerned even though you weren't employed by that sponsor agency?

HARTNETT: Not to my knowledge, no sir.

. . . .

NIZER: Is it not a fact, Mr. Hartnett, that on your own, without anybody asking you for any information, you wrote to employers of John Henry Faulk complaining about his background of Communist affiliation? That is a fact, isn't it?

HARTNETT: No, not to my knowledge, it is not a fact.

NIZER: I show you Exhibit 58-A. Are you the writer of this letter to Young & Rubicam, the agency? In 1955?

HARTNETT: Yes.

NIZER: I read to you from your letter of November 27, 1955: "Since the name of Louise Allbritton was proposed, she has been announced as a candidate for the Independent ticket of AFTRA, New York Local board. I find no Communist or Communist-front record on her, however, and therefore conclude that she is just a liberal. The coleader of this ticket is John Henry Faulk. He has a significant Communist-front record." Did you write that to Young & Rubicam?

HARTNETT: Yes.

NIZER: At that time, had Young & Rubicam asked you for any opinion about John Henry Faulk?

HARTNETT: No.

Hartnett had justified his collecting of fees for clearing performers on the grounds that he was an expert, and that he investigated with great care and accuracy. He had stated time and again that he knew that any mistakes he made could result in serious harm to the artist. It was in this area of his activities that Nizer began his cross-examination. Just how much care had Mr. Hartnett taken in the case of me, for instance, how well had he checked my background, what had he omitted and what had he made up?

There had been a rather laudatory article about me in *Newsweek* Magazine back in 1952. A careful researcher could certainly have found it. Lou, holding a file card in his hand that Hartnett had kept on me in his files, stood in front of Hartnett and asked:

NIZER: There is a reference on your file card, is there not, to "Newsweek," December 29, 1952; is that correct?

HARTNETT: I believe that's the date there was a reference to "Newsweek."

NIZER: And there was an article you found out in "Newsweek" about Mr. Faulk, correct?

HARTNETT: That's correct.

NIZER: Did you look at that article before you published Exhibit 41?

HARTNETT: No.

NIZER: You say you didn't look for the "Newsweek" article at all, even though you knew there was one?

HARTNETT: I did not know there was one prior to the publication.

NIZER: You did not?

HARTNETT: No sir. . . .

NIZER: Mr. Hartnett, you have a stamp, have you not, which you plant on these file cards on which you keep your records. A stamp?

HARTNETT: A rubber stamp.

NIZER: And that rubber stamp has about 13 different sources that you check off; is that correct?

HARTNETT: I wouldn't be sure there were 13, sir, without looking. It varied as more publications were issued.

NIZER: And when you made this card for John Henry Faulk, among the items on the rubber stamp were N.Y.P.L., what does that stand for?

HARTNETT: New York Public Library.

NIZER: Before you wrote Exhibit 41, did you go through all of these rubber stamp sources for information?

HARTNETT: I'd have to look at that, sir, just to make sure. It would be marked if I had.

NIZER: You mean that you would occasionally not even check at all? . . . on these sources which are listed on the rubber stamp?

HARTNETT: I would not always check on all those sources.

NIZER: Then you would never know whether you had turned up everything that was either for or against the man, would you?

BOLAN: I object.

THE COURT: Sustained.

NIZER: You have told us how thoroughly you checked in your practice of checking on a person's record, that you were very thorough and careful, have you not?

HARTNETT: Yes, I would say that I was thorough and careful.

NIZER: And even though you were thorough and careful, you tell us that there were occasions when you would send in a report about the people that you were reporting about, without checking all of the items which you had for sources on this card?

HARTNETT: Yes. . . .

NIZER: Did you go through all the sources which you had placed on your rubber stamp for checking?

HARTNETT: No, not in every case.

NIZER: Therefore, isn't it true that when you handed in these reports, in those instances where you didn't check all, you couldn't be sure that you had given a complete report, could you? That's correct, isn't it?

HARTNETT: As complete as was asked for.

NIZER: As asked for?

HARTNETT: Yes.

NIZER: Do you mean to say, Mr. Hartnett, that when your so-called client asked for a name, that he told you what sources to check?

HARTNETT: No, he didn't tell me.

NIZER: Then he didn't ask you for specific information. He asked you for your report on this man's alleged affiliations, didn't he? Wasn't that the meaning of it?

HARTNETT: Yes, if there were any alleged Communist or Communist-front affiliations.

NIZER: And unless you checked all the sources, you couldn't be sure either that you had all of the alleged Communist-front affiliations or things which were favorable to the man which would negate that. Isn't that so?

HARTNETT: No, I could not be 100 per cent sure.

NIZER: But you knew at the time you submitted the report that the man might lose his job, didn't you?

HARTNETT: No, not necessarily at all.

NIZER: You knew that in many instances in which you submitted reports the people lost their jobs, didn't you?

HARTNETT: I don't think that's precisely correct, because they didn't already have a job.

NIZER: You mean they didn't already have a job? Didn't you submit reports on many occasions where the man was trying to get a job and you were giving a report about him? That's right, isn't it?

HARTNETT: No, that's not right.

NIZER: Well, either the man was working or he was trying to get work. One of those two alternatives applied?

HARTNETT: No, I don't think that is correct.

NIZER: When you submitted your report about these people, if the report was adverse, you knew that there was a real likelihood that these people would not get that job on that television show, didn't you?

HARTNETT: If it was really adverse, yes.

NIZER: Yes, and yet when you submitted that report there were occasions when you hadn't even looked all the sources up with respect to these people, did you? Isn't that so? Yes or no to that.

HARTNETT: That's correct.

NIZER: Did you consider it important to find the affirmative things, the good parts of a man's record, as well as any meeting he might have attended, let's say, of a Wallace rally? Didn't you want to know whether he had served in the Army and other things that might be helpful to the patriotic record?

HARTNETT: I certainly did, so much that I spent over 750 hours in the public library checking for such information.

NIZER: Did you go to the New York Public Library with respect to John Faulk before you published Exhibit 41?

HARTNETT: I most certainly did.

NIZER: Did you look up in the public library any publications such as "Newsweek" that had been published about him?

HARTNETT: I initially found no references whatever to "Newsweek."

NIZER: You say that you found out about "Newsweek" four months after

Exhibit 41 was published on February 10, 1956; approximately four months?

HARTNETT: That's my best recollection, four or five months.

NIZER: So that would make it what—March, April, May, June or July of 1956?

HARTNETT: I would say so.

NIZER: Haven't you testified that the first time you found out about "Newsweek" was in December 1957?

HARTNETT: I don't recall that, sir.

Lou then read from Hartnett's examination before trial a clear and unequivocal statement that he had first learned about the *Newsweek* article on December 5, 1957. Then turning to Hartnett he asked:

Did you make that answer?

HARTNETT: Apparently I did, yes.

NIZER: Was it correct when you made it?

HARTNETT: It must have been. I apparently had the document in my hand.

NIZER: Do you take back your answer that you found out about it four or five months—

BOLAN: Objection.

THE COURT: Sustained.

NIZER: Were you correct when you testified a few moments ago that you found out about "Newsweek" in June or July 1956?

HARTNETT: Apparently not, no.

Lou then got from Hartnett the admission that he had checked all the indexes of the House Un-American Activities Committee hearings. He had found my name in only one place, the Sixth Edition of the Cumulative Index of the HUAC hearings, and it appeared there as John B. Faulk, which Hartnett characterized as a typographical error or a garbled version.

NIZER: This reference was to the item of those several hundred names that were supposed to be sponsors of what was called the United States Sponsors of American Continental Congress for Peace; is that the reference?

HARTNETT: Yes.

NIZER: Did you ever check with any of those several hundred names as to whether Faulk had attended that Peace Congress?

HARTNETT: No.

NIZER: Had you ever lifted the telephone or personally talked to Mr. Faulk and asked him whether he had authorized his name or attended that conference? Did you do that as a check?

HARTNETT: No, I did not.

Nizer then got a very interesting admission from Mr. Hartnett.

NIZER: Weren't you a member of the American Civil Liberties Union under your own name?

HARTNETT: Yes, I had a membership card in the American Civil Liberties Union.

NIZER: Was that union at a later time cited by the very California committee you have been citing in this case a Communist front?

HARTNETT: Yes, it was cited by the California committee [the Tenney Committee]. . . .

NIZER: . . . Therefore, if you were still publishing "Red Channels," you would have listed yourself, if you were following regular procedure?

HARTNETT: I would never list anybody for membership in the American Civil Liberties Union. . . .

NIZER: One of the charges, one of the facts, one of the flags you would wave to warn a sponsor is that this man appeared, was a member of a committee condemned by the Un-American Activities Committee, the investigating committee of California called the Tenney Committee?

HARTNETT: I would list it, sir.

NIZER: Therefore, if you prepared such a list, you would list yourself, wouldn't you?

HARTNETT: I was never called upon to bring a report home on myself.

NIZER: If you were preparing such a list, you would list yourself if you were consistent?

HARTNETT: No, because I never listed anyone solely for that one thing. I differ with the Tenney Committee. I don't know if it has characterized the National A.C.L.U., but I wouldn't list anybody merely because of that.

NIZER: If you had only one listing against somebody else, you wouldn't list it at all?

HARTNETT: I don't think I ever did in publication, but I would so state in a report to a client.

Nizer elicited from Hartnett some of the standards he used in listing people.

NIZER: Now, being listed in the index of the House Un-American Activities Committee can be of no significance whatsoever, isn't that so?

HARTNETT: It can be of no significance.

NIZER: As a matter of fact, you testified that President Eisenhower's name is listed, haven't you?

HARTNETT: Former President Eisenhower's name is, I believe, listed in the Cumulative Index.

NIZER: Isn't it a fact that the House Un-American Activities Committee Index will list the name of anybody that anybody has testified to, or any letterhead that has been offered with all the names is put into the index; isn't that a general practice?

HARTNETT: Yes, the general practice is that there is included in the Cumulative Index of the House Un-American Ac—the House Committee on Un-American Activities any reference in published testimony to persons or organizations, and to names listed on exhibits entered in evidence.

NIZER: Have you not testified that if President Eisenhower wanted to go on radio or television, since he has become ex-President, that you would list him on your citation, that you would list in your report these citations in the House Un-American Activities Committee?

HARTNETT: Yes.

If we could show and prove that the defendants had attacked my patriotism and loyalty without even believing their own allegations against me, it would go a long way toward proving malice and establishing the chances of our recovering punitive damages from them. Lou set out to do this.

NIZER: You have testified on direct examination that you were the author of "Red Channels," is that correct?

HARTNETT: Co-author.

NIZER: What year was that published in?

HARTNETT: 1950.

NIZER: All of the seven specifications against Mr. John Henry Faulk are with respect to occasions—right or wrong they are with respect to occasions that took place before 1950, aren't they, every one of them?

HARTNETT: Yes, we all know that.

NIZER: And in "Red Channels" you listed the names of a number of television and radio entertainers who you charged had pro-Communist affiliations, didn't you?

HARTNETT: That's a generally accurate characterization.

NIZER: And nevertheless, you never mentioned John Henry Faulk in "Red Channels," did you?

HARTNETT: I did not.

NIZER: In addition to "Red Channels," you prepared, as you claimed, a far more comprehensive summary of the alleged Communist-front affiliations of actors and entertainers which you called File 13; right?

HARTNETT: . . . I did.

NIZER: Again, prior to that publication of File 13, all the alleged seven specifications against Mr. John Henry Faulk, true or not, all of them preceded File No. 13, that first volume; right?

HARTNETT: That's right.

NIZER: And you never included the name of John Henry Faulk in your comprehensive File 13, did you?

HARTNETT: No. . . .

NIZER: In addition to that File 13, you kept personal notes from your personal file in which you intended to include virtually every entertainer with Communist-front affiliations according to you, didn't you keep such a file?

HARTNETT: Yes.

NIZER: And prior to Exhibit 41, had you ever included Mr. Faulk's name in that file?

HARTNETT: Yes.

NIZER: In your File 13?

HARTNETT: Yes.

BOLAN: I object.

NIZER: All right, let's see if you testify to that (p. 605, Harnett's examination before trial). At the bottom:

NIZER: I believe at one time during this examination, you defined File 13 to include not only the publications you released but your own personal file?

HARTNETT: Yes, I used it as a cover term for all that.

NIZER: Did you have any reference to Mr. Faulk in File 13 which you published in 1951?

HARTNETT: No.

Did you make that answer?

HARTNETT: Yes, I have just so testified.

NIZER: Was it correct when you made it?

HARTNETT: Surely.

NIZER: And you have stated that "Red Channels" was the most comprehensive listing of persons with alleged Communist-front affiliations that had ever been published by a private organization, haven't you?

HARTNETT: . . . Yes.

NIZER: Then you prepared Volume 2 of your File 13, didn't you?

HARTNETT: Yes.

NIZER: And that again listed any actor with an alleged Communist-front affiliation, didn't it? . . .

HARTNETT: No, not any actor.

NIZER: Only some actors?

HARTNETT: I think about 90 in all, performers, directors, producers, writers.

NIZER: And together between Volume 1 of File 13 and Volume 2 of File 13, you were intending to cover all of those that you could file who had, according to you, Communist-front affiliations?

HARTNETT: Oh, no, no.

NIZER: Did the volume have 200 names in it?

HARTNETT: Give or take 10 or 20, it had 200 names.

NIZER: Was Mr. Faulk's name listed in that at all?

HARTNETT: No.

NIZER: You have testified that you read at least a large majority of the government's publications having any relation to Communist-front participations, haven't you?

HARTNETT: Of people in the entertainment industry and the literary field, not all fields of endeavor.

NIZER: Mr. Faulk is in that field, of course?

HARTNETT: Yes.

NIZER: You have not seen Mr. Faulk's name mentioned by any witness in those publications, did you?

HARTNETT: Yes, he was mentioned by a witness.

NIZER: The only time he was mentioned after Exhibit 41 was by Mr. Milton who testified that he brought a suit which you are testifying in now: isn't that the only other reference?

HARTNETT: Yes, that is the reference I had in mind.

.   .   .   .

NIZER: After the period between 1949 and 1955, six years preceding your writing of Exhibit 41, you yourself attended a number of Communist-front meetings, didn't you?

HARTNETT: Yes.

NIZER: Those meetings were attended by persons in groups who were connected with the radio and television industry, weren't they?

HARTNETT: Yes.

NIZER: The subject matter of some of those meetings was in connection with the radio and television industry?

HARTNETT: Yes.

NIZER: You never saw Mr. Faulk at a single one of those meetings, did you?

HARTNETT: I don't recall that I did. I never knew him.

NIZER: You never heard his name mentioned at any of those meetings, did you?

HARTNETT: I can't recall that I did.

NIZER: Even if Mr. Faulk had attended any of the functions which you referred to in Exhibit 41, he could have done so without the slightest knowledge of the alleged Communist-front nature of the event and been there innocently, correct?

HARTNETT: Well, that would be difficult to concede to the Jefferson School of Social Science.

NIZER: So as to make progress, let us for the moment leave out the Jefferson School, which Mr. Faulk, you know, denies he ever heard of or went to. With the exception of that, take the other six affiliations, affiliated fronts that you say he attended even though there is a dispute about it. Have you not testified that he could have done so without the slightest knowledge of the alleged Communist-front nature of the events that had been there innocently?

HARTNETT: There is so much testimony, Mr. Nizer, I don't recall. I really don't recall it.

NIZER: Which one of the seven items do you say are those that he could have attended innocently even if he had been there? Just give us the ones that you would say, even assuming he had attended, that could have been very innocent, a loyal American going there.

HARTNETT: Club 65. . . . The Independent Citizens Committee of Arts, Sciences and Professions, Year One Salute to the United Nations, Stage for Action, Headline Cabaret. Sending greetings to People's Song on its second anniversary. . . . Showtime for Wallace, contributed cabaret material.

NIZER: The Jefferson School you excluded, that is fixed?

HARTNETT: Yes.

NIZER: And the possible sponsorship, his name on some kind of document of the American Continental Congress for Peace, or the claim that it was, would you include that as an innocent one possibly?

HARTNETT: It could possibly be.

NIZER: So you have mentioned six out of the seven as being innocent.

HARTNETT: No no, possibly.

NIZER: Possibly innocent. And have you not testified not merely that those were possibly innocent, but that they could have been attended in good faith?

HARTNETT: I can't—.

NIZER: Let me read it [Hartnett's examination before trial] so you don't trouble yourself.

HARTNETT: Would you please?

Lou then read from Hartnett's EBT a direct quote of Hartnett saying, "I had no knowledge, I had no evidence to back up a charge that he [Faulk] was pro-Communist. He might have attended those things in good faith."

NIZER: Did you make that answer?

HARTNETT: Yes.

NIZER: At the time you signed and swore to this testimony, was that still a correct answer?

HARTNETT: Yes. . . .

NIZER: Let me ask you, during the entire time prior to Exhibit 41 and when you wrote it, did you have any authority from any governmental agency to do this kind of work . . . of checking records of alleged Communist affiliations of any artist?

HARTNETT: Was I authorized by any government body? No.

NIZER: You were acting entirely as a private citizen in doing this checking, weren't you?

HARTNETT: In doing this checking, yes.

NIZER: Did you have any authority from the F.B.I. to do the checking that you were doing for these sponsors, associations, television companies, or advertising agencies?

HARTNETT: No.

I was impressed by Hartnett's ability to keep up a front as Nizer carried him through his embarrassing testimony. In spite of the fact that he admitted that he had not found my name in any of the favorite spots in which he looked for subversives, he answered each question precisely and confidently.

I had noticed that, from his first day on the stand, Hartnett would occasionally take a card from his inside pocket and jot down a note on it after looking at the clock on the wall. Eventually it became clear that he was noting the arrival or departure of certain spectators. He continued doing it when Nizer was cross-examining him; yet he did it so unobtrusively that Nizer, who might be preoccupied with his notes or arguing a point before the judge, didn't notice it. It became obvious, however, that Hartnett was plying his trade right in the witness box—he was writing down the names of actors and actresses who were attending the trial, and he was recording the times at which they came or went. What possible use he could make of this information could only be surmised.

I mentioned this behavior of Hartnett's to Nizer at lunch that day. Later in the afternoon, he began the cross-examination by asking Hartnett about the notes he was making. He asked the question in a tone of voice that would not have been inappropriate had the notes been an execution list. Hartnett's admission that he was writing people's names on his cards brought a gasp from the judge and the jury, who leaned forward and peered at Hartnett as though he had admitted to a monstrous crime. Lou asked no further questions about the cards.

There were times when Hartnett's testimony caused me to become so tense with anger that I would have to take a walk in the corridor to calm myself enough to sit and listen to any more of it. I don't believe my anger was personal; that is, it stemmed not from the fact that I had been the target of Hartnett's calculated plan, but rather from the fact that Hartnett symbolized the poison that had seeped through the entire country from Hollywood to New York. I had had the good luck to be able to do something about him. I knew that there were many hundreds of honorable citizens who had not been so fortunate, and I felt deeply for them.

Lou kept Hartnett's testimony to the matter of whether he had been motivated by malice.

NIZER: You never met John Henry Faulk before you wrote Exhibit 41, did you?

HARTNETT: Not to my knowledge, sir. I don't believe I did.

NIZER: Did you make any effort whatsoever to get in touch with him before publishing Exhibit 41, to check any of the things that you were going to say about him?

HARTNETT: No.

. . . .

NIZER: You knew, of course, with respect to these items in Exhibit 41 that you were alleging a onetime alleged appearance, not a regular association?

HARTNETT: A onetime scheduled appearance of sponsorship or sending greeting, yes.

. . . .

NIZER: Was it your policy, in making these reports or in writing bulletins, to limit yourself to charges which were supported by documents?

HARTNETT: Yes.

NIZER: In how many of these seven charges did you not have in your physical possession the document which is referred to in the charges at the time you wrote Exhibit 41?

HARTNETT: I did not have in my physical possession 4 or 5 of the supporting documents.

NIZER: And I call your attention to the middle of that paragraph, "Faulk was reported to have stated that the victorious slate's principal platform was opposition to AWARE and to have said: 'The first interest of a union's officers should be employment of members, not blacklisting them.' "

The only newspaper which is referred to in that item by name is the

"Daily Worker," correct?

HARTNETT: By name, yes.

NIZER: This quote appears there under the beginning of a paragraph which says: "On December 15, the Communist organ," meaning the "Daily Worker"—this quote comes from the "Herald Tribune," doesn't it?

HARTNETT: Yes it does.

NIZER: And you had the New York "Herald Tribune" in front of you when you wrote those words, didn't you?

HARTNETT: I most likely did, yes.

NIZER: You didn't mention the name of the "Herald Tribune" as a source of that quote, did you?

HARTNETT: No I didn't.

NIZER: And it was your purpose, wasn't it, to give to the reader the impression, when he read in Exhibit 41, that it was the "Daily Worker" to whom Mr. Faulk had said these things which you were quoting, wasn't it?

HARTNETT: Yes.

Paul Martinson had extracted from Hartnett back in 1958, testimony to the effect that he had prepared an original draft of the AWARE bulletin which was much longer that the one mailed out. Paul had managed to get hold of one page of this original draft; it had far more pernicious things to say about me than the one which was actually mailed out, and he had questioned Hartnett about it extensively. Hartnett could only produce the one page at the time of his EBT, claiming that he had destroyed the rest of it.

NIZER: You knew when this suit was instituted, by talking to your attorneys, that one of the questions that would be involved in litigation would be any malice on your part or AWARE's part in preparation of this document; didn't you know that?

HARTNETT: I would say so, yes.

NIZER: You knew that this first draft, which was, and you so testified, about 50 per cent longer than the final Exhibit 41, would be an important document in this case, didn't you?

HARTNETT: No I didn't.

NIZER: Did you destroy it because you didn't have any file space?

HARTNETT: I had file space, certainly.

NIZER: Do you testify, sir, now, do I understand you to say that at the time that you destroyed Exhibit 41's first draft, you had no idea that that document might be of importance in this case?

HARTNETT: I didn't think this case would ever even come to trial, sir. I thought it was a publicity stunt.

NIZER: You heard your attorney state that there were many sessions, you tell me, of this examination at which you were examined?

HARTNETT: I believe 23.

NIZER: Twenty-three times that you came down to be examined under oath, is that right?

HARTNETT: That is correct.

NIZER: And you said you didn't think that this case would come to trial?

An objection to this question was sustained, but Nizer pursued the matter.

NIZER: You knew that Mr. Faulk was charging in this suit that he had not one cent from television or radio after the time he left CBS as the result of the Exhibit 41 that you published; that was his position in this suit was it not?

HARTNETT: No, he remained at CBS for over a year after the publication. A year and a half.

NIZER: With the exception of that, didn't you know that his position was that he had been deprived of work in his profession which he had been in for all those years? You knew that was his position in this suit, didn't you?

HARTNETT: I knew that that was—yes, that was his testimony.

NIZER: Yet you testified now that you felt that this suit was a publicity stunt?

HARTNETT: At the time originally filed, yes sir. . . .

NIZER: Did you search in the "Daily Worker" to find out if Faulk was mentioned after 1949 and before 1956?

HARTNETT: No.

NIZER: Didn't you think it was important to find out whether there was any record, according to you, in the "Daily Worker" which would make reference to him during the 7-year period between 1949 and at the time you published Exhibit 41? Didn't you think that was important?

HARTNETT: Yes, but I myself had read the "Daily Worker" for that period.

NIZER: You mean without looking again, just from reading it for 7 years, you knew he wasn't in it; is that it?

HARTNETT: At least I had no recollection of any reference to him in it from 1949 to 1956. . . .

NIZER: Did you ever make this statement about Mr. Faulk any place in writing or orally, "that it is no wonder the 'Daily Worker' refers to John Henry Faulk because the readers are so familiar with his name." Did you say that in 1955?

HARTNETT: In 1956 . . . I did.

NIZER: And even though his name had not appeared, according to your search, from 1948 to 1956 you thought the readers would recognize his name instantly because they were so familiar with it in the "Daily Worker," is that it?

HARTNETT: It must have been if I said that before. . . .

NIZER: Even though for 8 years, approximately 8 years, his name had not appeared in any way according to your search, you think that 8 years later readers would have recognized Faulk's name, it would be familiar to them in the "Daily Worker"? Is that right?

HARTNETT: Yes, I got that impression. . . .

NIZER: Did you ever write that AWARE, Inc., had solid control of AFTRA union?

HARTNETT: I don't recollect such a writing, no.

Lou then produced a letter written back in the Fifties from Vincent Hartnett to a John Dungey. Mr. Dungey was the head of the Onondaga County American Legion; he also was a close friend of Laurence Johnson and a Mr. Neuser, the fruit and vegetable buyer for Johnson supermarket, who headed the Veteran's Action Committee of Syracuse, which was composed of the veterans in Mr. Johnson's supermarkets. The letter, which had been written by Hartnett to Dungey, was read by Nizer to the jury.

NIZER [reading]: "Those of us who are on the spot and in a position to know the facts realize that Equity is virtually lost, and that we may well lose our solid control of AFTRA. . . . "

"That Equity is virtually lost and we may well lose our solid control of AFTRA," and you were writing this to Mr. Dungey of the Syracuse Post in Syracuse, right?

HARTNETT: Yes.

NIZER: And when you said "our solid control," none of the Syracuse groups were members of AFTRA, were they?

HARTNETT: Not to my knowledge, no.

NIZER: And AWARE wasn't, of course, a member of AFTRA was it?

HARTNETT: No. . . .

NIZER: And you weren't a member of AFTRA, were you?

HARTNETT: No.

Hartnett testified that the problem AFTRA had in enforcing its constitutional amendment against Communists was that there were no persons in the union who were proved to be Communists without certain procedures. He explained what he meant by that:

> The establishment of the Communist Party membership through certain court procedures are by identification by the State Department or by the F.B.I.: and therefore there had been no such procedure by the government resulting in such an identification of party members. . . .

NIZER: You, of course, approve of those proper procedures to establish that a person is a Communist or a pro-Communist, don't you? . . .

HARTNETT: I think—no, I think they are entirely unrealistic. They don't conform to realities.

NIZER: You think that instead of leaving it to the government and the F.B.I. and the government authorities, that to do that would be very unrealistic; correct?

HARTNETT: Absolutely.

NIZER: And you think that the realistic approach is not to depend upon the government authorities but to have you, for an example, as a so-called consultant, determine who is a Communist; right?

HARTNETT: No, sir, that is not correct.

NIZER: Or to have AWARE, Inc., decide and make recommendations as to who is a Communist?

HARTNETT: No, that's not correct, either.

But Nizer would not let him stop there. He proved that that was exactly what Mr. Hartnett indeed did believe.

NIZER: Did you write to the American Broadcasting Company "in my opinion, finally, you would run a serious risk of adverse public opinion of featuring on your network James Thurber, Kim Hunter, Olive Deering?"

HARTNETT: Yes.

NIZER: When you said to the American Broadcasting Company "you would run a serious risk," did you mean to suggest that they better not hire Mr. James Thurber to appear on the air?

HARTNETT: Yes, I obviously did.

NIZER: Had you gotten in touch with Mr. James Thurber before you wrote this?

BOLAN: I object your Honor.

THE COURT: Sustained.

NIZER: Did you also know that the general practice of the advertising agencies when they got a report from you was not to tell the artist about that report? You knew that was the general practice in the industry, didn't you?

HARTNETT: Yes, I would say that was the general legal practice . . .

NIZER: Did you not volunteer information to various companies with respect to the alleged record of Mr. Faulk, even though they didn't ask you about Mr. Faulk?

HARTNETT: No, indirectly they did ask me about Mr. Faulk. They asked me about performers who had been on the slate.

NIZER: The sponsor, the company asked you for performers who had been in the Middle-of-the-Road slate? That is not right, is it Mr. Hartnett?

HARTNETT: Yes, as shown by the exhibits. They asked me about performers who in fact had been in the Faulk slate, which was certainly relevant to mention Faulk's record.

NIZER: You show me a letter. Please call for any letter in which the company, Borden's, or Young & Rubicam, or the Kudner Agency, asked for the record of the people who were in the Middle-of-the-Road slate. Please show me that document. Have you got such a one?

Hartnett stirred up three exhibits, letters which he had written to the Young & Rubicam agency and the Kudner Agency and said they were the letters he referred to.

NIZER: You point, and you can read it out loud, to the language that indicates that any one of those companies asked you for a report on anyone who ran in the Middle-of-the-Road slate of AFTRA. Point to any such sentence that would so indicate.

HARTNETT: Yes, my letter of November 27, 1955, to Mr. William D. Thompson of Young & Rubicam. "Since the name of Louise Allbritton was proposed, she has been announced as a candidate on the Independent Ticket of AFTRA, New York Local 4."

NIZER: You were writing that. They didn't ask you whether she was running on any union slate, did they?

HARTNETT: No, they asked me what information I had on her.

NIZER: On Louise Allbritton?

HARTNETT: Yes.

NIZER: And you, giving what you thought was pertinent information, referred to the fact that she was running on the Middle-of-the-Road slate, as a pro-Communist allegation?

HARTNETT: No, not pro-Communist.

NIZER: This you volunteered?

HARTNETT: No, as a matter of fact, she was on the Middle-of-the-Road slate. I can't make it any plainer. . . . That's all I can say. He asked me for any record on Louise Allbritton and this was part of the record.

NIZER: Is it not a fact that no "client" of yours ever said, "Will you please give me the record of some people who ran on the Middle-of-the-Road slate." That is correct, they never did that, did they?

HARTNETT: Put in that form, that is correct, yes. . . .

NIZER: Read the reference to Mr. Faulk that you wrote.

HARTNETT: Yes. "The . . . leader of this ticket, John Henry Faulk, had a significant Communist-front record. I am afraid he is using the liberals."

NIZER: Did they ask you about Mr. Faulk at all in the list of names that they gave you to check? Did they mention the name of Faulk at all?

HARTNETT: Not to my recollection, no. . . .

NIZER: Nevertheless, when you wrote a report as to the people they did ask you to write about, you added the words "John Henry Faulk" and said he had a serious record, didn't you?

HARTNETT: Yes. . . .

NIZER: For each of the names that you submitted these reports on, you received an amount of money, $5, $20, $25, is that right?

HARTNETT: $5, sometimes $20, yes.

NIZER: But in the case of John Henry Faulk, in this case, you volunteered that without any compensation didn't you?

HARTNETT: No, I was compensated for the report on the person who was elected from the Middle-of-the-Road slate. . . .

NIZER: For each name, you were accustomed to receive a separate payment that you made a report on, right?

HARTNETT: Yes.

NIZER: But you did not get any payment for John Henry Faulk that you mentioned in that letter, did you?

HARTNETT: No, I wasn't paid for any report on Faulk.

NIZER: You volunteered and threw that in free?

.   .   .   .

HARTNETT: Mr. Nizer, I can't make it any plainer. That was part of the information on the given subject whose name was proposed to me and for which names I received compensation.

NIZER: That is interesting. Now answer my question.

BOLAN: I object to Mr. Nizer's comment.

THE COURT: Yes, Mr. Nizer. That is stricken from the record.

BOLAN: This question has been answered five times already.

THE COURT: No, no, overruled.

NIZER: My last question is: You volunteered the name of John Henry Faulk and your evaluation of him free; you threw that in free, didn't you?

HARTNETT: I can't say yes to that, Mr. Nizer.

NIZER: Well, you didn't get paid for it did you?

BOLAN: I object.

THE COURT: Overruled.

HARTNETT: I did not get paid for information about Faulk.

Lou then had Hartnett testify about a letter that he had written to the Kudner Agency in which he had volunteered the information about me.

NIZER: Did anybody in the Kudner Agency ask you for any opinion or any report about John Henry Faulk?

HARTNETT: Not directly.

NIZER: Did they ask you for it indirectly?

HARTNETT: Yes.

NIZER: How, by asking you about Luis Van Rooten?

HARTNETT: Yes.

NIZER: Did you make a report on Collingwood because they asked you about Van Rooten?

HARTNETT: No that would be extending it a little bit.

NIZER: The only place you would extend it was to John Henry Faulk; correct?

HARTNETT: Yes, he is obviously—he was the only one mentioned. . . .

NIZER: Did you in substance ever write to Mr. Larry Johnson of Syracuse asking him to help in your effort to see that certain artists did not appear on air in view of their records?

HARTNETT: None come to mind, sir.

NIZER: Let me see if I can refresh your recollection. Did you ever ask Mr. Larry Johnson to take action against Franchot Tone?

HARTNETT: I don't know whether I asked him to take action. I remember writing to him about Franchot Tone.

NIZER: Mr. Johnson is not in the theatrical profession, is he?

HARTNETT: No.

NIZER: He was in the grocery business, supermarkets; right?

HARTNETT: Yes.

NIZER: What were you writing to Mr. Laurence Johnson with respect to Mr. Franchot Tone? Will you reconstruct that for us?

HARTNETT: As best I recall, he had probably asked me for a report on Franchot Tone, which I furnished him; and I believe I had made inquiry to see if Franchot Tone had offset his past record, and had been told he had not done so, at least my source of information. Yet, as best I recall, I expressed an opinion that Franchot Tone should do more than—

NIZER: Before he could appear on television?

BOLAN: I object.

NIZER: He should do more before he could appear—he should appear or be allowed to appear on television? Isn't that the substance of it?

HARTNETT: Before he was allowed to appear on television?

NIZER: Yes.

HARTNETT: Could be. I am not sure of that.

NIZER: Could be. Did you ever write to him, "if he refused to take a public stand, then we can take the necessary measures?" Did you ever write that to Laurence Johnson?

HARTNETT: Yes, that sounds right.

NIZER: "We" in that case is you and Laurence Johnson, right?

HARTNETT: It would seem so. . . .

NIZER: So you asked groups, various individuals to write protests to try to get people off the air that in your opinion had pro-Communist affiliation; right?

HARTNETT: Yes, I did.

Back in June of 1958 when Nizer was conducting Hartnett's examination before trial, Hartnett made some concessions on the record which now came back to haunt him:

NIZER: In writing to the Young & Rubicam agency in November, 1955, did you refer to Mr. Faulk as a known leftist?

HARTNETT: I believe so, yes.

NIZER: You knew, of course, when you wrote that that he was not a known leftist, didn't you?

HARTNETT: No, I think he was known in certain quarters as a leftist.

Lou then took Hartnett's examination before trial from the session of June 17, 1958, when Godfrey Schmidt was still acting as attorney for the defendants. Schmidt had stated that AWARE never intended to charge me with subversion.

NIZER: I read to you from page 553 of your examination before trial:
  "Mr. Hartnett, so you don't think I misunderstand, let me repeat what your counsel has said and I will put it in the form of a question to you so you can state it on the record. As I understand your position, you never charged Mr. Faulk with being a Communist; is that right? That is what your counsel is saying.
  "Answer: Yes.
  "You adopt that, don't you?
  "Answer: Yes.
  And you had never charged him with being pro-Communist without

his being a party member, I mean, a pro-Communist sympathizer; you never charged him with that?

"Answer: I was once sold a barrel of false information."

Did you make those statements to those questions?

HARTNETT: Yes, later corrected.

NIZER: What was that?

HARTNETT: Later, I believe later there was a correction on that.

NIZER: When you testified on June 17, 1958, you made those answers under oath, didn't you?

HARTNETT: I did.

NIZER: And when you said that you were once sold a barrel of misinformation, whom were you referring to as having sold you the barrel of misinformation?

HARTNETT: The anonymous informer, Mr. Adams.

NIZER: You are, of course, an investigator, aren't you?

HARTNETT: A researcher, research consultant.

NIZER: You consider yourself a competent and thorough researcher?

HARTNETT: I think to the limit of my ability to be very competent, thoroughgoing.

NIZER: I say you hold yourself forth in writing to clients as a thorough and competent researcher, don't you?

HARTNETT: I have made—language to that effect, yes. . . .

Nizer then took Hartnett's EBT and read further from his testimony of June 17, 1958.

NIZER [reading from Hartnett's EBT]:

"Question: Aside from the fact that you say you were sold false information about him, you don't charge him with being a Communist today?

"Answer: No sir."

If there ever was such a charge, you would know it was false?

HARTNETT: I do.

NIZER: Did you make that answer?

HARTNETT: I did, later corrected.

NIZER: Did you make that answer—first answer my question—in 1958?

HARTNETT: Yes.

NIZER: At the time you gave these answers in 1958 did you feel that John Henry Faulk should be free to obtain employment?

HARTNETT: Yes, I did.

NIZER: Did you in answer to a question by me agree to send out a letter stating that he was a good and loyal American, had no pro-Communist affiliation at all, and therefore, that you had been in error in asserting these things in Exhibit 41? Had you agreed to that in substance?

HARTNETT: In substance, yes, without the addition of the phrase "in error."

NIZER: And had Mr. Schmidt, before Roy Cohn replaced him, had Mr. Schmidt agreed as the president of AWARE, Inc., to send out on behalf of AWARE, Inc., a letter to any sponsor or advertising agency or anyone else that I would select stating that this had all been a barrel of false information?

HARTNETT: No, there is no reference again to any false information. He agreed—Mr. Schmidt did agree to send out some—to the issuance of letters of that nature.

THE COURT: Issuance of letters of that nature without this expression of—

HARTNETT: Yes, without acknowledging any false information.

NIZER: But acknowledging that, so far as you and AWARE were concerned, he was a good and loyal American and ought to be employed without any besmirching of his loyalty by reference to alleged pro-Communist affiliations; that in substance was agreed to?

HARTNETT: Well, again you are adding language to it which I don't believe was there, but it was in substance.

NIZER: Yes, and then it was a short time—how long after that was Mr. Schmidt replaced by Mr. Roy Cohn as counsel?

HARTNETT: Well, somewhere between one and three months. . . .

NIZER: It was after Mr. Roy Cohn was substituted as counsel for Mr. Schmidt that you changed your position that you have given us in substance; is that right?

HARTNETT: I don't recall whether it was after that or not, sir. I may have changed it personally before.

Hartnett never testified as to why he had changed his mind and withdrawn his offer.

I was aware, back in 1958, when I received a subpoena from the

House Un-American Activities Committee, that Hartnett consulted with members of their staff quite frequently. But I did not know that he had sought to interest the House Un-American Activities Committee in me long before that.

NIZER: ... didn't you in November 1955, about two months before you published Exhibit 41, write to the chief clerk of the House Committee on Un-American Activities about Mr. Faulk?

HARTNETT: I did.

NIZER: You wrote that letter when you knew that Mr. Faulk was running on the Middle-of-the-Road slate and the campaign for the election was going on, didn't you?

HARTNETT: Yes, I did. . . .

NIZER: Mr. Beal didn't ask you for information about Mr. Faulk, did he?

HARTNETT: He did not.

NIZER: He didn't ask you for information concerning the candidates running in the AFTRA union, did he?

HARTNETT: He did not. . . .

NIZER: You stated to Mr. Beal that Mr. Faulk was listed as—and I am quoting—"was listed as a member of the Radio Division of the Progressive Citizens of America." You wrote that to the House Un-American Activities Committee in November 1955, didn't you?

HARTNETT: I did.

NIZER: That was an incorrect statement, wasn't it? Mr. Faulk was not listed as a member of the Radio Division of the Progressive Citizens of America, was he, to your knowledge?

HARTNETT: I believe it was my information that he was.

Lou then took Hartnett's EBT in 1958 and read the questions and answers from it:

NIZER [reading EBT]:

"Did you make any inquiry as to whether he was a member of the Radio Division of the Progressive Citizens of America?

"Answer: I don't believe so. . . .

"But you just made no attempt either way to verify that, is that right?

"Answer: It is one of those things that would be almost impossible

to verify. I don't have access to the membership list of either organization. Both of them are defunct long since. . . .

"Did you at any time know any other people who were members
of the Radio Division of either of those organizations?

"Answer: Yes I think I have.

"I take it you made no attempt to ask them whether Mr. Faulk
had been affiliated.

"Answer: No I don't believe I did."

Then I heard for the first time, from Hartnett's lips, what had
happened when I had been called for a job at the Mutual Broadcasting Company, late in 1957.

NIZER: After Mr. Faulk was let out of Columbia Broadcasting System,
you knew he was trying to get other jobs, didn't you?

HARTNETT: The only one that comes to mind is I knew that someone
had made application to Mutual Broadcasting System of offering a
job there or seeking a job for him.

NIZER: And you talked to an executive of the Mutual Broadcasting
System then, didn't you?

HARTNETT: Call him an executive. It amounts to that, yes.

NIZER: Did you discuss Mr. Faulk's background . . . with that gentleman? What was his name, incidentally?

HARTNETT: Mr. Pat Winkler.

NIZER: Yes, of WOR Mutual Broadcasting Company, . . . and he told
you that they were considering Mr. Faulk for a job on their network;
correct in substance?

HARTNETT: No. . . . Where, he said that, as I recall, someone was trying
to sell Mr. Faulk to the network, not that they were considering him.

NIZER: By someone, you mean an agent of some kind?

HARTNETT: That's right, yes.

NIZER: And that they were considering him for that job?

HARTNETT: Words to that effect, yes.

NIZER: Then do you recall that the statement by Mr. Winkler was: "We
are considering hiring him"; is that right?

HARTNETT: I don't recall, but it would amount to that.

NIZER: . . . did you tell him that he had a pro-Communist affiliation
record?

HARTNETT: A record of affiliation with pro-Communist groups, yes.

NIZER: You said that some agent or somebody was trying to sell him. I read to you from your testimony on your examination before trial, page 1337:

"What did Mr. Winkler say to you?"

"Answer: He said that somebody from the network proposed hiring Mr. Faulk."

NIZER: Do you recall making that answer?

HARTNETT: Yes, I do now, yes.

NIZER: Do you want to correct the impression that it was somebody trying to sell him; it was the network that was proposing to Mr. Winkler that he be hired; right?

HARTNETT: Probably both, probably both an agent and the network, yes.

The newspapers followed the case very closely. However, there was a significant bit of testimony which the newspapers never reported; it concerned Hartnett's relations with the New York Police Department. As far as I know, no one ever followed through on it. It came about thus:

NIZER: In January 1956, did you advise any member of the Police Department about the charges that you had made in Exhibit 41 against Mr. Faulk?

HARTNETT: At about that period of time I did convey information I had about Mr. Faulk to the Police Department.

NIZER: Did you call up a member of the Police Department of the City of New York to tell him you had information for him about Mr. Faulk?

HARTNETT: To my best recollection . . . it's not too clear, but I think I did tell him certain information I had about Mr. Faulk, yes.

NIZER: They hadn't asked you for any information about Mr. Faulk, had they?

HARTNETT: No.

NIZER: You are not a member of the Police Department?

HARTNETT: No.

NIZER: You have no association of any official kind with the City of New York, have you?

HARTNETT: No.

NIZER: Or did you have at that time, in January of 1956, any association with the Police Department or any other department in any official capacity?

HARTNETT: Not official; unofficial.

NIZER: Unofficial?

HARTNETT: Surely.

NIZER: With the Police Department of the City of New York?

HARTNETT: Yes.

NIZER: What was your capacity?

HARTNETT: Well, I furnished—frequently furnished them with information, the F.B.I., many agencies.

NIZER: I didn't ask you about the F.B.I.

I move to strike that out.

THE COURT: Strike that out. And do I understand by furnishing information you feel that you were unofficially connected with the Police Department?

HARTNETT: I think that's a connection, your Honor, yes.

THE COURT: That is a connection, but it is unofficial, you would say?

HARNETT: Yes, I mean it was no official relationship.

THE COURT: You mean anybody that gives information to the Police Department is unofficially connected with the Police Department? Is that what you are saying?

HARTNETT: I would suppose it is a connection your Honor. I am trying to answer that the best I can.

NIZER: Did you have any crime report with respect to Mr. Faulk?

HARTNETT: No.

NIZER: Did you ask the Police Department if they had anything about Mr. Faulk and to tell you?

HARTNETT: Yes.

NIZER: You did?

HARTNETT: Yes.

NIZER: Whom did you talk to?

HARTNETT: Lieutenant Crain.

NIZER: What is the full name, please?

HARTNETT: Thomas F. Crain.

NIZER: And when you called Lieutenant Crain, you told him of what you claimed were the past Communist-front affiliations of Mr. Faulk; is that right?

HARTNETT: As best I recall, yes.

NIZER: Did you tell Lieutenant Crain anything about the AFTRA election in the union and the Middle-of-the-Road slate? Did you tell him about that controversy?

HARTNETT: I believe I did make reference to that, yes, to the election in AFTRA.

NIZER: You thought the fact that Mr. Faulk had been elected on the Middle-of-the-Road slate of the union was a subject for you to advise the Police Department of the City of New York; is that right?

[Objection sustained]

NIZER: Did you ask him for any information that he might have against . . . about Mr. Faulk so that you could use it in connection with the AFTRA controversy?

HARTNETT: Well, I asked him about it, and I did intend to use it in connection with the AFTRA controversy, yes. . . .

NIZER: You told Lieutenant Crain of the Police Department of the City of New York that the Middle-of-the-Road slate was helping Communism, didn't you?

HARTNETT: I don't recall saying that they were helping Communism. Did I so testify? I don't recall it, sir.

Nizer then read the following question and answer from Hartnett's examination before trial:

Did you say anything to the effect that the Middle-of-the-Road slate was helping Communism?

"Answer: Yes I think I did."

So that was what you told Lieutenant Crain, that the Middle-of-the-Road slate was helping Communism, right. You explained that to him?

HARTNETT: Apparently so, yes. . . .

NIZER: You have claimed, have you not, that Inspector Robb of the Police Department gave an authorization to give or receive information of the pertinent public nature to and from AWARE?

HARTNETT: Yes, that was my understanding.

NIZER: And was it your understanding that the Police Department of the City of New York had the right or duty to give this information if it had any?

HARTNETT: They had the right.

NIZER: They had the right?

HARTNETT: Yes.

NIZER: On what did you base that understanding that they had such a right?

HARTNETT: I can't say on what I based it. I just felt that they had.

NIZER: You claimed that such an understanding was had with Mr. Milton who testified here previously, of AWARE, with Inspector Robb; is that your position under oath?

HARTNETT: That such an understanding was had with . . . Inspector Robb . . .

NIZER: Concerning Inspector Robb's authorization to talk to you and give you information or receive information; that that was an arrangement made with Mr. Milton, the witness who testified here?

HARTNETT: I believe so, yes.

NIZER: Don't you know that Mr. Milton under oath has denied that?

HARTNETT: I don't know that he did. . . .

NIZER: How many times do you say you talked to Lieutenant Crain about artists trying to get information from the Police Department of the City of New York?

HARTNETT: . . . about 70.

NIZER: And you initiated all those 70 conversations; Lieutenant Crain didn't call you, you called him in every instance on your own?

HARTNETT: Or in virtually all instances, yes. . . .

NIZER: So you initiated calls about artists on television and radio, and you claim that Lieutenant Crain of the Police Department gave you, as a private citizen, information about those artists on 30 occasions; is that correct?

HARTNETT: Yes that is my testimony. . . .

NIZER: Don't you know, Mr. Hartnett, that Mr. Milton has contradicted your entire story that there was any understanding or arrangement with Inspector Robb in this matter?

BOLAN: Your Honor, I object to that statement.

THE COURT: Sustained.

Whereupon Lou took Milton's examination before trial and read from it on exactly this subject.

NIZER [reading from Milton's EBT]:

"As to the . . . part of AWARE getting information from the Police Department, I doubt very much if we had asked for and certainly would have no right to expect it."

"Question: On what do you base that conclusion?

"Answer: Simply that the average citizen is not in a position to demand information from the Police files, as I understand it. AWARE never did receive any information from that source."

Lou then looking steadily at Mr. Hartnett asked:

Now I ask you having read that testimony from Mr. Milton, do you still say that Mr. Milton made this arrangement with Inspector Robb for you to get this information?

[Objection sustained]

Lou tried again. He wasn't about to give up this plum.

NIZER: Do you say in this court that it was Mr. Milton who sat with Inspector Robb and made an arrangement with the Police Department of New York to exchange information with you?

HARTNETT: It was my understanding that there was such a luncheon with Godfrey Schmidt and Paul Milton and with Inspector Robb, and that certain authorization was given. That was my understanding, sir.

NIZER: After this examination before trial at which this Police Department matter came up, you had a conversation with the Police Department, didn't you?

HARTNETT: I believe after that or some time around that particular examination, yes.

NIZER: And don't you know that Commissioner Stephen Kennedy called in Inspector Robb to ask whether there was any truth to your statements in this matter? Weren't you informed of that?

BOLAN: Your Honor, I submit this is highly—

THE COURT: Sustained and strike it out, the jury will draw no inferences from that question.

Lou was forced to drop this line of questioning and turn to the association between Johnson and Hartnett, a close, harmonious and congenial relationship, during which they frequently exchanged information on artists and performers, as well as compliments on each other's fine character. The information they exchanged was rather detailed and they went to some lengths to obtain it; on one occasion Hartnett wrote to Johnson that he had called Jack Wren about a woman in a crowd scene on a Robert Montgomery television show.

NIZER: And the woman in the crowd scene, just a person in a crowd scene, you protested against because you felt she had a Communist-front affiliation?

Whether Hartnett could remember his testimony on this matter or not wasn't important, but Lou took his examination before trial and read from Hartnett's EBT:

"You would go after them if they were in crowd scenes, even though they didn't take any speaking parts?

"Answer: If they were Communist Party members, someone with a significant party record, and if they were in a crowd scene, yes, I would consider that of importance."

Then Nizer turned to him and asked:

Did you also protest the appearance of children on television if their parents or one of their parents, had a Communist-front affiliation record, according to you and your research?

HARTNETT: Yes.

NIZER: Did you make a report about the Kraft Television Theatre program to Mr. Laurence Johnson in June in 1954 in which you listed Susan Strasberg, daughter of Lee Strasberg . . . is that the language you used protesting Miss Strasberg?

. . . .

HARTNETT: Well, I didn't protest her, but I did say Susan Strasberg, daughter of Lee Strasberg, who is in file 13, but there is no protest here. . . .

NIZER: How old was Susan Strasberg in 1954, do you know?

HARTNETT: I would say in '54, about . . . about 15.

Nizer then took up Hartnett's examination before trial and read from questions asked him back in 1958.

NIZER [reading from EBT]:

"Did you in the course of these duties for any client also clear child actors?

"Answer: Yes.

"You charged the same fee for them?

"Answer: I would not know it was a child actor until I checked the identity as a rule.

"When you found out it was a child, did you charge a fee?

"Answer: A minimum fee, yes.

"A minimum fee, you mean the same $5?

"Answer: I believe so, yes."

NIZER: So you considered it a stratagem if there was a child like Susan Strasberg, who was trying to get employment; you considered that a stratagem on behalf of the father, who, you said, belonged in file 13? Is that what you mean as an illustration of it?

HARTNETT: It was a stratagem more generally than that.

Hartnett would waver at times in his answers, but for the most part he held up pretty well, I thought, under the rather severe examination. He was wary in his answers but Nizer would not let him go until he got him to admit the whole truth about his associations and his activities back in the Fifties. He asked Hartnett about a magazine article he had written back in the early Fifties for the *American Legion Magazine* which was critical of the Borden Company for hiring Communist-front entertainers on their program. Hartnett testified:

HARTNETT: I did write an article for the "American Legion Magazine" in which I was critical of the past employment practices of the Borden Company.

NIZER: And that article, before it was published, was brought to the attention of the Borden Company, wasn't it?

HARTNETT: No, I don't think it was.

NIZER: You had a conference with the Borden Company before that article was published, didn't you?

HARTNETT: I did. . . .

NIZER: And you were hired by the Borden Company before that article in which you criticized the Borden Company was published, weren't you?

HARTNETT: I was.

NIZER: Then the article came out thereafter and praised the Borden Company, didn't it?

HARTNETT: Both criticized and praised, I would say.

NIZER: By criticized, you mean they had once had not so good a record, but now they were very patriotic?

HARTNETT: It told the facts about the past infiltration and praised the Borden Company for taking measures.

NIZER: The measure which you praised that they had taken was that they had hired you; correct?

HARTNETT: No, that they had instituted their own policies. Part of this was retaining me. . . .

NIZER: In 1955 didn't you get $10,000 from the Borden Company? Didn't you receive that?

HARTNETT: I did.

NIZER: That was for your checking work, your so-called screening and security work?

HARTNETT: That is correct.

Nizer then read from Hartnett's EBT, where Hartnett had testified that he had written the article for the *American Legion Magazine*. Before it was published, he had a conference with Mr. Stuart Peabody, the advertising director of the Borden Company. As a result of the conference Hartnett had been placed on a retainer to do the checking for the Borden Company and had rewritten the article. Nizer took a copy of the article and read the two paragraphs which Hartnett had added to it just prior to its publication. In both paragraphs Hartnett was extravagant in his praise of the Borden Company and its new security measures. He then turned to Hartnett and asked:

The only thing that had been done before you wrote these two additions was that the Borden Company had engaged you to do their security work; isn't that right?

HARTNETT: That is not right. I can explain it if you wish.

NIZER: I will let you explain it, Mr. Hartnett.

HARTNETT: Yes. A triple-checking policy was inaugurated by the Borden Company. . . .

NIZER: So the great . . . patriotic service for which all Americans should be grateful was that not only you but two other people, two other organizations had been hired to tell the Borden Company whether any actor or actress should be on their programs according to their pro-Communist affiliations?

BOLAN: I object.

THE COURT: Sustained in that form.

An aspect of Johnson and Hartnett's cooperation which up to this point had not been explored was now taken up.

NIZER: Mr. Laurence Johnson, you have told us, was close to Mr. Stuart Peabody of Borden, wasn't he?

HARTNETT: Yes, I so testified in the EBT. . . .

NIZER: And didn't Mr. Laurence Johnson have something to do with your being engaged by the Borden Company?

HARTNETT: I have recently learned, he did.

NIZER: How recently did you learn that?

HARTNETT: I would say three, four weeks ago. . . .

NIZER: Didn't you know that approximately the time that this incident occurred, that Mr. Johnson had a meeting with Mr. Peabody just prior to your being retained by the Borden Company?

HARTNETT: He had had a meeting with Mr. Peabody shortly before, yes. . . .

NIZER: You say that you found out only three weeks ago that Mr. Johnson had helped get you that job at Borden's?

HARTNETT: Three or four weeks ago, yes, sir.

NIZER: By talking with Mr. Johnson?

HARTNETT: No sir.

NIZER: Who have you talked with? Just mention the name of the person.

HARTNETT: Mr. William B. Campbell of the Borden Company.

NIZER: And prior to three weeks ago, he had never told you that Mr. Johnson had visited him to hire you as a consultant?

HARTNETT: That is correct.

NIZER: Did you ask him about that fact 3 weeks ago?

HARTNETT: No sir.

NIZER: Are you still retained by Borden's?

HARTNETT: I am not.

NIZER: You went up to see Mr. Campbell of that company 3 weeks ago?

HARTNETT: No, I did not go to see him. He telephoned me.

NIZER: To tell you that Mr. Johnson had helped you in getting that job?

[Objection sustained]

NIZER: Mr. Laurence Johnson had also criticized the casting of Borden's "Treasury Men in Action" program before you were hired, hadn't he?

HARTNETT: Yes, I recall he did. . . .

NIZER: And after you were retained by the Borden Company, the protest of the Syracuse Post of the American Legion, the Veterans' Action Committee, and Mr. Johnson, in regard to the "Treasury Men in Action" stopped, didn't they?

HARTNETT: Yes, I think they surely must have.

NIZER: Did Mr. Johnson and the Syracuse groups, to your knowledge, know that you had been retained by the Borden Company? . . .

HARTNETT: Some time not long after that, they did, yes.

On the final day of Hartnett's cross-examination—that is, Tuesday, June 19—the judge announced that the forelady of the jury, Miss Tindale, was ill and that her doctor said that she could not return to the trial. By the drawing of a slip from the jury drum the alternate Ralph Rosenfeld was chosen to take her place; he became foreman.

I didn't think that Nizer could come up with anything on Hartnett that would prove any more embarrassing or contradictory than the matters that he had already gone over in the past week. But on that last day Nizer asked him:

Did you hold yourself forth as an independent producer, a radio and television producer in 1950?

HARTNETT: That was the field I was in, sir, yes.

NIZER: What program did you ever produce as an independent radio producer? Can you mention one?

HARTNETT: No sir. The show actually did not sell. It was scheduled to go on the air on ABC Television. At the last minute it was canceled.

NIZER: Incidentally, you described your association with Phillips H. Lord as what? What did you testify you were at Phillips H. Lord?

HARTNETT: I was an assistant to the executive producer, John O. Ives, and supervisor of "Gang Busters" program.

NIZER: Supervisor? Weren't you just script man, hired for $100? Wasn't that your duty at that place?

HARTNETT: No sir, I was the supervisor. . . . I was the supervisor as I have evidence to prove, and I was not at $100.

NIZER: What was your salary at Phillips H. Lord?

HARTNETT: My salary when I left was $150 a week.

NIZER: Wasn't your salary at Phillips H. Lord no more than $110 a week, sir?

HARTNETT: No sir, my top salary was $150.

NIZER: Did you ever write an article under an assumed name of Foreman?

HARTNETT: I did.

NIZER: And did you in that article claim that "Red Channels" was a blacklist, that it was so charged by various people as a blacklist?

HARTNETT: Not in that language, sir. I wrote that some critics had assailed it as a blacklist.

NIZER: And then did you praise, under the name of Foreman, a man by the name of Vincent Hartnett?

HARTNETT: Whether I praised him or not, sir, I don't recall.

NIZER: Under the name of Foreman, you were referring to Vincent Hartnett as a fine man who was doing a good service on "Red Channels," didn't you, in substance?

HARTNETT: Sir, I don't recall that is so.

When Lou started cross-examining Hartnett on his finances, I nearly went to sleep. It was the most boring part of the trial for me. Backward and forward and around and around they went, Hartnett explaining deposits and cash receipt books, et cetera, ad infinitum. Lou, questioning, questioning, questioning. However, several interesting things did come out of it.

NIZER: You charged as high as $200 and $300 for some of the reports, and not only $5, didn't you?

HARTNETT: In one case $300 and possibly. . . . I can't tell exactly . . . possibly 8 cases, $200.

. . . .

NIZER: Now will you tell us who paid you the $300? That was Arthur Miller, you reported, wasn't it?

HARTNETT: It was.

NIZER: The playwright. Who paid it?

[Objection sustained]

NIZER: Did you ever charge $5 for checking Santa Claus? . . . Did you list James Thurber, $20; Santa Claus no record, $5? Did you charge for him?

HARTNETT: Yes, he is a model in New York.

NIZER: He is a what?

HARTNETT: A model.

NIZER: A model?

HARTNETT: He is a well-known model used by advertisers.

NIZER: Isn't it a fact that someone . . . do you recall Mr. Susskind testifying that, in order to embarrass the agency, he put in all sorts of fictitious names and you charged $5 for those?

[Objection sustained]

. . . .

NIZER: Do you recall that there was a group in AFTRA that met at the Blue Ribbon Restaurant to hold a meeting?

HARTNETT: Not a group in AFTRA as such, no. It included members of AFTRA. . . .

NIZER: You attended that meeting without telling them who you were, and carried this hidden microphone to record it, didn't you?

HARTNETT: I did.

Hartnett then testified that he gave excerpts from the secret recording he made to various people including members of AWARE and to some of his clients.

NIZER: Did you have a detective license that authorized you to carry hidden microphones in your holster?

[Objection sustained]

NIZER: Did you have any license at all as a private detective?
HARTNETT: No. . . .

During one of the days of the cross-examination I noticed that two of Hartnett's sons, fine young boys, clean-cut, neatly scrubbed and neatly dressed, were in court. I regretted that they were there to see their father humiliated and embarrassed on the witness stand. Then, as I got to speculating on why he had brought them, it occurred to me that perhaps he wanted them to observe the sufferings that their father must go through for his principles. It also occurred to me that had I had my children there, they would have been there for the same purpose.

The weather grew warmer and warmer as June progressed, and the courtroom became uncomfortable. The huge fans which had been put up to cool off the jury were inadequate. Justice Geller made some pointed remarks about the lack of modern facilities in the courtroom. He also urged Nizer to cut short his cross-examination. Lou wanted to cooperate, but there was still a great deal of important material to be gone over with Hartnett. One night, however, he said that he felt we were taking advantage of the court's patience; perhaps we should bring the cross-examination to a halt. I looked at Paul and George and the voluminous material they had worked up, which was still unused. After a discussion of the matter, they agreed with Lou.

Nizer turned Hartnett back to Bolan. Bolan, anxious to repair some of the harm done on the cross-examination, went through a hopeless redirect examination. He made one telling mistake. Realizing that Nizer's question, several days before, about Hartnett's taking down the names of persons coming into the courtroom had left Hartnett in a bad light, Bolan sought to turn it to the defendant's advantage by asking Hartnett "Whose names were you writing down?" Nizer objected strenuously to this, but he was overruled. After all, as Justice Geller pointed out, Nizer himself had opened the door to this line of questioning by asking Hartnett about the matter. He directed Hartnett to proceed with his answer. Hartnett promptly replied that he was noting the presence of actors who came into court —"like Eliot Sullivan, who was sitting next to Mrs. Faulk; John Randolph; Alan Manson; Jack Gilford." Had some of them refused to answer questions before HUAC? They had. He had made this point. They were associated with me; my wife sat next to them.

Nizer on his recross-examination of Hartnett, a little later, backed off across the room, and his voice took on a sarcastic tone as he asked Mr. Hartnett: "You have testified that Eliot Sullivan sat down next to Mrs. Faulk. Do you see Mrs. Faulk in the courtroom now?" Spectators, judge, jury, and reporters, all leaned forward expectantly as Hartnett frantically scanned the rows of spectators. At length he pointed out a lady and said, "I believe she is the lady over here. I am not sure."

Nizer turned dramatically to the lady spectator and asked, "What is your name, please?"

The lady stood up and said, "My name is Helen Soffer. S-O-F-F-E-R."

Pandemonium broke out. Even Judge Geller could not escape the emotional impact of Hartnett's blunder. Lou waited for a lull and then cried in a searing voice, "Sir, is that an example of the accuracy with which you have identified your victims for the past ten years?" Hartnett mumbled something to the effect that John Sibley, a reporter for *The New York Times,* who was present in court, had pointed out the lady to him as Mrs. Faulk. By this time, however, no explanation that Hartnett could give would in any way have gotten him off the hook on which Nizer had fastened him.

Bolan announced a short time later that Mr. Hartnett was excused from the stand.

25

During the whole course of the trial I had been worrying about CBS and what its role would be. Would its representatives testify in behalf of the defendants? Of course, if they were subpoenaed, they would have to take the stand. Lou had pointed out, however, that if CBS was firm enough with the defendants' attorneys no one would be subpoenaed; it would be too risky. Lou had a strong conviction that it was never wise to subpoena a hostile witness.

The question of whether CBS people would come or not was soon answered; one morning when I walked into the courthouse I saw Carl Ward and another gentleman, who turned out to be a CBS attorney, standing in the corridor outside the courtroom. As I went in to take my place at the counsel table, Lou told me, "Ward is here and is going to testify all right—for the defendants." I felt a sudden resentment toward Ward, but I realized it was unjustified. He had not come willingly. He had been subpoenaed. I could tell from his expression that he did not particularly relish the role he was playing.

On the stand, Ward was the very model of a Madison Avenue executive. He was neatly dressed, and he had the air of complete detachment from the goings on in the court. In answer to Bolan's question, he said that he was now vice-president and director of affiliate relations for CBS television network. He had been general manager of Station WCBS from 1951 until April 1957. Bolan had obviously brought him in to prove that my position at CBS had been shaky back in 1955, long before the defendants' attack on me. Ward testified that he had had discussions of my sagging ratings in February of 1955 and that he had discussed with my agent the possibility that I might be let out at WCBS. However, my ratings had gone up and

I had been kept on. It was obvious that he was doing his best to be completely neutral in the case; he neither wanted to do me harm nor to be helpful to me.

Things picked up considerably when his cross-examination started. Although he was the defendants' witness, Lou made him sound as if he was ours.

NIZER: Did you consider his [Faulk's] personality unique?
WARD: Yes, sir, I did.
NIZER: And very effective as a professional performer?
WARD: I do.
NIZER: You did at that time, too, did you not, Mr. Ward?
WARD: I felt that Mr. Faulk, by virtue of being an unusual personality, represented an opportunity for the station to develop some unusual audience attraction and radio following.

Lou then, to Bolan's obvious dismay and over his vigorous objection, introduced a whole batch of promotional material that CBS had sent out on me.

NIZER: Did WCBS, when you were general manager, attempt, in accordance with good management of a radio station, attempt to exploit Mr. Faulk's personality by issuing special folders featuring Mr. Faulk? I show you Exhibit 17 in evidence and ask you if you recognize that as one of the folders issued by WCBS with respect to Mr. Faulk's skills as a salesman of goods.

This set off a crossfire of objections and rulings between the court and Bolan. Finally Ward was allowed to answer.

NIZER: Is the answer to that that you recognize it, that CBS did that?
WARD: Yes sir.
NIZER: As a promotion for this artist. I show you also Exhibit 15 some 21 sheets which are in evidence. . . . I would like to hold this up for a second so that jury will see what it is I showed them.

I was keeping my fingers crossed, hoping against hope that Ward would give a clear and unequivocal account of our April 1956 conferences, at which he told me that Laurence Johnson was in town knocking my sponsors off. He had, at that time, asked me to give the affidavit which I had presented, and I wanted the jury to be very clear on exactly what happened. His memory of those conferences was, alas, rather hazy, it turned out.

WARD: During that time [April 1956] I had discussions on occasion with Mr. Faulk, with the station program director [Sam Slate] and with the station sales manager.

These conversations ensued primarily from the information that had been brought to my office by a salesman as to certain statements that had been made about Mr. Faulk, as I recall it, to the effect that he was a pro-Communist or that he had appeared before pro-Communist groups or had appeared with pro-Communist groups, and so on. . . .

NIZER: Statements by whom, Mr. Ward?

WARD: As a result of this information having been brought to the station by one of our sales personnel. I don't know which one.

NIZER: Who was the person who was making these statements about Mr. Faulk? Was that stated to Mr. Faulk?

WARD: I do not recall the specific information I saw, whether it was a letter or whether it was printed matter, or what it may have been, beyond the fact that a salesman brought to my office this information in which, as I said, there were certain statements made to the effect that Mr. Faulk had appeared for certain Communist groups or with them; and as a result of this information being brought into my office, we had—I had discussions with Mr. Faulk regarding his actual position on this thing.

I discussed the same matter with our program director at a later time. Particularly in the area of sales, I discussed it with our sales manager from the standpoint of what effect this information would have on the sales acceptability of Mr. Faulk as a personality.

In one of the conversations, I believe Mr. Faulk asked if it would be helpful if he prepared an affidavit in which he stated his position in connection with this situation. I told him that I thought it might be very helpful for salesmen to have some item of this type in their hands that they could take out to show clients, and such a document was prepared. These are—I assumed that the—my immediate recollections of the conversations.

NIZER: Yes, I understand it is a long time. Did you in that conversation report that a salesman had been talking about Mr. Laurence Johnson being on Madison Avenue?

. . . .

WARD: I became cognizant of certain names in connection with the entire incident. I don't recall specifics of how I learned that one individual was involved in one way or another. I was aware of an overall picture.

NIZER: Do you recall whether Mr. Howard Lally of CBS sat in on any of these conferences?

WARD: I believe Mr. Lally was present at some of these meetings, yes.

NIZER: Who is Mr. Lally?

WARD: Mr. Lally was the sales representative of the station at that time.

NIZER: Do you recall whether Mr. Lally or any other source there was discussed at this time? Any particular individual, the name of any individual—not any incident but the name of any individual in connection with this difficulty?

WARD: I remember in some manner the names of certain individuals coming into the conversation. I do not recall how they developed in the conversation.

NIZER: Not how, but do you recall the names of any?

WARD: I recall the names of Mr. Hartnett and Mr. Johnson. . . . Mr. Laurence Johnson, and the organizational name of "AWARE" was in the conversations.

It turned out that Ward could remember after a while that it was Libby's who had canceled their time on my program. Then he couldn't remember whether he had sent my affidavit to any specific agencies or sponsors in an effort to offset Johnson's attack on me. However, when Lou presented him with a letter that he had written himself to Young & Rubicam agency in June 1956, his memory was refreshed again.

NIZER: Did you send, over your own signature, at any time in June 1956, this affidavit, defendant's Exhibit 20, to any leading agency?

WARD: On the basis of what I have just seen, yes.

Lou then asked Ward the big question:

NIZER: Can you describe with reasonable certainty the effect in and since 1956 on the status of an artist or performer, of the publication of charges of pro-Communism or pro-Communist affiliations?

To which Ward gave the institutional answer:

WARD: At WCBS or within CBS where he was already an employee, no effect.

THE COURT: No?

WARD: No effect. For a prospective new employer a reluctance, a concern. The individual would be less employable.

. . . .

NIZER: There was an effect at WCBS to the extent, at least, that you have testified that you got out a special affidavit and gave it to salesmen, wasn't there?

WARD: My statement applies to the continuing employment or the employing of Mr. Faulk at WCBS, on which there was no effect.

NIZER: You mean at that time?

WARD: At that time. Well, there was no effect as far as I know.

. . . .

NIZER: Was it customary to give salesmen affidavits about performers, affidavits which stated that the performers were loyal and good Americans and patriotic Americans? Was that a practice or very extraordinary.

WARD: It was an unusual circumstance.

It was Bolan, after Lou had completed Ward's cross-examination, who on redirect got from Ward the most definitive statement of CBS's—indeed the industry's—position on the matter of performers who were under attack:

BOLAN: If the sponsors had reacted negatively or had reacted against Mr. Faulk as a result of these statements you referred to, and canceled Mr. Faulk's spots with them, would CBS nevertheless have continued with Mr. Faulk?

WARD: If commercial sponsorship on the program had dropped below a certain level—I wouldn't know what they would be—but below a certain level his commercial value to us would have ended.

BOLAN: In other words the primary consideration with CBS was the commercial value of Mr. Faulk to CBS?

. . . .

WARD: That would have been a factor, yes.

Ward left the stand looking as proper and unruffled as when he first got on it. He nodded curtly to me and departed from the courtroom along with several CBS lawyers. The court then adjourned for lunch.

Over at Gasner's during lunch I quipped, "Well, if Ward arrived can Slate be far behind?" and Lou agreed that Sam Slate probably would be the next witness. It turned out that we were wrong: after lunch, Bolan put Sidney Roslow, president of Pulse, Inc., on the stand.

Mr. Roslow testified that he was the creator of the Pulse rating system, which is used by the broadcasting stations, advertising agencies and sponsors to gauge the size of their radio and television audiences. Until the moment he took the stand I really didn't believe that there was any such person as Mr. Roslow. As far as I had ever been able to tell, the whole business of audience ratings was something of a myth based on mythical listeners and compiled by mythical statisticians. I had been wrong. Here was Mr. Roslow, an acknowledged expert in his particular field, sitting there on the witness stand. Bolan had brought him in to prove that my ratings had slipped at CBS in 1957, and during his direct examination Mr. Roslow testified to exactly that. However, on his cross-examination his testimony as to my slipping ratings was not so persuasive, but neither Mr. Roslow nor Mr. Bolan knew that Mr. Nizer had spent the entire night before with some leading experts on program ratings and had managed to master an amazing amount of detail on this intricate business.

What the Pulse ratings actually did was to attempt to reflect the listening habits of some four million families in the Metropolitan area by taking a sampling of .0037 of one per cent of that audience. The whole thing became a blur to me and apparently to Judge Geller and both attorneys as they tried to follow the arithmetic of the discussion that was going on bweeen Lou and the witness. I do not know about the jury. But about the only thing I understood clearly from Roslow's testimony was that the defendants were paying him fifty dollars an hour to come and testify.

During a recess after Roslow's testimony I saw Sam Slate, flanked by two CBS attorneys, in the corridor outside the courtroom. He, like Ward, seemed to have little enthusiasm for the business at hand.

An odd ambivalence stole over me as Sam was sworn in and took his seat on the witness stand. Here we were in the same courtroom, me at the counsel table, Sam on the stand ready to give testimony as a defense witness. He had known me longer than any person in that courtroom. And, I reflected, in all likelihood he actually liked me as much as anyone in the courtroom did. I thought back over the dozens of times that Sam Slate had proved himself a good friend to me, and I felt certain that, whether his testimony would hurt my cause or not, Sam Slate had not the slightest desire to do me harm.

In answer to Bolan's first question, he stated that he was vice-president of the radio division of CBS and general manager of WCBS. I guessed that he was under considerable strain, for he testified that he became general manager of WCBS in or about April 1956, and I knew as a matter of fact that he had become general manager of WCBS in April 1957, just a few months before I was fired. Bolan was not long in getting to the reason for having Sam as a witness. He wanted Sam to give the official CBS reasons for firing me. Sam testified that he had had a conversation with me in July of 1957.

BOLAN: Will you tell us what that discussion was, what you said to Mr. Faulk and what he said to you?

SLATE: I told Mr. Faulk that we were going to have to make some basic program changes on WCBS because of a number of things, and unfortunately . . .

THE COURT: Keep your voice up please.

SLATE [continuing]: I told Mr. Faulk that we would have to make some basic changes in the program structure of the station and that unfortunately we were going to have to not—

THE COURT: Mr. Slate, you will have to do better than that. You're just talking to Mr. Bolan. Talk to the jury and speak up.

SLATE: Yes.

THE COURT: I barely hear you, and I am sitting very close to you.

SLATE: Can you hear me?

BOLAN: Maybe we can turn off the fan.

THE COURT: No, the fan is not noisy at all.

BOLAN: I think Mr. Slate by nature doesn't have a loud voice.

SLATE: To the best of my recollection, I had a conversation with Mr. Faulk that went something like this. I told Mr. Faulk that we were faced with a number of problems at the station which meant that we would unfortunately have to not renew his 13-week option on his contract. These—if you want me to explain what those problems were?

BOLAN: Yes.

NIZER: I object.

THE COURT: No, we want the conversation.

BOLAN: Did you discuss what those problems were with Mr. Faulk?

SLATE: To the best of my recollection, I did.

BOLAN: Will you tell us what you said?

SLATE: Yes. I told Mr. Faulk that we had a network commercial coming on at five o'clock, which automatically reduced the Faulk program, which was from five to six, to a half hour. We had also had some problems in the afternoon between the four and six period with a slight or gradual decline in the audience. . . . Well, as well as I remember, I simply told Mr. Faulk because of a number of changes that we were making in the program schedule, we would not be in a position to continue his services, and this is the gist of the conversation, to the best of my recollection.

Sam then went on to explain at some length and in some detail the changes they had contemplated making on the station's programming. As his answers became inaudible, I became embarrassed for him. But Judge Geller became impatient, and repeatedly he would order Sam to speak up. At one point the judge declared:

The jurors are motioning to me that they don't know what you're saying. Speak up, will you please, Mr. Slate? Shout.

SLATE: Yes, sir, I will shout.

THE COURT: That's it, shout right out.

SLATE: All right. I'm sorry. I will do the best I can. I am not a broadcaster, as you obviously realize.

Sam then testified that one of the factors that was responsible for my dismissal was my drop in Pulse ratings.

SLATE: The factors that we considered which led to a change in the afternoon programming, which included the Faulk show, showed a gradual decline in audience for the four-to-six period in 1957, roughly starting in January, and a slow decline the rest of the nine-month period, I believe.

BOLAN: In CBS's decision to let Mr. Faulk go, was any consideration given whatsoever to a bulletin which was published by the defendant AWARE, Inc., concerning Mr. Faulk?

[Objection sustained]

BOLAN: Were there any other factors other than those you have mentioned, Mr. Slate?

[Objection sustained]

. . . .

BOLAN: Did you give Mr. Faulk all of the reasons why CBS decided to let him go?

SLATE: To the best of my recollection, yes.

While it was perfectly true that Sam Slate had told me prior to my vacation in 1957 that there were plans afoot to bring in a Godfrey network show that would take up thirty minutes of my time on the air, he had assured me that I had nothing to worry about. I was puzzled as to why he would testify that he had told me before I went to Jamaica that I would be let out at CBS. He was bound to remember as clearly as I did that the first inkling I had that I was being fired came after I returned from Jamaica in August. By that time I had already been fired. I wondered if Sam was honestly confused.

As I pondered this I knew that I would soon find out, for Nizer rose to start his cross-examination.

Lou didn't start on the subject of my firing, however; he started on the meeting in April 1956, in Carl Ward's office, concerning Laurence Johnson's attack on me. Lou asked him to tell about the meeting.

SLATE: Mr. Nizer, to the best of my recollection, Mr. Ward talked to Mr. Faulk about this "AWARE" bulletin and asked him certain questions about it, and Mr. Faulk denied some of the allegations that were in the bulletins; and out of this conference came the affidavit that Mr. Faulk gave to WCBS.

. . . .

NIZER: Was there any mention concerning the Libby or cancellation of any other accounts?
SLATE: Not at this meeting, Mr. Nizer, to the best of my recollection.

. . . .

NIZER: Was there a discussion with respect to the impact upon CBS in any way with respect to Exhibit #41? Was there any such discussion?
SLATE: Yes, there was a discussion at that time and we expressed concern about what might be the effect of this bulletin.

Lou then asked him if he could explain or remember what was said in general about the effect on CBS.

SLATE: Well, the substance of the conversation was that we had no way of knowing at this time what effect it might have on the commercial sponsorship of the Faulk show, and as I remember, I believe that Mr. Ward felt that if we lost a great number of sponsors, why then we'd have to take a good hard look at the show again to determine whether we would continue it or not.

Sam's memory seemed to be considerably clearer than Carl Ward's on the matter of Laurence Johnson's participation in my sponsors' affairs back in April 1956.

NIZER: At any of these conferences or talks, at any of these talks preceding or around this period on this subject matter, were the names of any outside persons mentioned who were making these accusations?

SLATE: The name that I remember is Mr. Johnson.

NIZER: Is that Laurence Johnson of Syracuse?

SLATE: I believe that's correct, Mr. Nizer.

NIZER: What was said about Mr. Laurence Johnson at any of these talks, the substance of it?

SLATE: The reports that we had was that Mr. Johnson was making certain allegations against Mr. Faulk as in this bulletin, and also that he, I believe, was instrumental in having letters written to agencies and advertisers who were operating on the Faulk show.

NIZER: Did the jury hear that?

THE COURT: I am going to let this witness stand, but you must promise that you are going to speak louder. Stand up if it's going to make you speak louder.

SLATE: I will do my best.

And from that point on, Sam testified standing up, the first witness to have done so. At first Sam didn't seem to remember Tom Murray very well.

NIZER: Do you recall a gentleman by the name of Tom Murray bringing a letter to you from a sponsor who was on CBS?

SLATE: Yes, I have a vague recollection of that.

NIZER: Is Tom Murray—perhaps this is leading, but with your Honor's permission—associated with the Grey Agency? Does that bring it back to you, sir?

SLATE: I don't know, Mr. Nizer.

NIZER: Did Mr. Murray represent the Hoffman division of the Pabst Blue Ribbon Beer? Does that come back to you?

SLATE: At the time, he did.

NIZER: At the time. I would like to show this to you, Mr. Slate, so that it can refresh your recollection.

Lou thereupon handed to Sam a copy of the letter which had been written to the president of the Pabst Brewing Company and passed on to Tom Murray for action. Sam said that he recalled seeing the letter.

NIZER: As to the letter that you do remember, which is Exhibit 35, that was a sponsor on the Faulk show wasn't it?

SLATE: I believe that's correct.

NIZER: Then Mr. Murray was the agency's representative of that show: Do you recall that now?

SLATE: That is correct.

.   .   .   .

NIZER: What did he [Murray] say to you on that occasion, in substance?

SLATE: Mr. Murray expressed concern about this type of letter and frankly was . . . He wanted to know what CBS's position would be on it.

NIZER: What did you tell him? If you recall?

SLATE: I told him, as I recall, I told him I'd let him know.

NIZER: Did you have any doubt personally about Mr. Faulk's loyalty and patriotism at that time?

SLATE: No, sir.

NIZER: Was there anything said about Mr. Johnson making the rounds of Madison Avenue, in substance? . . . By any of the salesmen giving information.

SLATE: Salesmen said or reported that Mr. Johnson was calling—to use their expression—the agencies all up and down Madison Avenue.

NIZER: Was that about Mr. Faulk?

SLATE: About Mr. Faulk.

NIZER: Were any steps taken in order to strengthen the position of CBS with respect to this problem you have described?

SLATE: The step taken was the affidavit in which Mr. Faulk denied the allegations in these two documents, Mr. Nizer. . . .

.   .   .   .

NIZER: What was done with this affidavit after it was prepared?

SLATE: Mr. Nizer, directly I don't know.

NIZER: I don't mean directly. Was it given to the salesmen?

SLATE: I believe it was, Mr. Nizer.

NIZER: And it was given to the salesmen with what instructions, sir, generally?

SLATE: To my recollection, the general instructions were to use this letter to vindicate or to— In case the question of these charges are brought up against Mr. Faulk, to use this letter in his sales talk.

THE COURT: Use this letter or affidavit?

SLATE: I mean the affidavit, I'm sorry, the affidavit.

The last several days in court had been very uncomfortable. Summer had set in although it was still officially a couple of days away. Judge Geller promised the jurors that he would adjourn promptly at 4 P.M., which he did. Sam, looking somewhat relieved to be finished testifying for the day, left the stand, joined the CBS lawyers, and departed. The following morning his appearance started off on an odd note. Sam was no sooner in the witness chair than Justice Geller looked at him kindly and asked:

Mr. Slate, do you feel better this morning?

SLATE: Judge, I will do my best to project. I am sorry I embarrassed the court.

THE COURT: I am sure you will. We have a very noisy courtroom. Don't feel any compunction about speaking up loudly.

SLATE: Yes, I will do my best. If I don't I will—

THE COURT: If you don't, I will let you know.

SLATE: If I don't, I will ask permission to stand again.

THE COURT: If it is necessary, I will make that exception.

SLATE: Thank you, sir.

Everybody in the courtroom connected with the lawsuit in any way knew that Sam Slate was the defendants' ace-in-the-hole. If his testimony could persuade the jury that my firing at CBS was in no way attributable to pressure from the defendants it would cut sharply into my claim for damages. It struck me that calling Sam as a witness had been a bold move on Bolan's part. He must have known that Sam Slate was a close friend of mine, and he must have known further that Sam Slate had little appetite for the kind of goings on that the defendants indulged in. In many respects my sympathies were with Sam; he was in a difficult position. A feeling of gratitude and real affection would creep over me at various points in his testimony.

NIZER: Did you, at all times that Mr. Faulk was with you on WCBS, consider him an outstanding radio personality?

SLATE: I considered him one of our better people, Mr. Nizer.

NIZER: Did you consider him also a very effective salesman on the air in addition to being an entertainer?

SLATE: Yes, I did.

NIZER: In your opinion, was Faulk a unique and attractive personality in television as well, sir?

SLATE: On certain types of television shows, I thought Mr. Faulk was an excellent performer.

. . . .

NIZER: Would a charge of his being affiliated with pro-Communist organizations make him (the performer) a controversial figure in the industry?

SLATE: That would be one thing that would make him one, yes.

NIZER: What is the effect of such controversiality on his getting new employment?

SLATE: It certainly wouldn't help him any.

NIZER: No, I am sure of that, but would he become generally, in the practice of the industry, virtually unemployable for new jobs?

SLATE: I would say it would be very, very difficult for him to get new jobs, Mr. Nizer.

. . . .

NIZER: Can you state with only reasonable certainty, sir, that if a man becomes controversial, whether it turns out ultimately that he is innocent or guilty, the very controversiality makes it very, very difficult, to use your words, for him to get a job? Is that correct?

SLATE: In a general way that's correct.

. . . .

NIZER: After Mr. Faulk was let out at WCBS, it came to your attention that there was a station in Minneapolis that was trying to engage him? Do you recall that incident?

SLATE: Yes, through conversations with Mr. Faulk.

NIZER: Did you give Mr. Faulk advice with respect to accepting that offer if he could obtain it?

351

SLATE: I believe I did, Mr. Nizer. . . . As I remember the conversation, I advised Mr. Faulk to accept this job because, as long as this suit was pending and the—the combination of AWARE attack and the suit, and no one could predict how long this would last, and it might be a good idea for him to take the best job he could get.

. . . .

NIZER: Was the fact that this station WCCO was west as far as Minneapolis, in any event, a factor in your advice to him as to getting out of the orbit, so to speak, in substance of this AWARE bulletin?
SLATE: I have no recollection of giving Johnny that advice. I have no recollection of giving Johnny that advice. (He says it twice.)
NIZER: In substance, did you tell him something about getting beyond the city of New York, going away from the East?
SLATE: The only advice that I can remember giving Johnny, that it would be a good idea to get out of New York City. I don't remember where or what part of the country.

However, at this point Sam's memory began to fail him badly. For instance, I remember very vividly the time in June 1958 when he called me down to his office and told me he had heard from Wendell Campbell who was offering me a job with KFRC in San Francisco. He was a good friend of Wendell's; but he didn't seem to have any recollection of the incident.

NIZER: Did there come a time when you were called by Mr. Wendell Campbell of KFRC in San Francisco?
SLATE: No, sir.
NIZER: Did you ever talk to Mr. Wendell Campbell about Mr. Faulk?
SLATE: No, sir.
NIZER: Did you have any talks with Mr. Faulk about that San Francisco station?
SLATE: Yes, sir.
NIZER: What did you tell Mr. Faulk?
SLATE: I gave him practically the same advice that I did on the WCCO situation, Mr. Nizer.
NIZER: Did you not tell him in all candor that you had to advise Mr. Campbell that, that due to his being a controversial figure—

SLATE: Mr. Nizer, I have no recollection of having any direct conversation with Mr. Campbell.

. . . .

NIZER: Do you mean to say, sir, that your best recollection is that you never had any talk with anyone in KFRC, if those are the initials of it, in San Francisco, concerning Mr. Faulk in or about June of 1958 or any period around that time?

SLATE: I had, to the best of my recollection, I had no conversations directly with Mr. Campbell.

NIZER: Or with anyone else at the station?

SLATE: Or anyone else at the station.

NIZER: Did you talk to any representative of that station, either in New York or on long-distance telephone, sir?

SLATE: No, sir.

After this last answer Lou stood looking at Sam Slate for a long moment and then turned to a new subject, one that was, perhaps, just as uncomfortable for Sam.

NIZER: You testified, Mr. Slate, that you became general manager of WCBS in April of 1956; is that right?

SLATE: If I did I made an error, Mr. Nizer. It was in April of 1957.

NIZER: Did you not, in error, testify throughout your direct examination that you obtained the general managership in April 1956? Did you not on a number of occasions make that error yesterday?

SLATE: Mr. Nizer, if you say so, I accept it, but the facts are that I became in 1957—

NIZER: And in June of 1957, shortly after becoming the general manager, do you recall having a conference with Mr. Gerald Dickler, Mr. Faulk's manager, and Mr. Faulk, concerning the possibility of the Godfrey show taking over part of Mr. Faulk's hour?

SLATE: I am sure I did, Mr. Nizer.

NIZER: At that time, did you not tell both of these gentlemen that, so far as Mr. Faulk is concerned, he didn't have to be concerned at all, he would either continue on with the remaining half, or some other time that you would try to make available? Was that your position?

NIZER: I don't want you to raise your hand, Mr. Bolan. I protest against this.

BOLAN: I was talking to . . . referring to Mr. Lang.

NIZER: No, you weren't talking to Mr. Lang. I want to put upon the record that this is not the first time that this has been done.

BOLAN: That is a completely unwarranted statement, Mr. Nizer. Mr. Lang made a statement to me about something, and I told him to forget it.

NIZER: No, you put your hand to the witness.

BOLAN: I did not. I have never talked to Mr. Slate in my life before yesterday on the witness stand.

Judge Geller smoothed out the ruffled tempers of Mr. Bolan and Mr. Nizer, and Sam answered the question in the negative.

NIZER: When did you say yesterday you had a conversation with Mr. Faulk in which you gave him this explanation of his being discharged? You said it was July 1957, right?

SLATE: To the best of my recollection, Mr. Nizer, I said I didn't know. I said it was in July, August. It was after Mr. Faulk returned from Jamaica.

NIZER: Did you find out since yesterday that Mr. Faulk wasn't in the city of New York during the month of July from the seventh on?

SLATE: Yes.

NIZER: By whom was it called to your attention, sir?

SLATE: By one of my associates at CBS.

NIZER: Did you not yesterday time and again testify that this conversation with Mr. Faulk took place in July of 1957? Yesterday you did so testify. Just that is my question.

SLATE: I don't remember, Mr. Nizer.

NIZER: You don't remember since yesterday whether you so testified?

SLATE: I am sorry, sir. I don't remember the exact date.

COURT: No, no that's not the question whether you don't remember the exact date. The question is, do you remember that you so testified yesterday, that it was July, 1957? Do you remember that?

SLATE: I believe that's correct.

NIZER: Did the same associate advise you also yesterday that after you left the stand that you became a general manager a year after you said you were general manager?

SLATE: That's correct.

NIZER: So you had no conversation with Mr. Faulk concerning the subject matter you testified to yesterday in July of 1957, did you?

SLATE: I did not have any conversations with him until he returned from Jamaica, Mr. Nizer.

NIZER: Isn't it a fact, sir, that you knew that Mr. Faulk was going off for a long vacation in the beginning of July to Jamaica?

SLATE: Yes, sir, that's correct.

In May of 1957, shortly after Sam had become general manager, I had given a party in his honor at my home. Lou and Mildred Nizer were both guests. Sam had made a statement that night that now came back to plague him. The statement was to the effect that whatever happened in regard to the Arthur Godfrey show taking part of my time I had nothing to worry about. Nizer asked him if he remembered the party. He said yes, but he did not remember who was there. Nizer asked him if he didn't remember making this statement in the presence of those present. Sam said no.

Lou at this point was looking at Sam with disdain. His questions to him fairly rang through the courtroom. The night before I departed for Jamaica, in July 1957, Sam Slate, Murray Kempton and his wife and I had had dinner together, and Murray Kempton was now sitting at the press table. Nizer turned to this subject.

NIZER: Was there a dinner at the Sun Luck Restaurant with Mr. Kempton and his wife and Mr. Faulk?

SLATE: At what?

NIZER: Sun Luck Restaurant. You have no recollection, sir?

SLATE: This I don't remember, Mr. Nizer.

NIZER: At 49th Street, a Chinese restaurant, sir?

SLATE: Could be, Mr. Nizer.

. . . .

NIZER: You say you talked to Mr. Faulk about the conversation you were telling us about yesterday when he came back from Jamaica in August? Is that your correction now?

SLATE: That is correct.

NIZER: By that time, he had already been discharged, had he not?

SLATE: We had sent a notification to Mr. Dickler.

NIZER: And you sent the notification of discharge to Mr. Gerald Dickler his general manager, didn't you?

SLATE: That is right.

NIZER: And you and Mr. Dickler met for a drink because he was astonished at this, wasn't he?

[Objection sustained]

NIZER: Did Mr. Dickler ask to see you when he got this notice that his client, Mr. Faulk, was discharged?

SLATE: We saw each other, Mr. Nizer.

NIZER: Yes, and did he tell you how astonished, in substance, he was at having received this notice when you had assured Mr. Faulk before he left on vacation that his position was secure?

SLATE: I don't remember Mr. Dickler making that statement.

NIZER: Not in those particular words, but didn't he in substance express that to you, Mr. Slate?

SLATE: Mr. Dickler was unhappy over the situation, Mr. Nizer.

NIZER: But in addition to being unhappy, didn't he say, in substance, that this comes as a great shock to him? Didn't Mr. Dickler tell you that at that meeting at the bar?

SLATE: I don't remember.

NIZER: You say you don't remember. You mean you don't remember one way or the other, he might have said that, but you don't recall?

SLATE: That is correct.

Lou continued to press Sam hard on this important meeting between him and Dickler at the Waldorf-Astoria Men's Bar. All Sam could remember was that Dickler was very unhappy. He agreed that Dickler was surprised. At this point Lou got down to a very crucial aspect of my firing.

NIZER: So that it is clear to you when you told him [Dickler] "I am sorry I have to do this," that Mr. Faulk being all the way down in Jamaica didn't know about his discharge at that time, did he?

SLATE: That is correct.

NIZER: So far as the legal reason for doing it on July the 30th, you could, at the end of August 30, the same cycle, have done this on August 30th after Mr. Faulk returned here, couldn't you?

SLATE: Mr. Nizer, I don't know, sir. I know that I was told by legal—I remember that Mr. Faulk's contract, there was something about a 30-day notice in case of a network show, and we sent the letter out at that time.

NIZER: Your instructions about this came from the home office upstairs; is that right?

SLATE: No, sir.

Lou's voice had begun to betray irritation with Sam. He launched into the matter of my ratings and my share of audience, comparing them with those of WCBS generally as well as with those of several other performers during the 1956–57 period. Lou had mastered enough of the hocus-pocus of ratings to prove one thing once and for all for me. I don't know about the jury. But as I listened to the testimony I became more convinced than ever that ratings were whatever one chose to say they were. Then he picked Sam up on the matter of blacklisting in the industry.

NIZER: The CBS organization, during the years from 1952 to 1956 and thereabouts—from 1951 to 1956—had an executive whose duty it was also to act as what has been called screening or security officer; is that right?

SLATE: I believe that is correct.

NIZER: And his name was Dan O'Shea?

SLATE: I think so, Mr. Nizer.

.   .   .   .

NIZER: Was not CBS sensitive to the entire area of the possible Communist affiliations of any artist who appeared upon it, if there was any such report?

SLATE: I think all broadcasting organizations were, Mr. Nizer.

.   .   .   .

NIZER: Would the artist be informed of this report, or would the executives act upon it without advising the artist? Do you know?

SLATE: I don't know.

NIZER: You don't know. How many years were you with WCBS, sir, altogether?

SLATE: Eleven.

NIZER: Was the CBS station sensitive to criticism from Mr. Laurence Johnson, whom you referred to before?

SLATE: We were concerned about it, Mr. Nizer.

NIZER: Yes, during these years, and if you got a report from any source that there was such a possible affiliation, Communist-front affiliation, would you take that up with the artist, or would you just pass upon it within the executive personnel at CBS?

SLATE: Mr. Nizer, I never met Mr. O'Shea, and I never cleared anything with him.

Lou wanted to know if Sam hadn't had to clear people himself, hadn't had to take the responsibility for clearing people himself.

SLATE: Mr. Nizer, I never blacklisted anyone from appearing on WCBS shows, and to the best of my knowledge this was not done.

However, Lou had conclusive evidence that Oscar Hammerstein II and Moss Hart and Marc Connelly had been prevented from going on the Emily Kimbrough show and that Sam had personally had to take action in the matter. Sam's memory of that was very vague and he said as far as he knew both Mr. Hammerstein and Mr. Connelly had appeared on the Emily Kimbrough show. Lou sought to sharpen his memory of the situation. Sam denied knowing anything about it.

NIZER: What do you recall, if anything, about Oscar Hammerstein or Marc Connelly's situation?

SLATE: Mr. Nizer, as I remember, the producer on the show was—let's see if I can't—was a little concerned about the possible appearance of these people, but it was adjudicated or worked out and they appeared.

. . . .

NIZER: And by adjudicated, you mean that Mr. O'Shea sent down some
suggestion or order about it; is that right?
SLATE: I don't know what Mr. O'Shea did.

Bolan obviously sensed that Sam Slate, a vital defense witness, was
not doing the defense's cause much good. When he got up to conduct
the redirect examination he sought to shore up the places in Sam's
testimony that were sagging sadly from the pounding of Lou's cross-
examination. He had Sam recite in great detail once again, the official
reasons for my being fired. Then, realizing that his own witness had
stated quite clearly in previous testimony that my being controversial
was a reason for my being unemployable, he sought to establish that
I was controversial not because of the defendants' attack on me but
because I had brought the lawsuit. In this instance, however, it was
not Lou who objected, but Judge Geller.

THE COURT: In your experience in the industry, Mr. Slate, does a performer become controversial by bringing a lawsuit of the type which
is involved in this action?
SLATE: A lawsuit of this type would tend to make a performer controversial.
BOLAN: Would you read that back please?

[The last answer was read back]

THE COURT: I think it is appropriate to advise the jury that it is the absolute right under our jury system of government for anyone who has a
claim to bring a lawsuit so that the courts may determine the merits of
the lawsuit.
BOLAN: The defendants readily concede that, your Honor.
THE COURT: All right. The jury said that they didn't hear me. Let me
state it again. Under our system, it is absolutely the privilege of any
citizen, if he has a claim, to sue, to bring a lawsuit, so that the courts
may determine the validity or lack of validity of the lawsuit.
    That is the privilege that we have under our system, and Mr. Bolan
just conceded that that is correct.

Then Bolan went back to the matter of my ratings and from Sam's
testimony proved just the opposite of what Nizer had proved some

ten minutes before. Lou, taking up the recross-examination, went over the same ground again with Sam. After that, he made his final thrust.

NIZER: You testified that a lawsuit of this type. repeating your exact words, would aid in making a man controversial. By this type, I take it one that involves the loyalty and patriotism of a performer; is that right?

SLATE: That is correct.

NIZER: And the controversiality, to use that word again, the controversiality which was the subject matter of the lawsuit, both of them being merged for this purpose, was in existence at the time he was let out, wasn't it?

SLATE: That's correct.

NIZER: And that factor was a factor in letting him out, wasn't it, that controversiality?

SLATE: No, sir.

NIZER: Was it not, sir?

SLATE: No, sir.

NIZER: You mean to say that of all the factors you considered, Mr. Slate, you are telling us that the one factor you didn't consider was the controversiality of this pending lawsuit and the subject matter of it? Is that your testimony?

SLATE: That is my testimony.

NIZER: That is all, sir.

BOLAN: Thank you very much, Mr. Slate.

[Witness excused]

As Sam stepped down from the witness stand I felt a genuine embarrassment for him, and in a way genuine compassion. The two CBS attorneys rose from their seats among the spectators and the three marched out of the courtroom.

During a recess I saw Donald Conaway and Morty Becker standing in the corridors of the courthouse. Conaway had been hired as national secretary of AFTRA by the Jaffe faction of the union back in February of 1956 shortly after our slate had taken office in the New York local. Becker, a former law associate of Henry Jaffe, was at-

torney for the New York local. He was the man whom the union had
fired Judge Pecora to hire.

A bitter resentment swept over me as I realized Conaway was
down there to testify in the defendants' behalf. He was a paid employee of the union; his salary was paid by the members of the union
and, thus, in part by me. When he got on the stand it developed that
Bolan had brought him down there to testify that our slate, when we
were in the union, had not been as diligent as Mr. Conaway thought
we should have been in bringing charges against other union members
for having defied the House Un-American Activities Committee. Conaway testified that he had sent a letter to Charles Collingwood, who
was president of the New York local on June 18, 1956, in which he,
Conaway, had brought charges against a member of the union for refusing to answer questions before the House Un-American Activities
Committee. Lou stopped that bit of testimony very quickly by forcing
Conaway to admit that he had written the letter on his personal
initiative and with no official authority of the national union.

As Conaway was dismissed from the stand, Judge Geller announced
that he had made arrangements for the trial to continue in the Criminal Courts Building, 100 Centre Street, Room 1523, which was an
air-conditioned room, and that we should all meet there the next day.
He asked for the attorneys' consent for this arrangement. Lou, mop-
ping his brow, commented, "I give my consent retroactively as of six
weeks ago, your Honor."

The next day, June 21, we gathered in the new courtroom, which
was to be ours for the remainder of the trial. Judge Geller had assured
the jury that the case would be in its hands by June 28, one week
away. The jury had looked very pleased at this news; but no one was
more pleased than I.

Throughout the trial there had been a running controversy between
Bolan and Nizer over whether or not Laurence Johnson would testify.
These arguments had taken place in the judge's chambers, outside the
hearing of the jury. Bolan had maintained that Mr. Johnson was too
ill to come and testify. Lou was not convinced. Lou pointed out that
if Mr. Johnson indeed was too ill, he certainly did not want him to
come, but he had had word that Johnson had been traveling about the
country. Nizer wanted Johnson to submit to a medical examination by
a specialist of Nizer's choosing. The judge explained to the jury the

importance of the question. If a party to a suit fails to appear at a trial, without valid excuse, the jury is entitled to draw the strongest inference against him; they have the right to infer that he would not have been able to refute the evidence against him or substantiate charges made on his behalf.

This led to a duel of doctors. The defense announced that it would present a physician who would testify on Johnson's inability to come to the stand. Nizer chose as his specialist the foremost authority in New York on Johnson's particular disorder, Dr. Jerome Marks; Johnson agreed to come to New York for the examination.

The defendants called to the witness chair Dr. Wardner D. Ayer from Syracuse, a distinguished and learned physician with many degrees and an unimpeachable professional record.

Nizer had sat with Dr. Marks for hours going over in detail the nature of Johnson's disorder and familiarizing himself with all the medical terminology in the case. His cross-examination of Dr. Ayer reflected the thoroughness of his preparation; although Dr. Ayer was the very model of a thoroughly competent physician on the stand, Nizer was able to throw serious doubt on Ayer's evaluation of Johnson's physical condition.

Dr. Jerome Marks, in his turn on the stand, testified that in his opinion Johnson was fully able to come to court. I watched the jury's reaction to the conflicting testimony of these two distinguished doctors, and it seemed that they regarded Dr. Ayer as a fine gentleman but that they considered Dr. Marks the better qualified authority on Johnson's particular disorder; it seemed clear that they accepted his judgment that Johnson was well enough to appear as a witness if he wanted to.

However, either Bolan did not want to put Johnson on the stand, or Johnson refused to go through the ordeal of testifying. He did not make an appearance.

After Dr. Marks was dismissed from the stand the defense stated that it had no more witnesses to call. Justice Geller announced that he expected both sides to finish off all presentation of evidence by the next day. He again assured the jury that the case would be given to them not later than Wednesday or Thursday of the next week.

Lou had several rebuttal witnesses ready to go and he ran them off in fairly rapid order. First there was John Sibley, a reporter from *The*

New York Times, who had been covering the case from the first; it was he who, Vincent Hartnett had claimed, pointed out my wife to him. His testimony was brief and to the point.

NIZER: Did you ever point out Mrs. Faulk to Mr. Hartnett?
SIBLEY: I did not.

Lou then called Ted Poston, a long-time friend of mine, and a reporter on the *New York Post.* Ted and I had known each other since I first arrived in New York in 1946. We were both interested in interracial affairs and had seen each other socially as well as at public affairs gatherings. One of the allegations against me in the AWARE bulletin had been that I had appeared—presumably to entertain—at a place called Club 65 on a certain date in 1946. The affair had been given under the auspices of the *Amsterdam News* unit of the Newspaper Guild of New York. I had denied having entertained at the gathering or even being present, although it would have made little difference one way or the other had I been there for it was a perfectly respectable social affair, as Ted Poston, who had been there, testified. However, he made it perfectly clear that I had not been there and stood firmly by that answer during Bolan's cross-examination of him.

The following day, Friday, June 23, Nizer presented his final rebuttal witnesses. Hartnett, in an effort to prove that he had at least relied on ordinarily belief-worthy sources for the statements he had published about me, had claimed that he had based one of those statements—namely, that I had appeared at a function at the Jefferson School—on information he had received from a Mr. Jack Wren, an advertising executive with the firm of Batten, Barton, Durstine, and Osborn. Hartnett had further testified that he had been a friend of Jack Wren's, who had been something of a clearance officer for B.B.D.&O. in the early Fifties, and that they had frequently exchanged derogatory information on various television personalities. When Wren came into the courtroom, Bolan and Hartnett evidenced considerable surprise. By the time he had been sworn in and had taken the stand their surprise had turned to chagrin.

NIZER: Prior to February 1956, did you have any conversation with Mr. Vincent Hartnett in which you gave him any information about Mr.

John Henry Faulk, supposedly appearing or scheduled to appear at
the Jefferson School on or about February 16, 1948? . . . Did you
have any such conversation with Mr. Hartnett?

WREN: Absolutely not, sir.

NIZER: Your witness.

Bolan and Hartnett huddled for a few moments, then Bolan
launched his cross-examination. His attitude and that of Hartnett,
sitting directly across the table from me, suggested that they were
furious with Mr. Wren.

BOLAN: Mr. Wren, what were your duties at B.B.D.&O. in late 1955?

WREN: Well, my duties, among other things, was to protect our clients
against false charges made that we loaded our shows with Communists,
by Vincent Hartnett, who made these charges against us, who wrote
poison-pen letters behind our backs to our clients, wrote to our officers
accusing us of loading our shows with Communists.

BOLAN: Anything else in your duties, Mr. Wren?

WREN: Yes, my duties were to read television scripts to make sure that
they were accurate, especially dealing with realism.

BOLAN: Did you ever exchange information with Mr. Hartnett during the
year 1955?

WREN: No, sir.

BOLAN: Was your relationship with Mr. Hartnett in the year 1955 and
early 1956 a friendly one?

WREN: Unfriendly.

Bolan then produced a letter dated February 16, 1956, from Hartnett to Wren.

BOLAN: Did you have any communication at all with Mr. Hartnett
toward the latter part of 1955 and early 1956?

WREN: Absolutely not. None to my recollection.

BOLAN: Did you ever call his office on the telephone?

WREN: Not in that year.

BOLAN: 1955?

WREN: Not in that year, sir.

BOLAN: How about in 1956?

WREN: Not in that year, sir.

BOLAN: Are you positive of that?

WREN: Quite.

BOLAN: Did you ever send any communications to Mr. Hartnett at any time?

WREN: It is entirely possible I sent communications in the early '50s especially when Mr. Hartnett was engineering picket lines around our clients' shows, and I had to treat with him as a merchant treats with a racketeer who sells protection.

Lou, through Fred Mitchell, had secured the expert of experts on the subject of Pulse ratings, a genial, soft-spoken but very persuasive gentleman, Marvin Antonowsky. Antonowsky had taken his B.A. and M.A. degrees in statistics and was working on his Doctorate of Philosophy in statistics. Lou had worked with him for several nights mastering all the details of the mysterious items called ratings. Then Lou had had them construct huge charts so that the jury could easily see what was being discussed from the illustrations on the charts. It was Lou's thought that we should once and for all clear from the jury's mind any question about my falling ratings having been responsible for my being dismissed from CBS.

The large charts were placed in a strategic spot before the jury, and Mr. Antonowsky held forth under Lou's questioning like a professor explaining a diagram to a class. He was a thorough scholar in the matter. With his charts and his testimony Lou proved precisely the opposite of what the defendants had sought to maintain. As a matter of fact, he rather startled me; I had no idea that my ratings had been so high until Antonowsky started testifying. I got mad at WCBS all over again. Bolan, of course, knew that Antonowsky's testimony was doing a great deal of harm to the cause of the defendants but he hadn't spent the time mastering the matter that Nizer had and was unable to shake any of Antonowsky's testimony on cross-examination.

After Antonowsky was dismissed, Bolan called Hartnett back to the stand to rebut some of the strong testimony that Jack Wren had given.

BOLAN: Mr. Hartnett, was your relationship with Mr. Wren in January and February, 1956, a friendly relationship?

HARTNETT: It was.

The jury was left to decide whether Mr. Hartnett or Mr. Wren was to be believed. We were getting down toward the end of the day and Judge Geller was urging the lawyers to cut short any further discussion; he wanted to let the jury go home. But Bolan was anxious to get more direct rebuttal testimony from Hartnett concerning his finances. He also wanted to get a stipulation from Nizer that the defense counsel's accountant could go over my recent financial records, to ascertain my income since I had been fired. At one point it looked as though things were going to blow up in the courtroom. Mr. Bolan appeared to be verging on tears as he exploded at the judge:

BOLAN: . . . I wish you wouldn't be shouting at me throughout the trial as you have done from the very beginning. It gets to the point where the pressure is too great for me, your Honor. You have done it from the beginnning.

THE COURT: Nonsense, you put the court under pressure.

BOLAN: It's not nonsense.

THE COURT: Just a moment. We're going to stop this right now.

After a brief recess, Mr. Bolan returned to the courtroom, his composure regained.

BOLAN: . . . Your Honor, may I say that I apologize for getting excited a few moments ago.

THE COURT: Your apology is accepted.

Within a matter of moments thereafter I heard the welcome words from Nizer, "That is all. The plaintiff rests." The defense rested, too. Darkness was gathering over Manhattan as the jury was excused until Tuesday, June 26, at which time Bolan would give his summation.

26

I woke up at dawn Tuesday morning and lay in bed thinking. As far as I was concerned, school was out. All that remained now was the graduation exercises. Each side had had its say. All the evidence was in. Nothing could be added, nothing taken away. No surprise turns now. Bolan's summation of the defendants' case today and Lou's summation of ours tomorrow; the judge's charge to the jury, the jury's deliberation and its verdict on Thursday. I had no thought past that moment.

I remembered the final statement in Bolan's opening speech before the jury nearly three months before. He had said, "Above all, I do urge you to give your most careful attention to all of the evidence, and I am sure that when all the evidence is in, you will have found that the defendants did nothing which in any way damaged the reputation or professional career of the plaintiff." I wondered how he was going to get around that in his summation, but I was feeling too well to think about it for long. I started down to court that morning feeling as if I were going on a fishing trip.

When we arrived in court, first thing I noticed was that Vincent Hartnett was there with his wife and six lovely, bright-faced children. I felt a strong impulse to go up and congratulate them. They looked as though they had come to see their father receive a diploma of some kind. They were arrayed up near the front of the courtroom in front of the jury. Lou took exception to what he regarded as a crass bit of staging for the benefit of the jury. He spoke to the judge in chambers, and the Hartnett family was moved back several rows to a less conspicuous place. I smiled and reflected that Lou never let his opponent get the slightest advantage, even a seemingly innocent one.

Vincent Hartnett left his family and moved up to his place at the counsel table. While we were waiting for court to convene he dropped the sheaf of papers that he had been holding. I retrieved them for him from under the table. He gave me a tight smile of thanks and a curt nod. I smiled back at him pleasantly.

When court convened, Judge Geller stated from the bench that it was the responsibility of the court to dismiss from consideration by the jury all issues which had not been supported by evidence on the trial; and then, to my considerable amazement, he proceeded to state that the defendants' two affirmative defenses—namely, truth and fair comment—were stricken: the defendants had presented no evidence that would establish the truth of their charges against the plaintiff; and the defendants had not proved that their libel had been provoked. He then proceeded to strike their first partial defense of partial truth and partial fair comment, and instructed the jury that they could not consider these issues. He stated, "This leaves as the affirmative defense of the defendants, AWARE, Inc., and Hartnett, the partial defense of reliance on sources, which goes to mitigation of punitive damages. These defendants, you will recall, offered no direct proof of truth, but did present evidence of alleged reliance on sources, mostly in the form of documents which were not admitted for the truth of their content but merely for the limited purpose of claimed reliance on sources."

Judge Geller then turned his attention to the matter of the summations, pointing out that the function of the summation by the lawyers was to sum up or draw together the various lines of evidence and to argue and try to convince the jury to arrive at conclusions which each lawyer advanced. He warned them not to be swayed by the oratory of the two lawyers. "So listen carefully to both counsel. Reject what you consider to be unfounded or unsupported arguments and accept what you deem to be fair and reasonable inferences based on the believable evidence as you find it in this case."

He then told Mr. Bolan to proceed with his summation. Bolan moved up to the table which had been placed in front of the jury, set his papers out in front of him on the table and started in a low, easy voice. After telling them that he was going to give them the highlights of the case he said:

Why has this case lasted so long? It is probably a record for a libel case in New York County. And the answer is simple: because the plaintiff

at the outset knew he was not going to be able to prove his case. . . .
Had we confined this case to Mr. Faulk and the defendants, we would
have been out of here many weeks ago.

Why was somebody like Tony Randall the movie actor brought in
here before you to testify? What did he testify to? Did he know Mr.
Faulk? Did he have anything to do with Exhibit 41 or any of the issues
in the case? All Mr. Randall testified to was that he was afraid to go to
AFTRA meetings because he didn't want to be seen publicly taking a
position against AWARE. That's all he testified to. . . .

The plaintiff's plan here was obvious. That he sought to saturate
you with a mass of irrelevancies; week after week of testimony having
nothing to do with Exhibit 41; weeks and weeks of testimony to the
effect that blacklisting is a bad thing, that this is a general practice in
the industry, and it is a bad thing. . . .

Now, did the plaintiff, however, produce the key witnesses, the
important witnesses in this case? Namely, his employers at CBS. No,
he did not. He did not produce one witness from CBS. The defendants
did. The plaintiff had the burden to show his damages, but he did not
produce anybody from CBS. . . . We subpoenaed for you all of the
records at CBS relating to Mr. Faulk, and you may consider that very
seriously, ladies and gentlemen, in your deliberation, why didn't the
plaintiff produce anybody from CBS?"

I was beginning to feel drowsy again as Bolan droned on. The jury
was listening with interest, however, and I tried to do the same. Suddenly his summation took another turn as I heard him say:

. . . Mr. Faulk, has deliberately lied to you on numerous occasions
in this case on matters of great importance. There are so many lies
that it is hard to list them all. I will give you about nine or ten for a
start and mention many more throughout my summation.

I was suddenly wide-awake and furious. I was not prepared for
this turn in events. To sit and listen to a man calling me a liar and be
unable to do anything about it was a grim experience. I glanced at
Martinson and Nizer and Berger; they seemed to be taking it all very
calmly. I became angry at them. Bolan was riding along citing instance after instance where, he claimed, I had lied. He said that I
had lied about how well I had been doing at WCBS in 1955, had lied

about my loss of sponsors, had lied about my popularity as a TV
performer, had lied about the reasons for my being fired from CBS.

. . . I submit that just on this series of lies, they are so deliberate,
so flagrant, that you could question anything Mr. Faulk told you at this
trial, but I am going to give you quite a few others that are almost as
bad, if not worse in some cases. . . .

And as is evident throughout much of his testimony Mr. Faulk lied
when he knew that—when he believed that there wasn't any occasion
to contradict him. . . . He wanted to show you that he was quite a
performer before the alleged libel, before the publication of Exhibit 41.
The fact is that it wasn't until after the publication of Exhibit 41 that
Mr. Faulk really got sponsors. . . .

I submit that Mr. Faulk got more publicity out of this lawsuit, as a
result of this lawsuit, than he had ever had before in his life. He had
never been mentioned to any extent at all in the New York papers.

As I sat there in my chair, immobilized by court rules, listening as
he heaped opprobrium upon me, a feeling of despair and loneliness
crept over me. I realized that it would be impossible ever to communicate to anyone, even my dearest friends, how utterly crushing this
experience was for me. Although intellectually I understood that to
Bolan I was only a symbol and not a person, it was still impossible
for me to shake off the terrifying pain of his brutal attack on my
character.

. . . Mr. Faulk's lies spread over a tremendous area. Every area in
which he testified, he lied or exaggerated. . . .

I resented the fact that neither my lawyers nor my family could
share this experience with me. As Bolan read from Ward's testimony,
which supposedly contradicted statements that I had made, I grew
furious at Ward. His weaseling answers hit me between the eyes. Why
hadn't he stood up like a man, I thought bitterly.

When at long last Judge Geller announced a lunch recess I rose
numbly from my chair. Friends were smiling sympathetically, but I
regarded their sympathy as a smirk. A reporter for whom I had a
genuine respect nervously undertook to jest, "Why John, I didn't
realize you were such a liar." He of course was embarrassed by

Bolan's speech and was trying to joke it off. I pushed by him, stony-faced. Out of the entire group of spectators only one person seemed to understand my state of mind. That was Mildred Nizer. She came forward and caught my hands and kissed me warmly and looked at me steadily, squeezing my hands affectionately.

As I walked across Foley Square toward Gasner's Lou joined me. He discerned at once that I was in a grim state of mind and said cheerfully, "That viciousness is going to cost Bolan dearly. I'm really surprised that he chose that route. I would have thought that he would have been smarter than that. He's done his case no good with that violent attack upon you." I said nothing. Lou patted me affectionately on the shoulder and said, "Don't listen today. Let it go in one ear and out the other. Prepare to listen tomorrow." At lunch I sat with Lou, Paul and George, but had no appetite. I felt a mild resentment at them all for accepting the rules of the game and dismissing Bolan's viciousness with "That's the way Bolan plays." Paul Martinson seemed to understand fully how I felt. He looked at me for a long moment and then observed thoughtfully, "I've long felt there should be some restraint placed upon lawyers and their privilege of personally vilifying a man in open court."

When I got back to the courtroom Vincent Hartnett's children and family were gone. I realized why he had brought them: he had wanted them to hear about the evil man who had caused their father so much trouble. Bolan slashed into me again in the afternoon session, at first citing Sam Slate's testimony as evidence of what a hard-hearted liar I was. He then began to ridicule my ability as an entertainer, pointing out that I was never more than fourth-rate at best. After reviewing my various shows he said:

> This is another hoax which the plaintiff is seeking to perpetrate at this trial. The plaintiff, from the start of his career, has been primarily a radio disc jockey and nothing else. . . . His ability or lack of ability was very well known in the industry . . . The fact is that Mr. Faulk was not a star performer. He was ranked third or fourth amongst the radio disc jockeys in New York.

Bolan started in on my witnesses. He described David Susskind as "probably the most hypocritical witness that was produced in this trial." He gave Mark Goodson and Garry Moore's testimony the back of his hand. At some length he undertook to justify the defendants' efforts to police the political sentiments of radio and television performers. He made little headway with that.

. . . The plaintiff seeks to put the blame on the defendants for what he calls blacklisting, but he is dead wrong. It is the American public that does not want identified Communist Party members on its radio programs or television programs. It does not want people who invoke the Fifth Amendment concerning Communism on its program. It does not want people with records of Communist-front affiliations that have never been repudiated, appearing on their programs.

And since the public does not want it, the sponsors don't want it, the advertising agencies don't want these people on their programs. . . . Experts, such as Mr. Hartnett, in this field, were employed, and I don't think there is any doubt Mr. Hartnett is an expert in this field. He knows the workings of the Communist Party. He has tremendous files on the Communist Party, Communist fronts and its operations. . . .

They [Nizer, Susskind and the plaintiff] feel that activities by people such as Hartnett and AWARE contribute to the Communist Party in the United States. Eliminate them, and they feel that this will help get rid of the Communist Party. This is their attitude.

That is what is behind this whole lawsuit, and I feel there has been a tremendous amount of time, talent and effort marshaled here against these defendants, with this one aim, to eliminate private opposition to Communist infiltration in the United States.

The defendants here are not without support. You have seen from Exhibit 41 that the House Un-American Activities Committee backs the activities of the defendant. There has been testimony by Mr. Collingwood that the Catholic War Veterans, the Jewish War Veterans and the American Legion, branches of those organizations support the defendants. Mr. Collingwood described it as part of the blacklisting apparatus.

Bolan eulogized Donald Conaway, national Executive Secretary of AFTRA, and Rex Marshall, another AFTRA member who strongly supported AWARE, for their fine work in the union; and he contrasted that fine work with the weakness of the Middle-of-the-Road slate in relation to Communism. He delivered a splendid eulogy of Vincent Hartnett and AWARE, Inc., and their fine work, and he pointed out that there was a need for their services. At one point he said, "Is there anything wrong about Mr. Hartnett's getting paid for this work?" I wondered if his words sounded as ironic to the jury as they did to me. During the latter part of Bolan's summation the sky darkened, a thunderstorm developed, and flashes of lightning rent the skies. At one point there was a mighty clap of thunder, and George Berger leaned over to me and whispered, "Even the heavens are mad at Bolan now." However, I could manage only a faint smile; I was so numb and aching that I felt as if I had been physically pummeled. I was emotionally exhausted, without even the strength to be angry. When court finally adjourned that afternoon a grim taciturnity had settled over me. I nodded curtly to my friends and departed for the hotel. I had no appetite for conversation. I desired only solitude and the release that only sleep can bring.

The effects of Bolan's unbridled attack on me still hung over me the next morning. My mood wasn't improved any when I saw *The New York Times,* which carried the full story of the diatribe against me.

However, by the time I got down to the courthouse that morning my spirits had been raised. I was astonished to discover there were hundreds and hundreds of people gathered at the courthouse long before the court was to convene. I saw dozens of friends I had not seen for a long time. They had all come down to hear Nizer's summation of the case. The courtroom would not hold even half of them, and there was some confusion about setting up chairs and what not. I slipped into the courtroom as soon as possible and took my seat at the counsel table. I was in no mood to stand around being the premature victor. Vincent Hartnett sat down opposite me stiffly. He began to read *The New York Times,* smiling to himself as he read of Bolan's attack on me.

Nizer was all business, arranging huge piles of exhibits on the table in front of the jury, checking his notes, and making sure that everything was in order. He seemed to be in perfect form, fresh and alert. George leaned over to me and commented, "You'd never know that he has not been to bed at all last night, would you? He worked on this summation the entire night. Only finished it a couple of hours ago."

There was an air of climax in the room, one that suggested "This is it." I studied the faces of the jurors as they took their seats, to see if there was a trace of any sympathy for me after the drubbing I had received yesterday. Not one of them looked at me. They were chatting amiably and then quieted down as the court came to order.

Lou began quietly addressing the jury, thanking them for their extraordinary dedication to duty and for the patience that they had shown in serving on this case. He pointed out that this was not an ordinary service that these jurors had rendered. He said perhaps the jurors would derive some compensation from the extraordinary nature of their service, from the fact that this was a historic case with historic implications.

It is a case by John Henry Faulk against these defendants, but certain cases involve extraordinary principles. There are in the history of litigation just a few of these, sometimes only one in a generation, and I stand here with a very deep sense of responsibility because I have upon me the burden of presenting this case to you. . . . For six years we have waited for this day, six years. We have worked during those six years day and night. You see the exhibits, the documents, the unraveling of that which was very difficult to prove in a courtroom under oath; and so we too have been under strain. It has been a great responsibility, which we take very earnestly and you ought to have, I hope, the satisfaction that your work, whatever it be when this case is over, will have significance in the history of litigation nationally and, I think, internationally.

The last day was a very bitter day, because we would have thought that, after everything that happened in this courtroom, there could have been a different position taken by the defendants. I would expect them to defend themselves, but they didn't have to spill their malice and hate in this courtroom until I felt that I was neck-deep in mud. When a man has no generosity in his heart, he has real heart disease; and I think the defendants yesterday demonstrated the malice with which this case from the first moment has been steeped.

Here we were with the learned court, whose research and learning on the complicated question of libel law have awed us all, instructing you that the defenses of truth were stricken out of this case; they couldn't plead the truth because there wasn't a shred of evidence to show that there was any truth. . . .

There wasn't even partial truth. There was a defense of partial truth; that was stricken out. There wasn't even a defense left of fair comment; as his Honor instructed you learnedly, in certain libel cases you can say, "Well, I was wrong but it was a comment, a fair comment." That was stricken out because it must meet certain standards which are missing here. . . .

So they stood bare in this courtroom as libelers who had destroyed this man and his family. Don't you think it would have been the decent thing under those circumstances for the defendants to take the usual, proper position for a defendant, "I was wrong; I am sorry"? . . . But no! even under those circumstances they came into this court and called my client a liar for coming into court and testing his rights. . . . I admire Mr. Faulk for keeping silent under that attack, because I had to grip my seat. At the last moment we were libeled again.

And who is it that is held forth as a truthful man? Mr. Bolan says, "I gambled my case on the integrity, on the truth of Mr. Hartnett." I accept that unhesitatingly. Why, Exhibit 41, the bulletin that he wrote, has already been held to be a complete lie, and he is the author of it. So how can he be a truthful man? At least he ought to say, "I lied about this whole exhibit, but forgive me, I was mistaken. I didn't mean to." . . . I repeat that when the defense of truth is stricken out of a case and the defense of partial truth is stricken out of a case, the document is not only libelous but a complete lie. I stand by that, and I wouldn't be as strong about it if they hadn't called Mr. Faulk a liar. And I repeat it. . . . The whole summation was symbolic of this case.

In the first place, there is no issue of Communism in this case. John Henry Faulk, from the first moment he could understand and breathe, has been anti-Communist, and no one has proved otherwise. . . . So Communism is not an issue. . . .

The question is whether we will permit our government to protect us under proper judicial and other procedures, or whether we're going to permit private vigilantes like this gentleman seated here with the thin mouth and the blue suit [pointing at Hartnett] who sneaks into a restaurant, the Blue Ribbon Restaurant, when there is a meeting of some union people, with a hidden microphone in his lapel. That is the question, or are you going to permit private vigilantism for profit? If he was a real patriot and he dug up any evidence, he would have sent it to the F.B.I. like all of us should, against a Communist. . . .

If any citizen has any evidence of any kind and he is really a good-natured and proper and loyal citizen he sends it to the governmental authorities, not to this gentleman; he charged $20.00 a throw.

There was some laughter at this bit of grim humor, and Judge Geller immediately warned the spectators that he would clear the courtroom if there was any more of it.

The issue is not Communism at all. It is private vigilantism, and the only time that Mr. Bolan came near to touching the issue in this case is when he told you yesterday all about the Fifth Amendment fellows. He said, "If a fellow takes a Fifth Amendment, haven't we a right, when I want to employ the man, to take it into consideration?" Why, you don't need the Fifth Amendment. I as an individual employer can refuse to hire anybody because I don't like the color of his tie. I can refuse to hire anybody because I don't like his speech, I don't like the way he dresses. That is my privilege as an American, but that isn't blacklisting. That doesn't mean that I send around a list to all the employers that this man will go to, and they all agree that they can't hire this man. That is what is evil about it. As an individual, cannot the electric company say, "I want to charge twice as much as my competitor?" They're fixing a price. That is legal. But what they can't do is get together with all their people and fix prices among them. That is a crime under our law, not only an antitrust violation, it's a crime under the criminal law.

And the question is not whether somebody should have a right to reject a man who took the Fifth Amendment. The question is whether Mr. Hartnett can send around a list to all the agencies and sponsors and put them into their grips and say, "If you use this man we're going to see to it that you get pressure from the American Legion Post 41 and the Veteran's Action Committee, and thus, by concerted conspiracy, hit a man behind his back when he doesn't know what has hit him, and deprive him of his livelihood, and send him, like Mr. Faulk, away from New York and back to his home town. . . . And why? He never faced any accuser. The only time we have had a chance is by waiting six years to come into this courtroom and struggle through every witness, objection after objection, and then we are maligned for coming into an American court. We are told we're liars. We have no right to be here, I suppose.

And incidentally, the issue is not the American Legion. . . . That is not the issue. No one is attacking the American Legion. We are attacking Post 41 in Syracuse, Mr. Dungey, who is the tool of Mr. Johnson. You can get a local of any kind to be corrupt, and this is a conspiracy between Mr. Johnson, who controlled Mr. Dungey, and the reason they didn't bring Mr. Dungey into court is that we would have found out what his financial arrangements are with Mr. Johnson. We would have had a chance. Why didn't they bring Mr. Dungey down to say, "Oh, I didn't know Mr. Johnson was doing this. I did it on my own." Why isn't he here?

And why isn't the Veteran's Action Committee of Syracuse Super-Markets here, Mr. Neuser? After all, he is an employee of Johnson; that is conceded. He is his fruit and vegetable buyer. But notice these letterheads. You saw them, red, white and blue. After all, if you were a sponsor of a television company and you get a letter of that kind, American Legion Post 41, Syracuse, Onondaga County, red, white and blue, well, you get scared. This is how this conspiracy worked. But this was just a tool of Mr. Johnson. He ordered these letters sent, as I will prove to you. There is no question about it. We have it in writing. . . .

And the Veteran's Action Committee is another tool of Mr. Johnson. That also has a beautiful red, white and blue letterhead, and it's signed with this auspicious signature, "Chairman of the Internal Subversion Committee, Francis W. Neuser." And who is Neuser? The fruit and vegetable buyer of Mr. Johnson.

But when the sponsor gets this letter, he doesn't know that. He says, "My God, I'm paying one hundred thousand dollars for two weeks of this program and I have got the Veterans and the American Legion after me." . . .

The real issue in this case, ladies and gentlemen, is that there are people who try to take the law into their hands. They try to, because they believe fanatically and in this case there was no fanaticism; it was malice. They didn't think Faulk, even fanatically, was a Communist. They struck at Faulk for another reason which I am going to give you. That is what makes it malicious. But when they struck at other people, they did it fanatically, and if people can take the law into their own hands that way, then the Ku Klux Klan is a good organization. They too, think the government isn't doing enough. Then the Silver Shirt organization, that is Pelley's group, that is a very good group if that's right, because they say, "We are impatient."

You heard Mr. Hartnett testify that is the philosophy of these people. Mr. Hartnett said it's unrealistic to depend on the government. I couldn't believe my ears. He actually said it from the witness stand. . . . And there you had an insight into the evil that we're striking at, private vigilantes taking the law into their own hands. . . .

When you and your neighbor are not safe from somebody who does not like you, and he tips off Mr. Milton or Mr. Johnson and Mr.

Hartnett and he can, through these organizations, ruin you and your enterprise and your business by writing a letter behind your back to your employer, and you suddenly find yourself economically strangled, which is what happened to Mr. Faulk (he didn't earn one cent in his profession from 1958, 1959, 1960)—Mr. Bolan forgot all about that—when you are strangled because your neighbor or someone who is fanatical can take these measures against you without recourse, without your facing an accuser, without your showing you are innocent, then you have Communism under the guise of fighting Communism. . . .

This man was shipped off to Siberia. I don't mean to malign Austin, Texas, but that is not where he belongs now after he had been in New York living in a beautiful apartment and becoming one of the great stars of our culture. . . .

We allege a conspiracy to control the radio and television industry, and it was our duty to show you that this happens to all sorts of artists.

Why, one man, Mr. Dickler, testified that he knew of two people who committed suicide. I think he mentioned Philip Loeb, and this woman, Mady Christians, a wonderful actress, because they didn't know what hit them. They were great stars. Then suddenly they got into an agency—"No, we are sorry, we can't use you."

Although the room had more than its capacity of spectators, there was not a whisper as Nizer delivered his summation. It was a wonder to watch the skill with which he could reach for an exhibit, display it to the jury, and talk about it, all at the same time. At those times when he referred to Hartnett's conduct, Hartnett sat tight-lipped, writing away as though he had no connection whatever with what was going on in the courtroom. Lou spoke of the terrible difficulties that Kim Hunter experienced as the result of Hartnett's activities. He recalled her testimony and the hardships she had suffered.

. . . And what was the price for her continuing working? She had to meet Mr. Hartnett's demand to send a telegram to the union not to condemn AWARE. And this man who, if you hadn't met him in the courtroom and seen him cross-examined, you would think this was some great powerful figure—All these dictators, they shrink when you see them.

Lou then recited dramatically how the courageous Tom Murray of the Grey Advertising Agency had stood up to Johnson when Johnson had come down to New York threatening reprisals if the agency continued to buy commercial time on my program. Lou went through the whole thing, repeating the conversations between Johnson and Murray. He told of Johnson's threat to have the American Legion write a letter to my sponsor and how he fulfilled that threat. Then, solemnly:

That is the kind of action and conspiracy which operates here, and there are bones on these roads, of wonderful artists, men and women in their profession, crushed by this.

And we have had the courage—I say "we"; I mean Mr. John Henry Faulk— You rarely find them. The reason I'm spilling out my heart and feelings in this case is—well, when do you find that kind of American? Everybody rushes to shelter. Why put up the fight? Why should I starve with my children for the industry? I know Americanism is being violated, but why is it my duty to be a martyr?

But this man, from the first moment, said, "I am going to see this thing through if I have to drive a taxi." And, incidentally, he couldn't even do that. He tried to sell the "Encyclopaedia Britannica"; he failed. He went into mutual welfare funds; he failed.

And the thing that touched me most, I must admit to you I had to stop, I am sure you didn't notice, but I cried when he was on the stand and said, "I finally got to the point where I went over, . . . and said, 'Have you got any kind of a job for me in television?' and the fellow said, 'You know, let's be blunt about it. You are controversial. I can't take the chance.' " . . . And the result of that situation is that Faulk asked for a $10 sit-in job and the fellow said, "We have got a sit-in," and he can't earn $10 to sit in a chair because these people have crushed him. And yet he wouldn't surrender this lawsuit, nor would we.

And we examined these people. Mr. Bolan told it to you as if this were a crime on our part, 27 sessions of Mr. Hartnett. Tens of thousands of dollars for these huge mountains of minutes, yes, and we did it and we are proud of it, and we finally have reached the day of vindication, and your word is going out to all the world that Americanism will not stand for this kind of corruption, of private vigilantism.

Lou mentioned the difficulty we had in getting any advertising executive to testify. As he put it:

They don't want to put themselves on the stand. Every advertising executive we had, we had to spit blood to get him here because they don't want to be involved. They were all part of this blacklisting. They had to be. They couldn't help it, and nobody likes to confess that, and that is the answer to the CBS business which we will come to a little later.

Lou then described how Wren had called Hartnett a liar from the stand and accused him of being a blackmailer and a racketeer. He then reminded the jury that this was an issue in the case, whether Hartnett, Johnson working in conspiracy with Post 41 of the American Legion, and Mr. Neuser, his own fruit and vegetable buyer, could control the entire radio and television industry. He said:

This is dangerous, ladies and gentlemen. It is far more dangerous, dangerous as Communists are. This is far more dangerous to permit the culture, the entertainment medium to be controlled by a few people for profit. That is the real issue; that is the framework.

Lou then turned his attention to me. He began to paint my background in glowing colors. He described my schooling, my dedication to folklore, my learning. I became so uncomfortable I couldn't look at the jury or Lou. I gazed out the high window. I studied my hands. I stole furtive glances back over the crowded courtroom. I squirmed. I did everything to keep from appearing to be the person that Lou was talking about. I wanted to leave the room. I knew that would be too obvious, so I sat there feeling silly.

At recess, I slipped outside to smoke my pipe. In the corridor there were hundreds of people who hadn't been able to get in—every seat in the courtroom had been taken, and a number of people had been lined up along the walls. Kim Hunter was there in the corridor; she had been unable to get into the courtroom. She came forward and kissed me and asked me how it was going. She squeezed my hand tightly and whispered, "This is your day, you waited so long." Many other performers who had suffered at the hands of AWARE were on hand. They had come to witness the day of reckoning. I made it a point to see to it that Kim Hunter was able to get into the courtroom so that she could hear the remainder of Nizer's summation. As he took up again, he related my wartime activities—service in the Merchant Marine, then in the Red Cross overseas, and later as a GI in the Army. Then he got around to my career in radio and television and how I had been fired.

> I want to stop there and say no matter what you do, and I hope you are going to do full justice, punitive damages as well as regular damages, which I will come to—no matter what you do and even if he can get back to work in his profession, it will take him another three or five years to get back, you can not be off radio or television or pictures and just step back. The experts testify to that there is a momentum that is built up that is lost. He has lost five years no matter what you do. That you can't give him back.

I winced as Lou recited what I knew were facts and reflected again that I had not even thought past the end of this trial. For a fleeting moment I toyed with the idea, What am I going to do? But now Nizer had cause to turn on Hartnett again and I listened.

> If he [Hartnett] is a good investigator and he is so precise, he knew about it, and he deliberately omitted it, that man with the thin mouth and the blue suit, as somebody said, who goes to the Police Department. There was something here that shocked us out of our wits, and I think it should shock any American. He sets up, he claims, an alliance with the Police Department of New York. He says he had 60 or 70 conferences, secretly, with a certain gentleman whose name I will mercifully omit. You remember it, Lieutenant—I will mention it; there is no reason to shield him—Lieutenant Crain. Mr. Milton who has more sense, says that's untrue, Mr. Hartnett couldn't have done that because it's illegal to do it. So Mr. Milton calls Mr. Hartnett a liar, not we. Mr. Milton calls him a liar.
>
> And isn't that a terrible thing? A private vigilante works his way— you see how this works—works his way into the Police Department. He gives them information which is misleading. They may arrest you or your neighbor or your husband or your sister because he thinks she is pro-Communistic, and he has given them some data on her, and on the other hand they are supposed to feed him, he says.
>
> So here is a brilliant student, a teacher at Texas, a liberal democrat —yes, liberal, very liberal in the greatest tradition of the south. You have heard his testimony. . . . He is a liberal democrat, always was. . . . When that Middle-of-the-Road slate won Mr. Hartnett was in

trouble with that collection agency of his for patriotism, because they were going to stop blacklisting if they had to go to the courts or to the government to stop this.

That's why Mr. Hartnett and all the directors of AWARE and Mr. Johnson met. I am going to show you the meeting. I am going to piece together the writings in this case that we were able to dig out of their hide. They met and decided to destroy this man before he destroyed their income, their illegitimate income. That is the reason for the malice in this case.

Lou then went into detail on some of the other persons that the defendants had attacked—Kim Hunter and James Thurber, a dangerous figure according to Mr. Hartnett, who collected twenty dollars for saying it; even Santa Claus, as Lou said:

So first he [Santa Claus] was a model, and in ten seconds, when he didn't pass models, it was a gag. But he collected $5 for passing as Santa Claus. That is how preposterous and evil this thing is.

You know, this thing would be funny except for the fact that every artist in America was frightened to death. Every artist gave up his dignity, every artist gave up his self respect. You either knuckled under to the Hartnetts or the Johnsons, or you were out of work, and very few people wanted to do what Faulk did and not have food to eat in order to bring this case to trial. I am not exaggerating. The record shows, the last days we read in, he is in the so-called advertising business in Austin, Texas. . . .

How many artists want to do that in order to stand up to these people? And you have a chance; that is why I say this case is historic. You have a chance in this case to give a clarion call to the world on this, to make an award of punitive damages in several million dollars, of compensatory damages of over a million dollars.

It doesn't matter whether it can be collected or not. Let the word get out that this kind of thing must stop. Give, by your verdict, a clear answer to the kind of un-Americanism which this case represents. Aren't we free people? Do we have to knuckle under? Would you, before you get a job, want Mr. Jones or Mr. Smith to pass upon you so that you can't earn your livelihood if he thinks you're not a good American?

Behind his [the artist's] back he suddenly becomes unemployable, unemployable, unemployable. That word never passed Mr. Bolan's lips. They did not use that word "unemployable" in their entire summation of the whole day. The word "unemployable" wasn't mentioned, and it is the most important word in this case. When a man becomes controversial, he becomes unemployable. Let's not forget that word. They forgot it. Don't you forget it.

Lou knew how to wring every bit of the value out of the testimony of such witnesses as Kim Hunter, Ken Roberts and Everett Sloan. After recapitulating the testimony of Sloan as to how he had gotten clearance from the United States Government and still been turned down by the defendants, Lou said:

The United States Government says he is loyal, but he still can't get a job because Mr. Hartnett didn't say he was loyal. . . . Milton . . . says, "This isn't good enough." And Sloan is amazed. Remember him on the witness stand? He says, "Isn't good enough, what do you mean?" He [Milton] says, "Well, our standards are different." You see, this is unrealistic. This is the same as Hartnett. "This government stuff is unrealistic. We have different standards, but I'll tell you what I will do for you. I will make an appointment for you to see Mr. Hartnett." You see, that is the acme. Lord knows who Mr. Hartnett is until you get him into a courtroom and see his size. . . . An incident which ought to make an American hang his head in shame.

Then Lou recapitulated my entire experience with the union—how I had heard of the serious goings on, and how AWARE dominated the union; how I helped form a Middle-of-the-Road slate, got elected, became an official of the union, and then was attacked.

For the next hundred years the name of Faulk against AWARE and Johnson and Hartnett I think will be in the books.

Lou was building up a real head of steam now. The courtroom was entirely silent as he highlighted the conspiracy against me. He went back to 1955 when John Crosby in the New York *Herald Tribune* had written, "Not long ago the American Federation of Television and Radio Artists, the terror-stricken union of radio and television performers took a courageous and long overdue stand by condemning the viciously un-American practice of blacklisting actors." Lou referred to AWARE and Hartnett as a wolf pack of vigilantes. Then he quoted from another article. "Unholy alliance, AFTRA and the blacklist. Something like a state of terror spreads through the union. Actors who might have sought after office were afraid to do so. Many members have told me that they were afraid to speak at AFTRA meetings for fear that their names would be noted and their opportunities for work would diminish. Several have told me they were afraid even to attend meetings."

He quoted a line from Robert Frost: "The people I am most scared of are the people who are scared." He told how Hartnett, when I was running for office in AFTRA in November of 1955, had written to the House Un-American Activities Committee. "He [Hartnett] is trying to get Faulk in trouble with the House Un-American Activities Committee because Faulk is a candidate, and if the Middle-of-the-Road slate is elected the House Un-American Activities Committee should call Mr. Faulk and they would issue statements to that effect, that would crush the Middle-of-the-Road ticket." He pointed out to the jury that the reason I hung on a year after I had been attacked at CBS was because Collingwood and Ed Murrow had stepped in in my behalf and spoken to executives at CBS.

Every once in a while Lou would pause and shake his head as he would mutter, "Malice, malice, deliberate deception," or, "Now, isn't this horrendous?" He tells how Hartnett "has the *Herald Tribune* in front of him; he uses the quote of the *Herald Tribune,* and he ascribes it to the *Daily Worker*. Is that just a mistake, or is it malicious and vicious? Then punitive damages should be granted for malice." He read excerpts from letters between Hartnett and Johnson congratulating each other when they had succeeded in destroying an artist's career.

Lou was sailing along through the testimony, pointing out first Hartnett's then Johnson's malice, when suddenly Judge Geller declared a short recess. This was about four o'clock in the afternoon. Kim Hunter and Andrew Amsbach, manager of the Algonquin Hotel and Ben Bodne's son-in-law, came forward to chat with me, and we were commenting on Nizer's summation, when a reporter, Miss Stephanie Gervis, touched my elbow and drew me aside. "Laurence Johnson just died," she said. I stared at her. She was deadly serious and nodded her head as a kind of reaffirmation. "It's true," she said.

"That's the reason for this recess. The lawyers and the judge are try-ing to decide whether to go on or not."

"But how could he? Now?" I mumbled. Somehow, I knew that it was a fact. I moved over to the counsel table and sat down heavily in my chair. Paul and George entered from the judge's chamber, somber-faced. My eyes met theirs as they took their places beside me. They nodded sympathetically and looked straight ahead. Lou came in and walked behind my chair. He leaned over and put his hand on my shoulder. "They have just found a body in a Bronx motel," he whis-pered. "They think it is that of Larry Johnson."

I sat pondering—trying to come to some conclusion, trying to grasp the meaning of this strange turn. I could only think, over and over, "What a frail thing life is!" What would Johnson's death mean to our case? I was suddenly embarrassed with myself to think that I only considered the effect of this man's death on my interest. What a cold-blooded lot lawsuits make of all of us! I glanced at Lou. He was busily going over his remaining notes. The jury came back in, completely unaware of the news, and took their places. Judge Geller came in, took his place, and nodded for Lou to resume his summation.

George Berger told me later what had happened in the judge's chamber. Mr. Bolan's secretary had called him shortly before four o'clock and informed him that a body identified as that of Mr. Laurence Johnson had been found in a motel in the Bronx and was at that moment at the morgue in the Bronx. The judge asked that this information be withheld from the press until a positive identification of the body could be made, but Mr. Bolan had already informed two reporters. The judge called these two in and asked them if they could withhold the story until it was positively established that it was Mr. Johnson who had died. The reporters refused, saying that they had already called in the story. Bolan moved for a severance of Johnson as a defendant. To keep the jury from being influenced by the news of Johnson's death, Judge Geller arranged to have them sent to a hotel that night. The judge then instructed both attorneys to prepare memoranda on how they thought the matter should be handled.

Lou continued his summation without giving the slightest hint that anything had gone awry. He dwelt at length on the matter of damages, both compensatory and punitive. He then called upon the jury to award one million dollars in compensatory damages and a million dollars separately against each of the defendants for punitive damages. He ended up on the resounding note:

> I will not go on with the rest of the terrible story of this man's ordeal, but now I place his life in your hands. I place his wife's life and his three children's lives in your hands, very literally, because this man's reputation is either going to be restored by a verdict that will ring to the world, or he will be besmirched all over again.
> I leave to your hands the doing of full justice, and if you do that, ladies and gentlemen, you can sleep well because God will be awake. Thank you.

When Nizer had completed his summation the judge informed the jury that they would all go together to a hotel for the night, and they were not to read any newspaper or to listen to any radio or television. The jury was understandably mystified and obviously distressed at this news. The judge assured them that the case would be through by tomorrow, and accompanied by several court attendants they left for their hotel.

I could scarcely wait to hear from Nizer just exactly what this development would do to our suit. He explained it to me in detail. He also said that he was going to put every available man in his office to work on research relating to the legal problems that Johnson's death had raised. Poor Paul Martinson and George Berger, who had been planning a night of relaxation with their families, were included in the draft. I returned to the hotel with completely mixed feelings. I would be dishonest if I pretended that I was concerned about Johnson's death for his family's sake, but I was a little shocked at myself for thinking only of my own interest in the matter. I assumed that his family had been devoted to him, and they were at that very moment no doubt grieving their loss.

Later I went up to Nizer's office. He had all hands available working on the case. The consensus seemed to be that there was not precedent for such a situation.

The next morning's papers carried the news of Johnson's death under such headlines as "Faulk Case Figure Dead." They reported little that I hadn't already learned. Mr. Johnson's body, clad in pajamas, had been discovered in a Bronx motel. He had died, apparently, of natural causes.

Since a dead man cannot be party to a lawsuit, but his estate may, a legal mechanism had to be found whereby the position of the late Laurence Johnson as defendant could be immediately transferred to his estate, without any discontinuation of the proceedings. After an all-night session, Paul Martinson and George Berger submitted next morning to Judge Geller a Creditor's Petition; they argued that as the New York Supreme Court is a court of general jurisdiction, Justice Geller was entitled to accept this as a Surrogate, and to grant letters of Temporary Administration to an executor of his choice. He agreed with this course, and named an independent lawyer as administrator, who then sat in that afternoon when the court reconvened, as a defendant in the place of the late Laurence Johnson.

I went down to court that afternoon with Lou, Paul and George. We were astonished to see Bolan and Lang sitting at their ease on a table which had been placed before the judge's bench. They were sitting there cross-legged, laughing gaily and chatting, facing the spectators' section and apparently counting the number of persons entering the courtroom. Nizer was indignant. He observed that their posture and attitude "is of such arrogance as I've never seen in court before." The courtroom quickly filled up and as the spectators composed themselves we sat at the counsel table waiting for Justice Geller to enter. Paul and George chatted amiably with me as Louis Nizer sat and sketched the faces of court attendants and others. Bolan and Lang, still laughing, continued to swing their legs from the table and look out over the spectators. Finally Mr. Bolan tore a crossword puzzle from *The New York Times* and took his place at the counsel table, where he proceeded to work out the puzzle.

After what seemed to me an eternity, Justice Geller took his place on the bench. The jury was brought in and Justice Geller informed them of Johnson's death. One woman juror gasped and placed her hands over her mouth, but there was no noticeable reaction by the other jurors. Justice Geller then proceeded to deliver his charge to the jury.

"Now we have reached the hour of decision," he said, and he carefully explained that the verdict must be based solely on the evidence the jury had heard in the case. It was up to the jury to decide what were the true facts of the case and what inferences should reasonably be drawn from them. They were the sole and exclusive judges of the facts. The judge's function was to see to it that only legal evidence relevant to the issues of the case should be submitted to them, and to instruct them as to the principles of law to be applied to the case; on these they must accept the judge's direction.

Moving on to the subject of libel, he said:

The good reputation of a person has always been rightly regarded as a cherished possession among the peoples of the civilized communities.

Where action has been brought for alleged libel, it is for the defendants to bear the burden of proof; *in this case, the only defense remaining was that of the quality of proof on which the defendants had relied.*

With three defendants, it would be for the jury to determine the degree of conspiracy.

A conspiracy is an agreement or understanding between two or more persons, which may include a membership corporation, to do an illegal act. A libel is an illegal act.

If all three were found to be parties to a conspiracy, damages must be awarded against all of the conspirators.

The judge then discussed the two kinds of damages the jury must consider.

Compensatory damages are intended to compensate a plaintiff for all the damage he has suffered, that is, to make him whole. The damages awarded must be based upon the injury to his reputation and in his profession. He is also entitled to be compensated for the mental anguish, mortification and humiliation which you find and believe he experienced in his public and private life.

The amount of these damages was up to the jury to determine. They should use their common sense and good judgment. In respect of damages for loss of income, the judge referred to the testimony given by experts during the trial, and warned the jury to evaluate it as they did the testimony of other witnesses. Substantial damages could only be based on substantial injury. If the jury should consider there had been no substantial injury, then damages awarded should be only nominal.

Punitive damages, on the other hand, are to punish a defendant, to deter him from the repetition of an offense, and as a warning to others not to commit a like offense.

> Punitive damages are intended to protect the community and to vindi-
> cate public decency.

The award of punitive damages, in addition to compensatory damages, would depend on the extent to which the defendants had been ac-tuated by malice.

> Malice would include the notion of hostility or intent to injure. You
> may consider, if you deem it indicative of malice, any testimony given
> by either of the two defendants in this case.

Of course, now that Johnson was dead, he was no longer concerned in this consideration of punitive damages.

The judge carefully pointed out that the defendants' partial defense of reliance had no effect on their liability for compensatory damages. But there could be a mitigation of punitive damages if the defendants had shown great care, accuracy and truth in use of the information on which they had relied; again, it was for the jury to decide on this. The judge was careful to remind the jury of his ruling that, as a matter of law, none of the organizations described by the defendants as "officially designated a Communist front" was, in fact, so designated.

Finally, the judge explained that a unanimous verdict was not necessary in this case, and that as soon as ten of them were in agree-ment they should bring their deliberations to an end. If they found for the plaintiff, they must include in their verdict the amount of compensatory damages against all the defendants, and if they decided to award punitive damages, these must be named against each, Hart-nett and AWARE. "If your verdict is for the defendants, you must so state."

As the full meaning of Judge Geller's charge sank in, I was almost shocked. In this charge, he had literally ruled out Bolan's entire case, leaving the jury to decide but one thing—how much compensatory and punitive damages to award. In other words, the years of effort that the defendants had put into building their defenses, had been thrown out the window by Justice Geller in the last hour.

Bolan arose and made his exceptions to the charge and the judge then excused the alternate juror, Mr. King, who came over and shook my hand as he left the court. At exactly 5:35 P.M. Justice Geller said, "Members of the jury you may now retire and deliberate." And the jury rose and filed out. As they walked past the counsel table I tried desperately to get some clue from their faces as to their feelings. There was none. Each juror looked straight ahead.

Nizer suggested that I stay near him. Most of our friends went over to Gasner's to have cocktails and dinner. Lou suggested that we go to a Chinese restaurant nearby. Mildred, Ben Bodne and I agreed. Lynne, who had come to New York for the last days of the trial, joined us. George Berger was left in the courtroom to convey the news from the jury. The jury had gone out to dinner, so we were confident that they would not return a verdict for several hours. It was pointless for me to try to linger over the meal and feign indifference. I wanted to get back to the courtroom. Nizer speculated that if the jury were out a short time it would mean a good verdict for us. If the jury got locked up in wrangling there would have to be compromises and it would probably go badly for us. He offered no speculation whatever on whether the jury's verdict would be for us or against us.

At nine-thirty I could stand it no longer. I went back to the courtroom. There were several court attendants and a couple of reporters and good George Berger lolling around the tables and taking it easy. I sat down and jotted thoughts down on a piece of paper. Spectators wandered in and out. Suddenly an attendant called, "Will everybody be seated!" and word went out through the corridors and to the surrounding restaurants that something was about to happen in court. Merle Debuskey went dashing over to Gasner's to get our friends there. Bolan was summoned from his office several blocks away. When we were all seated and Bolan had arrived, Justice Geller asked an attendant to bring the jury in. My heart was pounding as they filed in and took their seats.

Justice Geller then said that the jury wanted to ask a question and he wanted it done in open court. The foreman rose and asked, "Can the jury award more damages than the plaintiff's attorney asked?" There was complete consternation on the face of everyone in the courtroom. George Berger and Paul Martinson stared at one another in disbelief. Louis Nizer fell back in his chair in amazement. In his entire legal career a jury had never come in and asked to give more than he, Nizer, had asked them for. The judge was obviously astonished by this question too. However, he carefully explained to the jury the law on this point.

The newsmen at their table and the spectators quickly got word out through the public that a historic event was about to take place. Nizer remarked to me that the record libel verdict in history was half a million dollars. He warned me, however, not to become too sanguine now. "Let's wait until the verdict's in," he said.

I sat at the table alone, thinking of the long, long road I had come along from South Austin, Texas, to this moment, in a courtroom in New York where a decision was being made that could possibly make history. Whether it was favorable or unfavorable to me, it would forever change my life. The soft June night outside was filled with the sounds of Manhattan after dark. Some of my friends wandered down to the night court, several floors below, to watch the never-ending drama there. Anything to while away the time. Scenes from my childhood kept floating before me. What would Daddy and Mama think about this? And Dobie? I realized how important the approval of those I loved was to me.

At last, word came out that the jury had reached a decision. It was necessary to send to Bolan's office for him again. The courtroom filled up quickly. Some minutes later Bolan came in. Hartnett sat opposite me, in his accustomed place. The jury filed back into their box. It was twenty minutes before midnight when the clerk of the court addressed the foreman of the jury, "Have you agreed upon a verdict?" "We have," he replied. "How do you find?" "We, the jury, have arrived at our decision in favor of Mr. Faulk. We have awarded the plaintiff, Mr. Faulk, compensatory damages in the sum of one million dollars against AWARE, Inc., Mr. Vincent Hartnett and the estate of the late Mr. Laurence Johnson. We have also awarded the plaintiff, Mr. Faulk, punitive damages in the sum of $1,250,000 against AWARE, Inc. and $1,250,000 against Mr. Hartnett." Bolan immediately jumped to his feet and demanded that the jury be polled. One juror had voted against the decision. Since only ten jurors were necessary for a verdict, this made no difference. The judge thanked them and excused them. The full impact of the verdict had not fully hit me as I went up to shake hands with each one as they left the jury box. For the first time in three months their faces betrayed their genuine feelings. As I clasped the hand of each, we could only smile and bob our heads. Several were weeping. I was near tears myself.

Suddenly, photographers and reporters were all over the place. The courtroom wheeled about me in a great blur. I tried to be honest, answering reporters that the decision numbed me. Lou suggested that we should have a quiet celebration. We left the courthouse for the last time and adjourned to the Algonquin Hotel. I still couldn't comprehend the meaning of such a settlement—three and a half million dollars! Lynne, Chris, Merle, the Kanes joined the Nizers and the Bodnes at a long table. Myrna Loy phoned, too ecstatic to do other than repeat, "Wonderful, wonderful." I called Cactus Pryor, my sister Mary and my sister Texana, and J. Frank Dobie, in Austin, to relate the news to them. Lynne and I decided that it was too late at night to call the children.

I slept more soundly than I had in many, many, many days.

27

The reaction to the news of the verdict was immediate and widespread. When I woke up the next morning and called the operator at the Algonquin, she told me that she had been swamped with calls from all over the country since daylight. She was even holding a couple from London and Paris. She hadn't let them through because she knew I was sleeping late. She said that the lobby was full of newspapermen, TV cameramen and radio newsmen. I was astonished. I had fantasied, but never really believed, there would be such a reaction to the verdict. Ben Bodne sent up the *Times* and the *Herald Tribune*. Both carried the story under big headlines on their front pages. The day became a blur of radio and TV interviews, newspaper interviews, telephone calls and telegrams. All the networks and local stations, except CBS, came for interviews, which were broadcast throughout the country.

By bedtime I still had scores of unanswered telephone calls, telegrams and cablegrams. The next morning Ben Bodne greeted me with: "Well, you've arrived, Johnny. The *Times* has an editorial on you." The editorial was headed "The Faulk Verdict," and it said, among other things:

> . . . The libel verdict should have a healthy effect in curbing the excesses of the superpatriots who sometimes show no more concern for the rights of individuals than the Communists they denounce. The case should assist in establishing a judicial delimitation on the lengths to which private groups, arrogating to themselves the mantle of public protector against subversion, can go in blacklisting and defaming their

fellow citizens. We do nothing to strengthen democracy if American-ism is distorted into a device for undermining the freedom the Con-stitution guarantees to every American.

All that day, and for the next several days, messages poured in from all across the land. Many contained clippings from local news-papers, editorials and cartoons on the verdict. People whom I had not heard from in six years called me. They were all excited and solicitous. Several offered me their summer homes to vacation in. One offered me his yacht, complete with a crew, to cruise around Nantucket and Martha's Vineyard. Other friends wanted to plan vic-tory parties for me. Good will and loud cheers were in the air.

But, for some reason, I couldn't get with it. A vague sort of melan-choly came over me. I wanted to get away—to be alone and think. When I spoke to Lou about it, he counseled me to stay in New York and take advantage of the job offers that would surely pour in. He knew that I was flat broke, and he figured the best cure for that was to be on hand while things were hot. As it turned out, things weren't that hot. I fell to, however, and started trying to hustle a job. The response was high on congratulations, but low on results. Most of the people I talked to were not very clear on just what it was that I did as a performer. Did I tell jokes, sing folk songs, or what?

I stayed around New York for two weeks, going for interviews and looking. Nothing happened. The urge to get away to myself became very strong. I was desperately anxious to get back to Austin to see the children and the rest of my family. On the other hand, I dreaded going back to face my creditors in Austin empty-handed. We were not only months behind in all our household debts, but our advertising business was swamped in a mire of debt. Most of my creditors were small-business people and good personal friends. They couldn't carry us without great inconvenience, and I knew it.

Lou had explained to me that it would be a long time before we realized anything from the judgment. The defendants had given notice of appeal. Of course, they wouldn't win it, he said, but there would be endless delays. Our big hope was to collect a good part of the compensatory judgment from the million dollar estate. After all, Laurence Johnson was worth millions, we had been told by one and all of the big companies which had caved in before his threats. But executing that judgment was a long way off. In the meantime, I did not have a vestige of a job—only a debt-ridden business to return to in Texas.

I drove back to Austin in the middle of July. The reunion with family and friends there was joyous, but dampened somewhat by the fact that I did not have the slightest notion of how I was going to meet our day-to-day expenses. After a spell of hugging and kissing and handshaking, I got busy on my finances. As much as I hated to do it, I had to call a friend in New York, Lawrence Kane, and borrow enough money to pay our most pressing debts and to live on for a while. A mild depression set in on me. I didn't seem to be able to think clearly on just what I would do next. Trying to keep our business afloat was out of the question. Going back to New York before I had made up my mind on exactly how I would go about climbing back into my profession was not very desirable either. So I decided to get off by myself and clear up my thoughts.

I went up to a houseboat on Lake Travis, far away from everybody, to live for a while. I was completely alone. The dog days were on Texas with a vengeance, holding the temperature around 105 degrees every day. I didn't mind the heat though. It tended to dissipate my depression—as if by evaporation. I finally realized that my chief trouble was rather to be expected: I was suffering from the letdown after six years of intense pushing in one direction. After that realization, my spirits livened up, and before long I was back on the track again. I resolved to take a flyer at New York again.

Oddly enough, within a day after I had made this decision, Mark Goodson called me from New York and asked me to go on one of their panel shows, *To Tell the Truth,* for a week. In typical Mark Goodson fashion, he said that he thought that instead of everybody sitting around feeling good about the big victory we had won, somebody ought to do something about getting me started again. I went to New York in August, and did the show. Bud Collyer was the M.C. of it, and he treated me with great civility. We had lunch one day and agreed that ours had never been a personal fight; we just didn't see issues in the union the same way. Shortly afterward, David Susskind gave me a part in a movie he was producing. Then Simon and Schuster bought the idea of this book. Martha Rountree started using me on a television show and pushing my interests with a determination. I got a daily radio show on a Westinghouse station in New

York. The world began to look promising. I was earning money, but best of all, my creative juices began to flow once more. The radio show was not my particular dish of tea and took up so much of my time in preparation that I was neglecting the writing of this book, so it was decided to let it go.

In February 1963, Nizer called me in and broke the sad news that our estimates of the Johnson estate had been completely inaccurate. Its entire value was much less than a quarter of a million dollars. It was disappointing to hear but I could not help feeling good about the irony of it. Every network and advertising agency in town had trembled at Mr. Johnson's tread on Madison Avenue, yet any of them could have bought him out with a week's advertising budget. It didn't take much to make them run. The administrators of the estate indicated that they would like to settle their end of the matter, so Lou negotiated a settlement with them. My share of the settlement enabled me to pay off at least part of my debts.

Hartnett and AWARE went through with their appeal. It was argued before the Appellate Division of the New York Supreme Court on October 1, 1963. In November, about six weeks later, the Appellate Division handed down its decision. It was a resounding victory for us. The Appellate Division had upheld all the law and fact in the case, unanimously. However, as we had anticipated, they had differed with the jury on the amount of damages. They felt the verdict of three and a half million was excessive. They cut it down to five hundred and fifty thousand dollars. Inasmuch as our chances of ever collecting the three and a half million were nonexistent (or even the interest on it for that matter), I could not really work up much concern for the reduction. In fact, I was personally rather happy to be rid of the huge sum in the case. Its magnitude had so overshadowed the issues in the case that I felt perhaps now the issues which had been so strongly affirmed by the higher court would become better known. The real importance of what had been legally resolved in the case would begin to emerge more clearly. The Appellate Division's decision had been as strong as it had been unanimous. It had said:

The proof in support of plaintiff's case was overwhelming. He conclusively established that the defendants planned to destroy his professional career through the use of libelous publications directed to the places where they would do him the most harm. He proved that they succeeded in doing so. The proof established that the libelous statements were not made recklessly but rather that they were made deliberately. The acts of the defendants were proven to be as malicious as they were vicious. The defendants were not content merely with publishing the libelous statements complained of, knowing that injury to the plaintiff must follow such publication. They pursued the plaintiff with the libel, making sure that its poison would be injected into the wellspring of his professional and economic existence. They did so with deadly effect. He was professionally destroyed, his engagements were canceled and he could not gain employment in his field, despite every effort on his part.

And what of the defenses? There was absolutely no support for them —to the point where the defendants admit that, except for the partial defense of truth and the partial defense of reasonable reliance, the court properly dismissed them. The partial defense of reasonable reliance was properly rejected by the jury, and the court, we believe, acted rightly in dismissing the partial defense of truth. . . . So we have, as found by the jury and amply supported by the evidence, a vicious libel, deliberately and maliciously planned and executed with devastating effect upon the plaintiff, all without a semblance of justification. . . . The guilt of the defendants was so clearly established by the other evidence in the case as to have left the jury no choice but to find the defendants liable.

Hartnett and AWARE, Inc, filed notice of appeal from the decision. The New York Court of Appeals will consider their appeal this spring (1964), and the decision will be in before this book is finally published.* They will have to go up to the higher court on even narrower issues than those that were argued before the Appellate Division. Their chances are slim indeed. As of this writing, as far as I'm concerned, the game is over and the score is in on *Faulk* v. *AWARE, V. Hartnett and L. Johnson.*

AWARE has just about ceased to function. I have heard that Vincent Hartnett is engaged in some sort of research work for the law offices of Roy Cohn and Thomas Bolan. He sends in a few

* As this book goes to press, word has been received that today (July 10, 1964) the New York State Court of Appeals has upheld, by a vote of 6–0, the Appellate Division's decision.

dollars each month to us toward paying off the judgment against him. Mr. Laurence Johnson has gone to his reward. It will be, perhaps, a matter of ironic interest to the reader that two of the defendants' attorneys, Godfrey Schmidt and Roy Cohn, have been separately indicted by the Federal government—on charges, of course, not related to my lawsuit. And I am galloping about the country on lecture tours, doing fairly well. Whether or not the rest of my bobbed-off judgment is collectable remains to be seen. I feel good about the fact that somebody owes *me* that much money, instead of my owing somebody that much. A half million dollars is a lot of money.

There is an illusion in our country that "money cures everything." It would be childish of me to deny that I am delighted to have won a monetary victory. Of course I am. But I did not enter into combat with the defendants as a monetary investment. The six-year fight against their destructive conspiracy has been crowned with victory. And I honor the courts, my attorneys, and those friends who stood by me and who lent me the large sums of money necessary to see the case through.

But there is a grim fact that I now have to face. The victory was a personal one. Without depreciating its significance, I feel that it was but a step—and *only* a step—in the right direction. I have won *my* case, but the noxious elements of blacklisting still permeate many areas of American life. We like to think that the heyday of McCarthyism is over. And it is true that the air is clearing somewhat. But despite this, and despite the decisive victory in my case, the poison of that dark era still runs through the land. It is embodied in the many superpatriots and the dozens of self-appointed vigilante outfits that still flourish. Indeed, the chief shield and sword of all such groups, the chief source of the poison they peddle, sits in Washington today, still tolerated by the American people and supported by their tax money. Herblock calls it the oldest floating crap game in the country, the House Un-American Activities Committee. So long as the HUAC and its coterie of camp followers have the power and the viciousness to destroy the reputation and careers of citizens who have done *nothing* more than exercise their rights to question and doubt, the poison will continue to plague and sicken our society.

America has always been a society of doubters and questioners. Most of our honored forebears were doubters and questioners of our economic, political and social institutions. They demanded and effected changes which strengthened and improved our country. They founded, joined and supported organizations which sought to achieve their purposes. We have always honored and respected a citizen who felt strongly enough about his country's problems to join with his neighbors, meet and discuss how best to solve them. Once we got our right peaceably to assemble and to petition the Government for a redress of grievances nailed down good and solid in the Bill of Rights of our Constitution, we started joining and we haven't slowed down since. That is, we didn't slow down until after World War II, when we were suddenly told that we had better stop this joining or we would get hauled in before a committee and made to apologize or get publicly pilloried, blacklisted. We suddenly lost our appetite for joining. And most of us quit joining. And we quit questioning and doubting. If we didn't quit, we kept quiet about it. We knew the vigilantes were riding.

To me, the most sinister aspect of that whole period was the systematic way respectable educators, ministers, artists, writers, librarians—Americans from every walk of life—were hauled in by some committee or publicly denounced by some vigilante group, and pronounced "guilty." Guilty for having thought and acted like responsible citizens. The terrible thing is that many of those so victimized, and the American people as a whole, accepted this sentence of "guilty." They accepted the right of the vigilantes to bring the charges, to make the decision, and to pronounce the sentence. Those very attributes which had for so long been held to be marks of civic virtue in a citizen, suddenly became sufficient cause to suspect and punish him. Citizens came to accept the dictum that a concern about injustices was a greater crime than the injustices themselves. And we all kept quiet. Silence became our greatest virtue. We felt that silence would make us safe. What a paradox! Silence was precisely what exposed us to the worst ravages of vigilantes. The habit of keeping quiet is still on us. Blacklisting still goes on.

It would be gratifying indeed to think that if my lawsuit served no other purpose, it demonstrated that one does not *have* to keep quiet when the vigilantes come riding.